becoming

THE WISDOM BOOKS

NCV
NEW CENTURY VERSION

Nelson Bibles
A Division of Thomas Nelson Publishers
Since 1798

www.thomasnelson.com

becoming

THE WISDOM BOOKS

Managing Editors: Carrie Hagar and Margaret Feinberg

Cover Model: April Barr

Page Design and Layout: Emily Keafer & Kristi Smith, Anderson Thomas Design

Cover Design: Jay Smith, JuiceBox Designs

Cover Photo: ©2005 Wolf Hoffman

Hair and makeup stylist: Rebecca Slaughter

Contributors: Margaret Feinberg, Valerie Gibbs, Natalie Gillespie, Emily Corser, Jessica E. King, Lisa Lauffer, Mary Scott Geis, Melinda Sloan, Susan Cole, Marcia Ford, Carrie Hagar, Jennifer Hesse

Stories of survival are actual stories. The writers' identities have been protected.

EVERY WOMAN IS IN THE PROCESS OF "BECOMING" IN ONE WAY OR ANOTHER.

You're becoming wiser with every lesson you learn. You're becoming stronger with every challenge you face. And you're becoming more attractive as God's presence grows in your life. That's why we have developed *Becoming*, a Bible intended to help you live a vibrant Christian life.

Where does *Becoming Wisdom Books* come from? Well, the Bible itself is divided into two major sections—the Old Testament and the New Testament. The Old Testament is then divided into five parts: the Books of the Law (also called "The Pentateuch"), Historical Books, Wisdom Books (also called "Books of Poetry"), Major Prophets, and Minor Prophets. The Wisdom Books—Job, Psalms, Proverbs, Ecclesiastes, and Song of Songs—are brimming with insight and wisdom about how life is meant to be lived.

The book of Job follows a man who experiences a string of personal disasters. His compelling story is a reminder that God's wisdom is greater than our own and his provision outpaces our deepest needs. The book of Psalms is an intimate, soul-searching journey of worship and praise. The book of Proverbs enables you to live the best life possible through God-given wisdom and life lessons. The book of Ecclesiastes raises questions about life's meaning and answers them with a resounding message that it's all about God. And Song of Songs reminds us that God is the creator of romance and love. Together, these books impart hope, strength, and wisdom into the Christian journey.

If you've ever felt disconnected from the Bible or read a scripture verse and wondered how to apply it to your own life, you're not alone! We all struggle to make sense of Scripture from time to time, and *Becoming* is packed with features, insights, notes, and practical tips that will help you connect with the Scriptures in a whole new way.

Relationships discusses ways to strengthen your friendships and interpersonal skills. Stories of Survival features ten candid testimonies from women who have faced tough situations and everyday struggles. What's the Point? focuses on Scripture passages and their relevance to today. Wise Words outlines principles from Proverbs that apply to everyone's life. Life Issues tackles some of the toughest questions women face today. We have also added extra features, including Quizzes and Calendars. And don't miss the special studies on Beauty and Purpose tucked into the back of the Bible!

Sure, the Bible may have been written thousands of years ago, but it carries a contemporary message that transcends time and circumstance. The Bible is a rich treasury of God-inspired, life-imparting wisdom and comfort that remains relevant to Christ-followers today. It is our prayer that God's Word will become more alive to you each day and that you'll find yourself in a deeper, more intimate relationship with Jesus.

—THE EDITORS OF BECOMING

A Note about the New Century Version

God never intended the Bible to be too difficult for his people. To make sure God's message was clear, the authors of the Bible recorded God's Word in familiar everyday language. These books brought a message that the original readers could understand. These first readers knew that God spoke through these books. Down through the centuries, many people wanted a Bible so badly that they copied different Bible books by hand!

Today, now that the Bible is readily available, many Christians do not regularly read it. Many feel that the Bible is too hard to understand or irrelevant to life.

The New Century Version captures the clear and simple message that the very first readers understood. This version presents the Bible as God intended it: clear and dynamic.

A team of scholars from the World Bible Translation Center worked together with twenty-one other experienced Bible scholars from all over the world to translate the text directly from the best available Greek and Hebrew texts. You can trust that this Bible accurately presents God's Word as it came to us in the original languages.

Translators kept sentences short and simple. They avoided difficult words and worked to make the text easier to read. They used modern terms for places and measurements. And they put figures of speech and idiomatic expressions ("he was gathered to his people") in language that even children understand ("he died").

Following the tradition of other English versions, the New Century Version indicates the divine name, Yahweh, by putting Lord, and sometimes God, in capital letters. This distinguishes it from Adonai, another Hebrew word that is translated Lord.

We acknowledge the infallibility of God's Word and yet our own frailty. We pray that God will use this Bible to help you understand his rich truth for yourself. To God be the glory.

TABLE OF CONTENTS

Job

If you've ever had a bad day, week, month, or even year, the story of Job is a comforting reminder that you are not alone. In one short time span, Job loses just about everything—his family, his financial security, and even his health. Yet throughout this incredibly difficult time, Job still manages to hold on to his faith.

The story of Job touches on a universal human experience: suffering. It also raises the question "Why?"—Why would God allow one righteous man to suffer, seemingly just to prove something to Satan?

However, nowhere in the forty-two chapters that comprise Job's story is an answer given. The age-old question of why God allows the righteous to suffer is raised but not resolved. Instead, the book provides fresh insight into the nature and power of God. Through Job's ordeal, we learn more about God's ability to handle the things that are both seen and unseen and discover that God is worthy to be trusted even when we don't understand. That's a tough lesson for anyone to learn, but Job's faithfulness portrays it beautifully for all to see. The book of Job reveals that God's actions are sometimes beyond our ability to fathom and that the sufferings we endure are not always a result of personal sin.

The good news is that even with unanswered questions, it is possible to trust God and live righteously, just like Job.

Job, the Good Man

1 A man named Job lived in the land of Uz. He was an honest and innocent man; he honored God and stayed away from evil. ²Job had seven sons and three daughters. ³He owned seven thousand sheep, three thousand camels, five hundred teams of oxen, and five hundred female donkeys. He also had a large number of servants. He was the greatest man among all the people of the East.

⁴Job's sons took turns holding feasts in their homes and invited their sisters to eat and drink with them. ⁵After a feast was over, Job would send and have them made clean. Early in the morning Job would offer a burnt offering for each of them, because he thought, "My children may have sinned and cursed God in their hearts." Job did this every time.

Satan Appears Before the Lord

⁶One day the angels came to show themselves before the LORD, and Satan" was with them. ⁷The LORD said to Satan, "Where have you come from?"

Satan answered the LORD, "I have been wandering around the earth, going back and forth in it."

⁸Then the LORD said to Satan, "Have you noticed my servant Job? No one else

▶▶ **1:6 Satan** Or "the accuser."

"The LORD gave these things to me, and he has taken them away. Praise the name of the LORD."

BOOKS & MUSIC

BOOKS

A RESILIENT LIFE

by Gordon MacDonald

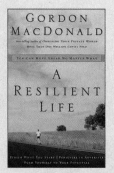

Gordon MacDonald has good news for women who fear that life is all downhill after forty: God has big plans for middle age and beyond! *A Resilient Life* teaches you to get ready for greatness by applying a few life lessons that MacDonald learned from a high school track coach. The lessons include not looking back except to learn from mistakes, maintaining self-discipline, running with a vision of the outcome, and joining in with others to make big things happen. *A Resilient Life* will help prepare you for the amazing things God wants to do in the second half of your life!

THE PILGRIM'S PROGRESS

by John Bunyan

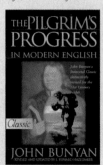

Even though this beautiful allegory is more than 325 years old, John Bunyan's *The Pilgrim's Progress* paints a realistic and relevant picture of struggles and temptations that continue to plague God's followers today. It tells the story of "Christian" as he journeys on a narrow road to a promised land. Bunyan writes the story as a dream and personalizes the different areas of temptation people experience by making them supporting characters in the book. Christian encounters these characters along the way, overcoming each temptation and remaining on the narrow path. This is a must-read classic for every generation.

MUSIC

SIMPLY NOTHING

by Shawn McDonald

Shawn McDonald's first album is a perfect combo of acoustic soul angst and passionate modern worship. This album is the one to reach for when you feel misunderstood, when you are down and need to grab on to some hope, or when you simply want to pour out your adoration to God. You'll probably recognize the catchy first hit "Gravity," which has enjoyed great success on Christian radio. But that just scratches the surface of McDonald's heartfelt pleas to God to stay with him, guide him, and take care of him, desires that everyone can relate to.

"A must-read classic for every generation."

WHAT'S IN A word?

Job 2:3 "Satan" means "adversary." In the story of Job, Satan remains true to his name by accusing Job and afflicting him with suffering of every kind.

on earth is like him. He is an honest and innocent man, honoring God and staying away from evil."

⁹But Satan answered the LORD, "Job honors God for a good reason. ¹⁰You have put a wall around him, his family, and everything he owns. You have blessed the things he has done. His flocks and herds are so large they almost cover the land. ¹¹But reach out your hand and destroy everything he has, and he will curse you to your face."

¹²The LORD said to Satan, "All right, then. Everything Job has is in your power, but you must not touch Job himself." Then Satan left the LORD's presence.

¹³One day Job's sons and daughters were eating and drinking wine together at the oldest brother's house. ¹⁴A messenger came to Job and said, "The oxen were plowing and the donkeys were eating grass nearby, ¹⁵when the Sabeans attacked and carried them away. They killed the servants with swords, and I am the only one who escaped to tell you!"

¹⁶The messenger was still speaking when another messenger arrived and said, "Lightning from God fell from the sky. It burned up the sheep and the servants, and I am the only one who escaped to tell you!"

¹⁷The second messenger was still speaking when another messenger arrived and said, "The Babylonians sent three groups of attackers that swept down and stole your camels and killed the servants. I am the only one who escaped to tell you!"

¹⁸The third messenger was still speaking when another messenger arrived and said, "Your sons and daughters were eating and drinking wine together at the oldest brother's house. ¹⁹Suddenly a great wind came from the desert, hitting all four corners of the house at once. The house fell in on the young people, and they are all dead. I am the only one who escaped to tell you!"

²⁰When Job heard this, he got up and tore his robe and shaved his head to show how sad he was. Then he bowed down to the ground to worship God.

²¹He said:

"I was naked when I was born,
  and I will be naked when I die.
The LORD gave these things to me,
  and he has taken them away.
  Praise the name of the LORD."

²²In all this Job did not sin or blame God.

Satan Appears Before the Lord Again

2 On another day the angels came to show themselves before the LORD, and Satan was with them again.

Love the Lord's Teaching

Do you get excited when you learn something new from the Lord? Are you in awe when you see God's Word becoming real in your life? Psalm 1:1-2 teaches that we shouldn't listen to sinners or imitate their behaviors; instead, we should love the Lord's teachings and think about them day and night. The psalm goes on to describe the rewards of loving the Lord's wisdom: we will live strong, fruitful lives that are destined for success. Letting God's Word soak in changes everything, so delve deeply into the Scriptures and listen up when your pastor is preaching! Learn to love the Lord's teachings; your life will be more productive, and your heart will be more fulfilled.

WISE WORDS

Choose Your Friends Wisely

You may think that your choice of companions has little to do with your spiritual life, but your friends rub off on you more than you realize! If you have godly friends, people who strive to put God first in their lives, they will naturally challenge you to grow in your faith. But if your inner circle of friends is filled with people who tear you down or ask you to compromise what you believe, you're going to eventually end up giving in. That's why Proverbs 1:10 says not to follow people who lead you into tempting situations. Instead, surround yourself with people who bring out the best in you! By choosing your friends wisely, you're choosing a better you.

²The LORD said to Satan, "Where have you come from?"

Satan answered the LORD, "I have been wandering around the earth, going back and forth in it."

³Then the LORD said to Satan, "Have you noticed my servant Job? No one else on earth is like him. He is an honest and innocent man, honoring God and staying away from evil. You caused me to ruin him for no good reason, but he continues to be without blame."

⁴"One skin for another!" Satan answered. "A man will give all he has to save his own life. ⁵But reach out your hand and destroy his flesh and bones, and he will curse you to your face."

⁶The LORD said to Satan, "All right, then. Job is in your power, but you may not take his life."

⁷So Satan left the LORD's presence. He put painful sores on Job's body, from the top of his head to the soles of his feet. ⁸Job took a piece of broken pottery to scrape himself, and he sat in ashes in misery.

⁹Job's wife said to him, "Why are you trying to stay innocent? Curse God and die!"

¹⁰Job answered, "You are talking like a foolish woman. Should we take only good things from God and not trouble?" In spite of all this Job did not sin in what he said.

Job's Three Friends Come to Help

¹¹Now Job had three friends: Eliphaz the Temanite, Bildad the Shuhite, and Zophar the Naamathite. When these friends heard about Job's troubles, they agreed to meet and visit him. They wanted to show their concern and to comfort him. ¹²They saw Job from far away, but he looked so different they almost didn't recognize him. They began to cry loudly and tore their robes and put dirt on their heads to show how sad they were. ¹³Then they sat on the ground with Job seven days and seven nights. No one said a word to him because they saw how much he was suffering.

Job Curses His Birth

3 After seven days Job cried out and cursed the day he had been born, ²saying:

³"Let the day I was born be destroyed,
   and the night it was said, 'A boy
      is born!'
⁴Let that day turn to darkness.
   Don't let God care about it.
   Don't let light shine on it.
⁵Let darkness and gloom have that
      day.
   Let a cloud hide it.
   Let thick darkness cover its
      light.
⁶Let thick darkness capture that
      night.
   Don't count it among the days of
      the year
   or put it in any of the months.
⁷Let that night be empty,
   with no shout of joy to be
      heard.
⁸Let those who curse days curse that
      day.
   Let them prepare to wake up the
      sea monster Leviathan.
⁹Let that day's morning stars never
      appear;
   let it wait for daylight that
      never comes.
   Don't let it see the first light of
      dawn,
¹⁰because it allowed me to be
      born
   and did not hide trouble from
      my eyes.
¹¹"Why didn't I die as soon as I was
      born?
   Why didn't I die when I came
      out of the womb?
¹²Why did my mother's knees receive
      me,
   and my mother's breasts feed
      me?
¹³If they had not been there,
   I would be lying dead in
      peace;
   I would be asleep and at rest
¹⁴with kings and wise men of the
      earth
   who built places for themselves
      that are now ruined.
¹⁵I would be asleep with rulers
   who filled their houses with
      gold and silver.
¹⁶Why was I not buried like a child
      born dead,

like a baby who never saw the
light of day?
[17]In the grave the wicked stop
making trouble,
and the weary workers are at
rest.
[18]In the grave there is rest for the
captives
who no longer hear the shout of
the slave driver.
[19]People great and small are in the
grave,
and the slave is freed from his
master.

[20]"Why is light given to those in
misery?
Why is life given to those who
are so unhappy?
[21]They want to die, but death does
not come.
They search for death more than
for hidden treasure.
[22]They are very happy
when they get to the grave.

[23]They cannot see where they are
going.
God has hidden the road
ahead.
[24]I make sad sounds as I eat;
my groans pour out like water.
[25]Everything I feared and dreaded
has happened to me.
[26]I have no peace or quietness.
I have no rest, only trouble."

Eliphaz Speaks

4 Then Eliphaz the Temanite answered:
[2]"If someone tried to speak with you,
would you be upset?
I cannot keep from speaking.
[3]Think about the many people you
have taught

BE STILL & KNOW

Praying Scripture

One great way to get to know God is to talk to him using his own words. Praying the Scriptures—reciting Bible verses back to God as a form of prayer—honors God and helps you memorize verses that will provide comfort and strength throughout your life. Another term you may have heard is "meditating" on Scripture. This simply means to think about and reflect on specific chapters or verses. If you want to try praying the Scriptures, Psalm 3:3 or Psalm 18:1–2 are great places to start. The book of Psalms overflows with praises and pleas that celebrate God and beg for his help. You can even sing Scripture, and you may recognize verses in worship choruses you already know.

WHAT'S IN A word?

Job 3:1 "Cursed" means "held in contempt." Job's pain drove him to anger, but he refused to reject his faith. In the entire book of Job, you'll never find him cursing God or those who had hurt his family.

and the weak hands you have
made strong.
[4]Your words have comforted those
who fell,
and you have strengthened
those who could not stand.
[5]But now trouble comes to you, and
you are discouraged;
trouble hits you, and you are
terrified.
[6]You should have confidence because
you respect God;
you should have hope because
you are innocent.

[7]"Remember that the innocent will
not die;
honest people will never be
destroyed.
[8]I have noticed that people who plow
evil
and plant trouble, harvest it.
[9]God's breath destroys them,
and a blast of his anger kills
them.
[10]Lions may roar and growl,
but when the teeth of a strong
lion are broken,
[11]that lion dies of hunger.
The cubs of the mother lion are
scattered.

[12]"A word was brought to me in
secret,
and my ears heard a whisper of it.
[13]It was during a nightmare
when people are in deep sleep.
[14]I was trembling with fear;
all my bones were shaking.

ETIQUETTE 101

BE A GREAT PARTY GUEST

Want to make sure you're invited to the best parties? Know how to be a great guest! RSVP early and inquire about attire if the invitation does not specify. Make the hostess aware of dietary restrictions or food allergies, but don't demand specific dishes—organic, vegan, low-carb, and the like. If you're unhappy with the food, don't eat it. (Proverbs 15:17 says it's not about the food—it's about the company.) Bring the hostess a modest gift, such as flowers or food. Never arrive early, as your host may be unprepared. After the party, send a note thanking the hostess for her hospitality.

¹⁵A spirit glided past my face,
and the hair on my body stood
on end.
¹⁶The spirit stopped,
but I could not see what it was.
A shape stood before my eyes,
and I heard a quiet voice.
¹⁷It said, 'Can a human be more right
than God?
Can a person be pure before his
maker?
¹⁸God does not trust his angels;
he blames them for mistakes.
¹⁹So he puts even more blame on people
who live in clay houses,"
whose foundations are made of
dust,
who can be crushed like a moth.
²⁰Between dawn and sunset many
people are broken to pieces;
without being noticed, they die
and are gone forever.
²¹The ropes of their tents are pulled
up,
and they die without wisdom.'

5 "Call if you want to, Job, but no
one will answer you.
You can't turn to any of the holy
ones.
²Anger kills the fool,
and jealousy slays the stupid.
³I have seen a fool succeed,
but I cursed his home
immediately.
⁴His children are far from safety
and are crushed in court with no
defense.
⁵The hungry eat his harvest,
even taking what grew among
the thorns,

and thirsty people want his
wealth.
⁶Hard times do not come up from
the ground,
and trouble does not grow from
the earth.
⁷People produce trouble
as surely as sparks fly upward.

⁸"But if I were you, I would call on
God
and bring my problem before
him.
⁹God does wonders that cannot be
understood;
he does so many miracles they
cannot be counted.
¹⁰He gives rain to the earth
and sends water on the fields.
¹¹He makes the humble person
important
and lifts the sad to places of
safety.
¹²He ruins the plans of those who
trick others
so they have no success.
¹³He catches the wise in their own
clever traps
and sweeps away the plans of
those who try to trick
others.
¹⁴Darkness covers them up in the
daytime;
even at noon they feel around in
the dark.
¹⁵God saves the needy from their
lies
and from the harm done by
powerful people.
¹⁶So the poor have hope,
while those who are unfair are
silenced.

fun FACTS

In 2003, 23% of women ages 30 to 34 had never been married, nearly quadruple the percentage from 1970.

(Census Bureau)

➤ **4:19 clay houses** This is probably talking about people's bodies.

BIBLE Women & Men

Lydia

Do you love to have everybody over to your place? Lydia did. In fact, her hospitality is legendary. When she met Paul and the followers of Christ outside Philippi, "She worshiped God, and he opened her mind to pay attention to what Paul was saying" (Acts 16:14). In other words, she accepted the story of Jesus and believed in him. Then she went home, spread the news, and all the people in her house were baptized. After that, she invited Paul and other believers in Christ to stay in her home. Lydia's house became a place of ministry and encouragement.

Your Whole Being

Do you feel restrained when you worship? Perhaps you long to stretch your hands to heaven or shout praises, but you are afraid of appearing undignified or inappropriate. The Bible describes many acceptable forms of worship. In Psalm 34:2, David tells of praising God with his whole being, and we read throughout the psalms that he sang and danced before the Lord. You may not be ready to dance like David did, but you can begin by worshiping with your *whole being*—whatever that means for you—during your private time with God.

17"The one whom God corrects is happy,
  so do not hate being corrected by the Almighty.
18God hurts, but he also bandages up;
  he injures, but his hands also heal.
19He will save you from six troubles;
  even seven troubles will not harm you.
20God will buy you back from death in times of hunger,
  and in battle he will save you from the sword.
21You will be protected from the tongue that strikes like a whip,
  and you will not be afraid when destruction comes.
22You will laugh at destruction and hunger,
  and you will not fear the wild animals,
23because you will have an agreement with the stones in the field,
  and the wild animals will be at peace with you.
24You will know that your tent is safe, because you will check the things you own and find nothing missing.
25You will know that you will have many children,
and your descendants will be like the grass on the earth.
26You will come to the grave with all your strength, like bundles of grain gathered at the right time.

27"We have checked this, and it is true,
  so hear it and decide what it means to you."

Job Answers Eliphaz

6 Then Job answered:
2"I wish my suffering could be weighed
and my misery put on scales.
3My sadness would be heavier than the sand of the seas.
No wonder my words seem careless.
4The arrows of the Almighty are in me;
  my spirit drinks in their poison;
  God's terrors are gathered against me.
5A wild donkey does not bray when it has grass to eat,
  and an ox is quiet when it has feed.
6Tasteless food is not eaten without salt,
  and there is no flavor in the white of an egg.

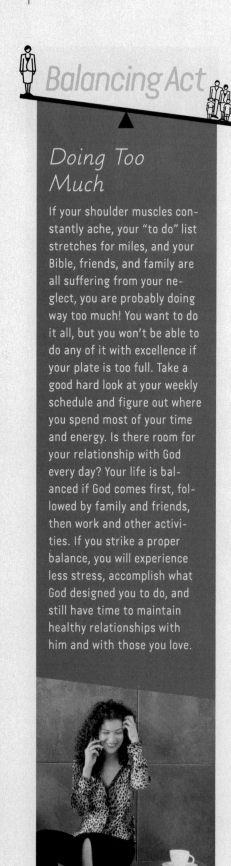

Balancing Act

Doing Too Much

If your shoulder muscles constantly ache, your "to do" list stretches for miles, and your Bible, friends, and family are all suffering from your neglect, you are probably doing way too much! You want to do it all, but you won't be able to do any of it with excellence if your plate is too full. Take a good hard look at your weekly schedule and figure out where you spend most of your time and energy. Is there room for your relationship with God every day? Your life is balanced if God comes first, followed by family and friends, then work and other activities. If you strike a proper balance, you will experience less stress, accomplish what God designed you to do, and still have time to maintain healthy relationships with him and with those you love.

7I refuse to touch it;
    such food makes me sick.

8"How I wish that I might have what I ask for
    and that God would give me what I hope for.
9How I wish God would crush me
    and reach out his hand to destroy me.
10Then I would have this comfort
    and be glad even in this unending pain,
    because I would know I did not reject the words of the Holy One.

11"I do not have the strength to wait.
    There is nothing to hope for,
    so why should I be patient?
12I do not have the strength of stone;
    my flesh is not bronze.
13I have no power to help myself,
    because success has been taken away from me.

14"They say, 'A person's friends should be kind to him when he is in trouble,
    even if he stops fearing the Almighty.'
15But my brothers cannot be counted on.
    They are like streams that do not always flow,
    streams that sometimes run over.
16They are made dark by melting ice
    and rise with melting snow.
17But they stop flowing in the dry season;
    they disappear when it is hot.
18Travelers turn away from their paths
    and go into the desert and die.
19The groups of travelers from Tema look for water,
    and the traders of Sheba look hopefully.
20They are upset because they had been sure;
    when they arrive, they are disappointed.
21You also have been no help.
    You see something terrible, and you are afraid.
22I have never said, 'Give me a gift.
    Use your wealth to pay my debt.
23Save me from the enemy's power.
    Buy me back from the clutches of cruel people.'

24"Teach me, and I will be quiet.
    Show me where I have been wrong.
25Honest words are painful,
    but your arguments prove nothing.
26Do you mean to correct what I say?
    Will you treat the words of a troubled man as if they were only wind?
27You would even gamble for orphans
    and would trade away your friend.

28"But now please look at me.
    I would not lie to your face.
29Change your mind; do not be unfair;
    think again, because my innocence is being questioned.
30What I am saying is not wicked;
    I can tell the difference between right and wrong.

7 "People have a hard task on earth,
    and their days are like those of a laborer.
2They are like a slave wishing for the evening shadows,
    like a laborer waiting to be paid.
3But I am given months that are empty,
    and nights of misery have been given to me.
4When I lie down, I think, 'How long until I get up?'
    The night is long, and I toss until dawn.
5My body is covered with worms and scabs,
    and my skin is broken and full of sores.

⁶"My days go by faster than a
weaver's tool,
and they come to an end
without hope.
⁷Remember, God, that my life is only
a breath.
My eyes will never see happy
times again.
⁸Those who see me now will see me
no more;
you will look for me, but I will
be gone.
⁹As a cloud disappears and is gone,
people go to the grave and never
return.
¹⁰They will never come back to their
houses again,

and their places will not
know them anymore.
¹¹"So I will not stay quiet;
I will speak out in the
suffering of my spirit.
I will complain because I am so
unhappy.
¹²I am not the sea or the sea
monster.
So why have you set a guard over
me?
¹³Sometimes I think my bed will
comfort me
or that my couch will stop my
complaint.
¹⁴Then you frighten me with dreams
and terrify me with visions.
¹⁵My throat prefers to be choked;
my bones welcome death.

WHAT'S IN A word?

Job 8:1 "Bildad" means "son of contention." Bildad was one of Job's friends who came to help him, but his stern, accusatory comments did not provide the comfort or wise counsel that Job needed.

¹⁶I hate my life; I don't want to live
forever.
Leave me alone, because my days
have no meaning.
¹⁷"Why do you make people so
important
and give them so much
attention?
¹⁸You examine them every morning
and test them every moment.
¹⁹Will you never look away from me
or leave me alone even long
enough to swallow?
²⁰If I have sinned, what have I done to
you,
you watcher of humans?
Why have you made me your
target?
Have I become a heavy load for
you?
²¹Why don't you pardon my wrongs
and forgive my sins?
I will soon lie down in the dust of
death.
Then you will search for me, but
I will be no more."

Bildad Speaks to Job

8 Then Bildad the Shuhite answered:
²"How long will you say such things?
Your words are no more than
wind.
³God does not twist justice;
the Almighty does not make
wrong what is right.
⁴Your children sinned against God,

Beauty BECOMES HER

Lips of Praise

Lipstick comes in all forms these days—pencils, tubes, and wands—and all kinds of funky designs. Whatever form you choose, you should begin by outlining your natural lip line with a neutral-colored pencil. Next, apply your favorite color and blend the two shades with a lip brush. If you'd like to add fullness to your lips, choose a light lipstick color. Remember, though, that what comes out of your lips is far more important than what you put on them. As Job 8:21 says, "God will yet fill your mouth with laughter and your lips with shouts of joy."

and he punished them for their sins.

[5]But you should ask God for help and pray to the Almighty for mercy.

[6]If you are good and honest, he will stand up for you

and bring you back where you belong.

[7]Where you began will seem unimportant, because your future will be so successful.

[8]"Ask old people; find out what their ancestors learned,

[9]because we were only born yesterday and know nothing.

HEALTH

Insomnia

Most people have trouble sleeping from time to time, but for some, low-quality sleep is an ongoing or even lifelong issue. It's estimated that temporary insomnia—which can last from several days to several weeks—affects half of all adults. For those suffering from insomnia, medications and behavior therapies are available. But if you are among those who experience the occasional restless night, you can help quiet your mind and heart by reflecting on the nature of God. Instead of counting sheep, meditate on his blessings. Use the time—even the wee hours of the morning—to praise him and tell him what's on your heart.

Our days on earth are only a shadow.

[10]Those people will teach you and tell you and speak about what they know.

[11]Papyrus plants cannot grow where there is no swamp, and reeds cannot grow tall without water.

[12]While they are still growing and not yet cut, they will dry up quicker than grass.

[13]That is what will happen to those who forget God; the hope of the wicked will be gone.

[14]What they hope in is easily broken; what they trust is like a spider's web.

[15]They lean on the spider's web, but it breaks. They grab it, but it does not hold up.

[16]They are like well-watered plants in the sunshine that spread their roots all through the garden.

[17]They wrap their roots around a pile of rocks and look for a place among the stones.

[18]But if a plant is torn from its place, then that place rejects it and says, 'I never saw you.'

[19]Now joy has gone away; other plants grow up from the same dirt.

[20]"Surely God does not reject the innocent or give strength to those who do evil.

[21]God will yet fill your mouth with laughter and your lips with shouts of joy.

[22]Your enemies will be covered with shame, and the tents of the wicked will be gone."

What's the POINT?

Job Answers Bildad

9 Then Job answered:
² "Yes, I know that this is true,
but how can anyone be right in
the presence of God?
³ Someone might want to argue with
God,
but no one could answer God,
not one time out of a thousand.
⁴ God's wisdom is deep, and his
power is great;
no one can fight him without
getting hurt.
⁵ God moves mountains without
anyone knowing it
and turns them over when he is
angry.
⁶ He shakes the earth out of its place
and makes its foundations
tremble.
⁷ He commands the sun not to shine
and shuts off the light of the
stars.
⁸ He alone stretches out the skies
and walks on the waves of the
sea.
⁹ It is God who made the Bear, Orion,
and the Pleiades[n]
and the groups of stars in the
southern sky.
¹⁰ He does wonders that cannot be
understood;
he does so many miracles they
cannot be counted.
¹¹ When he passes me, I cannot see
him;
when he goes by me, I do not
recognize him.
¹² If he snatches something away, no
one can stop him
or say to him, 'What are you
doing?'
¹³ God will not hold back his anger.
Even the helpers of the monster
Rahab lie at his feet in fear.
¹⁴ So how can I argue with God,
or even find words to argue with
him?
¹⁵ Even if I were right, I could not
answer him;
I could only beg God, my Judge,

Job 9:5–6

God is big. Very, very big. Bigger than King Kong or any giant in any movie you have ever seen. Just how big is he? Try this. Close your eyes and picture the tallest building on earth. Then imagine a huge giant towering over it. Nope—that doesn't even come close to the vastness of God. When it comes to capturing the true image of God, Job painted a pretty accurate picture of him. Job described him as the one who "shakes the earth out of its place and makes its foundations tremble" (Job 9:6). He turns mountains upside down, tells the sun not to shine, and turns off the stars. Wow! That's some pretty awesome power. You know what? That is the kind of power you have at your side and in your daily life, if you are in a relationship with him. While God is the creator of the universe, he is also the God who wants to get up close and personal with each and every person—including you! He loves you more than you can know and wants you to reciprocate his love. God is a big God, but he's not too big to have a relationship with you.

9:9 Bear . . . Pleiades Names of well-known groups
of stars.

Love

Monogamy

Monogamy. It's a word that is often mocked these days. But, despite the Old Testament prevalence of multiple wives and the popular notion that monogamy is old-fashioned and unrealistic in the twenty-first century, God's plan for marriage is that "each man should have his own wife, and each woman should have her own husband" (1 Corinthians 7:2). And it *is* realistic! The bride's words in Song of Songs 7:10 demonstrate God's design for romantic relationships: "I belong to my lover, and he *desires only me*" (emphasis added). While our capacity to love may seem limitless, going outside God's boundaries for intimacy will only cause heartache. Making a total commitment to each other—in God's way and with God's help—will form a strong, lasting marriage relationship.

for mercy.
¹⁶If I called to him and he answered,
    I still don't believe he would
        listen to me.
¹⁷He would crush me with a storm
    and multiply my wounds for no
        reason.
¹⁸He would not let me catch my
        breath
    but would overwhelm me with
        misery.
¹⁹When it comes to strength, God is
        stronger than I;
    when it comes to justice, no one
        can accuse him.
²⁰Even if I were right, my own mouth
        would say I was wrong;
    if I were innocent, my mouth
        would say I was guilty.

²¹"I am innocent,
    but I don't care about myself.
    I hate my own life.
²²It is all the same. That is why I say,
    'God destroys both the innocent
        and the guilty.'
²³If the whip brings sudden death,
    God will laugh at the suffering
        of the innocent.
²⁴When the land falls into the hands
        of evil people,
    he covers the judges' faces so
        they can't see it.
    If it is not God who does this,
        then who is it?

²⁵"My days go by faster than a
        runner;
    they fly away without my seeing
        any joy.
²⁶They glide past like paper
        boats.
    They attack like eagles
        swooping down to feed.
²⁷Even though I say, 'I will forget my
        complaint;
    I will change the look on my face
        and smile,'
²⁸I still dread all my suffering.
    I know you will hold me guilty.
²⁹I have already been found guilty,
    so why should I struggle for no
        reason?

³⁰I might wash myself with soap
    and scrub my hands with strong
        soap,
³¹but you would push me into a dirty
        pit,
    and even my clothes would hate
        me.

³²"God is not human like me, so I
    cannot answer him.
    We cannot meet each other in
        court.
³³I wish there were someone to make
        peace between us,
    someone to decide our case.
³⁴Maybe he could remove God's
        punishment
    so his terror would no longer
        frighten me.
³⁵Then I could speak without being
        afraid,
    but I am not able to do that.

10 "I hate my life,
    so I will complain without
        holding back;
    I will speak because I am so
        unhappy.
²I will say to God: Do not hold me
        guilty,
    but tell me what you have
        against me.
³Does it make you happy to trouble
        me?
    Don't you care about me, the
        work of your hands?
    Are you happy with the plans of
        evil people?
⁴Do you have human eyes
    that see as we see?
⁵Are your days like the days of humans,
    and your years like our years?
⁶You look for the evil I have done
    and search for my sin.
⁷You know I am not guilty,
    but no one can save me from
        your power.

⁸"Your hands shaped and made me.
    Do you now turn around and
        destroy me?
⁹Remember that you molded me like
        a piece of clay.

RELATIONSHIPS

What a Friend Needs...

Have you ever had a friend in crisis and weren't sure how to react? The book of Job offers amazing insight—on what *not* to do. Job lost his livestock, his family, and even his health (Job 1:13-19, 2:7). His friends may have had good intentions, but they certainly had a questionable view of God—and a distinct lack of tact. Their first blunders were minimizing Job's pain and assuming they could relate to his losses (4:5-6, 5:8). Perhaps their worst mistake was insinuating that Job's trials were the result of his sin (11:10-11, 14-15). What a friend in crisis often needs most is a non-judgmental sounding board for her emotions, not accusations or rationalizations. Listen, offer a hug, and commit to pray for her.

Will you now turn me back into dust?
¹⁰You formed me inside my mother
like cheese formed from milk.
¹¹You dressed me with skin and flesh;
you sewed me together with bones and muscles.
¹²You gave me life and showed me kindness,
and in your care you watched over my life.

¹³"But in your heart you hid other plans.
I know this was in your mind.
¹⁴If I sinned, you would watch me
and would not let my sin go unpunished.
¹⁵How terrible it will be for me if I am guilty!
Even if I am right, I cannot lift my head.
I am full of shame
and experience only pain.
¹⁶If I hold up my head, you hunt me like a lion
and again show your terrible power against me.
¹⁷You bring new witnesses against me
and increase your anger against me.
Your armies come against me.

¹⁸"So why did you allow me to be born?
I wish I had died before anyone saw me.
¹⁹I wish I had never lived,
but had been carried straight from birth to the grave.
²⁰The few days of my life are almost over.
Leave me alone so I can have a moment of joy.
²¹Soon I will leave; I will not return
from the land of darkness and gloom,
²²the land of darkest night,
from the land of gloom and confusion,
where even the light is darkness."

Zophar Speaks to Job

11 Then Zophar the Naama-thite answered:
²"Should these words go unanswered?
Is this talker in the right?
³Your lies do not make people quiet;
people should correct you when you make fun of God.
⁴You say, 'My teachings are right,
and I am clean in God's sight.'
⁵I wish God would speak
and open his lips against you
⁶and tell you the secrets of wisdom,
because wisdom has two sides.
Know this: God has even forgotten some of your sin.

⁷"Can you understand the secrets of God?
Can you search the limits of the Almighty?
⁸His limits are higher than the heavens; you cannot reach them!
They are deeper than the grave; you cannot understand them!
⁹His limits are longer than the earth
and wider than the sea.

¹⁰"If God comes along and puts you in prison
or calls you into court, no one can stop him.

Seven ways to...

Say "I Love You"

1. List the things you love about someone and give it to the person.

2. Write a poem and send it by e-mail.

3. Make a favorite meal or bake a fantastic sweet treat for that special someone.

4. Express your feelings in ways that are meaningful to the one you love.

5. Send an old-fashioned, hand-made, and handwritten card.

6. Find an item on eBay that the person you love has always wanted.

7. Express your love creatively: Write a love letter. Sing a song. Paint a picture.

¹¹God knows who is evil,
and when he sees evil, he takes note of it.
¹²A fool cannot become wise
any more than a wild donkey can be born tame.

¹³"You must give your whole heart to him
and hold out your hands to him for help.
¹⁴Put away the sin that is in your hand;
let no evil remain in your tent.
¹⁵Then you can lift up your face without shame,
and you can stand strong without fear.
¹⁶You will forget your trouble
and remember it only as water gone by.
¹⁷Your life will be as bright as the noonday sun,
and darkness will seem like morning.
¹⁸You will feel safe because there is hope;
you will look around and rest in safety.
¹⁹You will lie down, and no one will scare you.
Many people will want favors from you.
²⁰But the wicked will not be able to see,
so they will not escape.
Their only hope will be to die."

Job Answers Zophar

12 Then Job answered:
²"You really think you are the only wise people
and that when you die, wisdom will die with you!
³But my mind is as good as yours;
you are not better than I am.
Everyone knows all these things.
⁴My friends all laugh at me
when I call on God and expect him to answer me;
they laugh at me even though I am right and innocent!
⁵Those who are comfortable don't care that others have trouble;
they think it right that those people should have troubles.

⁶The tents of robbers are not bothered,
and those who make God angry are safe.
They have their god in their pocket.
⁷"But ask the animals, and they will teach you,
or ask the birds of the air, and they will tell you.
⁸Speak to the earth, and it will teach you,
or let the fish of the sea tell you.
⁹Every one of these knows
that the hand of the LORD has done this.
¹⁰The life of every creature
and the breath of all people are in God's hand.
¹¹The ear tests words
as the tongue tastes food.
¹²Older people are wise,
and long life brings understanding.

¹³"But only God has wisdom and power,
good advice and understanding.
¹⁴What he tears down cannot be rebuilt;
anyone he puts in prison cannot be let out.
¹⁵If God holds back the waters, there is no rain;
if he lets the waters go, they flood the land.
¹⁶He is strong and victorious;
both the one who fools others and the one who is fooled belong to him.
¹⁷God leads the wise away as captives
and turns judges into fools.
¹⁸He takes off chains that kings put on
and puts a garment on their bodies.
¹⁹He leads priests away naked
and destroys the powerful.
²⁰He makes trusted people be silent
and takes away the wisdom of elders.

²¹He brings disgrace on important
people
and takes away the weapons of
the strong.
²²He uncovers the deep things of
darkness
and brings dark shadows into
the light.
²³He makes nations great and then
destroys them;
he makes nations large and then
scatters them.
²⁴He takes understanding away from
the leaders of the earth
and makes them wander
through a pathless desert.
²⁵They feel around in darkness with
no light;
he makes them stumble like
drunks.

13 "Now my eyes have seen
all this;
my ears have heard and
understood it.
²What you know, I also know.
You are not better than I am.
³But I want to speak to the Almighty
and to argue my case with
God.
⁴But you smear me with lies.
You are worthless doctors, all of
you!
⁵I wish you would just stop talking;
then you would really be wise!
⁶Listen to my argument,
and hear the pleading of my lips.
⁷You should not speak evil in the
name of God;
you cannot speak God's truth by
telling lies.
⁸You should not unfairly choose his
side against mine;
you should not argue the case
for God.
⁹You will not do well if he examines
you;
you cannot fool God as you
might fool humans.
¹⁰God would surely scold you
if you unfairly took one person's
side.

¹¹His bright glory would scare you,
and you would be very much
afraid of him.
¹²Your wise sayings are worth no
more than ashes,
and your arguments are as weak
as clay.
¹³"Be quiet and let me speak.
Let things happen to me as they
will.
¹⁴Why should I put myself in danger
and take my life in my own
hands?
¹⁵Even if God kills me, I have hope in
him;
I will still defend my ways to his
face.
¹⁶This is my salvation.
The wicked cannot come before
him.
¹⁷Listen carefully to my words;
let your ears hear what I say.
¹⁸See, I have prepared my case,
and I know I will be proved right.
¹⁹No one can accuse me of doing
wrong.

If someone can, I will be quiet
and die.
²⁰"God, please just give me these two
things,
and then I will not hide from
you:
²¹Take your punishment away from
me,
and stop frightening me with
your terrors.
²²Then call me, and I will answer,
or let me speak, and you answer.
²³How many evil things and sins have
I done?
Show me my wrong and my sin.
²⁴Don't hide your face from me;
don't think of me as your
enemy.
²⁵Don't punish a leaf that is blown by
the wind;
don't chase after straw.
²⁶You write down cruel things
against me
and make me suffer for my
boyhood sins.
²⁷You put my feet in chains

**Q: THE BIBLE SAYS IN MATTHEW 7:7 TO "ASK, AND GOD
WILL GIVE TO YOU," SO WHY AM I STILL SINGLE?**

**A: Singleness is a tough one, with no magic formula. First,
make sure you've lined up your desires with what God wants
for you. God wants you to desire him more than anyone else.
Ask him how you can have a healthy, whole, fulfilled life with
him whether or not you are married. Although some days are
easier than others, make the choice to trust him—he will take
care of you in the best way, right now and in the future.**

WISE WORDS

Always Seek Wisdom

The entire book of Proverbs makes a pretty convincing case that wisdom is worth its weight in gold. In fact, Proverbs 2:4 says that wisdom is like a hidden treasure. Wisdom protects you, guides you, and leads you to a better way of living. According to Proverbs 2:20, wisdom will help you do what is right and good—what is best. When you're in a tough situation, remember to ask God for wisdom. He knows the situation in and out, and he has an answer for every circumstance. If you just take a few moments to pray, you'll find yourself embracing wisdom in your life. Treat wisdom as if it were a golden treasure—definitely worth the search!

and keep close watch wherever I go.
You even mark the soles of my feet.

28"Everyone wears out like something rotten,
like clothing eaten by moths.

14 "All of us born to women live only a few days and have lots of trouble.

2We grow up like flowers and then dry up and die.
We are like a passing shadow that does not last.
3Lord, do you need to watch me like this?
Must you bring me before you to be judged?
4No one can bring something clean from something dirty.
5Our time is limited.
You have given us only so many months to live
and have set limits we cannot go beyond.
6So look away from us and leave us alone
until we put in our time like a laborer.

7"If a tree is cut down,
there is hope that it will grow again
and will send out new branches.
8Even if its roots grow old in the ground,
and its stump dies in the dirt,
9at the smell of water it will bud
and put out new shoots like a plant.
10But we die, and our bodies are laid in the ground;
we take our last breath and are gone.
11Water disappears from a lake,
and a river loses its water and dries up.
12In the same way, we lie down and do not rise again;
we will not get up or be awakened
until the heavens disappear.

13"I wish you would hide me in the grave;
hide me until your anger is gone.
I wish you would set a time
and then remember me!
14Will the dead live again?
All my days are a struggle;
I will wait until my change comes.
15You will call, and I will answer you;
you will desire the creature your hands have made.
16Then you will count my steps,
but you will not keep track of my sin.
17My wrongs will be closed up in a bag,
and you will cover up my sin.

18"A mountain washes away and crumbles;
and a rock can be moved from its place.
19Water washes over stones and wears them down,
and rushing waters wash away the dirt.
In the same way, you destroy hope.
20You defeat people forever, and they are gone;
you change their appearance and send them away.
21Their children are honored, but they do not know it;
their children are disgraced, but they do not see it.
22They only feel the pain of their body
and feel sorry for themselves."

Eliphaz Answers Job

15 Then Eliphaz the Temanite answered:
2"A wise person would not answer with empty words
or fill his stomach with the hot east wind.
3He would not argue with useless words
or make speeches that have no value.
4But you even destroy respect for God
and limit the worship of him.
5Your sin teaches your mouth what to say;
you use words to trick others.
6It is your own mouth, not mine, that shows you are wicked;

Stories of SURVIVAL

Secondary Infertility
NATASHA'S STORY

Many women have struggled with infertility, and nearly everyone knows at least one of those women. However, fewer people are familiar with secondary infertility—the inability to have a child after successfully giving birth to one or more children.

My husband and I rode an emotional roller coaster for more than two years as we tried to conceive our second child. We wondered why we couldn't have another baby, especially since we had succeeded once before. Was God using our infertility to tell us that we were bad parents? Was there a lesson he was trying to teach us? Why wouldn't he answer our desperate prayers for another joyous addition to our family?

The heartbreak was compounded by the people around me. Well-meaning friends kept asking when we were going to have another child, and my sister became pregnant with her fifth baby. It was so hard seeing pregnant mothers or hearing that other parents I knew were now expecting again. I finally found comfort in Psalm 113:9: "He gives children to the woman who has none and makes her a happy mother. Praise the LORD!"

While God had not promised me more children, this verse helped me hope that he wanted to bless me somehow. Even though I continued to face disappointment month after month, I began to believe that God hadn't forgotten me. Perhaps God had a project he wanted to birth through me. Maybe I'd be the mother of just one child and be blessed with special opportunities to nurture and minister to others outside my biological family. I felt I could trust God to take away the empty ache in my heart.

My husband and I eventually conceived a second child, a beautiful baby girl who completes our family. Even if God had not chosen to answer my prayers with another baby, I learned a valuable lesson along our journey of infertility. I now fully trust that God has a great plan in store for me and those I love, even when life doesn't go the way I want it to.

> THIS VERSE HELPED ME HOPE THAT HE WANTED TO BLESS ME SOMEHOW.

january

New Year's Day. Set new spiritual goals. What can you learn about God this year? **1**	Donate anything you don't need to a charity. **2**	**3**	Do Internet research on a place you'd like to visit one day. **4**	**5**
Find someone you can mentor. **6**	Pray for a person of influence: It's Katie Couric's birthday. **7**	Spend ten minutes in silence today. **8**	January is National Soup Month. Give away some Campbell's! **9**	Reconnect with a long-lost friend. **10**
Embrace technology! Learn how to use a new computer program. **11**	Try to find faith-related themes in a movie you watch. **12**	Pray for a person of influence: It's Orlando Bloom's birthday. **13**	**14**	*Start a prayer journal.* **15**
16	**17**	Pray for a person of influence: It's Kevin Costner's birthday. **18**	**19**	Memorize Psalm 23. Recite it out loud the next time you're afraid! **20**
21	*Organize a game night with friends.* **22**	**23**	Get active! Don't let your gym membership go to waste. **24**	**25**
Pray for a person of influence: It's Kirk Franklin's birthday. **26**	**27**	**28**	Pray for a person of influence: It's Oprah Winfrey's birthday. **29**	**30**
31				

"Prayer is reaching out after the unseen."
–*Andrew Murray*

your own lips testify against
you.

⁷"You are not the first man ever
born;
you are not older than the hills.
⁸You did not listen in on God's secret
council.
But you limit wisdom to
yourself.
⁹You don't know any more than we
know.
You don't understand any more
than we understand.
¹⁰Old people with gray hair are on
our side;
they are even older than your
father.
¹¹Is the comfort God gives you not
enough for you,
even when words are spoken
gently to you?
¹²Has your heart carried you away
from God?
Why do your eyes flash with
anger?
¹³Why do you speak out your anger
against God?
Why do these words pour out of
your mouth?

¹⁴"How can anyone be pure?
How can someone born to a
woman be good?
¹⁵God places no trust in his holy ones,
and even the heavens are not
pure in his eyes.
¹⁶How much less pure is one who is
terrible and rotten
and drinks up evil as if it were
water!

¹⁷"Listen to me, and I will tell you
about it;
I will tell you what I have seen.
¹⁸These are things wise men have
told;
their ancestors told them, and
they have hidden nothing.
¹⁹(The land was given to their fathers
only,
and no foreigner lived among
them.)

²⁰The wicked suffer pain all their
lives;
the cruel suffer during all the
years saved up for them.
²¹Terrible sounds fill their ears,
and when things seem to be
going well, robbers attack
them.
²²Evil people give up trying to escape
from the darkness;
it has been decided that they
will die by the sword.
²³They wander around and will
become food for vultures.
They know darkness will soon
come.
²⁴Worry and suffering terrify them;
they overwhelm them, like a
king ready to attack,

²⁵because they shake their fists at
God
and try to get their own way
against the Almighty.
²⁶They stubbornly charge at God
with thick, strong shields.

²⁷"Although the faces of the wicked
are thick with fat,
and their bellies are fat with
flesh,
²⁸they will live in towns that are
ruined,
in houses where no one lives,
which are crumbling into ruins.
²⁹The wicked will no longer get rich,
and the riches they have will not
last;
the things they own will no
longer spread over the land.

³⁰They will not escape the
darkness.
A flame will dry up their
branches;
God's breath will carry the
wicked away.
³¹The wicked should not fool
themselves by trusting what
is useless.
If they do, they will get nothing
in return.
³²Their branches will dry up before
they finish growing
and will never turn green.
³³They will be like a vine whose
grapes are pulled off before
they are ripe,
like an olive tree that loses its
blossoms.

**More than 8.7 million peo-
ple underwent cosmetic
surgery in 2003, up 33%
from 2002.**

(American Society of Plastic
Surgery)

³⁴People without God can produce
nothing.
Fire will destroy the tents of
those who take money to do
evil,
³⁵who plan trouble and give birth to
evil,
whose hearts plan ways to trick
others."

Job Answers Eliphaz

16 Then Job answered:
²"I have heard many
things like these.
You are all painful comforters!
³Will your long-winded speeches
never end?
What makes you keep on arguing?
⁴I also could speak as you do
if you were in my place.

RELATIONSHIPS

Sleep on It

Psalm 4:4 reminds us not to sin when we are angry. When your temper flares, one of the best ways to avoid sinning is to take a step back before responding. Through his servant David, God essentially tells us to take a deep breath, count to ten, and think through our circumstances before reacting. Better yet, pray before responding to a situation. Anger in itself is not harmful; in fact, it is a God-given emotion that can motivate us to confront injustice or wrongdoing. But left unchecked, anger can be explosive, dangerous, and destructive to priceless relationships. So the next time you find yourself angry with someone, take a moment to cool down before you respond. It's in your best interest!

I could make great speeches against you
and shake my head at you.
⁵But, instead, I would encourage you,
and my words would bring you relief.

⁶"Even if I speak, my pain is not less,
and if I don't speak, it still does not go away.
⁷God, you have surely taken away my strength
and destroyed my whole family.
⁸You have made me thin and weak,
and this shows I have done wrong.
⁹God attacks me and tears me with anger;
he grinds his teeth at me;
my enemy stares at me with his angry eyes.
¹⁰People open their mouths to make fun of me
and hit my cheeks to insult me.
They join together against me.
¹¹God has turned me over to evil people
and has handed me over to the wicked.

¹²Everything was fine with me,
but God broke me into pieces;
he held me by the neck and crushed me.
He has made me his target;
¹³ his archers surround me.
He stabs my kidneys without mercy;
he spills my blood on the ground.
¹⁴Again and again God attacks me;
he runs at me like a soldier.

¹⁵"I have sewed rough cloth over my skin to show my sadness
and have buried my face in the dust.
¹⁶My face is red from crying;
I have dark circles around my eyes.
¹⁷Yet my hands have never done anything cruel,
and my prayer is pure.

¹⁸"Earth, please do not cover up my blood.
Don't let my cry ever stop being heard!

¹⁹Even now I have one who speaks for me in heaven;
the one who is on my side is high above.
²⁰The one who speaks for me is my friend.
My eyes pour out tears to God.
²¹He begs God on behalf of a human
as a person begs for his friend.

²²"Only a few years will pass
before I go on the journey of no return.

17 My spirit is broken;
the days of my life are almost gone.
The grave is waiting for me.
²Those who laugh at me surround me;
I watch them insult me.

³"God, make me a promise.
No one will make a pledge for me.
⁴You have closed their minds to understanding.
Do not let them win over me.
⁵People might speak against their friends for money,

but if they do, the eyes of their
children go blind.

6"God has made my name a curse
word;
people spit in my face.
7My sight has grown weak because of
my sadness,
and my body is as thin as a
shadow.
8Honest people are upset about this;
innocent people are upset with
those who do wrong.
9But those who do right will
continue to do right,
and those whose hands are not
dirty with sin will grow
stronger.

10"But, all of you, come and try again!
I do not find a wise person
among you.
11My days are gone, and my plans
have been destroyed,
along with the desires of my
heart.
12These men think night is day;
when it is dark, they say, 'Light
is near.'
13If the only home I hope for is the
grave,
if I spread out my bed in
darkness,
14if I say to the grave, 'You are my
father,'
and to the worm, 'You are my
mother' or 'You are my
sister,'
15where, then, is my hope?
Who can see any hope for me?
16Will hope go down to the gates of
death?
Will we go down together into
the dust?"

Bildad Answers Job

18 Then Bildad the Shuhite
answered:
2"When will you stop these speeches?
Be sensible, and then we can
talk.
3You think of us as cattle,
as if we are stupid.

4You tear yourself to pieces in your
anger.
Should the earth be vacant just
for you?
Should the rocks move from
their places?

5"The lamp of the wicked will be put
out,
and the flame in their lamps will
stop burning.
6The light in their tents will grow
dark,

and the lamps by their sides will
go out.
7Their strong steps will grow weak;
they will fall into their own evil
traps.
8Their feet will be caught in a net
when they walk into its web.
9A trap will catch them by the heel
and hold them tight.
10A trap for them is hidden on the
ground,
right in their path.

Become INVOLVED

Food for the Hungry

Food for the Hungry (FFTH) provides food, clean water, education, medical care, agricultural projects, building projects, child development programs, health and nutrition programs, micro-enterprise loans, and emergency relief for forty-seven countries around the world. Founded in 1971, this evangelistic organization gives ninety-three percent of all donations directly to the countries in need.

FFTH offers many ways for volunteers to get plugged in to their programs. One way is through their child sponsorship program that is similar to those of World Vision and Compassion International. For about a dollar a month, this program enables people to sponsor a child in another country and provide for his basic needs. It's amazing what one dollar can do for a child in need!

In addition to child sponsorship, volunteers can also make a short-term or long-term commitment to missions through FFTH's Hunger Corps. Volunteers can also train to be advocates for the poor in their own communities or sign up to become a prayer partner with FFTH. Prayer partners receive monthly e-mail updates highlighting a different country and its needs.

To find out more about getting involved with Food for the Hungry, check out their Web site at www.fh.org or call 1-800-2-HUNGER.

¹¹Terrible things startle them from every side
and chase them at every step.
¹²Hunger takes away their strength,
and disaster is at their side.
¹³Disease eats away parts of their skin;
death gnaws at their arms and legs.
¹⁴They are torn from the safety of their tents
and dragged off to Death, the King of Terrors.
¹⁵Their tents are set on fire,
and sulfur is scattered over their homes.
¹⁶Their roots dry up below ground,
and their branches die above ground.
¹⁷People on earth will not remember them;
their names will be forgotten in the land.
¹⁸They will be driven from light into darkness
and chased out of the world.
¹⁹They have no children or descendants among their people,
and no one will be left alive where they once lived.
²⁰People of the west will be shocked at what has happened to them,
and people of the east will be very frightened.
²¹Surely this is what will happen to the wicked;
such is the place of one who does not know God."

Job Answers Bildad

19 Then Job answered:
²"How long will you hurt me
and crush me with your words?
³You have insulted me ten times now
and attacked me without shame.
⁴Even if I have sinned,
it is my worry alone.
⁵If you want to make yourselves look better than I,
you can blame me for my suffering.
⁶Then know that God has wronged me
and pulled his net around me.
⁷"I shout, 'I have been wronged!'
But I get no answer.
I scream for help
but I get no justice.
⁸God has blocked my way so I cannot pass;
he has covered my paths with darkness.
⁹He has taken away my honor
and removed the crown from my head.
¹⁰He beats me down on every side until I am gone;
he destroys my hope like a fallen tree.
¹¹His anger burns against me,
and he treats me like an enemy.
¹²His armies gather;
they prepare to attack me.
They camp around my tent.
¹³"God has made my brothers my enemies,
and my friends have become strangers.
¹⁴My relatives have gone away,
and my friends have forgotten me.
¹⁵My guests and my female servants treat me like a stranger;
they look at me as if I were a foreigner.
¹⁶I call for my servant, but he does not answer,
even when I beg him with my own mouth.
¹⁷My wife can't stand my breath,
and my own family dislikes me.
¹⁸Even the little boys hate me
and talk about me when I leave.
¹⁹All my close friends hate me;
even those I love have turned against me.

Life Issues

Parent Problems

Honoring and obeying your parents can be hard—especially if your parents don't recognize that you're an adult. How can you honor your parents and still maintain healthy boundaries? First, forgive them for anything they did wrong in your younger years. Children don't come with instructions, and all parents unintentionally make mistakes (unfortunately, some do so intentionally). Ephesians 6:2 says to "Honor your father and mother," and it doesn't set a time limit or put any conditions on the command. When you honor your parents, regardless of their meddling and mistakes, the character of Christ becomes refined in you. It also shows your parents just how much you've matured—physically and spiritually. Yes, you can have your own life, but you need to leave room in it for the parents God gave you.

²⁰I am nothing but skin and bones;
  I have escaped by the skin of my
  teeth.
²¹Pity me, my friends, pity me,
  because the hand of God has hit
  me.
²²Why do you chase me as God does?
  Haven't you hurt me enough?

²³"How I wish my words were written
  down,
  written on a scroll.
²⁴I wish they were carved with an
  iron pen into lead,
  or carved into stone forever.
²⁵I know that my Defender lives,
  and in the end he will stand
  upon the earth.
²⁶Even after my skin has been
  destroyed,
  in my flesh I will see God.
²⁷I will see him myself;
  I will see him with my very own
  eyes.
  How my heart wants that to
  happen!

²⁸"If you say, 'We will continue to
  trouble Job,
  because the problem lies with
  him,'
²⁹you should be afraid of the sword
  yourselves.
  God's anger will bring
  punishment by the sword.
  Then you will know there is
  judgment."

Zophar Answers

20 Then Zophar the Naama-
thite answered:
²"My troubled thoughts cause me to
  answer,
  because I am very upset.
³You correct me and I am insulted,
  but I understand how to answer
  you.

⁴"You know how it has been for a
  long time,
  ever since people were first put
  on the earth.
⁵The happiness of evil people is brief,

What's the POINT?

Job 19:1–3

Have you ever been blamed for something you didn't do? It's the worst feeling, isn't it? Let's say some people you thought were friends spread a story about you, and now the rumors are running rampant. The people you trusted are urging you to "come clean," but you know you've done nothing wrong. They have judged you prematurely, and it's tough to convince them you are innocent. Job knew exactly what that felt like. When he was at the lowest point in his life, his friends just shook their heads, pointed their fingers, and asked him what he had done to deserve his punishment. No sympathy, no assistance, no encouragement. Just a heaping dose of criticism and judgment. What Job needed was someone to believe in him, love him, and stand by him. Instead, he got the third degree! Job's story serves as a reminder not to jump to conclusions the next time you hear a rumor. If a friend falls on hard times, be sure that your reaction is not one of accusation or criticism. What hurting people need most is compassion and care, someone to stand by their side and assure them things will all work out. Will that be you the next time you see someone in need? Now that's real friendship!

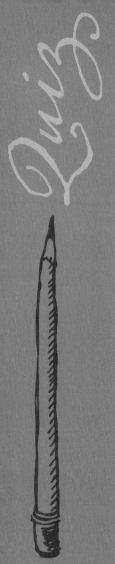

how high maintenance are you?

1. YOU'RE GOING OUT TO RUN A FEW ERRANDS. BEFORE YOU WALK OUT THE DOOR, YOU:

❏ A. Put on a casual outfit and spend five minutes or so on your hair and makeup.

❏ B. Throw on some sweatpants and put your hair in a ponytail.

❏ C. Take more than an hour picking out your clothes, putting on your makeup, and styling your hair. After trying on at least three pairs of shoes, you're finally ready to run those errands.

2. YOU ARE HAVING LUNCH WITH A FEW FRIENDS. WHEN THE SERVER ASKS FOR YOUR ORDER, YOU:

❏ A. Begin grilling the server about every option and substitution. When you can't get exactly what you want, you silently vow to never eat there again.

❏ B. Ask for one substitution with your meal and a slice of lemon in your beverage.

❏ C. Quickly pick something off the menu and return to the conversation.

3. A FRIEND SENDS YOU FLOWERS. YOU NOTICE THAT SOME OF THE FLOWERS ARE ALREADY WILTING. YOU ARE:

❏ A. So excited that you overlook the problem. You immediately call your friend and thank her for her thoughtfulness.

❏ B. Disappointed with the arrangement. You call the florist and ask what can be done to correct the situation. Regardless of the response, you decide your friend's kindness deserves a double dose of gratitude. You not only call her but also send a handwritten note of thanks.

❏ C. In a state of shock. How could the florist deliver wilted flowers? You call immediately but refuse the florist's offer to replace the arrangement. You ask that your friend receive a full refund. You call and thank your friend, explaining the situation. You feel good about your decision.

Scoring:

1. A=2, B=1, C=3
2. C=3, B=2, C=1
3. A=1, B=2, C=3

IF YOU SCORED 1-4, YOU ARE DEFINITELY LOW MAINTENANCE. You're laid-back, easy to please, and comfortable with yourself. You're okay with imperfection, and your relaxed attitude makes you a joy to be around.

IF YOU SCORED 5-7, YOU ARE MEDIUM MAINTENANCE. You want to take care of yourself, but not at the cost of making other people uncomfortable. You recognize that there are boundaries of acceptable behavior, and you are willing to compromise when it's warranted.

IF YOU SCORED 8 OR HIGHER, YOU ARE PROBABLY HIGH MAINTENANCE. You have high expectations of yourself and others, and you're not afraid to let people know when they don't meet those expectations. You're picky and see your high standards as a reflection of who you are. The problem occurs when your high-maintenance moments cause you to put your needs above the needs of others. Your words and actions can inadvertently push away the people who love and care about you.

WHAT'S IN A word?

Job 20:1 "Zophar" means "chirping." Like a bird chirping noisily in the early morning, Zophar—also a friend of Job—offered some of the harshest comments on Job's situation.

and the joy of the wicked lasts only a moment.
[6]Their pride may be as high as the heavens,
and their heads may touch the clouds,
[7]but they will be gone forever, like their own dung.
People who knew them will say, 'Where are they?'
[8]They will fly away like a dream and not be found again;
they will be chased away like a vision in the night.
[9]Those who saw them will not see them again;
the places where they lived will see them no more.
[10]Their children will have to pay back the poor,
and they will have to give up their wealth.
[11]They had the strength of their youth in their bones,
but it will lie with them in the dust of death.

[12]"Evil may taste sweet in their mouths, and they may hide it under their tongues.
[13]They cannot stand to let go of it; they keep it in their mouths.
[14]But their food will turn sour in their stomachs,
like the poison of a snake inside them.
[15]They have swallowed riches, but they will spit them out;
God will make them vomit their riches up.

[16]They will suck the poison of snakes, and the snake's fangs will kill them.
[17]They will not admire the sparkling streams
or the rivers flowing with honey and cream.
[18]They must give back what they worked for without eating it;
they will not enjoy the money they made from their trading,
[19]because they troubled the poor and left them with nothing.
They have taken houses they did not build.

[20]"Evil people never lack an appetite, and nothing escapes their selfishness.
[21]But nothing will be left for them to eat;
their riches will not continue.
[22]When they still have plenty, trouble will catch up to them,
and great misery will come down on them.
[23]When the wicked fill their stomachs,
God will send his burning anger against them,
and blows of punishment will fall on them like rain.
[24]The wicked may run away from an iron weapon,
but a bronze arrow will stab them.
[25]They will pull the arrows out of their backs
and pull the points out of their livers.
Terrors will come over them;
[26]   total darkness waits for their treasure.
A fire not fanned by people will destroy them
and burn up what is left of their tents.
[27]The heavens will show their guilt,

Q: WHAT ARE SOME WAYS I CAN GET CLOSER TO GOD?

A: First Thessalonians 5:17 simply says, "Pray continually." Talk with God constantly throughout the day, just as you would talk to a friend (or even yourself!). Develop a daily habit of picking up your Bible and reading it, along with a devotional or Christian classic. Create a prayer journal with pictures of those you are praying for, and write down your thoughts and prayers along with the answers you receive. This is a great way to record how God is working in your life!

WISE WORDS

Give Generously

It doesn't take too many holiday seasons before you begin to realize that the biggest joy in any gift exchange is giving rather than receiving. Even though new gadgets and gizmos are fun to receive, there's nothing like putting a smile on someone else's face. God is a big fan of giving! Not only does he lavish you with his love, grace, and provision, he invites you to experience the joy of giving. Proverbs 3:9 encourages believers to honor the Lord with their wealth and the "firstfruits" of their crops. You may not have a garden to share, but you do have income, time, talents, and encouragement that you can share generously for God's glory. Participate in the joy of giving today!

and the earth will rise up against them.
28A flood will carry their houses away,
    swept away on the day of God's anger.
29This is what God plans for evil people;

this is what he has decided they will receive."

Job Answers Zophar

21 Then Job answered:
2"Listen carefully to my words,
    and let this be the way you comfort me.
3Be patient while I speak.
    After I have finished, you may continue to make fun of me.

4"My complaint is not just against people;
    I have reason to be impatient.
5Look at me and be shocked;
    put your hand over your mouth in shock.
6When I think about this, I am terribly afraid
    and my body shakes.
7Why do evil people live a long time?
    They grow old and become more powerful.
8They see their children around them;
    they watch them grow up.
9Their homes are safe and without fear;
    God does not punish them.
10Their bulls never fail to mate;
    their cows have healthy calves.
11They send out their children like a flock;
    their little ones dance about.
12They sing to the music of tambourines and harps,
    and the sound of the flute makes them happy.
13Evil people enjoy successful lives
    and then go peacefully to the grave.
14They say to God, 'Leave us alone!
    We don't want to know your ways.
15Who is the Almighty that we should serve him?
    What would we gain by praying to him?'
16The success of the wicked is not their own doing.

Their way of thinking is different from mine.
17Yet how often are the lamps of evil people turned off?
    How often does trouble come to them?
    How often do they suffer God's angry punishment?
18How often are they like straw in the wind
    or like chaff that is blown away by a storm?
19It is said, 'God saves up a person's punishment for his children.'
    But God should punish the wicked themselves so they will know it.
20Their eyes should see their own destruction,
    and they should suffer the anger of the Almighty.
21They do not care about the families they leave behind
    when their lives have come to an end.

22"No one can teach knowledge to God;
    he is the one who judges even the most important people.
23One person dies while he still has all his strength,
    feeling completely safe and comfortable.
24His body was well fed,
    and his bones were strong and healthy.
25But another person dies with an unhappy heart,
    never enjoying any happiness.
26They are buried next to each other,
    and worms cover them both.

27"I know very well your thoughts
    and your plans to wrong me.
28You ask about me, 'Where is this great man's house?
    Where are the tents where the wicked live?'
29Have you never asked those who travel?

Have you never listened to their stories?
³⁰On the day of God's anger and punishment,
it is the wicked who are spared.
³¹Who will accuse them to their faces?
Who will pay them back for the evil they have done?
³²They are carried to their graves,
and someone keeps watch over their tombs.
³³The dirt in the valley seems sweet to them.
Everybody follows after them,
and many people go before them.

³⁴"So how can you comfort me with this nonsense?
Your answers are only lies!"

Eliphaz Answers

22 Then Eliphaz the Temanite answered:
²"Can anyone be of real use to God?
Can even a wise person do him good?
³Does it help the Almighty for you to be good?
Does he gain anything if you are innocent?
⁴Does God punish you for respecting him?
Does he bring you into court for this?
⁵No! It is because your evil is without limits
and your sins have no end.
⁶You took your brothers' things for a debt they didn't owe;
you took clothes from people and left them naked.
⁷You did not give water to tired people,
and you kept food from the hungry.
⁸You were a powerful man who owned land;
you were honored and lived in the land.
⁹But you sent widows away empty-handed,

and you mistreated orphans.
¹⁰That is why traps are all around you
and sudden danger frightens you.
¹¹That is why it is so dark you cannot see
and a flood of water covers you.

¹²"God is in the highest part of heaven.
See how high the highest stars are!
¹³But you ask, 'What does God know?
Can he judge us through the dark clouds?
¹⁴Thick clouds cover him so he cannot see us
as he walks around high up in the sky.'
¹⁵Are you going to stay on the old path where evil people walk?
¹⁶They were carried away before their time was up,
and their foundations were washed away by a flood.
¹⁷They said to God, 'Leave us alone!
The Almighty can do nothing to us.'
¹⁸But it was God who filled their houses with good things.
Their way of thinking is different from mine.

¹⁹"Good people can watch and be glad;
the innocent can laugh at them and say,
²⁰'Surely our enemies are destroyed,
and fire burns up their wealth.'

²¹"Obey God and be at peace with him;
this is the way to happiness.
²²Accept teaching from his mouth,
and keep his words in your heart.
²³If you return to the Almighty, you will be blessed again.
So remove evil from your house.
²⁴Throw your gold nuggets into the dust
and your fine gold among the rocks in the ravines.

Corporate Time

Intimate times of worship with God are vital to the spiritual life of a believer. But quiet time alone is not enough. You were created to join with other believers who have the common goal of worshiping Christ. David writes of praising the Lord "in the great meeting" with other worshipers (see Psalm 22:25). The New Testament talks about believers strengthening one another in the faith. Corporate worship encourages the hearts of believers and is a precious gift that pleases God.

²⁵Then the Almighty will be your gold
and the best silver for you.
²⁶You will find pleasure in the Almighty,
and you will look up to him.
²⁷You will pray to him, and he will hear you,

MONEY

Becoming Debt-Free

Consumer debt has more than doubled to over $2 trillion in the last ten years. According to the Federal Reserve Board, that figure translates into $18,700 per U.S. household—and that doesn't include home mortgages. Now that's a lot of debt! Credit card companies want us to be comfortable with debt so that we will spend more and continue to increase their profits. But debt isn't your friend. Interest, fees, and excess charges cause debt to grow even if you buy something on sale.

Say you find a beautiful necklace for $500. If you buy it now, you'll save twenty percent, making it only $400. You decide to go for the bling-bling and charge it on your credit card. If your card's interest rate is eighteen percent and you make only the minimum payments, it will take you about 5.2 years to pay off the necklace! In the end, you'll pay $215.42 in interest—a total of $115.42 more than the full price. And that's no bargain!

The good news is that no matter how much debt you have, it's never too late to make a change. Agencies are available to help you consolidate your debt at lower interest rates. You may have to get creative, downsize, take on a second job, carpool, or give up extras like cable TV, but you *can* be debt-free. It's worth it. Romans 13:7 says, "Pay everyone, then, what you owe." Begin taking the necessary steps toward financial freedom today!

and you will keep your promises
  to him.
28Anything you decide will be done,
  and light will shine on your
    ways.
29When people are made humble and
    you say, 'Have courage,'
  then the humble will be saved.
30Even a guilty person will escape
  and be saved because your hands
    are clean."

Job Answers

23 Then Job answered:
2"My complaint is still
    bitter today.
  I groan because God's heavy
    hand is on me.
3I wish I knew where to find God
  so I could go to where he lives.
4I would present my case before him
  and fill my mouth with
    arguments.
5I would learn how he would answer
    me
  and would think about what he
    would say.
6Would he not argue strongly
    against me?
  No, he would really listen to me.
7Then an honest person could
    present his case to God,
  and I would be saved forever by
    my judge.

8"If I go to the east, God is not there;
  if I go to the west, I do not see
    him.
9When he is at work in the north, I
    catch no sight of him;
  when he turns to the south, I
    cannot see him.
10But God knows the way that I
    take,
  and when he has tested me, I
    will come out like gold.
11My feet have closely followed his
    steps;
  I have stayed in his way;
  I did not turn aside.
12I have never left the commands he
    has spoken;

I have treasured his words more
than my own.

¹³"But he is the only God.
Who can come against him?
He does anything he wants.
¹⁴He will do to me what he said he
would do,
and he has many plans like this.
¹⁵That is why I am frightened of him;
when I think of this, I am afraid
of him.
¹⁶God has made me afraid;
the Almighty terrifies me.
¹⁷But I am not hidden by the
darkness,
by the thick darkness that
covers my face.

24 "I wish the Almighty would
set a time for judging.
Those who know God do not see
such a day.
²Wicked people take other people's
land;
they steal flocks and take them
to new pastures.
³They chase away the orphan's
donkey
and take the widow's ox when
she has no money.
⁴They push needy people off the
path;
all the poor of the land hide
from them.
⁵The poor become like wild donkeys
in the desert
who go about their job of
finding food.
The desert gives them food for
their children.
⁶They gather hay and straw in the
fields
and pick up leftover grapes from
the vineyard of the wicked.
⁷They spend the night naked,
because they have no
clothes,
nothing to cover themselves in
the cold.
⁸They are soaked from mountain
rains

and stay near the large rocks
because they have no
shelter.
⁹The fatherless child is grabbed
from its mother's breast;
they take a poor mother's baby
to pay for what she owes.
¹⁰So the poor go around naked
without any clothes;
they carry bundles of grain but
still go hungry;
¹¹they crush olives to get oil
and grapes to get wine, but they
still go thirsty.
¹²Dying people groan in the city,
and the injured cry out for help,
but God accuses no one of doing
wrong.

¹³"Those who fight against the
light
do not know God's ways
or stay in his paths.
¹⁴When the day is over, the
murderers get up
to kill the poor and needy.
At night they go about like
thieves.

Don't Fall Too Hard!

Proverbs 5 is more than just a warning against adultery; it's a caution to use your head—not just your heart—when falling in love. The writer says to use good sense (verse 2) and not to give your love away to just anyone (verse 16). This may seem like obvious advice, but when emotions are involved, even the most level-headed person can become a bit starry-eyed. Remember that loving someone is a choice. You may respond emotionally to someone, but to truly love—*love* as a verb—you must add your intellect and rationality to the equation. Be wise in choosing a mate, and seek the objective opinions of those you trust before you take the plunge!

¹⁵Those who are guilty of adultery
watch for the night,
thinking, 'No one will see us,'
and they keep their faces
covered.
¹⁶In the dark, evil people break into
houses.
In the daytime they shut
themselves up in their own
houses,
because they want nothing to do
with the light.
¹⁷Darkness is like morning to all
these evil people

who make friends with the
terrors of darkness.

¹⁸"They are like foam floating on the
water.
Their part of the land is cursed;
no one uses the road that goes
by their vineyards.
¹⁹As heat and dryness quickly melt
the snow,
so the grave quickly takes away
the sinners.
²⁰Their mothers forget them,
and worms will eat their bodies.
They will not be remembered,
so wickedness is broken in
pieces like a stick.
²¹These evil people abuse women who
cannot have children
and show no kindness to widows.
²²But God drags away the strong by
his power.
Even though they seem strong,
they do not know how long
they will live.

²³God may let these evil people feel
safe,
but he is watching their ways.
²⁴For a little while they are
important, and then they
die;
they are laid low and buried like
everyone else;
they are cut off like the heads of
grain.
²⁵If this is not true, who can prove I
am wrong?
Who can show that my words are
worth nothing?"

{ fun FACTS }

Adding 30 minutes to your daily commute increases your risk of becoming obese by 3%.

(American Journal of Preventative Medicines)

Bildad Answers

25 Then Bildad the Shuhite
answered:
²"God rules and he must be honored;
he set up order in his high
heaven.
³No one can count God's armies.
His light shines on all people.
⁴So no one can be good in the
presence of God,
and no one born to a woman can
be pure.
⁵Even the moon is not bright
and the stars are not pure in his
eyes.
⁶People are much less! They are like
insects.
They are only worms!"

Job Answers Bildad

26 Then Job answered:
²"You are no help to the
helpless!
You have not aided the weak!
³Your advice lacks wisdom!

You have shown little
understanding!
⁴Who has helped you say these
words?
And where did you get these
ideas?

⁵"The spirits of the dead tremble,
those who are beneath and in
the waters.
⁶Death is naked before God;
destruction is uncovered before
him.
⁷God stretches the northern sky out
over empty space
and hangs the earth on nothing.
⁸He wraps up the waters in his thick
clouds,
but the clouds do not break
under their weight.
⁹He covers the face of the moon,
spreading his clouds over it.
¹⁰He draws the horizon like a circle
on the water
at the place where light and
darkness meet.
¹¹Heaven's foundations shake
when he thunders at them.
¹²With his power he quiets the sea;
by his wisdom he destroys
Rahab, the sea monster.
¹³He breathes, and the sky clears.
His hand stabs the fleeing
snake.
¹⁴And these are only a small part of
God's works.
We only hear a small whisper of
him.
Who could understand God's
thundering power?"

27 And Job continued speaking:
²"As surely as God lives, who has
taken away my rights,
the Almighty, who has made me
unhappy,
³as long as I am alive
and God's breath of life is in my
nose,
⁴my lips will not speak evil,
and my tongue will not tell a lie.

⁵I will never agree you are right;
    until I die, I will never stop
        saying I am innocent.
⁶I will insist that I am right; I will
        not back down.
    My conscience will never bother
        me.

⁷"Let my enemies be like evil
        people,
    my foes like those who are
        wrong.
⁸What hope do the wicked have
        when they die,
    when God takes their life away?
⁹God will not listen to their cries
    when trouble comes to them.
¹⁰They will not find joy in the
        Almighty,
    even though they call out to God
        all the time.

¹¹"I will teach you about the power of
        God
    and will not hide the ways of the
        Almighty.
¹²You have all seen this yourselves.
    So why are we having all this
        talk that means nothing?

¹³"Here is what God has planned for
        evil people,
    and what the Almighty will give
        to cruel people:
¹⁴They may have many children, but
        the sword will kill them.
    Their children who are left will
        never have enough to eat.
¹⁵Then they will die of disease and be
        buried,
    and the widows will not even cry
        for them.
¹⁶The wicked may heap up silver like
        piles of dirt
    and have so many clothes they
        are like piles of clay.
¹⁷But good people will wear what evil
        people have gathered,
    and the innocent will divide up
        their silver.
¹⁸The houses the wicked build are
        like a spider's web,
    like a hut that a guard builds.

¹⁹The wicked are rich when they go
        to bed,
    but they are rich for the last
        time;
    when they open their eyes,
        everything is gone.
²⁰Fears come over them like a flood,
    and a storm snatches them away
        in the night.
²¹The east wind will carry them away,
        and then they are gone,
    because it sweeps them out of
        their place.
²²The wind will hit them without
        mercy
    as they try to run away from its
        power.
²³It will be as if the wind is clapping
        its hands;
    it will whistle at them as they
        run from their place.

28

"There are mines where
        people dig silver
    and places where gold is made
        pure.
²Iron is taken from the ground,
    and copper is melted out of
        rocks.
³Miners bring lights
    and search deep into the mines
        for ore in thick darkness.

⁴Miners dig a tunnel far from where
        people live,
    where no one has ever walked;
    they work far from people,
        swinging and swaying from
        ropes.
⁵Food grows on top of the earth,
    but below ground things are
        changed as if by fire.
⁶Sapphires are found in rocks,
    and gold dust is also found
        there.
⁷No hawk knows that path;
    the falcon has not seen it.
⁸Proud animals have not walked
        there,
    and no lions cross over it.
⁹Miners hit the rocks of flint
    and dig away at the bottom of
        the mountains.
¹⁰They cut tunnels through the rock
    and see all the treasures there.
¹¹They search for places where rivers
        begin
    and bring things hidden out
        into the light.

Job

Job is a good man, yet he suffers terribly. He loses his wealth, his servants—even his children—though he did nothing wrong. His wife and his friends turn on him. Still, Job praises God. He vents his frustration toward God but still trusts God to handle the situation. He is the perfect example of bad things happening to good people, and his story teaches that God can handle our big questions and will remain faithful even when we don't get it. Ultimately, Job hangs on for the ride, and God restores what was taken from him.

BIBLE
Women & Men

What's the
POINT?

Job 28:15

Isn't beautiful jewelry fantastic? Bright gold necklaces, spectacular earrings with diamonds and rubies, and gorgeous bracelets covered with opals or pearls...wearing them makes you feel like someone special. Yet all the gems in the world won't make you wise. God made precious metals and gemstones because he loves beauty and wants you to appreciate it, but he never wants you to put your faith in it. Gold is just a metal, and diamonds are just rocks. They are both pulled from the dusty, dirty ground that God also created. Job talks about miners working underground, giving their all to get to the precious gemstones. But wisdom is far more valuable than any gemstone. Riches are great, but wisdom keeps your life on track. There are plenty of people whose wrists and necks are dripping with diamonds who can't keep their relationships together, who feel miserable and empty inside, and who do not have a personal relationship with God. They may look as if they have it all, but they have nothing that will sustain them when trouble comes. Enjoy the fine things God gives you, but realize that they are still just stuff! They will never give you the same satisfaction and peace that come when you pursue a daily relationship with God and continually ask him for wisdom in your life.

12"But where can wisdom be found,
 and where does understanding live?
13People do not understand the value of wisdom;
 it cannot be found among those who are alive.
14The deep ocean says, 'It's not in me;'
 the sea says, 'It's not in me.'
15Wisdom cannot be bought with gold,
 and its cost cannot be weighed in silver.
16Wisdom cannot be bought with fine gold
 or with valuable onyx or sapphire gems.
17Gold and crystal are not as valuable as wisdom,
 and you cannot buy it with jewels of gold.
18Coral and jasper are not worth talking about,
 and the price of wisdom is much greater than rubies.
19The topaz from Cush cannot compare to wisdom;
 it cannot be bought with the purest gold.

20"So where does wisdom come from,
 and where does understanding live?
21It is hidden from the eyes of every living thing,
 even from the birds of the air.
22The places of destruction and death say,
 'We have heard reports about it.'
23Only God understands the way to wisdom,
 and he alone knows where it lives,
24because he looks to the farthest parts of the earth
 and sees everything under the sky.
25When God gave power to the wind
 and measured the water,
26when he made rules for the rain
 and set a path for a thunderstorm to follow,

27then he looked at wisdom and
decided its worth;
he set wisdom up and tested it.
28Then he said to humans,
'The fear of the Lord is wisdom;
to stay away from evil is
understanding.' "

Job Continues

29 Job continued to speak:
2"How I wish for the months
that have passed
and the days when God watched
over me.
3God's lamp shined on my head,
and I walked through darkness
by his light.
4I wish for the days when I was
strong,
when God's close friendship
blessed my house.
5The Almighty was still with me,
and my children were all around
me.
6It was as if my path were covered
with cream
and the rocks poured out olive
oil for me.
7I would go to the city gate
and sit in the public square.
8When the young men saw me, they
would step aside,
and the old men would stand up
in respect.
9The leading men stopped speaking
and covered their mouths with
their hands.
10The voices of the important men
were quiet,
as if their tongues stuck to the
roof of their mouths.
11Anyone who heard me spoke well of
me,
and those who saw me praised
me,
12because I saved the poor who called
out
and the orphan who had no one
to help.
13The dying person blessed me,
and I made the widow's heart
sing.

14I put on right living as if it were
clothing;
I wore fairness like a robe and a
turban.
15I was eyes for the blind
and feet for the lame.
16I was like a father to needy people,
and I took the side of strangers
who were in trouble.
17I broke the fangs of evil people
and snatched the captives from
their teeth.

18"I thought, 'I will live for as many
days as there are grains of
sand,
and I will die in my own house.
19My roots will reach down to the
water.
The dew will lie on the branches
all night.
20New honors will come to me
continually,
and I will always have great
strength.'

21"People listened to me carefully
and waited quietly for my
advice.
22After I finished speaking, they
spoke no more.
My words fell very gently on
their ears.
23They waited for me as they would
for rain
and drank in my words like
spring rain.
24I smiled at them when they doubted,
and my approval was important
to them.
25I chose the way for them and was
their leader.
I lived like a king among his
army,
like a person who comforts sad
people.

30 "But now those who are
younger than I
make fun of me.
I would not have even let their
fathers
sit with my sheep dogs.

2What use did I have for their
strength
since they had lost their
strength to work?
3They were thin from hunger
and wandered the dry and
ruined land at night.
4They gathered desert plants among
the brush
and ate the root of the broom
tree.
5They were forced to live away from
people;
people shouted at them as if
they were thieves.
6They lived in dried-up streambeds,
in caves, and among the rocks.
7They howled like animals among
the bushes
and huddled together in the
brush.
8They are worthless people without
names
and were forced to leave the
land.

9"Now they make fun of me with
songs;
my name is a joke among them.
10They hate me and stay far away
from me,
but they do not mind spitting in
my face.
11God has taken away my strength
and made me suffer,
so they attack me with all their
anger.

WHAT'S IN A word?

Job 29:6 "Covered with cream"
may not describe a path you'd
like to walk down, but the
cream and oil mentioned in
this verse actually refer to
wealth!

¹²On my right side they rise up like a
    mob.
    They lay traps for my feet
    and prepare to attack me.
¹³They break up my road
    and work to destroy me,
    and no one helps me.
¹⁴They come at me as if through a
    hole in the wall,
    and they roll in among the ruins.
¹⁵Great fears overwhelm me.
    They blow my honor away as if
    by a great wind,
    and my safety disappears like a
    cloud.

¹⁶"Now my life is almost over;
    my days are full of suffering.
¹⁷At night my bones ache;
    gnawing pains never stop.
¹⁸In his great power God grabs hold
    of my clothing
    and chokes me with the collar of
    my coat.

¹⁹He throws me into the mud,
    and I become like dirt and ashes.

²⁰"I cry out to you, God, but you do
    not answer;
    I stand up, but you just look at
    me.
²¹You have turned on me without
    mercy;
    with your powerful hand you
    attacked me.
²²You snatched me up and threw me
    into the wind
    and tossed me about in the
    storm.
²³I know you will bring me down to
    death,
    to the place where all living
    people must go.

BE STILL & KNOW

Let It All Out

God doesn't want you to try to hide your true feelings from him when you pray (as if you can hide anything from God!). He isn't looking for flowery phrases or fake cheerfulness when things are going wrong. The book of Job clearly shows that honesty with God is truly the best policy! As tragedies befall Job at every turn, he openly expresses his

feelings to God. When you surrender control of everything, even your anger and sorrow, you allow God to transform your heart through prayer. Even if your trial doesn't have a happy ending like Job's did, you will never regret being transparent with God.

²⁴"Surely no one would hurt those
    who are ruined
    when they cry for help in their
    time of trouble.
²⁵I cried for those who were in
    trouble;
    I have been very sad for poor
    people.
²⁶But when I hoped for good, only
    evil came to me;
    when I looked for light,
    darkness came.
²⁷I never stop being upset;
    days of suffering are ahead of
    me.
²⁸I have turned black, but not by the
    sun.
    I stand up in public and cry for
    help.
²⁹I have become a brother to wild
    dogs
    and a friend to ostriches.
³⁰My skin has become black and peels
    off,
    as my body burns with fever.
³¹My harp is tuned to sing a sad
    song,
    and my flute is tuned to
    moaning.

31 "But I made an agreement
    with my eyes
    not to look with desire at a girl.
²What has God above promised for
    people?
    What has the Almighty planned
    from on high?
³It is ruin for evil people
    and disaster for those who do
    wrong.
⁴God sees my ways
    and counts every step I take.

⁵"If I have been dishonest
    or lied to others,
⁶then let God weigh me on honest
    scales.
    Then he will know I have done
    nothing wrong.
⁷If I have turned away from doing
    what is right,
    or my heart has been led by my
    eyes to do wrong,

or my hands have been made unclean,

[8] then let other people eat what I have planted,
and let my crops be plowed up.

[9] "If I have desired another woman
or have waited at my neighbor's door for his wife,
[10] then let my wife grind another man's grain,
and let other men have sexual relations with her.
[11] That would be shameful,
a sin to be punished.
[12] It is like a fire that burns and destroys;
all I have done would be plowed up.

[13] "If I have been unfair to my male and female slaves
when they had a complaint against me,
[14] how could I tell God what I did?
What will I answer when he asks me to explain what I've done?
[15] God made me in my mother's womb,
and he also made them;
the same God formed both of us in our mothers' wombs.

[16] "I have never refused the appeals of the poor
or let widows give up hope while looking for help.
[17] I have not kept my food to myself
but have given it to the orphans.
[18] Since I was young, I have been like a father to the orphans.
From my birth I guided the widows.
[19] I have not let anyone die for lack of clothes
or let a needy person go without a coat.
[20] That person's heart blessed me,
because I warmed him with the wool of my sheep.
[21] I have never hurt an orphan
even when I knew I could win in court.

ETIQUETTE 101

HOSTING HOUSEGUESTS

You finally have a home of your own, and you're ready for overnight visitors! Being a gracious hostess begins with a willingness to share all that you have (see Proverbs 11:24–25). Provide a nightlight, alarm clock, clean towels, and a bed with clean sheets. (If you're in a one-bedroom apartment, offer to sleep on the couch.) Present a spotless bathroom, and take steps to guard the privacy of your guests. Keep pets away from guests who are allergic or not fond of animals. Prepare a light breakfast—coffee, cereal, and juice are good basics. Finally, part with hugs and an invitation for another visit.

[22] If I have, then let my arm fall off my shoulder
and be broken at the joint.
[23] I fear destruction from God,
and I fear his majesty, so I could not do such things.

[24] "I have not put my trust in gold
or said to pure gold, 'You are my security.'
[25] I have not celebrated my great wealth
or the riches my hands had gained.
[26] I have not thought about worshiping the sun in its brightness
nor admired the moon moving in glory
[27] so that my heart was pulled away from God.
My hand has never offered the sun and moon a kiss of worship.
[28] If I had, these also would have been sins to be punished,

because I would have been unfaithful to God.

[29] "I have not been happy when my enemies fell
or laughed when they had trouble.
[30] I have not let my mouth sin
by cursing my enemies' life.
[31] The servants of my house have always said,
'All have eaten what they want of Job's food.'
[32] No stranger ever had to spend the night in the street,
because I always let travelers stay in my home.
[33] I have not hidden my sin as others do,
secretly keeping my guilt to myself.
[34] I was not so afraid of the crowd
that I kept quiet and stayed inside
because I feared being hated by other families.

WISE WORDS

Positive Thinking

Whether you're a glass-half-full or glass-half-empty kind of woman, God wants you to look for the good in others and in your own life. Proverbs 4:23 says, "Be careful what you think, because your thoughts run your life." If you are constantly thinking negative and destructive thoughts, they are going to affect your attitude, behavior, and relationships in an unhealthy way. That's not what God wants for your life! That's why he asks you to "keep your eyes focused on what is right, and look straight ahead to what is good" (Proverbs 4:25). By meditating and acting on his Word and his ways, you can't help but have a positive impact on the world around you. Now *that's* a goal worth focusing on!

35("How I wish a court would hear my case!
Here I sign my name to show I have told the truth.
Now let the Almighty answer me;
let the one who accuses me write it down.

36I would wear the writing on my shoulder;
I would put it on like a crown.
37I would explain to God every step I took,
and I would come near to him like a prince.)

38"If my land cries out against me
and its plowed rows are not wet with tears,
39if I have taken the land's harvest without paying
or have broken the spirit of those who worked the land,
40then let thorns come up instead of wheat,
and let weeds come up instead of barley."
The words of Job are finished.

Elihu Speaks

32 These three men stopped trying to answer Job, because he was so sure he was right. 2But Elihu son of Barakel the Buzite, from the family of Ram, became very angry with Job, because Job claimed he was right instead of God. 3Elihu was also angry with Job's three friends who had no answer to show that Job was wrong, yet continued to blame him. 4Elihu had waited before speaking to Job, because the three friends were older than he was. 5But when Elihu saw that the three men had nothing more to say, he became very angry.

6So Elihu son of Barakel the Buzite said this:
"I am young,
and you are old.
That is why I was afraid
to tell you what I know.
7I thought, 'Older people should speak,
and those who have lived many years should teach wisdom.'
8But it is the spirit in a person,
the breath of the Almighty, that gives understanding.
9It is not just older people who are wise;

they are not the only ones who understand what is right.
10So I say, listen to me.
I too will tell you what I know.
11I waited while you three spoke,
and listened to your explanations.
While you looked for words to use,
12 I paid close attention to you.
But not one of you has proved Job wrong;
none of you has answered his arguments.
13Don't say, 'We have found wisdom;
only God will show Job to be wrong, not people.'
14Job has not spoken his words against me,
so I will not use your arguments to answer Job.

15"These three friends are defeated
and have no more to say;
words have failed them.
16Now they are standing there with no answers for Job.
Now that they are quiet, must I wait to speak?
17No, I too will speak
and tell what I know.
18I am full of words,
and the spirit in me causes me to speak.
19I am like wine that has been bottled up;
I am ready to burst like a new leather wine bag.
20I must speak so I will feel relief;
I must open my mouth and answer.
21I will be fair to everyone
and not flatter anyone.
22I don't know how to flatter,
and if I did, my Maker would quickly take me away.

33 "Now, Job, listen to my words.
Pay attention to everything I say.
2I open my mouth
and am ready to speak.
3My words come from an honest heart,

and I am sincere in saying what I
know.
[4]The Spirit of God created me,
and the breath of the Almighty
gave me life.
[5]Answer me if you can;
get yourself ready and stand
before me.
[6]I am just like you before God;
I too am made out of clay.
[7]Don't be afraid of me;
I will not be hard on you.

[8]"But I heard what you have said;
I heard every word.
[9]You said, 'I am pure and without
sin;
I am innocent and free from
guilt.
[10]But God has found fault with me;
he considers me his enemy.
[11]He locks my feet in chains
and closely watches everywhere I
go.'

[12]"But I tell you, you are not right in
saying this,
because God is greater than we
are.
[13]Why do you accuse God
of not answering anyone?
[14]God does speak—sometimes one way
and sometimes another—
even though people may not
understand it.
[15]He speaks in a dream or a vision of
the night

WHAT'S IN A word?

Job 32:2 "Elihu" means "whose
God is he." After the debate
between Job and his three
friends comes to a close, Elihu
makes an appearance to offer
his wise perspective on Job's
situation. Though he is a
young man, he speaks the
truth with confidence.

when people are in a deep sleep,
lying on their beds.
[16]He speaks in their ears
and frightens them with
warnings
[17]to turn them away from doing
wrong
and to keep them from being
proud.
[18]God does this to save people from
death,
to keep them from dying.
[19]People may be corrected while in
bed in great pain;
they may have continual pain in
their very bones.
[20]They may be in such pain that they
even hate food,
even the very best meal.
[21]Their body becomes so thin there is
almost nothing left of it,
and their bones that were
hidden now stick out.
[22]They are near death,
and their life is almost over.

[23]"But there may be an angel to speak
for him,
one out of a thousand, who will
tell him what to do.
[24]The angel will beg for mercy and say:
'Save him from death.
I have found a way to pay for his
life.'
[25]Then his body is made new like a
child's.
It will return to the way it was
when he was young.
[26]That person will pray to God, and
God will listen to him.
He will see God's face and will
shout with happiness.
And God will set things right
for him again.
[27]Then he will say to others,
'I sinned and twisted what was
right,
but I did not receive the
punishment I should have
received.
[28]God bought my life back from death,
and I will continue to enjoy life.'

[29]"God does all these things to a
person
two or even three times
[30]so he won't die as punishment for
his sins
and so he may still enjoy life.

What's the POINT?

Job 34:19

In a recent romantic comedy film, a prince came to America to attend college. There, he met a hardworking, middle-class farm girl determined to make it on her own. Their lives were very different because of their social standing. He was privileged; she had to work long hours to stay in school. One morning, the girl's mouth fell open in astonishment when she stopped by the prince's dorm room and found his servant cooking breakfast over a hotplate and waiting on him hand and foot. To her, that highlighted the differences in their status. He received special treatment. He had it easy in many ways. In the film, being a prince made him special, while she struggled to make ends meet. To God, everyone is special. It doesn't make any difference if you are a day laborer or a king, a professional or a student. God loves you no matter what your status is. To him, you are a princess, whether you were raised in a castle or a two-bedroom apartment. You were created in his "image and likeness" (Genesis 1:26) to be royalty in his kingdom. You can hold your head up high, no matter what your surroundings or circumstances, knowing you are a child of the King.

31"Job, pay attention and listen to me;
   be quiet, and I will speak.
32If you have anything to say, answer me;
   speak up, because I want to prove you right.
33But if you have nothing to say, then listen to me;
   be quiet, and I will teach you wisdom."

34 Then Elihu said:
2"Hear my words, you wise men;
   listen to me, you who know a lot.
3The ear tests words
   as the tongue tastes food.
4Let's decide for ourselves what is right,
   and let's learn together what is good.

5"Job says, 'I am not guilty,
   and God has refused me a fair trial.
6Instead of getting a fair trial,
   I am called a liar.
 I have been seriously hurt,
   even though I have not sinned.'
7There is no other man like Job;
   he takes insults as if he were drinking water.
8He keeps company with those who do evil
   and spends time with wicked men,
9because he says, 'It is no use
   to try to please God.'

10"So listen to me, you who can understand.
   God can never do wrong!
   It is impossible for the Almighty to do evil.
11God pays people back for what they have done
   and gives them what their actions deserve.
12Truly God will never do wrong;
   the Almighty will never twist what is right.
13No one chose God to rule over the earth

or put him in charge of the
whole world.
¹⁴If God should decide
to take away life and breath,
¹⁵then everyone would die together
and turn back into dust.

¹⁶"If you can understand, hear this;
listen to what I have to say.
¹⁷Can anyone govern who hates what
is right?
How can you blame God who is
both fair and powerful?
¹⁸God is the one who says to kings,
'You are worthless,'
or to important people, 'You are
evil.'
¹⁹He is not nicer to princes than
other people,
nor kinder to rich people than
poor people,
because he made them all with
his own hands.
²⁰They can die in a moment, in the
middle of the night.
They are struck down, and then
they pass away;
powerful people die without
help.

²¹"God watches where people go;
he sees every step they take.
²²There is no dark place or deep
shadow
where those who do evil can
hide from him.
²³He does not set a time
for people to come before him
for judging.
²⁴Without asking questions, God
breaks powerful people into
pieces
and puts others in their place.
²⁵Because God knows what people do,
he defeats them in the night,
and they are crushed.
²⁶He punishes them for the evil they
do
so that everyone else can watch,
²⁷because they stopped following
God
and did not care about any of his
ways.

²⁸The cry of the poor comes to God;
he hears the cry of the needy.
²⁹But if God keeps quiet, who can
blame him?
If he hides his face, who can see
him?
God still rules over both nations
and persons alike.
³⁰ He keeps the wicked from ruling
and from trapping others.

³¹"But suppose someone says to God,
'I am guilty, but I will not sin
anymore.
³²Teach me what I cannot see.
If I have done wrong, I will not
do it again.'
³³So, Job, should God reward you as
you want
when you refuse to change?
You must decide, not I,
so tell me what you know.

³⁴"Those who understand speak,
and the wise who hear me say,
³⁵'Job speaks without knowing what
is true;
his words show he does not
understand.'
³⁶I wish Job would be tested
completely,
because he answered like an evil
man!
³⁷Job now adds to his sin by turning
against God.
He claps his hands in protest,
speaking more and more against
God."

35 Then Elihu said:
²"Do you think this is fair?
You say, 'God will show that I am
right,'
³but you also ask, 'What's the use?
I don't gain anything by not
sinning.'

⁴"I will answer you
and your friends who are with
you.
⁵Look up at the sky
and see the clouds so high above
you.
⁶If you sin, it does nothing to God;

Balancing Act

All about Love

So there's this guy, and you're head over heels in love with him. Maybe he's your husband or your boyfriend—or let's just say he has serious potential. He's all you can think about. He is the only one you want to spend time with. Falling in love and being in love is glorious, no doubt about it. God designed women to love deeply, but too much of a good thing can become a bad thing. The beautiful gift of romantic love is best experienced when it's lived out in the context of other healthy and active relationships—with God, family, and friends. When you fall in love, your head may feel as if it's in the clouds, but ultimately you'll be glad if you keep your feet firmly planted on the ground.

even if your sins are many, they
do nothing to him.
[7]If you are good, you give nothing to
God;
he receives nothing from your
hand.
[8]Your evil ways only hurt others like
yourself,
and the good you do only helps
other human beings.

[9]"People cry out when they are in
trouble;
they beg for relief from
powerful people.
[10]But no one asks, 'Where is God, my
Maker,

who gives us songs in the night,
[11]who makes us smarter than the
animals of the earth
and wiser than the birds of the
air?'
[12]God does not answer evil people
when they cry out,
because the wicked are proud.
[13]God does not listen to their useless
begging;
the Almighty pays no attention
to them.
[14]He will listen to you even less
when you say that you do not see
him,
that your case is before him,
that you must wait for him,
[15] that his anger never punishes,
and that he doesn't notice evil.

[16]So Job is only speaking nonsense,
saying many words without
knowing what is true."

Elihu's Speech Continues

36 Elihu continued:
[2]"Listen to me a little
longer, and I will show
you
that there is more to be said for
God.
[3]What I know comes from far away.
I will show that my Maker is
right.
[4]You can be sure that my words are
not false;
one who really knows is with you.

[5]"God is powerful, but he does not
hate people;
he is powerful and sure of what
he wants to do.
[6]He will not keep evil people alive,
but he gives the poor their
rights.
[7]He always watches over those who
do right;
he sets them on thrones with
kings
and they are honored forever.
[8]If people are bound in chains,
or if trouble, like ropes, ties
them up,
[9]God tells them what they have done,
that they have sinned in their
pride.
[10]God makes them listen to his
warning
and commands them to change
from doing evil.
[11]If they obey and serve him,
the rest of their lives will be
successful,
and the rest of their years will
be happy.
[12]But if they do not listen,
they will die by the sword,
and they will die without
knowing why.

[13]"Those who have wicked hearts
hold on to anger.

Taking Time

Even if you brush twice a day, a hurried thirty-second cleaning isn't enough to keep your teeth clean from bacteria and plaque. You need to brush your teeth for two minutes to keep your mouth healthy and happy. Some days, you may feel like you only have thirty seconds to spend with God, but remember that building a strong relationship with him takes a commitment of your time and energy. See if you can carve out more time in your schedule to spend with God in prayer and Bible study. Next time you're polishing those pearly whites, try praying. And then continue the conversation!

february

February is Black History Month. Read a book about civil rights. **1**	*Groundhog Day. It's time to look forward to spring.* **2**	Track down and call a former classmate. **3**	**4**	Try a new outdoor winter sport. **5**
6	Invite a friend to go to church with you this week. **7**	**8**	**9**	Look for three ways to reduce expenses. Bless someone else with the savings. **10**
It's Make a New Friend Day. Reach out to someone you barely know. **11**	It's Abraham Lincoln's birthday. Research America's Christian heritage on-line. **12**	Read something new in your Bible today. Try the book of Ruth. **13**	*Valentine's Day!* Deliver small gifts to a single woman. **14**	**15**
16	**17**	Reflect on your New Year's resolutions. Are you keeping them? **18**	**19**	**20**
Pray for your pastor and church leaders today. **21**	**22**	Volunteer to baby-sit for someone who can't afford to pay you. **23**	**24**	*Get to know your neighbors.* **25**
Has someone hurt you lately? Forgive and pray for that person. **26**	**27**	Memorize Proverbs 15:4. Offer someone encouragement today. **28**		

Even when God punishes them,
they do not cry for help.
[14]They die while they are still young,
and their lives end in disgrace.
[15]But God saves those who suffer
through their suffering;
he gets them to listen through
their pain.

[16]"God is gently calling you from the
jaws of trouble
to an open place of freedom
where he has set your table full
of the best food.
[17]But now you are being punished
like the wicked;
you are getting justice.
[18]Be careful! Don't be led away from
God by riches;
don't let much money turn you
away.
[19]Neither your wealth nor all your
great strength
will keep you out of trouble.
[20]Don't wish for the night
when people are taken from
their homes.
[21]Be careful not to turn to evil,
which you seem to want more
than suffering.

[22]"God is great and powerful;
no other teacher is like him.

[23]No one has planned his ways for him;
no one can say to God, 'You have
done wrong.'
[24]Remember to praise his work,
about which people have sung.
[25]Everybody has seen it;

people look at it from far off.
[26]God is so great, greater than we can
understand!
No one knows how old he is.

[27]"He evaporates the drops of water
from the earth
and turns them into rain.
[28]The rain then pours down from the
clouds,
and showers fall on people.

fun FACTS

[29]No one understands how God
spreads out the clouds
or how he sends thunder from
where he lives.
[30]Watch how God scatters his
lightning around him,
lighting up the deepest parts of
the sea.
[31]This is the way God governs the
nations;
this is how he gives us enough
food.
[32]God fills his hands with lightning
and commands it to strike its
target.
[33]His thunder announces the coming
storm,
and even the cattle know it is
near.

37

"At the sound of his
thunder, my heart pounds
as if it will jump out of my
chest.
[2]Listen! Listen to the thunder of
God's voice
and to the rumbling that comes
from his mouth.
[3]He turns his lightning loose under
the whole sky
and sends it to the farthest
parts of the earth.
[4]After that you can hear the roar
when he thunders with a great
sound.
He does not hold back the
flashing
when his voice is heard.
[5]God's voice thunders in wonderful
ways;

BIBLE Women & Men

Job's Wife

When someone you love starts telling you her problems, are you a model of encouragement? Job's wife may have had a right to vent. After all, Satan took her children and her possessions and left her with a husband who was covered with boils. Yuck! Job's wife became angry with God and told her husband to "Curse God and die!" (Job 2:9). That's some show of moral support! Job kept trusting and praising God, while his wife turned away. She is a good example of what *not* to do the next time tragedy hits close to home.

he does great things we cannot
understand.
⁶He says to the snow, 'Fall on the
earth,'
and to the shower, 'Be a heavy
rain.'
⁷With it, he stops everyone from
working
so everyone knows it is the work
of God.
⁸The animals take cover from the
rain
and stay in their dens.
⁹The storm comes from where it was
stored;
the cold comes with the strong
winds.
¹⁰The breath of God makes ice,
and the wide waters become
frozen.
¹¹He fills the clouds with water
and scatters his lightning
through them.
¹²At his command they swirl around
over the whole earth,
doing whatever he commands.
¹³He uses the clouds to punish people
or to water his earth and show
his love.

¹⁴"Job, listen to this:
Stop and notice God's miracles.
¹⁵Do you know how God controls the
clouds
and makes his lightning flash?
¹⁶Do you know how the clouds hang
in the sky?
Do you know the miracles of
God, who knows everything?
¹⁷You suffer in your clothes
when the land is silenced by the
hot, south wind.
¹⁸You cannot stretch out the sky like
God
and make it look as hard as
polished bronze.
¹⁹Tell us what we should say to him;
we cannot get our arguments
ready because we do not
have enough understanding.
²⁰Should God be told that I want to
speak?

Would a person ask to be
swallowed up?
²¹No one can look at the sun
when it is bright in the sky
after the wind has blown all the
clouds away.
²²God comes out of the north in
golden light,
in overwhelming greatness.
²³The Almighty is too high for us to
reach.
He has great strength;
he is always right and never
punishes unfairly.
²⁴That is why people honor him;
he does not respect those who
say they are wise."

The Lord Questions Job

38 Then the LORD answered
Job from the storm. He said:
²"Who is this that makes my purpose
unclear
by saying things that are not
true?
³Be strong like a man!
I will ask you questions,
and you must answer me.
⁴Where were you when I made the
earth's foundation?
Tell me, if you understand.
⁵Who marked off how big it should
be? Surely you know!
Who stretched a ruler across
it?
⁶What were the earth's foundations
set on,
or who put its cornerstone in
place
⁷while the morning stars sang
together
and all the angels shouted with
joy?

⁸"Who shut the doors to keep the
sea in
when it broke through and was
born,
⁹when I made the clouds like a coat
for the sea
and wrapped it in dark clouds,

Seven ways to...

Jump-Start Your Faith

1. Schedule time for daily prayer and stick to it.

2. Ask God to make you more aware of him throughout the day.

3. Learn something new. Attend a church retreat.

4. Hang out with other Christians. Join a small group.

5. Serve others. Volunteer to help someone in need.

6. Listen to praise and worship music throughout the day.

7. Memorize Bible verses.

¹⁰when I put limits on the sea
and put its doors and bars in
place,
¹¹when I said to the sea, 'You may
come this far, but no
farther;
this is where your proud waves
must stop'?

Stories of SURVIVAL

Surviving Gang Rape and Abuse

KARINA'S STORY

I grew up with verbally, physically, and sexually abusive parents. For years I was hit, yelled at, and raped at home and by others outside our home. I was told I would never marry, have children, or amount to anything. At 17, I was gang-raped by three people I knew. As they held me at gunpoint, they threatened to find me and kill me if I ever told anyone. I kept it a secret for many years until God brought someone into my life I could trust with the information.

As a teen, I learned about Jesus through a friend who took me to church. I could tell by watching her family and their lifestyle that God was very real to them. I realized that I needed God and promised to give him the rest of my life.

Through years of counseling, I came to realize that I was angry with God for the abuse he allowed. Although he is God and holds all parents accountable for their actions, he revealed to me that he does not usurp parents' authority over their children. God showed me that my parents were in pain and that hurting people often hurt other people. Through God's grace, I have forgiven my parents. I pray for their salvation and his mercy on them.

God has also shown me that I was never alone. He was always there with me, giving me the will to live. I've held on to the truth expressed in Jeremiah 29:11: "I have good plans for you, not plans to hurt you. I will give you hope and a good future."

Because my parents were always angry with me, I'm still learning to believe that God loves me unconditionally and isn't angry with me. I want to believe God is trustworthy, even though my parents were not. As I continue to seek God, he gives me his sweet peace. At 47, I have been married just over a year. Jesus is teaching me more about himself through my husband's patient, consistent love.

> I REALIZED THAT I NEEDED GOD AND PROMISED TO GIVE HIM THE REST OF MY LIFE.

12"Have you ever ordered the
        morning to begin,
    or shown the dawn where its
        place was
13in order to take hold of the earth by
        its edges
    and shake evil people out of it?
14At dawn the earth changes like clay
        being pressed by a seal;
    the hills and valleys stand out
        like folds in a coat.
15Light is not given to evil people;
    their arm is raised to do harm,
        but it is broken.

16"Have you ever gone to where the
        sea begins
    or walked in the valleys under
        the sea?
17Have the gates of death been
        opened to you?
    Have you seen the gates of the
        deep darkness?
18Do you understand how wide the
        earth is?
    Tell me, if you know all these
        things.

19"What is the path to light's home,
    and where does darkness live?
20Can you take them to their places?
    Do you know the way to their
        homes?
21Surely you know, if you were
        already born when all this
        happened!
    Have you lived that many years?

22"Have you ever gone into the
        storehouse of the snow
    or seen the storehouses for hail,
23which I save for times of trouble,
    for days of war and battle?
24Where is the place from which
        light comes?
    Where is the place from which
        the east winds blow over the
        earth?
25Who cuts a waterway for the heavy
        rains
    and sets a path for the
        thunderstorm?
26Who waters the land where no one
        lives,

the desert that has no one in it?
27Who sends rain to satisfy the empty
        land
    so the grass begins to grow?
28Does the rain have a father?
    Who is father to the drops of
        dew?
29Who is the mother of the ice?
    Who gives birth to the frost
        from the sky
30when the water becomes hard as
        stone,
    and even the surface of the
        ocean is frozen?

31"Can you tie up the stars of the
        Pleiades
    or loosen the ropes of the stars
        in Orion?
32Can you bring out the stars on time
    or lead out the stars of the Bear
        with its cubs?
33Do you know the laws of the sky
    and understand their rule over
        the earth?

34"Can you shout an order to the clouds
    and cover yourself with a flood
        of water?
35Can you send lightning bolts on
        their way?
    Do they come to you and say,
        'Here we are'?
36Who put wisdom inside the mind
    or understanding in the heart?
37Who has the wisdom to count the
        clouds?
    Who can pour water from the
        jars of the sky
38when the dust becomes hard
    and the clumps of dirt stick
        together?

39"Do you hunt food for the female
        lion
    to satisfy the hunger of the
        young lions
40while they lie in their dens
    or hide in the bushes waiting to
        attack?
41Who gives food to the birds
    when their young cry out to God
    and wander about without food?

WISE WORDS

You Are Never Alone

Sometimes it's easy to think that you're on your own and that you have to tackle a situation single-handedly, but the truth is that you're never alone. God is always with you. His eyes are always on you. Proverbs 5:21 says, "The Lord sees everything you do, and he watches where you go." There isn't anything you're facing or going through that God doesn't know about. Whether you're facing a temptation, a trial, or a triumphant moment, God is with you—through thick and thin, good and bad. In fact, God says that he will not "leave you or forget you" (Deuteronomy 31:6). So the next time you're feeling alone, call out to the One who has promised to never leave you.

39 "Do you know when the mountain goats give birth?
    Do you watch when the deer gives birth to her fawn?
2Do you count the months until they give birth

and know the right time for them to give birth?
³They lie down, their young are born,
and then the pain of giving birth is over.
⁴Their young ones grow big and strong in the wild country.
Then they leave their homes and do not return.

⁵"Who let the wild donkey go free? Who untied its ropes?
⁶I am the one who gave the donkey the desert as its home;
I gave it the desert lands as a place to live.
⁷The wild donkey laughs at the confusion in the city,
and it does not hear the drivers shout.
⁸It roams the hills looking for pasture,
looking for anything green to eat.

⁹"Will the wild ox agree to serve you and stay by your feeding box at night?
¹⁰Can you hold it to the plowed row with a harness
so it will plow the valleys for you?
¹¹Will you depend on the wild ox for its great strength
and leave your heavy work for it to do?
¹²Can you trust the ox to bring in your grain
and gather it to your threshing floor?

¹³"The wings of the ostrich flap happily,
but they are not like the feathers of the stork.
¹⁴The ostrich lays its eggs on the ground
and lets them warm in the sand.
¹⁵It does not stop to think that a foot might step on them and crush them;
it does not care that some animal might walk on them.
¹⁶The ostrich is cruel to its young, as if they were not even its own.
It does not care that its work is for nothing,
¹⁷because God did not give the ostrich wisdom;
God did not give it a share of good sense.
¹⁸But when the ostrich gets up to run, it is so fast
that it laughs at the horse and its rider.

¹⁹"Job, are you the one who gives the horse its strength
or puts a flowing mane on its neck?
²⁰Do you make the horse jump like a locust?
It scares people with its proud snorting.
²¹It paws wildly, enjoying its strength,
and charges into battle.

HEALTH
Mini-Addictions

Is coffee your first (and only) thought as you roll out of bed? Is your favorite soda a permanent fixture in your hand? There are countless things, many of which are harmless in moderation, that can easily become addictions. Caffeine is a big one! Coffee isn't the only culprit, though; it's surprising how much caffeine is in sodas—including diet drinks—and teas. Sugar is another addiction that's easy to overlook because you may not notice it adding up throughout your day. Television can also become an addiction if you turn to it for comfort. Take an assessment of your life. Are you hooked on a food, beverage, or activity that you're using as a coping mechanism rather than turning to God to meet your needs? Could any of these mini-addictions compromise your long-term physical, emotional, or spiritual health? If so, make a move toward moderation today!

²²It laughs at fear and is afraid of
nothing;
it does not run away from the
sword.
²³The bag of arrows rattles against
the horse's side,
along with the flashing spears
and swords.
²⁴With great excitement, the horse
races over the ground;
and it cannot stand still when it
hears the trumpet.
²⁵When the trumpet blows, the horse
snorts, 'Aha!'
It smells the battle from far away;
it hears the shouts of
commanders and the battle
cry.
²⁶"Is it through your wisdom that the
hawk flies
and spreads its wings toward
the south?
²⁷Are you the one that commands the
eagle to fly
and build its nest so high?
²⁸It lives on a high cliff and stays
there at night;
the rocky peak is its protected
place.
²⁹From there it looks for its food;
its eyes can see it from far away.
³⁰Its young eat blood,
and where there is something
dead, the eagle is there."

40 The LORD said to Job:
²"Will the person who
argues with the
Almighty correct him?
Let the person who accuses God
answer him."

³Then Job answered the LORD:
⁴"I am not worthy; I cannot answer
you anything,
so I will put my hand over my
mouth.
⁵I spoke one time, but I will not
answer again;
I even spoke two times, but I will
say nothing more."

⁶Then the LORD spoke to Job from the
storm:
⁷"Be strong, like a man!
I will ask you questions,
and you must answer me.
⁸Would you say that I am unfair?
Would you blame me to make
yourself look right?
⁹Are you as strong as God?
Can your voice thunder like his?
¹⁰If so, then decorate yourself with
glory and beauty;
dress in honor and greatness as
if they were clothing.
¹¹Let your great anger punish;
look at the proud and bring
them down.
¹²Look at the proud and make them
humble.
Crush the wicked wherever they
are.
¹³Bury them all in the dirt together;
cover their faces in the grave.
¹⁴If you can do that, then I myself will
praise you,
because you are strong enough
to save yourself.

¹⁵"Look at Behemoth,ⁿ
which I made just as I made you.
It eats grass like an ox.
¹⁶Look at the strength it has in its
body;
the muscles of its stomach are
powerful.
¹⁷Its tail is like a cedar tree;
the muscles of its thighs are
woven together.
¹⁸Its bones are like tubes of bronze;
its legs are like bars of iron.
¹⁹It is one of the first of God's works,
but its Maker can destroy it.
²⁰The hills, where the wild animals
play,
provide food for it.
²¹It lies under the lotus plants,
hidden by the tall grass in the
swamp.
²²The lotus plants hide it in their
shadow;
the poplar trees by the streams
surround it.

Praising God in Adversity

Let's be honest, Job had it rough. God allowed Satan to take his wealth, obliterate his family, and even devastate his health. And Job certainly complained about his plight. But despite his groaning, his questioning, and his prevailing feeling of helplessness, Job never lost his faith. Did he doubt? Certainly. But he didn't allow his doubt to become unbelief. And most importantly, he never stopped worshiping God. Even to the end, Job acknowledged the Lord's sovereignty and power. When your world feels like it's tumbling down around you, follow Job's example of unbroken faith in the midst of adversity.

40:15 Behemoth A large land animal, exact identity unknown.

Life Issues

Looking Out for Number One

Road rage. Cutting in line. Grabbing the last item on the shelf. We live in an "all about me" society, and it can be tough to be a servant. Yet Philippians 2:3 says not to let "selfishness or pride be your guide" and instructs believers to think of others first. James 3:16 even goes so far as to say that selfishness goes hand in hand with "confusion and every kind of evil." Ask God to show you any areas in your life where selfishness might be an issue. Sometimes, even the things we are doing for others can be a form of selfishness, especially if we are doing it for recognition or praise. Do what David says in Psalm 51:10 and pray, "Create in me a pure heart, God, and make my spirit right again."

²³If the river floods, it will not be afraid;
it is safe even if the Jordan River rushes to its mouth.
²⁴Can anyone blind its eyes and capture it?
Can anyone put hooks in its nose?

41 "Can you catch Leviathan" on a fishhook
or tie its tongue down with a rope?
²Can you put a cord through its nose
or a hook in its jaw?
³Will it keep begging you for mercy
and speak to you with gentle words?
⁴Will it make an agreement with you
and let you take it as your slave for life?
⁵Can you make a pet of Leviathan as you would a bird
or put it on a leash for your girls?
⁶Will traders try to bargain with you for it?
Will they divide it up among the merchants?

⁷Can you stick darts all over its skin
or fill its head with fishing spears?
⁸If you put one hand on it,
you will never forget the battle,
and you will never do it again!
⁹There is no hope of defeating it;
just seeing it overwhelms people.
¹⁰No one is brave enough to make it angry,
so who would be able to stand up against me?
¹¹No one has ever given me anything
that I must pay back,
because everything under the sky belongs to me.

¹²"I will speak about Leviathan's arms and legs,
its great strength and well-formed body.
¹³No one can tear off its outer hide
or poke through its double armor.
¹⁴No one can force open its great jaws;
they are filled with frightening teeth.

¹⁵It has rows of shields on its back
that are tightly sealed together.
¹⁶Each shield is so close to the next one
that no air can go between them.
¹⁷They are joined strongly to one another;
they hold on to each other and cannot be separated.
¹⁸When it snorts, flashes of light are thrown out,
and its eyes look like the light at dawn.
¹⁹Flames blaze from its mouth;
sparks of fire shoot out.
²⁰Smoke pours out of its nose,
as if coming from a large pot over a hot fire.
²¹Its breath sets coals on fire,
and flames come out of its mouth.
²²There is great strength in its neck.
People are afraid and run away.
²³The folds of its skin are tightly joined;
they are set and cannot be moved.
²⁴Its chest is as hard as a rock,
even as hard as a grinding stone.
²⁵The powerful fear its terrible looks
and draw back in fear as it moves.
²⁶The sword that hits it does not hurt it,
nor the arrows, darts, and spears.
²⁷It treats iron as if it were straw
and bronze metal as if it were rotten wood.
²⁸It does not run away from arrows;
stones from slings are like chaff to it.
²⁹Clubs feel like pieces of straw to it,
and it laughs when they shake a spear at it.
³⁰The underside of its body is like broken pieces of pottery.
It leaves a trail in the mud like a threshing board.
³¹It makes the deep sea bubble like a boiling pot;

41:1 Leviathan A sea creature, exact identity unknown.

it stirs up the sea like a pot of oil.
³²When it swims, it leaves a shining
   path in the water
   that makes the sea look as if it
      had white hair.
³³Nothing else on earth is equal to it;
   it is a creature without fear.
³⁴It looks down on all those who are
      too proud;
   it is king over all proud
      creatures."

Job Answers the Lord

42 Then Job answered the LORD:
²"I know that you can do all things
   and that no plan of yours can be
      ruined.
³You asked, 'Who is this that made
      my purpose unclear by
      saying things that are not
      true?'
   Surely I spoke of things I did not
      understand;
   I talked of things too wonderful
      for me to know.
⁴You said, 'Listen now, and I will
      speak.
   I will ask you questions,
      and you must answer me.'
⁵My ears had heard of you before,
   but now my eyes have seen you.
⁶So now I hate myself;
   I will change my heart and life.
   I will sit in the dust and ashes."

End of the Story

⁷After the LORD had said these things to Job, he said to Eliphaz the Temanite, "I am angry with you and your two friends, because you have not said what is right about me, as my servant Job did. ⁸Now take seven bulls and seven male sheep, and go to my servant Job, and offer a burnt offering for yourselves. My servant

Q: HOW CAN I FORGIVE SOMEONE WHO HURTS ME?

A: First, acknowledge that no one is perfect. Then ask God to help you make an intentional decision to forgive, regardless of how you feel. Put yourself in the offender's shoes, trying to view the situation from that person's perspective. People usually hurt others as a result of the pain in their own lives. When you come to understand why people behave the way they do, you are more likely to have empathy for them. Forgiving others is always the right thing to do!

Job will pray for you, and I will listen to his prayer. Then I will not punish you for being foolish. You have not said what is right about me, as my servant Job did." ⁹So Eliphaz the Temanite, Bildad the Shuhite, and Zophar the Naamathite did as the LORD said, and the LORD listened to Job's prayer.

¹⁰After Job had prayed for his friends, the LORD gave him success again. The LORD gave Job twice as much as he had owned before. ¹¹Job's brothers and sisters came to his house, along with everyone who had known him before, and they all ate with him there. They comforted him and made him feel better about the trouble the LORD had brought on him, and each one gave Job a piece of silver and a gold ring.

¹²The LORD blessed the last part of Job's life even more than the first part. Job had fourteen thousand sheep, six thousand camels, a thousand teams of oxen, and a thousand female donkeys. ¹³Job also had seven sons and three daughters. ¹⁴He named the first daughter Jemimah, the second daughter Keziah, and the third daughter Keren-Happuch. ¹⁵There were no other women in all the land as beautiful as Job's daughters. And their father Job gave them land to own along with their brothers.

¹⁶After this, Job lived one hundred forty years. He lived to see his children, grandchildren, great-grandchildren, and great-great-grandchildren. ¹⁷Then Job died; he was old and had lived many years.

Psalms

Sing a song. Say a prayer. Write a poem. There are so many ways to connect with God. Reading the book of Psalms is like peeking into the prayer journals of King David and the other authors. These candid conversations with God provide a template for our own spiritual journey.

The book of Psalms uses songs, prayers, and poetry to express some of the deepest passions and longings of the human heart. Like a pendulum, its chapters swing from desperate heartache and pain to exquisite joy and satisfaction. In the process, Psalms teaches a valuable lesson: It's okay to be honest with ourselves and with God about our humanity.

Each of the 150 psalms records a personal response to God in a variety of situations. Together, they're a powerful reminder that when you face the hard stuff of life, you can go to God with your genuine emotions and be vulnerable with him. God knows all about your deep, intense emotions. After all, he created the female heart! You can run to God and pour out your heart to him—honestly, unreservedly, entirely. He will not only be with you in the situation but also reveal himself to you through it! Throughout the high and low points, the Psalms are a rich treasury of praise and recognition of God as ruler, king, and creator. That's something worth singing about.

BOOK 1

Two Ways to Live

1 Happy are those who don't
listen to the wicked,
who don't go where sinners go,
who don't do what evil people
do.
²They love the LORD's teachings,
and they think about those
teachings day and night.
³They are strong, like a tree planted
by a river.
The tree produces fruit in
season,
and its leaves don't die.
Everything they do will succeed.

⁴But wicked people are not like
that.
They are like chaff that the
wind blows away.
⁵So the wicked will not escape God's
punishment.
Sinners will not worship with
God's people.
⁶This is because the LORD takes care
of his people,
but the wicked will be
destroyed.

The Lord's Chosen King

2 Why are the nations so angry?
Why are the people making
useless plans?
²The kings of the earth prepare to
fight,
and their leaders make plans
together
against the LORD
and his appointed one.

Contents

Contents

"Because your love is better than life, I will praise you. I will praise you as long as I live."

BOOKS & MUSIC

BOOKS

A SHEPHERD LOOKS AT PSALM 23

by Philip Keller

This little book offers special insight into one of the most popular passages of Scripture—Psalm 23, which portrays God as the gentle shepherd of his people. Philip Keller, who once worked as a shepherd, provides new insight into God's role as your guide, caregiver, protector, owner, provider, and comforter. Because of his personal connection, the author helps you step into the metaphor and sense God's presence in your life as he leads you through dangers and into his loving arms.

PRAYER: FINDING THE HEART'S TRUE HOME

by Richard Foster

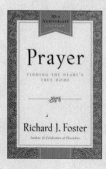

If you want to improve your communication with God, this book is a great place to start. Richard Foster explores different aspects and types of prayer, from the very simple prayers that express everyday concerns to the prayers that move beyond requests into a habit of conversation with God. Your prayer life will deepen as you incorporate prayers of adoration and rest, contemplation, sacrament, and meditation. Discover how prayer can motivate you to change and encourage you to reach out to others. By connecting more intimately with God through prayer, you will truly find your heart's home.

MUSIC

PASSION WORSHIP—SACRED REVOLUTION

Passion Worship is a live project recorded in front of more than twenty-thousand college students at a 2003 conference called OneDay. The album brims with infectious energy and enthusiasm. All thirteen songs are performed by popular worship leaders, including Chris Tomlin, the David Crowder Band, Charlie Hall, Nathan and Christy Nockels (also known as Watermark), Matt Redman, and others. It's difficult to pick one favorite, but Tomlin's "Holy Is the Lord" and Crowder's "O Praise Him (All This for a King)" are highlights. Also, don't miss Redman's "Blessed Be Your Name."

Keller "provides new insight into God's role as your guide, caregiver, protector, owner, provider, and comforter."

3They say, "Let's break the chains
that hold us back
and throw off the ropes that tie
us down."

4But the one who sits in heaven
laughs;
the Lord makes fun of them.
5Then the LORD warns them
and frightens them with his
anger.
6He says, "I have appointed my own
king
to rule in Jerusalem on my holy
mountain, Zion."

7Now I will tell you what the LORD
has declared:
He said to me, "You are my son.
Today I have become your father.
8If you ask me, I will give you the
nations;
all the people on earth will be
yours.
9You will rule over them with an iron
rod.
You will break them into pieces
like pottery."

10So, kings, be wise;
rulers, learn this lesson.
11Obey the LORD with great fear.
Be happy, but tremble.
12Show that you are loyal to his son,
or you will be destroyed by his
anger,
because he can quickly become
angry.
But happy are those who trust
him for protection.

A Morning Prayer

*David sang this when he ran away from his son
Absalom.*

3 LORD, I have many enemies!
Many people have turned
against me.
2Many are saying about me,
"God won't rescue him."   *Selah*

3But, LORD, you are my shield,
my wonderful God who gives me
courage.
4I will pray to the LORD,

What's the POINT?

Psalm 1:2

What do you fill your mind with each day? Is your time packed with e-mails, instant messages, cell phone calls, business meetings, and anxious thoughts about what you need to do next? Psalm 1:2 says that people who love God love his teachings and think about them "day and night." What do you think about all day and night? God wants you to fill your eyes, ears, and thoughts with what he can teach you through prayer, reading the Bible, and spending time with other believers. In order to think about his teachings day and night, you may have to change some things. You may have to turn off the iPod, television, and computer so you can spend time talking to God and listening for his voice. You may have to set your alarm for thirty minutes earlier so you have time to read God's Word before you start your day. You may need to listen to a Christian radio station in your car so you can hear scriptures reflected in the music and messages that drive important lessons home. These ideas may seem unnecessary, but think of them as spiritual water stops along each day's journey; your intentional efforts will help keep your mind focused on God all day long!

MONEY

The Money Trap

Did you know that money has a different meaning for everyone? Some people confuse their self-worth with their net worth. These people feel better about themselves when they have money. It's linked to their self-esteem. For others, money is a sign of security. Keeping money in the bank is a source of protection from the "what-ifs" of life. Other people enjoy the sense of power that money gives them. It makes them feel important and provides a measure of status. Other people try to find acceptance through money. They link money to accomplishment or view it as an affirmation of who they are.

What does money mean to you? It may be a good time for a heart check to make sure that your possessions don't possess you. It's important to recognize what you think money buys for you—whether it's self-worth, security, power, status, accomplishment, or an easier life. While money offers a showy façade of these things, only God can ultimately provide the authentic security and strength you seek. His desire is to show you your true value and worth, protect you, allow you to triumph over evil, and remind you that you are complete in him. As Proverbs 11:28 says, "Those who trust in riches will be ruined, but a good person will be healthy like a green leaf."

and he will answer me from his
   holy mountain.   *Selah*

⁵I can lie down and go to sleep,
   and I will wake up again,
   because the Lord gives me
      strength.
⁶Thousands of troops may surround
      me,
   but I am not afraid.

⁷Lord, rise up!
   My God, come save me!
You have struck my enemies on the
      cheek;
   you have broken the teeth of the
      wicked.
⁸The Lord can save his people.
   Lord, bless your people.   *Selah*

An Evening Prayer

For the director of music. With stringed instruments. A psalm of David.

4 Answer me when I pray to you,
   my God who does what is
      right.
Make things easier for me when I
      am in trouble.
   Have mercy on me and hear my
      prayer.

²People, how long will you turn my
      honor into shame?
   How long will you love what is
      false and look for new lies?
                                 Selah
³You know that the Lord has chosen
      for himself those who are
      loyal to him.
   The Lord listens when I pray to
      him.
⁴When you are angry, do not sin.
   Think about these things quietly
      as you go to bed.   *Selah*
⁵Do what is right as a sacrifice to the
      Lord
   and trust the Lord.

⁶Many people ask,
   "Who will give us anything
      good?"
   Lord, be kind to us.
⁷But you have made me very happy,
   happier than they are,

are you a
savvy shopper?

1. WHEN DECIDING WHICH PRODUCT TO BUY, YOU USUALLY BASE YOUR DECISION ON:

❏ A. Price.

❏ B. Quality and price.

❏ C. Ease of purchase.

2. THE MAJORITY OF ITEMS YOU BUY ARE:

❏ A. Full retail.

❏ B. On sale.

3. IF YOU NEED TO BUY AN ITEM THAT COSTS $100 OR MORE, YOU:

❏ A. Compare prices on-line then call or visit local stores to see if they can match the best price you find.

❏ B. Go to a store that carries the item and buy whatever they have in stock.

❏ C. Visit a mall or shopping center where you can compare prices and options at more than one store.

4. YOUR ATTITUDE TOWARD DISCOUNTS, COUPONS, AND REBATES IS:

❏ A. They're almost always worth using, as long as they don't tempt you to buy products you don't need.

❏ B. They're only worthwhile if they discount the item 20 percent or more.

❏ C. They're not worth it because they take too much time.

5. YOU SEE THE WEEKLY SALES FLYER FROM YOUR LOCAL GROCER IN THE NEWSPAPER. YOU:

❏ A. Throw it into the recycling bin.

❏ B. Immediately start a list of sale items that you need.

❏ C. Flip through the flyer and make a mental note of anything that's on sale.

Quiz

Scoring:

1. A=2, B=3, C=1
2. A=1, B=3
3. A=3, B=1, C=2
4. A=3, B=2, C=1
5. A=1, B=3, C=2

IF YOU SCORED 1-6, YOU SHOP FOR CONVENIENCE RATHER THAN FOR A DEAL. If it's easy and available, you'll buy the product no matter how much extra it costs you.

IF YOU SCORED 7-11, YOU TRY TO PAY ATTENTION TO PRICE WHEN YOU CAN. You like to find things on sale, but sometimes you choose to save time rather than money.

IF YOU SCORED 12 OR HIGHER, YOU ARE A SAVVY SHOPPER. You try to stretch your dollars to make them go further. You enjoy finding deals and saving money when you can.

What's the POINT?

Psalm 5:3

Do you consider yourself to be the "Can-Do Queen," capable of handling any crisis without help from anyone else? Many women strive for perfection, thinking that the way to win everyone's approval—including God's—is to do everything all by themselves, never wanting to be a burden and working hard to juggle too many balls in the air. However, meeting that standard all the time is impossible, and it limits what God can do in your life. It also limits your level of intimacy with others if you never share your needs and weaknesses with them. King David, the writer of this psalm, told God what his needs were every morning. He wasn't afraid God would berate him for not doing enough. There's no indication he felt selfish in asking for what he needed. Even though he was a great king with a great deal of authority and decision-making power of his own, David got it right when he simply told God his needs, then waited for an answer. He didn't jump right out of bed and try to do it all, and he didn't keep everything all bottled up. Follow David's example. Tell God each morning what you need, and then wait to see how he will answer.

even with all their grain and
new wine.
8 I go to bed and sleep in peace,
because, LORD, only you keep me
safe.

A Morning Prayer for Protection

For the director of music. For flutes. A psalm of David.

5 LORD, listen to my words.
Understand my sadness.
2 Listen to my cry for help, my King
and my God,
because I pray to you.
3 LORD, every morning you hear my
voice.
Every morning, I tell you what I
need,
and I wait for your answer.

4 You are not a God who is pleased
with the wicked;
you do not live with those who
do evil.
5 Those people who make fun of you
cannot stand before you.
You hate all those who do evil.
6 You destroy liars;
the LORD hates those who kill
and trick others.

7 Because of your great love,
I can come into your Temple.
Because I fear and respect you,
I can worship in your holy Temple.
8 LORD, since I have many enemies,
show me the right thing to do.
Show me clearly how you want
me to live.

9 My enemies' mouths do not tell the
truth;
in their hearts they want to
destroy others.
Their throats are like open graves;
they use their tongues for
telling lies.
10 God, declare them guilty!
Let them fall into their own
traps.
Send them away because their sins
are many;
they have turned against you.

WHAT'S IN A word?

Psalm 5:2 "My King" It isn't uncommon for the psalmist to refer to God as "King"—a welcome reminder that he is the sovereign ruler over everything.

11 But let everyone who trusts you be
happy;
let them sing glad songs forever.
Protect those who love you
and who are happy because of
you.
12 LORD, you bless those who do what
is right;
you protect them like a soldier's
shield.

A Prayer for Mercy in Troubled Times

For the director of music. With stringed instruments. Upon the sheminith. A psalm of David.

6 LORD, don't correct me when
you are angry;
don't punish me when you are
very angry.
2 LORD, have mercy on me because I
am weak.
Heal me, LORD, because my
bones ache.
3 I am very upset.
LORD, how long will it be?

4 LORD, return and save me;
save me because of your
kindness.
5 Dead people don't remember you;
those in the grave don't praise
you.

6 I am tired of crying to you.
Every night my bed is wet with
tears;
my bed is soaked from my crying.
7 My eyes are weak from so much
crying;
they are weak from crying about
my enemies.

⁸Get away from me, all you who do
evil,
   because the LORD has heard my
   crying.
⁹The LORD has heard my cry for help;
   the LORD will answer my prayer.
¹⁰All my enemies will be ashamed and
troubled.
   They will turn and suddenly
   leave in shame.

A Prayer for Fairness

*A shiggaion of David which he sang to the LORD about
Cush, from the tribe of Benjamin.*

7 LORD my God, I trust in you for
protection.
Save me and rescue me
   from those who are chasing me.
²Otherwise, like a lion they will tear
me apart.
   They will rip me to pieces, and
   no one can save me.

³LORD my God, what have I done?

Have my hands done something
   wrong?
⁴Have I done wrong to my friend
   or stolen without reason from
   my enemy?
⁵If I have, let my enemy chase me
   and capture me.
   Let him trample me into the
   dust
   and bury me in the ground.

Selah

⁶LORD, rise up in your anger;
   stand up against my enemies'
   anger.
   Get up and demand
   fairness.
⁷Gather the nations around you
   and rule them from above.
⁸LORD, judge the people.
   LORD, defend me because I am
   right,
   because I have done no wrong,
   God Most High.

Q: I HAVE BEEN HEARING ABOUT THE "NAMES" OF GOD. WHAT DOES THAT MEAN?

A: Throughout the Bible, there are many names for God, each of which reveals a different facet of his character. God told Moses one of his names: "I AM" (Exodus 3:14). That name implies God's immortality—that he has been, is today, and always will be. Matthew 1:23 says that Jesus would be called "Immanuel," which means "God is with us." Just as your name becomes part of your identity, getting to know God by studying his names will tell you a lot more about his identity and what he is like.

WISE WORDS

Honor Your Parents

Honoring your parents is one of the Ten Commandments that doesn't have a time limit. No matter your age, Proverbs 6:20 says that you should remember your parents' guidelines and training. God influences your life directly through the leadership of your parents. They are not perfect—no one is—but God calls you to respect them. If you harbor resentment over one of your parents' imperfect moments, forgive them today and ask God to mend your relationship. If you are close with your parents, treasure that relationship and their incredible influence in your life. Good parents provide wisdom, instill values, and teach lessons that last a lifetime. Honor your parents by learning from the positive lessons they taught you.

⁹God, you do what is right.
    You know our thoughts and
        feelings.
Stop those wicked actions done by
        evil people,
    and help those who do what is
        right.

¹⁰God protects me like a shield;
    he saves those whose hearts are
        right.
¹¹God judges by what is right,
    and God is always ready to
        punish the wicked.
¹²If they do not change their lives,
    God will sharpen his sword;

he will string his bow and take
    aim.
¹³He has prepared his deadly weapons;
    he has made his flaming arrows.

¹⁴There are people who think up evil
    and plan trouble and tell lies.
¹⁵They dig a hole to trap others,
    but they will fall into it
        themselves.
¹⁶They will get themselves into
        trouble;
    the violence they cause will hurt
        only themselves.

¹⁷I praise the LORD because he does
        what is right.
    I sing praises to the LORD Most
        High.

WHAT'S IN A word?

Psalm 9:1 "All my heart" This phrase is a wonderful reminder that real praise isn't halfhearted—it requires all of you. God deserves uncondi-tional, wholehearted worship!

The Lord's Greatness

For the director of music. On the gittith. A psalm of David.

8 LORD our Lord,
        your name is the most
            wonderful name in all
                the earth!
    It brings you praise in heaven
        above.
²You have taught children and
        babies
    to sing praises to you
        because of your enemies.
And so you silence your enemies
        and destroy those who try to get
            even.

³I look at your heavens,
    which you made with your
        fingers.
I see the moon and stars,
    which you created.
⁴But why are people even important
        to you?
    Why do you take care of human
        beings?
⁵You made them a little lower than
        the angels
    and crowned them with glory
        and honor.
⁶You put them in charge of
        everything you made.
    You put all things under their
        control:
⁷all the sheep, the cattle,
    and the wild animals,
⁸the birds in the sky,
    the fish in the sea,
    and everything that lives under
        water.

Beauty BECOMES HER

A Cut Above

Everyone experiences it sooner or later: the bad hair day. No matter what you do, there are times when your hair refuses to obey. Whether it's pouffy, flat, or sporting a rebellious strand or two, there are days when your hair seems to conspire against you. If you have time, try washing and blow-drying your hair again. If you don't have time, remember that tomorrow's hair may be better! Everyone has bad days—whether they're hair-related or not. It's important to remember that God is always with you, faithfully loving you on your best and worst days—and every day in between.

fun FACTS

Studies show that tanning bed bulbs emit up to a 10 times more wrinkle- and cancer-causing rays than the sun.

(Glamour)

⁹Lᴏʀᴅ our Lord,
your name is the most
wonderful name in all the
earth!

Thanksgiving for Victory

For the director of music. To the tune of "The Death of the Son." A psalm of David.

9 I will praise you, Lᴏʀᴅ, with all
my heart.
I will tell all the miracles you have
done.
²I will be happy because of you;
God Most High, I will sing
praises to your name.

³My enemies turn back;
they are overwhelmed and die
because of you.
⁴You have heard my complaint;
you sat on your throne and
judged by what was right.
⁵You spoke strongly against the
foreign nations and
destroyed the wicked;
you wiped out their names
forever and ever.
⁶The enemy is gone forever.
You destroyed their cities;
no one even remembers them.

⁷But the Lᴏʀᴅ rules forever.
He sits on his throne to judge,
⁸and he will judge the world in
fairness;
he will decide what is fair for
the nations.
⁹The Lᴏʀᴅ defends those who suffer;
he defends them in times of
trouble.
¹⁰Those who know the Lᴏʀᴅ trust him,
because he will not leave those
who come to him.

¹¹Sing praises to the Lᴏʀᴅ who is king
on Mount Zion.
Tell the nations what he has done.
¹²He remembers who the murderers
are;
he will not forget the cries of
those who suffer.
¹³Lᴏʀᴅ, have mercy on me.
See how my enemies hurt me.
Do not let me go through the
gates of death.
¹⁴Then, at the gates of Jerusalem, I
will praise you;
I will rejoice because you saved
me.

¹⁵The nations have fallen into the pit
they dug.
Their feet are caught in the nets
they laid.
¹⁶The Lᴏʀᴅ has made himself known
by his fair decisions;
the wicked get trapped by what
they do.   *Higgaion. Selah*

¹⁷Wicked people will go to the grave,
and so will all those who forget
God.
¹⁸But those who have troubles will
not be forgotten.
The hopes of the poor will never
die.

¹⁹Lᴏʀᴅ, rise up and judge the nations.
Don't let people think they are
strong.
²⁰Teach them to fear you, Lᴏʀᴅ.
The nations must learn that they
are only human.   *Selah*

Be Still & Know

Prayer Journals

Do you have a system for keeping track of how God has answered your prayers? A prayer journal can provide focus, organization, and encouragement in your prayer life. Creating a prayer journal can be as simple as picking up a spiral notebook or as elaborate as creating a scrapbook with pictures and mementos. The next time you sit down to pray, grab a pen and your prayer journal and write down the date, what you just read or studied in the Bible, and the things and people you are praying for. Leave space to add the answers you receive. Each day, go back and look at prior entries, and you will soon be able to clearly see God at work in your life!

march

Make a calendar of your friends' birthdays. **1**	**2**	*Start a budget today!* **3**	Bake a treat for someone who needs a pick-me-up. **4**	**5**
6	Listen to a worship CD during your daily drive. **7**	**8**	*Thank God for his goodness!* **9**	**10**
11	Read the Song of Songs today. What did you learn about love? **12**	Take time to dust those hard-to-reach places in your home. **13**	Open a dictionary and look up three unfamiliar words. **14**	**15**
16	*St. Patrick's Day.* Research the history of St. Patrick on-line. **17**	Pray for a person of influence: It's Queen Latifah's birthday. **18**	Read Proverbs 31. Share what you learned with another woman. **19**	**20**
Volunteer at a local soup kitchen or charity. **21**	**22**	**23**	Buy a new photo album and organize all of your loose photos. **24**	**25**
Pray for your husband or future husband. **26**	**27**	Make appointments for your annual physical exams. **28**	**29**	It's Norah Jones's birthday. Celebrate by praying for her. **30**
Request a free copy of your credit report on-line. **31**				

"No act of kindness, no matter how small, is ever wasted."
—*Aesop*

A Complaint About Evil People

10 LORD, why are you so far
away?
Why do you hide when there is
trouble?
2 Proudly the wicked chase down
those who suffer.
Let them be caught in their own
traps.
3 They brag about the things they
want.
They bless the greedy but hate
the LORD.
4 The wicked people are too proud.
They do not look for God;
there is no room for God in
their thoughts.
5 They always succeed.
They are far from keeping your
laws;
they make fun of their enemies.
6 They say to themselves, "Nothing
bad will ever happen to me;
I will never be ruined."

7 Their mouths are full of curses, lies,
and threats;
they use their tongues for sin
and evil.
8 They hide near the villages.
They look for innocent people to
kill;
they watch in secret for the
helpless.
9 They wait in hiding like a lion.
They wait to catch poor people;
they catch the poor in nets.
10 The poor are thrown down and
crushed;
they are defeated because the
others are stronger.
11 The wicked think, "God has
forgotten us.
He doesn't see what is
happening."

12 LORD, rise up and punish the
wicked.
Don't forget those who need help.

Life Issues

Faithfulness

People struggle to be faithful—in their marriages, in their friendships, and in their job. It takes effort to keep our relationships strong. At work, it can be tough to meet deadlines, always arrive on time, and do the job well day after day. But believers need to be faithful in everything so their lives reflect God's faithfulness. Matthew 25:14–30 tells the story of a master who gave three servants some money and told them to take care of it. He heaped praise and rewards on the servants who made wise investment choices and proved to be faithful stewards. In 1 and 2 Samuel, we learn that God blessed David in many ways when he was faithful to obey. In addition to the privilege of serving him, God rewards us with mercy and grace that far surpass what we deserve. Being faithful in everything takes work, but it's worth it.

Balancing Act

The Driver's Seat

Riding in the backseat is not as much fun as being the driver. Backseat passengers have no control over which way or how fast the car will go. It can be downright nerve-wracking to give up control. What happens when God wants to be the driver in your life? Do you ask him to get in the backseat? God wants you to let go of the steering wheel and let him take you where he wants you to go. That means you must slide into the passenger seat or even ride in the back at times. It also means you have to trust and rely on God rather than yourself. If you keep driving, you are bound to take a wrong turn. You may even "total" your life. Let him drive, and you'll always be safe—a little uncomfortable, maybe, but definitely headed in the right direction.

¹³Why do wicked people hate God?
  They say to themselves, "God
    won't punish us."
¹⁴LORD, surely you see these cruel and
    evil things;
  look at them and do something.
People in trouble look to you for
    help.
  You are the one who helps the
    orphans.
¹⁵Break the power of wicked people.
  Punish them for the evil they
    have done.

¹⁶The LORD is King forever and ever.
  Destroy from your land those
    nations that do not worship
    you.
¹⁷LORD, you have heard what the poor
    people want.
  Do what they ask, and listen to
    them.
¹⁸Protect the orphans and put an end
    to suffering

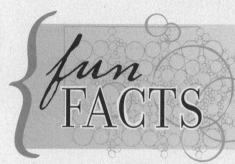

1 in 600. Those are your odds of a face-to-face encounter with the IRS.

(Kiplinger's)

so they will no longer be afraid
  of evil people.

Trust in the Lord

For the director of music. Of David.

11 I trust in the LORD for
    protection.
So why do you say to me,
  "Fly like a bird to your
    mountain.
²Like hunters, the wicked string
    their bows;
  they set their arrows on the
    bowstrings.

They shoot from dark places
  at those who are honest.
³When the foundations for good
    collapse,
  what can good people do?"

⁴The LORD is in his holy temple;
  the LORD sits on his throne in
    heaven.
He sees what people do;
  he keeps his eye on them.
⁵The LORD tests those who do right,
  but he hates the wicked and
    those who love to hurt
    others.
⁶He will send hot coals and burning
    sulfur on the wicked.
  A whirlwind is what they will
    get.
⁷The LORD does what is right, and he
    loves justice,
  so honest people will see his face.

A Prayer Against Liars

For the director of music. Upon the sheminith. A psalm of David.

12 Save me, LORD, because the
    good people are all gone;
  no true believers are left on
    earth.
²Everyone lies to his neighbors;
  they say one thing and mean
    another.

³The LORD will stop those flattering
    lips
  and cut off those bragging
    tongues.
⁴They say, "Our tongues will help us
    win.
  We can say what we wish; no one
    is our master."

⁵But the LORD says,

ETIQUETTE 101
RULES OF MODERN DATING

Speed dating. Personal matchmakers. Cyber dating. Modern dating can be complicated! Here are a few "rules" to dispel the confusion. Be courteous and complimentary, but don't force intimacy. If you choose to call, do so only once, and don't sit around waiting for him to call back. Regardless of your opinion about women asking men out, the general rule is that the person who asks is the one who plans the date and pays for it. If you're asked out and don't want to go, say no—politely but firmly. And remember that he has feelings, jitters, and doubts, so be sensitive!

"I will now rise up,
    because the poor are being hurt.
Because of the moans of the
    helpless,
    I will give them the help they
        want."
⁶The LORD's words are pure,
    like silver purified by fire,
    like silver purified seven times
        over.

⁷LORD, you will keep us safe;
    you will always protect us from
        such people.
⁸But the wicked are all around us;
    everyone loves what is wrong.

A Prayer for God to Be Near

For the director of music. A psalm of David.

13 How long will you forget
    me, LORD? Forever?
How long will you hide from me?
²How long must I worry
    and feel sad in my heart all day?
    How long will my enemy win
        over me?

³LORD, look at me.
    Answer me, my God;
    tell me, or I will die.
⁴Otherwise my enemy will say, "I
    have won!"
    Those against me will rejoice
        that I've been defeated.

⁵I trust in your love.
    My heart is happy because you
        saved me.
⁶I sing to the LORD
    because he has taken care of me.

The Unbelieving Fool

For the director of music. Of David.

14 Fools say to themselves,
    "There is no God."
Fools are evil and do terrible
    things;
    there is no one who does
        anything good.

²The LORD looked down from heaven
    on all people
    to see if anyone understood,

What's the POINT?

Psalm 13:5–6

Remember those bygone days of childhood and happy afternoons spent at the neighborhood park, riding carefree on the seesaw? Although you hoped your partner wouldn't hop off and send you crashing to the ground, there was always a chance that you may end up on your backside with a thud. You may feel that you're taking that same risk when you put your hope and confidence in God, but you can always trust him to look out for your best interest. He isn't going to let you come crashing down or leave you high and dry, your feet dangling in the air. He has it all under control. He wants to keep you balanced, and he wants to take good care of you. You may be tempted at times to argue with him, forget about him, or think that you know more than he does about what's best for you, but he wants you to follow his lead and depend on him no matter what he asks you to do. He is trustworthy, and he knows what he's doing. If you depend on his protection on the seesaw of life, sometimes you will be up and sometimes you will come down. You may not always be comfortable, but you can rest assured that with God as your partner, you will never be alone.

7 Seven ways to...

Make a Good First Impression

1. Take care of your appearance.

2. Smile warmly.

3. Maintain eye contact.

4. Be the first to reach out for a handshake.

5. Use good posture. Don't slouch!

6. Show interest in the other person by asking questions.

7. Restate the person's name as you close the conversation.

if anyone was looking to God for help.
³But all have turned away.
Together, everyone has become evil.
There is no one who does anything good,
not even one.

⁴Don't the wicked understand?

They destroy my people as if they were eating bread.
They do not ask the Lᴏʀᴅ for help.
⁵But the wicked are filled with terror,
because God is with those who do what is right.
⁶The wicked upset the plans of the poor,
but the Lᴏʀᴅ will protect them.

⁷I pray that victory will come to Israel from Mount Zion!
May the Lᴏʀᴅ bring them back.
Then the people of Jacob will rejoice,
and the people of Israel will be glad.

What the Lord Demands

A psalm of David.

15

Lᴏʀᴅ, who may enter your Holy Tent?
Who may live on your holy mountain?
²Only those who are innocent
and who do what is right.
Such people speak the truth from their hearts
³ and do not tell lies about others.
They do no wrong to their neighbors
and do not gossip.
⁴They do not respect hateful people
but honor those who honor the Lᴏʀᴅ.
They keep their promises to their neighbors,
even when it hurts.
⁵They do not charge interest on money they lend
and do not take money to hurt innocent people.

Whoever does all these things will never be destroyed.

Q: SOMETIMES IT SEEMS LIKE CHRISTIANITY IS ALL ABOUT RULES AND RESTRICTIONS. WHY IS GOD SO STRICT?

A: If you think being a Christian is a matter of obeying a list of "do's" and "don'ts," you're missing out on true Christianity! Sure, God gave a list of commandments (Exodus 20), but God's "rules" are meant to protect you, not limit you! He wants you to live a life of freedom and vibrancy, a life that brings glory to him. Christians should be the happiest, most fun-loving people on earth because we have even more reasons to celebrate than those who don't know Christ.

The Lord Takes Care of His People

A miktam of David.

16 Protect me, God,
because I trust in you.
[2]I said to the LORD, "You are my Lord.
Every good thing I have comes
from you."
[3]As for the godly people in the
world,
they are the wonderful ones I
enjoy.
[4]But those who turn to idols
will have much pain.
I will not offer blood to those
idols
or even speak their names.

[5]No, the LORD is all I need.
He takes care of me.
[6]My share in life has been pleasant;
my part has been beautiful.

[7]I praise the LORD because he advises
me.
Even at night, I feel his leading.
[8]I keep the LORD before me always.
Because he is close by my side,
I will not be hurt.
[9]So I rejoice and am glad.
Even my body has hope,
[10]because you will not leave me in the
grave.
You will not let your holy one
rot.
[11]You will teach me how to live a holy
life.
Being with you will fill me with
joy;
at your right hand I will find
pleasure forever.

A Prayer for Protection

A prayer of David.

17 LORD, hear me begging
for fairness;
listen to my cry for help.
Pay attention to my prayer,
because I speak the truth.
[2]You will judge that I am right;
your eyes can see what is true.

[3]You have examined my heart;
you have tested me all night.
You questioned me without finding
anything wrong;
I have not sinned with my
mouth.
[4]I have obeyed your commands,
so I have not done what evil
people do.
[5]I have done what you told me;
I have not failed.

[6]I call to you, God,
and you answer me.
Listen to me now,
and hear what I say.
[7]Your love is wonderful.
By your power you save those
who trust you
from their enemies.
[8]Protect me as you would protect
your own eye.
Hide me under the shadow of
your wings.
[9]Keep me from the wicked who
attack me,
from my enemies who surround
me.
[10]They are selfish
and brag about themselves.
[11]They have chased me until they
have surrounded me.
They plan to throw me to the
ground.
[12]They are like lions ready to kill;
like lions, they sit in hiding.
[13]LORD, rise up, face the enemy, and
throw them down.
Save me from the wicked with
your sword.
[14]LORD, save me by your power
from those whose reward is in
this life.
They have plenty of food.
They have many sons
and leave much money to their
children.
[15]Because I have lived right, I will see
your face.
When I wake up, I will see your
likeness and be satisfied.

WISE WORDS

Run from Temptation

When was the last time you were tempted to compromise your beliefs? Temptation comes in different forms. Proverbs 7 tells the story of a man who is walking down a road when a woman beckons to him and invites him back to her home. The young man foolishly follows her, leading to an immoral relationship. Commenting on the story, Proverbs 7:25 says, "Don't let yourself be tricked by such a woman; don't go where she leads you." Temptation can be tricky because it seems innocent or fun at first. But temptation is dangerous because it lures you into sin when your guard is down. That's why it's important to know your weaknesses and turn away at the first sign of temptation.

A Song of Victory

For the director of music. By the LORD's servant, David. David sang this song to the LORD when the LORD had saved him from Saul and all his other enemies.

18 I love you, LORD. You are
my strength.

[2]The LORD is my rock, my protection,
my Savior.

Stories of SURVIVAL

Separation and Reconciliation

SARAH'S STORY

Carly and I bonded as sorority sisters more than thirty years ago. Our friendship was largely based on parties and road trips. After college, I began growing in my faith and developed new interests. I was excited about what God was doing in my life, and I wanted to share my newfound joy with everyone, including Carly. She expressed an interest in God and even went to church with me a few times, but she eventually chose her lifestyle over God. I wanted to continue my friendship with Carly, but I felt torn. The more time I spent with her, the more I felt pulled into the very lifestyle I was trying to leave.

I realized that I needed to grow in my faith so I could make a positive impact on Carly's life. I finally had to make a tough decision and let the unhealthy friendship go. I found a special card to send her and included a note expressing my love, sadness, and con-

cerns—and my pledge to keep Carly in my thoughts and prayers.

I remember being affirmed, comforted, and instilled with hope when I read the following words from Ecclesiastes 3:1, 3: "There is a time for everything, and everything on earth has its special season. There is a time to tear apart and a time to sew together. There is a time to be silent and a time to speak."

> SHE EXPRESSED AN INTEREST IN GOD AND EVEN WENT TO CHURCH WITH ME A FEW TIMES, BUT SHE EVENTUALLY CHOSE HER LIFESTYLE OVER GOD.

Twelve years later, I saw Carly boarding the same plane I was on. I knew it was time to reconnect. When she saw me, she paused and then threw her arms up in the air with glee. While our lifestyles and core values still differ significantly, I'm now in a better position to be a beacon of God's love to Carly. Indeed, there is a time for everything!

RELATIONSHIPS

Listen More, Talk Less

Everyone needs a friend who can be counted on to listen without judging. Even more valuable is a friend in whom you can confide, knowing your privacy will be maintained. As women, we are often guilty of gossiping under the guise of "sharing concerns," but any way you present it, this is wrong. Proverbs tells us that a trustworthy friend can keep a secret (11:13), but foolish people talk too much (10:14). If a friend shares something personal with you, always ask permission before adding her to a prayer list or mentioning her problem to anyone—even another believer. Be respectful of the privacy of others, and you will be the trustworthy friend they can come to again and again.

My God is my rock.
I can run to him for safety.
He is my shield and my saving strength, my defender.
³I will call to the LORD, who is worthy of praise,
and I will be saved from my enemies.

⁴The ropes of death came around me;
the deadly rivers overwhelmed me.
⁵The ropes of death wrapped around me.
The traps of death were before me.
⁶In my trouble I called to the LORD.
I cried out to my God for help.
From his temple he heard my voice;
my call for help reached his ears.

⁷The earth trembled and shook.
The foundations of the mountains began to shake.
They trembled because the LORD was angry.
⁸Smoke came out of his nose,
and burning fire came out of his mouth.

Burning coals went before him.
⁹He tore open the sky and came down
with dark clouds under his feet.
¹⁰He rode a creature with wings and flew.
He raced on the wings of the wind.
¹¹He made darkness his covering, his shelter around him,
surrounded by fog and clouds.
¹²Out of the brightness of his presence came clouds
with hail and lightning.
¹³The LORD thundered from heaven;
the Most High raised his voice,
and there was hail and lightning.
¹⁴He shot his arrows and scattered his enemies.
His many bolts of lightning confused them with fear.
¹⁵LORD, you spoke strongly.
The wind blew from your nose.
Then the valleys of the sea appeared,
and the foundations of the earth were seen.

¹⁶The LORD reached down from above and took me;
he pulled me from the deep water.
¹⁷He saved me from my powerful enemies,
from those who hated me,
because they were too strong for me.
¹⁸They attacked me at my time of trouble,
but the LORD supported me.
¹⁹He took me to a safe place.
Because he delights in me, he saved me.

²⁰The LORD spared me because I did what was right.
Because I have not done evil, he has rewarded me.
²¹I have followed the ways of the LORD;
I have not done evil by turning away from my God.
²²I remember all his laws
and have not broken his rules.
²³I am innocent before him;
I have kept myself from doing evil.

²⁴The LORD rewarded me because I
did what was right,
because I did what the LORD said
was right.

²⁵LORD, you are loyal to those who are
loyal,

and you are good to those who
are good.
²⁶You are pure to those who are pure,
but you are against those who
are bad.
²⁷You save the humble,
but you bring down those who
are proud.
²⁸LORD, you give light to my lamp.
My God brightens the darkness
around me.

²⁹With your help I can attack an army.
With God's help I can jump over
a wall.
³⁰The ways of God are without fault.
The LORD's words are pure.
He is a shield to those who trust
him.
³¹Who is God? Only the LORD.
Who is the Rock? Only our God.
³²God is my protection.
He makes my way free from
fault.
³³He makes me like a deer that does
not stumble;
he helps me stand on the steep
mountains.
³⁴He trains my hands for battle
so my arms can bend a bronze
bow.
³⁵You protect me with your saving
shield.
You support me with your right
hand.
You have stooped to make me
great.
³⁶You give me a better way to live,
so I live as you want me to.
³⁷I chased my enemies and caught
them.
I did not quit until they were
destroyed.
³⁸I crushed them so they couldn't
rise up again.
They fell beneath my feet.
³⁹You gave me strength in battle.
You made my enemies bow
before me.
⁴⁰You made my enemies turn back,
and I destroyed those who hated
me.
⁴¹They called for help,
but no one came to save them.
They called to the LORD,
but he did not answer them.
⁴²I beat my enemies into pieces, like
dust in the wind.
I poured them out like mud in
the streets.

⁴³You saved me when the people
attacked me.
You made me the leader of
nations.

HEALTH
Panic Attacks

Panic attacks, a specific form of anxiety, are more common among women than men. While everyone occasionally experiences some degree of fear and anxiety, full-blown panic attacks are characterized by sudden fear for no apparent reason, as well as *extreme* anxiety or discomfort. For the millions of Americans who suffer from panic attacks every year, various treatments, including prescriptions and professional counseling, are available. It's important to remember that no matter what fear you face, God wants you to turn to him. Isaiah 43:1 says, "Don't be afraid, because I have saved you. I have called you by name, and you are mine." Run to God for safety. He is your protector.

People I never knew serve me.
⁴⁴As soon as they hear me, they obey me.
Foreigners obey me.
⁴⁵They all become afraid
and tremble in their hiding places.

⁴⁶The LORD lives!
May my Rock be praised.
Praise the God who saves me!
⁴⁷God gives me victory over my enemies
and brings people under my rule.
⁴⁸He saves me from my enemies.

You set me over those who hate me.
You saved me from violent people.
⁴⁹So I will praise you, LORD, among the nations.
I will sing praises to your name.
⁵⁰The LORD gives great victories to his king.
He is loyal to his appointed king,
to David and his descendants forever.

God's Works and Word

For the director of music. A psalm of David.

19 The heavens declare the glory of God,
and the skies announce what his hands have made.
²Day after day they tell the story;
night after night they tell it again.
³They have no speech or words;
they have no voice to be heard.
⁴But their message goes out through all the world;
their words go everywhere on earth.
The sky is like a home for the sun.
⁵ The sun comes out like a bridegroom from his bedroom.
It rejoices like an athlete eager to run a race.
⁶The sun rises at one end of the sky
and follows its path to the other end.
Nothing hides from its heat.

⁷The teachings of the LORD are perfect;
they give new strength.
The rules of the LORD can be trusted;
they make plain people wise.
⁸The orders of the LORD are right;
they make people happy.
The commands of the LORD are pure;
they light up the way.
⁹Respect for the LORD is good;
it will last forever.
The judgments of the LORD are true;
they are completely right.
¹⁰They are worth more than gold,
even the purest gold.
They are sweeter than honey,
even the finest honey.
¹¹By them your servant is warned.
Keeping them brings great reward.

¹²People cannot see their own mistakes.
Forgive me for my secret sins.
¹³Keep me from the sins of pride;
don't let them rule me.
Then I can be pure
and innocent of the greatest of sins.

¹⁴I hope my words and thoughts please you.
LORD, you are my Rock, the one who saves me.

A Prayer for the King

For the director of music. A psalm of David.

20 May the LORD answer you in times of trouble.
May the God of Jacob protect you.
²May he send you help from his Temple
and support you from Mount Zion.
³May he remember all your offerings
and accept all your sacrifices.
Selah

No Microphone Needed

Many churches have a group of musicians, often called the worship team, who lead the congregation in corporate worship. But even if you're not up on stage, *you* are on the worship team if you're praising the Lord! You don't have to be musically gifted—the entire congregation is a part of the team. Psalm 149, which is all about praising God, mentions nothing about musical talents. In fact, the chapter says that "God is honored by all who worship him" (verse 9). God isn't concerned about pitch or musical abilities, so make a joyful noise to the Lord!

⁴May he give you what you want
  and make all your plans
    succeed,
⁵and we will shout for joy when you
    succeed,
  and we will raise a flag in the
    name of our God.
May the LORD give you all that you
    ask for.

⁶Now I know the LORD helps his
    appointed king.
  He answers him from his holy
    heaven
  and saves him with his strong
    right hand.
⁷Some trust in chariots, others in
    horses,
  but we trust the LORD our God.
⁸They are overwhelmed and
    defeated,
  but we march forward and win.
⁹LORD, save the king!
  Answer us when we call for help.

Thanksgiving for the King

For the director of music. A psalm of David.

21 LORD, the king rejoices
      because of your
      strength;
  he is so happy when you save
    him!
²You gave the king what he wanted
  and did not refuse what he
    asked for.   *Selah*
³You put good things before him
  and placed a gold crown on his
    head.
⁴He asked you for life,
  and you gave it to him,
  so his years go on and on.

**In the United States, a
woman is sexually
assaulted or raped every
two minutes.**

(Oprah.com)

⁵He has great glory because you gave
    him victories;
  you gave him honor and praise.
⁶You always gave him blessings;
  you made him glad because you
    were with him.
⁷The king truly trusts the LORD.
  Because God Most High always
    loves him,
  he will not be overwhelmed.
⁸Your hand is against all your
    enemies;
  those who hate you will feel
    your power.
⁹When you appear,
  you will burn them as in a
    furnace.
 In your anger you will swallow
    them up,
  and fire will burn them up.
¹⁰You will destroy their families from
    the earth;
  their children will not live.
¹¹They made evil plans against you,
  but their traps won't work.
¹²You will make them turn their
    backs
  when you aim your arrows at
    them.
¹³Be supreme, LORD, in your power.
  We sing and praise your
    greatness.

The Prayer of a Suffering Man

*For the director of music. To the tune of "The Doe of
Dawn." A psalm of David.*

22 My God, my God, why
      have you abandoned
      me?
  You seem far from saving me,
    far away from my groans.
²My God, I call to you during the day,
    but you do not answer.
  I call at night;
    I am not silent.

³You sit as the Holy One.
  The praises of Israel are your
    throne.
⁴Our ancestors trusted you;
  they trusted, and you saved
    them.
⁵They called to you for help
  and were rescued.
 They trusted you
  and were not disappointed.

⁶But I am like a worm instead of a
    man.
  People make fun of me and hate
    me.
⁷Those who look at me laugh.
  They stick out their tongues and
    shake their heads.
⁸They say, "Turn to the LORD for
    help.
  Maybe he will save you.
 If he likes you,
    maybe he will rescue you."

⁹You had my mother give birth to me.
  You made me trust you
    while I was just a baby.
¹⁰I have leaned on you since the day I
    was born;

WHAT'S IN A word?

Psalm 20:7 "Chariots" Chariots provided a
significant advantage on ancient battlefields. The more chariots you
had, the more likely you were to win. But David knew that it wouldn't
matter how many chariots they had if they misplaced their trust and
took their eyes off God.

you have been my God since my
   mother gave me birth.
[11]So don't be far away from me.
   Now trouble is near,
   and there is no one to help.
[12]People have surrounded me like
   angry bulls.
   Like the strong bulls of Bashan,
   they are on every side.
[13]Like hungry, roaring lions
   they open their mouths at me.
[14]My strength is gone,
   like water poured out onto the
   ground,
   and my bones are out of joint.
 My heart is like wax;
   it has melted inside me.
[15]My strength has dried up like a clay
   pot,
   and my tongue sticks to the top
   of my mouth.
   You laid me in the dust of death.
[16]Evil people have surrounded me;
   like dogs they have trapped me.
   They have bitten my arms and
   legs.
[17]I can count all my bones;
   people look and stare at me.
[18]They divided my clothes among
   them,
   and they threw lots for my
   clothing.

[19]But, LORD, don't be far away.
   You are my strength; hurry to
   help me.
[20]Save me from the sword;
   save my life from the dogs.
[21]Rescue me from the lion's mouth;
   save me from the horns of the
   bulls.

[22]Then I will tell my brothers and
   sisters about you;
   I will praise you in the public
   meeting.
[23]Praise the LORD, all you who respect
   him.
   All you descendants of Jacob,
   honor him;
   fear him, all you Israelites.
[24]He does not ignore those in trouble.

He doesn't hide from them
   but listens when they call out to
   him.
[25]LORD, I praise you in the great
   meeting of your people;
   these worshipers will see me do
   what I promised.
[26]Poor people will eat until they are
   full;
   those who look to the LORD will
   praise him.
   May your hearts live forever!
[27]People everywhere will remember
   and will turn to the LORD.

All the families of the nations
   will worship him
[28]because the LORD is King,
   and he rules the nations.

[29]All the powerful people on earth
   will eat and worship.
   Everyone will bow down to him,
   all who will one day die.
[30]The people in the future will serve
   him;
   they will always be told about
   the Lord.

Become INVOLVED

Blood:Water Mission

Members of the pop/rock band Jars of Clay do a lot more than just make music. In fact, a major facet of their agenda as a band is to make a difference in the world by leaving a positive legacy of serving others.

Jars of Clay founded the Blood:Water Mission because they discovered that in many disadvantaged countries in Africa, clean water and clean blood are the two biggest needs in fighting the HIV/AIDS pandemic.

The Blood:Water Mission is dedicated to building clean water wells, supporting medical facilities, and focusing on community and worldwide transformation by addressing the underlying issues in Africa: poverty, injustice, and oppression.

In many African communities, women and children must walk as much as ten miles a day just for water. Jars of Clay wants to see that number drastically reduced through the 1,000 Wells Project. Churches, individuals, and communities are raising money to build or repair 1,000 clean water wells in 1,000 African villages. Clean water protects communities from life-threatening illnesses and enables HIV patients to live longer, stronger lives.

For more information on getting involved or to see if the band is holding an educational symposium near you, visit their Web site at www.bloodwatermission.org.

What's the POINT?

Psalm 23:1

God is compared to a shepherd in many places in the Bible, just as his followers are compared to sheep. The author of this psalm, King David, had firsthand experience with sheep and the role of a shepherd because he was a shepherd as a young man. He knew that sheep are not the most intelligent animals. They need someone to watch them constantly so they will not walk right into a hazardous situation. Sheep have a natural tendency to eat the wrong things, wander off into danger, and follow the crowd—even to their death. Sounds a lot like people, doesn't it? Like sheep, we all need God's guidance every day. You need God to point you in the right direction. You need him to stand guard over you and protect you from your enemies and those who would harm you physically, emotionally, or spiritually. You need him to monitor your "diet" and encourage you to take in a healthy portion of what his Word provides. You need him to come after you when you start wandering away. And you need the fellowship of the flock as you seek relationships with others who love him and follow him. With God as your shepherd, you will have everything you need.

³¹They will tell that he does what is
   right.
People who are not yet born
   will hear what God has done.

The Lord the Shepherd

A psalm of David.

23 The LORD is my shepherd;
      I have everything I need.
²He lets me rest in green pastures.
   He leads me to calm water.
³He gives me new strength.
 He leads me on paths that are right
   for the good of his name.
⁴Even if I walk through a very dark
   valley,
 I will not be afraid,
because you are with me.
   Your rod and your shepherd's
   staff comfort me.

⁵You prepare a meal for me
   in front of my enemies.
You pour oil of blessing on my head;ⁿ
   you fill my cup to overflowing.
⁶Surely your goodness and love will
   be with me
 all my life,
and I will live in the house of the
   LORD forever.

A Welcome for God into the Temple

A psalm of David.

24 The earth belongs to the
      LORD, and everything
      in it—
 the world and all its people.
²He built it on the waters
   and set it on the rivers.

³Who may go up on the mountain of
   the LORD?
 Who may stand in his holy
   Temple?
⁴Only those with clean hands and
   pure hearts,
 who have not worshiped idols,
 who have not made promises in
   the name of a false god.
⁵They will receive a blessing from
   the LORD;

the God who saves them will
   declare them right.
⁶They try to follow God;
   they look to the God of Jacob for
   help.   *Selah*

⁷Open up, you gates.
   Open wide, you aged doors
   and the glorious King will come
   in.
⁸Who is this glorious King?
   The LORD, strong and mighty.
   The LORD, the powerful warrior.
⁹Open up, you gates.
   Open wide, you aged doors
   and the glorious King will come
   in.
¹⁰Who is this glorious King?
   The LORD All-Powerful—
   he is the glorious King.   *Selah*

A Prayer for God to Guide

Of David.

25 LORD, I give myself to you;
      ² my God, I trust you.
 Do not let me be disgraced;
   do not let my enemies laugh at
   me.
³No one who trusts you will be
   disgraced,
   but those who sin without
   excuse will be disgraced.

⁴LORD, tell me your ways.
   Show me how to live.
⁵Guide me in your truth,
   and teach me, my God, my
   Savior.
 I trust you all day long.
⁶LORD, remember your mercy and love
   that you have shown since long
   ago.
⁷Do not remember the sins
   and wrong things I did when I
   was young.
 But remember to love me always
   because you are good, LORD.

⁸The LORD is good and right;
   he points sinners to the right
   way.
⁹He shows those who are humble
   how to do right,
   and he teaches them his ways.

➡➡ **23:5 pour oil . . . head** This can mean that God gave him great wealth and blessed him.

[10]All the LORD's ways are loving and
true
for those who follow the
demands of his agreement.
[11]For the sake of your name, LORD,
forgive my many sins.
[12]Are there those who respect the
LORD?
He will point them to the best
way.
[13]They will enjoy a good life,
and their children will inherit
the land.
[14]The LORD tells his secrets to those
who respect him;
he tells them about his
agreement.
[15]My eyes are always looking to the
LORD for help.
He will keep me from any traps.
[16]Turn to me and have mercy on me,
because I am lonely and hurting.
[17]My troubles have grown larger;
free me from my problems.

[18]Look at my suffering and troubles,
and take away all my sins.
[19]Look at how many enemies I
have!
See how much they hate me!
[20]Protect me and save me.
I trust you, so do not let me be
disgraced.
[21]My hope is in you,
so may goodness and honesty
guard me.
[22]God, save Israel from all their
troubles!

The Prayer of an Innocent Believer

Of David.

26 LORD, defend me because I
have lived an innocent
life.
I have trusted the LORD and
never doubted.
[2]LORD, try me and test me;

Q: WHY SHOULD I BE BAPTIZED IN WATER? WHY DOES IT MATTER?

A: Being baptized in water is a way to publicly acknowledge that you have accepted Jesus Christ as your Savior and that you want to live a life pleasing to God. While Jesus was on earth, he was baptized in the Jordan River by his cousin John the Baptist. When you are baptized, you are following the example of Jesus, and Matthew 3:17 says that Jesus' baptism pleased God. Baptism is also deeply meaningful because it is a powerful symbol of how God has washed away your sins.

WISE WORDS

Be Wise about Giving Advice

Have you ever offered someone advice? How did that person respond? It can be fun to give advice, but no matter how good or wise your advice may be, some people just aren't willing, ready, or in a place where they can receive it. Proverbs 9:8 advises, "Do not correct those who make fun of wisdom, or they will hate you. But correct the wise, and they will love you." The next time you're ready to give someone advice, stop and consider the other person. Does the person want advice or just a listening ear? Don't be discouraged by people who don't take your advice, but focus your energy and efforts on those who are ready to receive it!

look closely into my heart and
mind.
[3]I see your love,
and I live by your truth.
[4]I do not spend time with liars,
nor do I make friends with those
who hide their sin.
[5]I hate the company of evil people,
and I won't sit with the wicked.

Life Issues

Breaking Addictions

Alcoholism. Sexual addictions. Destructive relationships. Eating disorders. Anything you cannot control is an addiction that rules your life. Being a slave to your addictions makes them idols in your life by giving them power over you that they have no right. God wants your relationship with him to come first in your life, above and beyond any bad habits or addictions. God wants you to be set free from anything that controls you. In 2 Corinthians 10:5, Paul advises believers to "capture every thought and make it give up and obey Christ." *Every* thought—no exceptions. If you need to break free from an addiction, meditate on this verse, find someone you can be accountable to, and ask God to help you get rid of the behavior once and for all.

⁶I wash my hands to show I am
    innocent,
    and I come to your altar, LORD.
⁷I raise my voice in praise
    and tell of all the miracles you
    have done.
⁸LORD, I love the Temple where you
    live,
    where your glory is.
⁹Do not kill me with those sinners
    or take my life with those
    murderers.
¹⁰Evil is in their hands,
    and they do wrong for money.
¹¹But I have lived an innocent life,
    so save me and have mercy on me.
¹²I stand in a safe place.
    LORD, I praise you in the great
    meeting.

A Song of Trust in God

Of David.

27 The LORD is my light and
    the one who saves me.
So why should I fear anyone?
The LORD protects my life.
    So why should I be afraid?
²Evil people may try to destroy my
    body.
    My enemies and those who hate
    me attack me,
but they are overwhelmed and
    defeated.
³If an army surrounds me,
    I will not be afraid.
If war breaks out,
    I will trust the LORD.

⁴I ask only one thing from the LORD.
    This is what I want:

Let me live in the LORD's house
    all my life.
Let me see the LORD's beauty
    and look with my own eyes at his
    Temple.
⁵During danger he will keep me safe
    in his shelter.
    He will hide me in his Holy Tent,
    or he will keep me safe on a high
    mountain.
⁶My head is higher than my enemies
    around me.
I will offer joyful sacrifices in his
    Holy Tent.
    I will sing and praise the LORD.

⁷LORD, hear me when I call;
    have mercy and answer me.
⁸My heart said of you, "Go, worship
    him."
    So I come to worship you, LORD.
⁹Do not turn away from me.
    Do not turn your servant away
    in anger;
    you have helped me.
Do not push me away or leave me
    alone,
    God, my Savior.
¹⁰If my father and mother leave me,
    the LORD will take me in.
¹¹LORD, teach me your ways,
    and guide me to do what is right
    because I have enemies.
¹²Do not hand me over to my enemies,
    because they tell lies about me
    and say they will hurt me.

¹³I truly believe
    I will live to see the LORD's
    goodness.
¹⁴Wait for the LORD's help.
    Be strong and brave,
    and wait for the LORD's help.

fun FACTS

18 hours without sleep slows your reaction time from a quarter of a second to half of a second.

(Time)

A Prayer in Troubled Times

Of David.

28 Lord, my Rock, I call out
to you for help.
Do not be deaf to me.
If you are silent,
I will be like those in the grave.
²Hear the sound of my prayer,
when I cry out to you for help.
I raise my hands
toward your Most Holy Place.
³Don't drag me away with the
wicked,
with those who do evil.
They say "Peace" to their
neighbors,
but evil is in their hearts.
⁴Pay them back for what they have
done,
for their evil deeds.
Pay them back for what they have
done;
give them their reward.
⁵They don't understand what the
Lord has done
or what he has made.
So he will knock them down
and not lift them up.

⁶Praise the Lord,
because he heard my prayer for
help.
⁷The Lord is my strength and shield.
I trust him, and he helps me.
I am very happy,
and I praise him with my song.
⁸The Lord is powerful;
he gives victory to his chosen
one.
⁹Save your people
and bless those who are your
own.
Be their shepherd and carry
them forever.

God in the Thunderstorm

A psalm of David.

29 Praise the Lord, you
angels;
praise the Lord's glory and
power.

²Praise the Lord for the glory of his
name;
worship the Lord because he is
holy.

³The Lord's voice is heard over the
sea.
The glorious God thunders;
the Lord thunders over the
ocean.
⁴The Lord's voice is powerful;
the Lord's voice is majestic.
⁵The Lord's voice breaks the
trees;
the Lord breaks the cedars of
Lebanon.

⁶He makes the land of Lebanon
dance like a calf
and Mount Hermon jump like a
baby bull.
⁷The Lord's voice makes the
lightning flash.
⁸The Lord's voice shakes the
desert;
the Lord shakes the Desert of
Kadesh.
⁹The Lord's voice shakes the oaks
and strips the leaves off the
trees.
In his Temple everyone says, "Glory
to God!"

Forgiving All

It's a tough concept to wrap your brain around when you've been hurt, but Proverbs 10:12 tells us that "love forgives all wrongs." Not just the little ones, but all wrongs. From the point of view of the *forgiver*, that seems like a tough pill to swallow. But if you consider it from the standpoint of the forgiven, you can readily see how privileged you are to serve a God who believes so strongly in forgiveness. God, in his infinite love for us, forgives all of our sins. When forgiving others doesn't come easily, consider how often you have been on the receiving end of his immeasurable mercy and forgiveness.

What's Really Priceless?

A popular advertising campaign reminds us that there are some things money can't buy, but for everything else there's MasterCard. The catchy slogan is not only clever but also highlights something we often forget: some things shouldn't carry a price tag. For example, your dignity and self-worth are more important than all the wealth the world has to offer. Some popular television series today glamorize compromising your values by making it look fun and profitable. Contestants are willing to do outrageous things or exhibit ungodly behavior if that's what it takes to win the money.

You don't have to be a reality show contestant to find situations that test your integrity. Eventually, you're going to find yourself in a situation where you'll be tempted to cheat, lie, or steal for financial gain. You may tell yourself that it's not a big deal, but don't be deceived—it's never worth it to lower your standards for any sum of money. When temptation comes your way, remember that you're always better off with an empty wallet than to give away something priceless—your integrity. Proverbs 22:1 says, "Being respected is more important than having great riches. To be well thought of is better than silver or gold." Your integrity, dignity, and self-worth should never be for sale.

---

¹⁰The Lord controls the flood.
 The Lord will be King forever.
¹¹The Lord gives strength to his
   people;
 the Lord blesses his people with
   peace.

Thanksgiving for Escaping Death

A psalm of David. A song for giving the Temple to the Lord.

30 I will praise you, Lord,
   because you rescued me.
 You did not let my enemies
   laugh at me.
²Lord, my God, I prayed to you,
 and you healed me.
³You lifted me out of the grave;
 you spared me from going down
   to the place of the dead.

⁴Sing praises to the Lord, you who
   belong to him;
 praise his holy name.
⁵His anger lasts only a moment,
 but his kindness lasts for a
   lifetime.
 Crying may last for a night,
 but joy comes in the morning.

⁶When I felt safe, I said,
 "I will never fear."
⁷Lord, in your kindness you made my
   mountain safe.
 But when you turned away, I was
   frightened.

⁸I called to you, Lord,
 and asked you to have mercy on
   me.
⁹I said, "What good will it do if I die
 or if I go down to the grave?
 Dust cannot praise you;
 it cannot speak about your truth.
¹⁰Lord, hear me and have mercy on me.
 Lord, help me."

¹¹You changed my sorrow into
   dancing.
 You took away my clothes of
   sadness,
 and clothed me in happiness.
¹²I will sing to you and not be silent.

WHAT'S IN A word?

Psalm 30:11 "Sorrow into dancing" This is a wonderful expression of the transformation that has taken place in the psalmist's life. When you experience God's strength and comfort in your life, you can't help but be transformed!

LORD, my God, I will praise you
forever.

A Prayer of Faith in Troubled Times

For the director of music. A psalm of David.

31 LORD, I trust in you;
let me never be
disgraced.
Save me because you do what is
right.
[2] Listen to me
and save me quickly.
Be my rock of protection,
a strong city to save me.
[3] You are my rock and my protection.
For the good of your name, lead
me and guide me.
[4] Set me free from the trap they set
for me,
because you are my protection.
[5] I give you my life.
Save me, LORD, God of truth.

[6] I hate those who worship false gods.
I trust only in the LORD.
[7] I will be glad and rejoice in your
love,
because you saw my suffering;
you knew my troubles.
[8] You have not handed me over to my
enemies
but have set me in a safe place.

[9] LORD, have mercy, because I am in
misery.
My eyes are weak from so much
crying,
and my whole being is tired
from grief.
[10] My life is ending in sadness,
and my years are spent in crying.
My troubles are using up my
strength,

and my bones are getting
weaker.
[11] Because of all my troubles, my
enemies hate me,
and even my neighbors look
down on me.
When my friends see me,
they are afraid and run.
[12] I am like a piece of a broken pot.
I am forgotten as if I were
dead.
[13] I have heard many insults.
Terror is all around me.
They make plans against me
and want to kill me.

[14] LORD, I trust you.
I have said, "You are my
God."
[15] My life is in your hands.
Save me from my enemies
and from those who are chasing
me.
[16] Show your kindness to me, your
servant.
Save me because of your love.
[17] LORD, I called to you,
so do not let me be disgraced.
Let the wicked be disgraced
and lie silent in the grave.
[18] With pride and hatred
they speak against those who do
right.
So silence their lying lips.

BE STILL & KNOW

Pray for Protection

Throughout the book of Psalms, David shows people how to pray, especially when they are in trouble. For example, Psalm 3 and Psalm 5 are described as "morning prayers" for protection against enemies. David had the wisdom to know he could not make it on his own. He needed God's protection, and he wasn't afraid to ask for it. How good

are you at asking for God's protection in every situation? Are you asking him to lead the way? Women often fall into the trap of thinking they can do it all, but even the great King David knew better than that. Ask God to go before you and protect you in everything you do.

april

1 — *April Fool's Day!* Play a harmless joke on someone you love.

2 — Learn how to make a new recipe. Share it with your friends.

3 — The first Sunday of April marks the start of daylight saving time in most of the country. Turn clocks forward one hour at 2 A.M.

4 — Pray for a person of influence: It's Maya Angelou's birthday.

5

6 — Make a list of your immediate family members. Pray for them every night this week.

7

8

9 — Spend time today with someone who doesn't have many friends.

10 — Read the first five chapters of Proverbs. Share what you learned with someone.

11

12 — Take your vitamins—and calcium (with your doctor's approval).

13

14

15 — *Don't forget that your taxes are due today!*

16

17 — Make a new friend by reaching out to a person of a different race or nationality.

18

19 — Pray for a person of influence: It's Kate Hudson's birthday.

20

21

22 — *Earth Day.* Increase the amount of recycling in your home and workplace.

23 — April is National Humor Month. Be lighthearted. Make others laugh!

24

25

26 — Get involved! Join a walkathon. Promote literacy. Adopt a highway.

27

28 — *Deliver a bouquet of flowers to one of your neighbors.*

29

30 — Pray for a person of influence: Kirsten Dunst is celebrating a birthday today.

"Hold a true friend with both your hands." –*Nigerian Proverb*

¹⁹How great is your goodness
       that you have stored up for
           those who fear you,
   that you have given to those who
       trust you.
       You do this for all to see.
²⁰You protect them by your presence
       from what people plan against
           them.
       You shelter them from evil
           words.
²¹Praise the LORD.
       His love to me was wonderful
           when my city was attacked.
²²In my distress, I said,
       "God cannot see me!"
   But you heard my prayer
       when I cried out to you for help.
²³Love the LORD, all you who belong
       to him.
       The LORD protects those who
           truly believe,
       but he punishes the proud as
           much as they have sinned.
²⁴All you who put your hope in the
       LORD
       be strong and brave.

It Is Better to Confess Sin

A maskil of David.

32 Happy is the person
       whose sins are forgiven,
   whose wrongs are pardoned.
²Happy is the person
       whom the LORD does not
           consider guilty
       and in whom there is nothing
           false.

³When I kept things to myself,
       I felt weak deep inside me.
       I moaned all day long.
⁴Day and night you punished me.
       My strength was gone as in the
           summer heat.   *Selah*
⁵Then I confessed my sins to you
       and didn't hide my guilt.
   I said, "I will confess my sins to the
       LORD,"
       and you forgave my guilt.   *Selah*

⁶For this reason, all who obey you

What's the
POINT?

Psalm 31:5

Do you pursue what you want with a passion, or do you give most things only a halfhearted effort? King David comes across in the Bible as a man who poured himself fully into whatever he did. When he praised the Lord, he did it with abandon: singing, dancing, and throwing quite a party. When he was in despair, he hit bottom: weeping, wailing, and crying out to God. In Psalm 31:5, David gives everything he has to God. He hands his whole life over to God and asks God to save him. He repeats this request again and again throughout this psalm and others. He goes after God's favor with gusto, fully expecting an answer to his pleas. And God answered David time and time again. He placed David in the position of king, helped him defeat many surrounding nations, and gave him wealth and power. David was an ordinary man who made many mistakes, but God responded to David's passionate pursuit of him. He will do the same for you if you do what David did—give him everything. Hand over your life, and ask God to take control. Pursue him with passion as David did, and just see how God will meet your needs and beyond.

should pray to you while they
still can.
When troubles rise like a flood,
they will not reach them.
[7]You are my hiding place.
You protect me from my
troubles
and fill me with songs of
salvation.   *Selah*

[8]The LORD says, "I will make you wise
and show you where to go.
I will guide you and watch over
you.
[9]So don't be like a horse or donkey,
that doesn't understand.

They must be led with bits and reins,
or they will not come near you."

[10]Wicked people have many troubles,
but the LORD's love surrounds
those who trust him.
[11]Good people, rejoice and be happy
in the LORD.
Sing all you whose hearts are
right.

Praise God Who Creates and Saves

33 Sing to the LORD, you who
do what is right;
honest people should praise him.
[2]Praise the LORD on the harp;
make music for him on a
ten-stringed lyre.

[3]Sing a new song to him;
play well and joyfully.

[4]God's word is true,
and everything he does is right.
[5]He loves what is right and fair;
the LORD's love fills the earth.

[6]The sky was made at the LORD's
command.
By the breath from his mouth,
he made all the stars.
[7]He gathered the water of the sea
into a heap.
He made the great ocean stay in
its place.
[8]All the earth should worship the
LORD;
the whole world should fear
him.
[9]He spoke, and it happened.
He commanded, and it appeared.
[10]The LORD upsets the plans of
nations;
he ruins all their plans.
[11]But the LORD's plans will stand
forever;
his ideas will last from now on.
[12]Happy is the nation whose God is
the LORD,
the people he chose for his very
own.
[13]The LORD looks down from heaven
and sees every person.
[14]From his throne he watches
all who live on earth.
[15]He made their hearts
and understands everything
they do.
[16]No king is saved by his great
army.
No warrior escapes by his great
strength.
[17]Horses can't bring victory;
they can't save by their strength.
[18]But the LORD looks after those who
fear him,
those who put their hope in his
love.
[19]He saves them from death
and spares their lives in times of
hunger.
[20]So our hope is in the LORD.

Beauty BECOMES HER

Blemishes

If you want to hide your blemishes, concealers are available in a variety of colors and textures. But be wary of trying too hard to mask imperfections. Applying too much concealer or using a color that doesn't match your natural skin tone will actually highlight your blemishes. Find the best shade for you and avoid those thick makeup smudges by applying only a light layer of concealer. Makeup is great for masking blemishes, but don't try to conceal anything from God. He already sees and knows everything—flaws and all—and embraces you as his child, regardless of the imperfections you see.

WHAT'S IN A word?

Psalm 32:1 "Happy" is another way to say that you are pleased, blessed, content, or satisfied. In this psalm, David contrasts the draining effect of unconfessed sin with the true happiness and freedom that comes with having a clean slate with God.

He is our help, our shield to protect us.
²¹We rejoice in him,
  because we trust his holy name.
²²Lord, show your love to us
  as we put our hope in you.

Praise God Who Judges and Saves

David's song from the time he acted crazy so Abimelech would send him away, and David did leave.

34 I will praise the Lord at all times;
  his praise is always on my lips.
²My whole being praises the Lord.
  The poor will hear and be glad.
³Glorify the Lord with me,
  and let us praise his name together.

⁴I asked the Lord for help, and he answered me.
  He saved me from all that I feared.
⁵Those who go to him for help are happy,
  and they are never disgraced.
⁶This poor man called, and the Lord heard him
  and saved him from all his troubles.
⁷The angel of the Lord camps around those who fear God,
  and he saves them.

⁸Examine and see how good the Lord is.

Happy is the person who trusts him.
⁹You who belong to the Lord, fear him!
  Those who fear him will have everything they need.
¹⁰Even lions may get weak and hungry,
  but those who look to the Lord will have every good thing.
¹¹Children, come and listen to me.
  I will teach you to worship the Lord.
¹²You must do these things
  to enjoy life and have many happy days.
¹³You must not say evil things,
  and you must not tell lies.
¹⁴Stop doing evil and do good.
  Look for peace and work for it.

¹⁵The Lord sees the good people
  and listens to their prayers.
¹⁶But the Lord is against those who do evil;
  he makes the world forget them.
¹⁷The Lord hears good people when they cry out to him,
  and he saves them from all their troubles.
¹⁸The Lord is close to the brokenhearted,
  and he saves those whose spirits have been crushed.

¹⁹People who do what is right may have many problems,
  but the Lord will solve them all.
²⁰He will protect their very bones;
  not one of them will be broken.
²¹Evil will kill the wicked;
  those who hate good people will be judged guilty.
²²But the Lord saves his servants' lives;
  no one who trusts him will be judged guilty.

A Prayer for Help

Of David.

35 Lord, battle with those who battle with me.
  Fight against those who fight against me.

²Pick up the shield and armor.
  Rise up and help me.
³Lift up your spears, both large and small,
  against those who chase me.
  Tell me, "I will save you."

WISE WORDS

Hold Your Tongue

Do you love to talk? Many women do! It's fun to share, connect with others, and grow together. But sometimes all that talking can lead to some pretty unhealthy discussions that include slander and gossip. Proverbs 10:19 says, "If you talk a lot, you are sure to sin; if you are wise, you will keep quiet." Are you known for empty chatter or well-chosen words of wisdom? God calls you to be wise with your words. Your mouth was designed to encourage and build others up, not to shred reputations or spread gossip. So the next time you're about to say something you really shouldn't, stop talking! Remember that sometimes the best thing you can say is nothing at all.

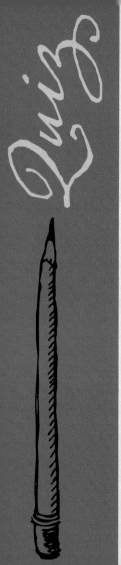

do you know your boundaries?

1. YOU HAVE AN EXTREMELY BUSY DAY AHEAD. A GIRLFRIEND CALLS TO CHAT FOR A WHILE. YOU:

☐ A. Decide not to tell her about your schedule. You spend more than an hour on the phone talking about random topics because she's a friend and you feel you should be there for her, even if it's just to talk.

☐ B. Let her know you're on a tight schedule but allow the conversation to come to a natural end nearly an hour later.

☐ C. Explain that you have a busy day and can only talk for a few minutes. Ten minutes later, you gently remind her of your schedule and offer to call her back at another time.

2. YOUR FRIEND'S COUSIN NEEDS A PLACE TO STAY UNTIL SHE GETS SETTLED. YOU:

☐ A. Immediately offer her your couch—rent-free and without any limitations or stipulations.

☐ B. Ask a few questions about the cousin and decide to let her stay with you for as long as she needs to. You tactfully encourage her to find a different place for her dogs and request that she doesn't smoke in your house.

☐ C. Ask a lot of questions about the cousin and offer to let her stay for two weeks. At that point, you know you can extend the offer if things are working out. But you clearly explain the rules: no pets, no smoking, and no boyfriends spending the night.

3. A COWORKER IS SHORT ON CASH WHENEVER YOU GO TO LUNCH WITH HER. YOU KNOW SHE HAS THE MONEY, BUT SHE ALWAYS SEEMS TO CONVENIENTLY FORGET HER PURSE. YOU:

☐ A. Continue paying for her lunches because you think it's a nice thing to do.

☐ B. Tell her you can't afford to keep buying her lunch but pull out your wallet anyway.

☐ C. Explain that this is the last time you can cover for her and insist that she repay you as soon as you return to the office.

MOSTLY A'S: YOU ARE A PUSHOVER. You don't know where to draw the line, and you're afraid to tell people when they've gone too far. As a result, you often get taken advantage of and find yourself in tough situations. Rather than helping people, you enable them to the point where they no longer see the need to help themselves.

MOSTLY B'S: YOU MAKE A SOLID EFFORT TO DRAW BOUNDARIES, but you let people walk all over you when it comes to follow-through. There are times when you know you're getting taken advantage of, but you don't know what to do about it. It's time to speak up and assert yourself.

MOSTLY C'S: YOU HAVE LEARNED TO DRAW AND DEFEND YOUR BOUNDARIES. You know what you're willing to give, and you look for ways to help people without making them dependent on you. You have learned to balance meeting your needs with meeting the needs of others.

⁴Make those who want to kill me
  be ashamed and disgraced.
 Make those who plan to harm me
  turn back and run away.
⁵Make them like chaff blown by the
   wind
  as the angel of the Lord forces
   them away.
⁶Let their road be dark and slippery
  as the angel of the Lord chases
   them.
⁷For no reason they spread out their
   net to trap me;
  for no reason they dug a pit for
   me.
⁸So let ruin strike them suddenly.
  Let them be caught in their own
   nets;
  let them fall into the pit and die.
⁹Then I will rejoice in the Lord;
  I will be happy when he saves
   me.
¹⁰Even my bones will say,
  "Lord, who is like you?
 You save the weak from the strong,
  the weak and poor from
   robbers."

¹¹Men without mercy stand up to
   testify.
  They ask me things I do not
   know.
¹²They repay me with evil for the
   good I have done,
  and they make me very sad.

WHAT'S IN A
word?

Psalm 34:9 "Fear" Fearing God
does not mean that you
should hide in a corner or walk
on eggshells, afraid that a
lightning bolt will hit you if you
make one misstep. Instead,
this command instructs you
to show God the honor and
respect that he deserves.

¹³Yet when they were sick, I put on
   clothes of sadness
  and showed my sorrow by
   fasting.
 But my prayers were not answered.
¹⁴ I acted as if they were my
   friends or brothers.
 I bowed in sadness as if I were
   crying for my mother.
¹⁵But when I was in trouble, they
   gathered and laughed;
  they gathered to attack before I
   knew it.
  They insulted me without
   stopping.
¹⁶They made fun of me and were
   cruel to me
  and ground their teeth at me in
   anger.
¹⁷Lord, how long will you watch this
   happen?
  Save my life from their attacks;
  save me from these people who
   are like lions.
¹⁸I will praise you in the great
   meeting.
  I will praise you among crowds
   of people.
¹⁹Do not let my enemies laugh at me;
  they hate me for no reason.
 Do not let them make fun of me;
  they have no cause to hate me.
²⁰Their words are not friendly
  but are lies about peace-loving
   people.
²¹They speak against me
  and say, "Aha! We saw what you
   did!"

²²Lord, you have been watching. Do
   not keep quiet.
  Lord, do not leave me alone.
²³Wake up! Come and defend me!
  My God and Lord, fight for
   me!
²⁴Lord my God, defend me with your
   justice.
  Don't let them laugh at me.
²⁵Don't let them think, "Aha! We got
   what we wanted!"
  Don't let them say, "We
   destroyed him."

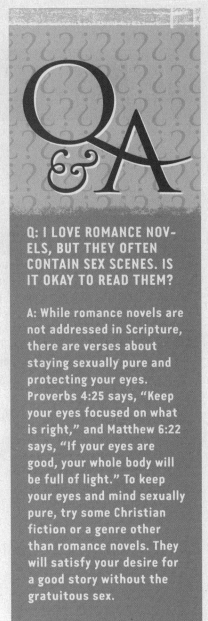

Q & A

**Q: I LOVE ROMANCE NOV-
ELS, BUT THEY OFTEN
CONTAIN SEX SCENES. IS
IT OKAY TO READ THEM?**

A: While romance novels are
not addressed in Scripture,
there are verses about
staying sexually pure and
protecting your eyes.
Proverbs 4:25 says, "Keep
your eyes focused on what
is right," and Matthew 6:22
says, "If your eyes are
good, your whole body will
be full of light." To keep
your eyes and mind sexually
pure, try some Christian
fiction or a genre other
than romance novels. They
will satisfy your desire for
a good story without the
gratuitous sex.

²⁶Let them be ashamed and
   embarrassed,
  because they were happy when I
   hurt.
 Cover them with shame and
   disgrace,
  because they thought they were
   better than I was.
²⁷May my friends sing and shout for
   joy.
  May they always say, "Praise the
   greatness of the Lord,

ETIQUETTE 101

E-MAIL PROTOCOL

E-mail is a great time saver, but it can be a minefield if you don't know the protocol. Be concise and answer any questions the sender asks, as well as further questions you anticipate. Use proper spelling, punctuation, and grammar, and always double-check your tone before hitting "Send." Don't use ALL CAPITALS—it looks as if you're yelling. Avoid marking messages "urgent" unless they truly are, and use "Cc:" and "Reply to All" sparingly. Never forward virus hoaxes, chain letters, confidential information, or libelous or defamatory remarks (see Proverbs 4:24 and 5:2). In short, don't lower your communication standards just because it's an e-mail.

who loves to see his servants do well."

28 I will tell of your goodness
and will praise you every day.

Wicked People and a Good God

For the director of music. Of David, the servant of the LORD.

36 Sin speaks to the wicked
in their hearts.
They have no fear of God.

2 They think too much of themselves
so they don't see their sin and
hate it.

3 Their words are wicked lies;
they are no longer wise or good.

4 At night they make evil plans;
what they do leads to nothing
good.
They don't refuse things that
are evil.

5 LORD, your love reaches to the
heavens,
your loyalty to the skies.

6 Your goodness is as high as the
mountains.
Your justice is as deep as the
great ocean.
LORD, you protect both people and
animals.

7 God, your love is so precious!
You protect people in the
shadow of your wings.

8 They eat the rich food in your
house,
and you let them drink from
your river of pleasure.

9 You are the giver of life.
Your light lets us enjoy life.

10 Continue to love those who know
you
and to do good to those who are
good.

11 Don't let proud people attack me
and the wicked force me
away.

12 Those who do evil have been
defeated.
They are overwhelmed;
they cannot do evil any longer.

God Will Reward Fairly

Of David.

37 Don't be upset because of
evil people.
Don't be jealous of those who do
wrong,

2 because like the grass, they will
soon dry up.
Like green plants, they will soon
die away.

3 Trust the LORD and do good.
Live in the land and feed on
truth.

4 Enjoy serving the LORD,
and he will give you what you
want.

5 Depend on the LORD;
trust him, and he will take care
of you.

6 Then your goodness will shine like
the sun,
and your fairness like the
noonday sun.

7 Wait and trust the LORD.
Don't be upset when others get
rich
or when someone else's plans
succeed.

fun FACTS

In 2003, nearly 35% of all births were to unmarried women.

(National Center for Heath Statistics)

What's the POINT?

⁸Don't get angry.
>Don't be upset; it only leads to trouble.

⁹Evil people will be sent away,
>but those who trust the LORD will inherit the land.

¹⁰In a little while the wicked will be no more.
>You may look for them, but they will be gone.

¹¹People who are not proud will inherit the land
>and will enjoy complete peace.

¹²The wicked make evil plans against good people.
>They grind their teeth at them in anger.

¹³But the Lord laughs at the wicked,
>because he sees that their day is coming.

¹⁴The wicked draw their swords and bend their bows
to kill the poor and helpless,
>to kill those who are honest.

¹⁵But their swords will stab their own hearts,
>and their bows will break.

¹⁶It is better to have little and be right
>than to have much and be wrong.

¹⁷The power of the wicked will be broken,
>but the LORD supports those who do right.

¹⁸The LORD watches over the lives of the innocent,
>and their reward will last forever.

¹⁹They will not be ashamed when trouble comes.
>They will be full in times of hunger.

²⁰But the wicked will die.
>The LORD's enemies will be like the flowers of the fields;
>they will disappear like smoke.

²¹The wicked borrow and don't pay back,
>but those who do right give freely to others.

Psalm 37:21

Too much debt leads to big trouble. You or someone you know may be teetering on the edge of bankruptcy because of mounting debt. Does God have anything to say about bankruptcy? He does, actually, and makes a pretty strong statement about that here: "The wicked borrow and don't pay back." Ouch! If you are among those who want to follow God but are drowning in debt, bankruptcy may give you the option of reorganizing what you need to pay back—but you still need to pay it back. Even if your debt is legally erased, you have a moral obligation to be faithful to the creditors who trusted you to pay them for the merchandise or services you used. Plus, if you begin to take good care of what God provides for you, you will see your efforts pay off. Even better, your creditors will probably begin to wonder what makes you so different and why you continue to pay when you don't have to. Even if the payments are very small, your debt will shrink little by little. Then you will have the peace and satisfaction of a job well done, and you will have a real incentive for not getting into that predicament again!

Seven ways to...

Get Out of Debt

1. Save one credit card for emergencies and cut up your remaining cards.

2. Talk to a debt counselor.

3. Consider consolidating your debt.

4. Establish a goal and timeline for becoming debt-free.

5. Ask a friend to hold you accountable.

6. Wait twenty-four hours before making sizable purchases.

7. Look for a second job.

²²Those whom the LORD blesses will
    inherit the land,
    but those he curses will be sent
      away.

²³When people's steps follow the
    LORD,
    God is pleased with their ways.
²⁴If they stumble, they will not fall,
    because the LORD holds their
      hand.

²⁵I was young, and now I am old,
    but I have never seen good
      people left helpless
    or their children begging for
      food.
²⁶Good people always lend freely to
    others,
    and their children are a blessing.

²⁷Stop doing evil and do good,
    so you will live forever.
²⁸The LORD loves justice
    and will not leave those who
      worship him.
  He will always protect them,
    but the children of the wicked
      will die.
²⁹Good people will inherit the land
    and will live in it forever.

³⁰Good people speak with wisdom,
    and they say what is fair.
³¹The teachings of their God are in
      their heart,
    so they do not fail to keep
      them.
³²The wicked watch for good people
    so that they may kill them.
³³But the LORD will not take away his
      protection
    or let good people be judged
      guilty.

³⁴Wait for the LORD's help
    and follow him.
  He will honor you and give you the
      land,
    and you will see the wicked sent
      away.

³⁵I saw a wicked and cruel man
    who looked strong like a healthy
      tree in good soil.
³⁶But he died and was gone;
    I looked for him, but he couldn't
      be found.

³⁷Think of the innocent person,
    and watch the honest one.
  The man who has peace
    will have children to live after
      him.
³⁸But sinners will be destroyed;
    in the end the wicked will die.

WHAT'S IN A word?

Psalm 37:34 "Wait" means more than just sitting around. Rather, waiting on the Lord is an active expression of faith that involves praying and believing that he will do what he has promised!

³⁹The LORD saves good people;
    he is their strength in times of
      trouble.
⁴⁰The LORD helps them and saves
    them;
    he saves them from the wicked,
    because they trust in him for
      protection.

A Prayer in Time of Sickness

A psalm of David to remember.

38 LORD, don't correct me
    when you are angry.
  Don't punish me when you are
    furious.
²Your arrows have wounded me,
    and your hand has come down
      on me.
³My body is sick from your
      punishment.
  Even my bones are not healthy
    because of my sin.
⁴My guilt has overwhelmed me;
    like a load it weighs me down.

⁵My sores stink and become infected
    because I was foolish.
⁶I am bent over and bowed down;
    I am sad all day long.
⁷I am burning with fever,
    and my whole body is sore.
⁸I am weak and faint.
    I moan from the pain I feel.

⁹Lord, you know everything I want;
    my cries are not hidden from
      you.
¹⁰My heart pounds, and my strength
    is gone.
  I am losing my sight.

¹¹Because of my wounds, my friends
and neighbors avoid me,
and my relatives stay far away.
¹²Some people set traps to kill me.
Those who want to hurt me plan
trouble;
all day long they think up lies.

¹³I am like the deaf; I cannot hear.
Like the mute, I cannot speak.
¹⁴I am like those who do not hear,
who have no answer to give.
¹⁵I trust you, LORD.
You will answer, my Lord and
God.
¹⁶I said, "Don't let them laugh at me
or brag when I am defeated."
¹⁷I am about to die,
and I cannot forget my pain.
¹⁸I confess my guilt;
I am troubled by my sin.
¹⁹My enemies are strong and healthy,
and many hate me for no reason.
²⁰They repay me with evil for the
good I did.
They lie about me because I try
to do good.

²¹LORD, don't leave me;
my God, don't go away.
²²Quickly come and help me,
my Lord and Savior.

Life Is Short

*For the director of music. For Jeduthun. A psalm of
David.*

39 I said, "I will be careful
how I act
and will not sin by what I say.
I will be careful what I say
around wicked people."
²So I kept very quiet.
I didn't even say anything good,
but I became even more upset.
³I became very angry inside,
and as I thought about it, my
anger burned.
So I spoke:
⁴"LORD, tell me when the end will
come
and how long I will live.
Let me know how long I have.
⁵You have given me only a short life;

my lifetime is like nothing to you.
Everyone's life is only a breath.
Selah

⁶People are like shadows moving
about.
All their work is for nothing;
they collect things but don't
know who will get them.

⁷"So, Lord, what hope do I have?
You are my hope.
⁸Save me from all my sins.
Don't let wicked fools make fun
of me.
⁹I am quiet; I do not open my mouth,
because you are the one who has
done this.
¹⁰Quit punishing me;
your beating is about to kill me.
¹¹You correct and punish people for
their sins;
like a moth, you destroy what
they love.
Everyone's life is only a breath.
Selah

¹²"LORD, hear my prayer,
and listen to my cry.
Do not ignore my tears.
I am like a visitor with you.
Like my ancestors, I'm only here
a short time.
¹³Leave me alone so I can be happy
before I leave and am no more."

Praise and Prayer for Help

For the director of music. A psalm of David.

40 I waited patiently for the
LORD.
He turned to me and heard my
cry.
²He lifted me out of the pit of
destruction,
out of the sticky mud.
He stood me on a rock
and made my feet steady.
³He put a new song in my mouth,
a song of praise to our God.
Many people will see this and
worship him.
Then they will trust the LORD.

⁴Happy is the person
who trusts the LORD,
who doesn't turn to those who are
proud
or to those who worship false
gods.
⁵LORD my God, you have done many
miracles.
Your plans for us are many.
If I tried to tell them all,
there would be too many to
count.

BIBLE Women & Men

Jochabed

Could you give up the one thing you love most? Jochabed faced a nearly impossible decision: keep her son and try to hide him from the Egyptians, who were killing all Hebrew baby boys, or let him drift away from her—literally—in a basket down the river (Exodus 2:3). Jochabed was the mother of Moses, the man God called to lead the Israelites out of four hundred years of slavery in Egypt. Moses' mission was set into motion when Jochabed released him in order to save his life. Her sacrifice saved her people, all because she was willing to let go!

What's the POINT?

Psalm 39:4–5

Life is short. You may hear that saying a lot, but have you ever really thought about it? If the earth was here for thousands of years before you were born, and your life will last an average of only seventy or eighty years before death ushers you into eternity, that's really not very much time. In light of all that came before and all that will come after your life, it is important to make every minute count. God's Word says you are to love him first, then love others. So ask yourself how you are fulfilling those two commands. Even people who don't know God usually demonstrate love to their families. Would your family say that you respond in a loving way to them? How about your friends and coworkers? Are you doing your very best to make your relationship with them a positive experience and to make each minute count? If you knew that this would be the last chance you had to resolve a conflict or mend a broken relationship, what would you want to do? Today is that day. Now is that time. Live like there is no tomorrow, and you will not face the sadness that comes with regret.

⁶You do not want sacrifices and offerings.
  But you have made a hole in my ear
  to show that my body and life are yours.
You do not ask for burnt offerings and sacrifices to take away sins.
⁷Then I said, "Look, I have come.
  It is written about me in the book.
⁸My God, I want to do what you want.
  Your teachings are in my heart."

⁹I will tell about your goodness in the great meeting of your people.
  LORD, you know my lips are not silent.
¹⁰I do not hide your goodness in my heart;
  I speak about your loyalty and salvation.
I do not hide your love and truth from the people in the great meeting.

¹¹LORD, do not hold back your mercy from me;
  let your love and truth always protect me.
¹²Troubles have surrounded me;
  there are too many to count.
My sins have caught me
  so that I cannot see a way to escape.
I have more sins than hairs on my head,
  and I have lost my courage.
¹³Please, LORD, save me.
  Hurry, LORD, to help me.
¹⁴People are trying to kill me.
  Shame them and disgrace them.
People want to hurt me.
  Let them run away in disgrace.
¹⁵People are making fun of me.
  Let them be shamed into silence.
¹⁶But let those who follow you be happy and glad.
  They love you for saving them.

Stories of SURVIVAL

Less Than Perfect

KARISSA'S STORY

I grew up with a very strict father who was a perfectionist. He constantly asked me to redo things—whether it was the way I folded clothes or the way I pronounced words. Much of what he told me was helpful, but he made me feel like I could never meet his standards. He was trying to be a good parent, but some things went too far. I began worrying about the most frivolous details in order to earn my father's approval.

As a result of my upbringing, I have struggled with perfectionism for many years. I always felt I had to earn the highest grades in school, and I tirelessly pursued one promotion after another in my career. While being well-organized and seeking excellence are good qualities, I've learned the hard way that the desire to be perfect and the tendency to obsess over details can separate you from the people you love.

Driven to be the very best I could be, I have struggled to accept myself as God created me. But slowly,

through God's Word and grace, I'm learning to come to terms with my imperfections and discovering how to let things go. I spend a lot of time quoting 2 Corinthians 12:9 to myself. It says, "'My grace is enough for you. When you are weak, my power is made perfect in you.' So I am very happy to brag about my weaknesses. Then Christ's power can live in me."

I've learned that sometimes it's good for me to face the reality of a messy room, an overcooked meal, or leaving the house without wearing makeup. It's healthy to let people see who I really am and drop the façade I've been trying to maintain for so many years. In the process, I'm learning to accept love and grace from God and from others on a whole new level. It's been a tough road, and I still have a long way to go. But I rest in the fact that God's perfect love embraces my imperfections and loves me just the way I am.

> THROUGH GOD'S WORD AND GRACE, I'M LEARNING TO COME TO TERMS WITH MY IMPERFECTIONS AND DISCOVERING HOW TO LET THINGS GO.

Balancing Act

Nine to Five

Most likely, your work follows you home at the end of the day. When you leave your job, you may find it difficult to switch gears and get on with your personal life. E-mails are waiting, cell phones are ringing, and that "one more thing" you want to do can eat up time that should be spent with God, other people, or just yourself. You want to be productive, of course, whether you work around the home or elsewhere. But your work shouldn't take over your life. After a full day, put your work down and leave it alone until the next morning. Take time to rest and recharge your batteries, and you'll be ready to face your work again.

May they always say, "Praise the LORD!"

[17]Lord, because I am poor and helpless,
please remember me.
You are my helper and savior.
My God, do not wait.

A Prayer in Time of Sickness

For the director of music. A psalm of David.

41 Happy are those who
think about the poor.
When trouble comes, the LORD
will save them.
[2]The LORD will protect them and
spare their life
and will bless them in the land.
He will not let their enemies
take them.
[3]The LORD will give them strength
when they are sick,
and he will make them well
again.

[4]I said, "LORD, have mercy on me.
Heal me, because I have sinned
against you."
[5]My enemies are saying evil things
about me.
They say, "When will he die and
be forgotten?"
[6]Some people come to see me,
but they lie.
They just come to get bad news.
Then they go and gossip.
[7]All my enemies whisper about me
and think the worst about me.
[8]They say, "He has a terrible
disease.
He will never get out of bed
again."
[9]My best and truest friend, who ate
at my table,
has even turned against me.

[10]LORD, have mercy on me.
Give me strength so I can pay
them back.
[11]Because my enemies do not defeat
me,
I know you are pleased with me.

[12]Because I am innocent, you support
me
and will let me be with you
forever.
[13]Praise the LORD, the God of Israel.
He has always been,
and he will always be.
Amen and amen.

BOOK 2

Wishing to Be Near God

For the director of music. A maskil of the sons of Korah.

42 As a deer thirsts for
streams of water,
so I thirst for you, God.
[2]I thirst for the living God.
When can I go to meet with him?
[3]Day and night, my tears have been
my food.
People are always saying,
"Where is your God?"
[4]When I remember these things,
I speak with a broken heart.
I used to walk with the crowd
and lead them to God's Temple
with songs of praise.

[5]Why am I so sad?
Why am I so upset?
I should put my hope in God
and keep praising him,
my Savior and [6]my God.

I am very sad.
So I remember you where the
Jordan River begins,
near the peaks of Hermon and
Mount Mizar.
[7]Troubles have come again and
again, sounding like
waterfalls.
Your waves are crashing all
around me.
[8]The LORD shows his true love every
day.
At night I have a song,
and I pray to my living God.
[9]I say to God, my Rock,
"Why have you forgotten me?
Why am I sad
and troubled by my enemies?"

¹⁰My enemies' insults make me feel
as if my bones were broken.
They are always saying,
"Where is your God?"

¹¹Why am I so sad?
Why am I so upset?
I should put my hope in God
and keep praising him,
my Savior and my God.

A Prayer for Protection

43

God, defend me.
Argue my case against
those who don't
follow you.
Save me from liars and those
who do evil.
²God, you are my strength.
Why have you rejected me?
Why am I sad
and troubled by my enemies?
³Send me your light and truth
to guide me.
Let them lead me to your holy
mountain,
to where you live.
⁴Then I will go to the altar of God,
to God who is my joy and
happiness.
I will praise you with a harp,
God, my God.

⁵Why am I so sad?
Why am I so upset?
I should put my hope in God
and keep praising him,
my Savior and my God.

A Prayer for Help

For the director of music. A maskil of the sons of Korah.

44

God, we have heard about
you.
Our ancestors told us
what you did in their days,
in days long ago.
²With your power you forced the
nations out of the land
and placed our ancestors here.
You destroyed those other
nations,

but you made our ancestors
grow strong.
³It wasn't their swords that took the
land.
It wasn't their power that gave
them victory.
But it was your great power and
strength.
You were with them because you
loved them.

⁴My God, you are my King.
Your commands led Jacob's
people to victory.
⁵With your help we pushed back our
enemies.
In your name we trampled those
who came against us.
⁶I don't trust my bow to help me,
and my sword can't save me.
⁷You saved us from our foes,
and you made our enemies
ashamed.
⁸We will praise God every day;
we will praise your name forever.

Selah

⁹But you have rejected us and shamed
us.
You don't march with our armies
anymore.
¹⁰You let our enemies push us back,
and those who hate us have taken
our wealth.
¹¹You gave us away like sheep to be
eaten
and have scattered us among the
nations.
¹²You sold your people for nothing
and made no profit on the
sale.
¹³You made us a joke to our neighbors;
those around us laugh and make
fun of us.
¹⁴You made us a joke to the other
nations;
people shake their heads.
¹⁵I am always in disgrace,
and I am covered with shame.
¹⁶My enemy is getting even
with insults and curses.

Q: I AM SINGLE, AND I WANT TO BE A MOTHER. IS IT OKAY TO THINK ABOUT ADOPTING?

A: Becoming a parent is both a privilege and a lot of work! Giving a child a family is a beautiful thing, but single parenting is an enormous task. Pray long and hard, and seek the wise advice of trusted family members and friends. Evaluate the big picture, making sure you have the finances, health and stamina, and support network to help you rear a child. Spend time with single parents to get a realistic picture of parenthood, and develop friendships with two-parent families so your child can see what healthy marriages look like.

RELATIONSHIPS

Feuding Friends—Should You Get Involved?

Two of your closest friends are at odds with each other. In your experience, both have been equally trustworthy and responsible, so it's difficult to know whom to believe. What should you do? One important thing to realize is that hearing only one side of the story will not present an accurate, complete picture of the truth (see Proverbs 18:17). Even if you hear both sides, it's almost impossible to know who is right. And that brings up another issue: *right* can be hard to define. One friend may have justifiable reasons for being upset, but the other may also have legitimate complaints. Your safest bet? Don't get involved (see Proverbs 26:17). Maintain separate relationships with both friends, and pray that they work things out.

¹⁷All these things have happened to us,
but we have not forgotten you
or failed to keep our agreement with you.
¹⁸Our hearts haven't turned away from you,
and we haven't stopped following you.
¹⁹But you crushed us in this place where wild dogs live,
and you covered us with deep darkness.
²⁰If we had forgotten our God
or lifted our hands in prayer to foreign gods,
²¹God would have known,
because he knows what is in our hearts.
²²But for you we are in danger of death all the time.
People think we are worth no more than sheep to be killed.
²³Wake up, Lord! Why are you sleeping?
Get up! Don't reject us forever.
²⁴Why do you hide from us?

Have you forgotten our pain and troubles?
²⁵We have been pushed down into the dirt;
we are flat on the ground.
²⁶Get up and help us.
Because of your love, save us.

A Song for the King's Wedding

For the director of music. To the tune of "Lilies." A maskil. A love song of the sons of Korah.

45 Beautiful words fill my mind.
I am speaking of royal things.
My tongue is like the pen of a skilled writer.

²You are more handsome than anyone,
and you are an excellent speaker,
so God has blessed you forever.
³Put on your sword, powerful warrior.
Show your glory and majesty.
⁴In your majesty win the victory
for what is true and right.
Your power will do amazing things.
⁵Your sharp arrows will enter the hearts of the king's enemies.
Nations will be defeated before you.
⁶God, your throne will last forever and ever.

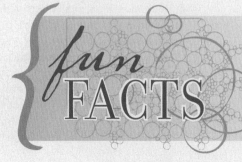

fun FACTS

Some 4,300 women under 35 develop breast cancer each year.

(Self.com)

You will rule your kingdom with
fairness.
⁷You love right and hate evil,
so God has chosen you from
among your friends;
he has set you apart with much
joy.
⁸Your clothes smell like myrrh, aloes,
and cassia.
From palaces of ivory
music comes to make you happy.
⁹Kings' daughters are among your
honored women.
Your bride stands at your right
side
wearing gold from Ophir.

¹⁰Listen to me, daughter; look and
pay attention.
Forget your people and your
father's family.
¹¹The king loves your beauty.
Because he is your master, you
should obey him.
¹²People from the city of Tyre have
brought a gift.
Wealthy people will want to
meet you.

¹³The princess is very beautiful.
Her gown is woven with gold.
¹⁴In her beautiful clothes she is
brought to the king.
Her bridesmaids follow behind
her,
and they are also brought to him.
¹⁵They come with happiness and joy;
they enter the king's palace.

¹⁶You will have sons to replace your
fathers.
You will make them rulers
through all the land.
¹⁷I will make your name famous from
now on,
so people will praise you forever
and ever.

God Protects His People

For the director of music. By alamoth. A psalm of the sons of Korah.

46 God is our protection and
our strength.

He always helps in times of
trouble.
²So we will not be afraid even if the
earth shakes,
or the mountains fall into the sea,
³even if the oceans roar and foam,
or the mountains shake at the
raging sea.   *Selah*

⁴There is a river that brings joy to
the city of God,
the holy place where God Most
High lives.
⁵God is in that city, and so it will not
be shaken.
God will help her at dawn.
⁶Nations tremble and kingdoms
shake.
God shouts and the earth
crumbles.

⁷The Lord All-Powerful is with us;
the God of Jacob is our defender.
Selah

⁸Come and see what the Lord has
done,
the amazing things he has done
on the earth.
⁹He stops wars everywhere on the
earth.
He breaks all bows and spears
and burns up the chariots with
fire.
¹⁰God says, "Be still and know that I
am God.
I will be praised in all the
nations;
I will be praised throughout the
earth."

¹¹The Lord All-Powerful is with us;
the God of Jacob is our defender.
Selah

God, the King of the World

For the director of music. A psalm of the sons of Korah.

47 Clap your hands, all you
people.
Shout to God with joy.
²The Lord Most High is wonderful.
He is the great King over all the
earth!

Worship through Writing

**Do you ever get the sense
while reading Psalms that
you are peeking into
David's personal journal?
In a way, you are! Psalms
offers a vivid picture of
the ups and downs David
faced in his relationship
with God. It is intimate
and candid, and it is *worship*. Writing your praise
to the Lord can be just as
worshipful as singing or
shouting it. A journal can
be a brilliant reminder of
where you've been and
what God has brought you
through. Try this form of
worship today!**

What's the POINT?

Psalm 46:1

What are you most afraid of? Do you jump at the sight of snakes or cockroaches, hide behind triple-locked doors at night, or keep a light on when you sleep to chase the dark away? No matter what your fears are, you do not have to face them on your own because God will never leave you. He is there in the dark with you. He is beside you when you are alone at night. He is always with you! But maybe it's not the dark of night that scares you. Maybe the storms of life that threaten to disrupt your tranquility are causing you the greatest concern. When the storms come, and they will, God will be right by your side, comforting you until you see the sun shining again. In Psalm 46, the author describes devastating natural disasters that would cause fear in even the most faithful believers. But the psalmist says that because of God's protection and strength, his people need not fear. When it feels like the mountains are falling into the sea of your life, rest in the fact that God can handle it. No stress, calamity, mishap, or blunder is too big for God. Go to him with your fears, your anxieties, and the cries of your heart. Then feel his arms wrapping around you, providing all that you need.

³He defeated nations for us
  and put them under our control.
⁴He chose the land we would inherit.
  We are the children of Jacob,
    whom he loved.   *Selah*

⁵God has risen with a shout of joy;
  the Lᴏʀᴅ has risen as the
    trumpets sounded.
⁶Sing praises to God. Sing praises.
  Sing praises to our King. Sing
    praises.
⁷God is King of all the earth,
  so sing a song of praise to him.
⁸God is King over the nations.
  God sits on his holy throne.
⁹The leaders of the nations meet
  with the people of the God of
    Abraham,
because the leaders of the earth
  belong to God.
  He is supreme.

Jerusalem, the City of God

A psalm of the sons of Korah.

48 The Lᴏʀᴅ is great; he
    should be praised
in the city of our God, on his
  holy mountain.
²It is high and beautiful
  and brings joy to the whole
    world.
Mount Zion is like the high
  mountains of the north;
  it is the city of the Great King.
³God is within its palaces;
  he is known as its defender.
⁴Kings joined together
  and came to attack the city.
⁵But when they saw it, they were
    amazed.
  They ran away in fear.
⁶Fear took hold of them;
  they hurt like a woman having a
    baby.
⁷You destroyed the large trading
    ships
  with an east wind.

⁸First we heard
  and now we have seen

that God will always keep his city
    safe.
  It is the city of the Lᴏʀᴅ
    All-Powerful,
  the city of our God.   *Selah*

⁹God, we come into your Temple
  to think about your love.
¹⁰God, your name is known
    everywhere;
  all over the earth people praise
    you.
  Your right hand is full of
    goodness.
¹¹Mount Zion is happy
  and all the towns of Judah
    rejoice,
because your decisions are fair.

¹²Walk around Jerusalem
  and count its towers.
¹³Notice how strong they are.
  Look at the palaces.
  Then you can tell your children
    about them.
¹⁴This God is our God forever and
    ever.
  He will guide us from now on.

Trusting Money Is Foolish

For the director of music. A psalm of the sons of Korah.

49 Listen to this, all you
    nations;
  listen, all you who live on earth.
²Listen, both great and small,
  rich and poor together.
³What I say is wise,
  and my heart speaks with
    understanding.
⁴I will pay attention to a wise saying;
  I will explain my riddle on the
    harp.

⁵Why should I be afraid of bad
    days?
  Why should I fear when evil
    people surround me?
⁶They trust in their money
  and brag about their riches.
⁷No one can buy back the life of
    another.
  No one can pay God for his own
    life,

WHAT'S IN A
word?

Psalm 47:2 "Most High" refers to God's stature above everything else on earth and in heaven. God is the creator of everything, our all-powerful defender, and the great King over all the earth.

⁸because the price of a life is high.
  No payment is ever enough.
⁹Do people live forever?
  Don't they all face death?

¹⁰See, even wise people die.
  Fools and stupid people also
    die
  and leave their wealth to others.
¹¹Their graves will always be their
    homes.
  They will live there from now
    on,
  even though they named places
    after themselves.
¹²Even rich people do not live
    forever;
  like the animals, people die.

¹³This is what will happen to those
    who trust in themselves
  and to their followers who
    believe them.   *Selah*
¹⁴Like sheep, they must die,
  and death will be their
    shepherd.
  Honest people will rule over them
    in the morning,
  and their bodies will rot in a
    grave far from home.
¹⁵But God will save my life
  and will take me from the grave.
                          Selah

¹⁶Don't be afraid of rich people
  because their houses are more
    beautiful.
¹⁷They don't take anything to the
    grave;

their wealth won't go down with
    them.
¹⁸Even though they were praised
    when they were alive—
  and people may praise you when
    you succeed—
¹⁹they will go to where their
    ancestors are.
  They will never see light
    again.
²⁰Rich people with no understanding
  are just like animals that
    die.

God Wants True Worship

A psalm of Asaph.

50 The God of gods, the
  LORD, speaks.
  He calls the earth from the
    rising to the setting sun.
²God shines from Jerusalem,
  whose beauty is perfect.
³Our God comes, and he will not be
    silent.
  A fire burns in front of him,

Become
INVOLVED

VolunteerMatch

If you want to try your hand at volunteering somewhere locally, VolunteerMatch could help you find the perfect fit. VolunteerMatch pairs up individuals who want to volunteer with organizations that need the help. They also offer a range of online services to support their community of volunteer, non-profit, and business leaders who are all committed to making a difference. The site's mission is to help everyone find a great place to volunteer. In fact, VolunteerMatch recently celebrated their two millionth volunteer referral!

All you have to do is stop by the site and type in your zip code to see which agencies in your area need your help. The opportunities are coded with symbols that tell if the tasks are appropriate for different age groups, such as children or seniors. You can change the geographical radius of your search to discover opportunities from within five miles of your home to your entire state.

A recent search of Hernando County, Florida, for example, turned up volunteer positions that ranged from families needed to host foreign exchange students to cosmetologists needed to do makeovers on female cancer patients for the American Cancer Society. To check out opportunities in your area, visit www.volunteer-match.org.

"If you can't feed a hundred people,
   then feed just one."
                    –*Mother Teresa*

may

It's *May Day!* Research its history on-line. **1**	Floss every day for the next week. **2**	**3**	*Jog or go for a brisk walk.* **4**	It's *Cinco de Mayo!* Celebrate by enjoying authentic Mexican food. **5**
This month honors Asian-American heritage. **6**	*Mother's Day* is the second Sunday in May. Plan a special surprise for your mother— or someone else's. **7**	Keep small weights near the television. Get in shape while you're watching TV. **8**	**9**	Pray for a person of influence: It's Bono's birthday. **10**
11	Read Job 42. Memorize a verse from the chapter. **12**	**13**	*Tell God three things you love about him.* **14**	Lots of women are graduating this month. Let them know you care. **15**
Take a look at your schedule. Do you need to slow down? **16**	Sleep in on your day off this week. Remember to take care of your body. **17**	Make a homemade gift for a friend just for fun. **18**	**19**	Read Psalm 8. Praise God for his greatness! **20**
Collect old Bibles from around your home and give them away. **21**	**22**	**23**	**24**	*Memorial Day* is observed on the last Monday in May. Take time to pray for our troops. **25**
26	**27**	Begin a prayer list in the back of this Bible and pray through it each day. **28**	**29**	**30**
31				

and a powerful storm surrounds
  him.
⁴He calls to the sky above and to the
  earth
  that he might judge his people.
⁵He says, "Gather around, you who
  worship me,
  who have made an agreement
  with me, using a sacrifice."
⁶God is the judge,
  and even the skies say he is
  right.   *Selah*

⁷God says, "My people, listen to me;
  Israel, I will testify against
  you.
  I am God, your God.
⁸I do not scold you for your
  sacrifices.
  You always bring me your burnt
  offerings.
⁹But I do not need bulls from your
  stalls
  or goats from your pens,

¹⁰because every animal of the forest
  is already mine.
  The cattle on a thousand hills
  are mine.
¹¹I know every bird on the mountains,
  and every living thing in the
  fields is mine.
¹²If I were hungry, I would not tell
  you,
  because the earth and
  everything in it are mine.
¹³I don't eat the meat of bulls
  or drink the blood of goats.
¹⁴Give an offering to show thanks to
  God.
  Give God Most High what you
  have promised.
¹⁵Call to me in times of trouble.
  I will save you, and you will
  honor me."

¹⁶But God says to the wicked,
  "Why do you talk about my
  laws?

Why do you mention my
  agreement?
¹⁷You hate my teachings
  and turn your back on what I say.
¹⁸When you see a thief, you join him.
  You take part in adultery.
¹⁹You don't stop your mouth from
  speaking evil,
  and your tongue makes up lies.
²⁰You speak against your brother
  and lie about your mother's son.
²¹I have kept quiet while you did
  these things,
  so you thought I was just like
  you.
  But I will scold you
  and accuse you to your face.

²²"Think about this, you who forget
  God.
  Otherwise, I will tear you apart,
  and no one will save you.
²³Those people honor me
  who bring me offerings to show
  thanks.
  And I, God, will save those who do
  that."

Life Issues

Handling Success

Have you ever heard the expression, "Too much of a good thing can be a bad thing"? It's definitely true, especially when it comes to success. It's easy to turn to God when life is falling apart all around you, but how about when you're on top of the world? Success can cause you to overwork, over-buy, and overcompensate—all out of a desire to feel the rush that comes with more success. Don't miss opportunities to draw closer to God and thank him for his blessings because you're so busy striving for that next level of success. You see, God measures true success on a very different scale. Truly successful people are humble, serve others, and don't hold on to their possessions too tightly. Deuteronomy 8:17–18 reminds us that our worldly wealth and success come from God, so don't let pride get the best of you.

A Prayer for Forgiveness

For the director of music. A psalm of David when the prophet Nathan came to David after David's sin with Bathsheba.

51 God, be merciful to me
  because you are loving.
  Because you are always ready to
  be merciful,
  wipe out all my wrongs.
²Wash away all my guilt
  and make me clean again.

³I know about my wrongs,
  and I can't forget my sin.
⁴You are the only one I have sinned
  against;
  I have done what you say is wrong.
  You are right when you speak
  and fair when you judge.
⁵I was brought into this world in sin.
  In sin my mother gave birth to
  me.

⁶You want me to be completely
  truthful,

so teach me wisdom.
⁷Take away my sin, and I will be
    clean.
Wash me, and I will be whiter
    than snow.

⁸Make me hear sounds of joy and
    gladness;
    let the bones you crushed be
    happy again.
⁹Turn your face from my sins
    and wipe out all my guilt.

¹⁰Create in me a pure heart, God,
    and make my spirit right again.
¹¹Do not send me away from you

or take your Holy Spirit away
    from me.
¹²Give me back the joy of your
    salvation.
    Keep me strong by giving me a
    willing spirit.
¹³Then I will teach your ways to those
    who do wrong,
    and sinners will turn back to
    you.

¹⁴God, save me from the guilt of
    murder,
    God of my salvation,
    and I will sing about your
    goodness.
¹⁵Lord, let me speak
    so I may praise you.
¹⁶You are not pleased by sacrifices, or
    I would give them.
    You don't want burnt offerings.
¹⁷The sacrifice God wants is a broken
    spirit.
    God, you will not reject a heart
    that is broken and sorry for
    sin.

¹⁸Do whatever good you wish for
    Jerusalem.
    Rebuild the walls of Jerusalem.
¹⁹Then you will be pleased with right
    sacrifices and whole burnt
    offerings,
    and bulls will be offered on your
    altar.

HEALTH
Migraines

It's estimated that 45 million Americans suffer from chronic headaches, and 28 million of those people suffer from migraines. According to the Web site WebMD.com, more women than men get migraines, and a quarter of all women with migraines experience four or more each month. Though the causes of these severe headaches are still unknown, trigger points include stress, certain food and beverages, caffeine, changes in the weather, and fatigue. If you think you suffer from migraines, you should visit your doctor. In addition, consider using the book of Psalms for comfort and as a launching pad for prayer and reflection. Psalm 38:8–9 says, "I am weak and faint. I moan from the pain I feel. Lord, you know everything I want; my cries are not hidden from you." You can be honest with God—even when things are tough. Remember that he is with you every step of the way.

God Will Punish the Proud

For the director of music. A maskil of David. When Doeg the Edomite came to Saul and said to him, "David is in Ahimelech's house."

52 Mighty warrior, why do
    you brag about the
    evil you do?
    God's love will continue
    forever.
²You think up evil plans.
    Your tongue is like a sharp razor,
    making up lies.
³You love wrong more than right
    and lies more than truth.   *Selah*
⁴You love words that bite
    and tongues that lie.

⁵But God will ruin you forever.

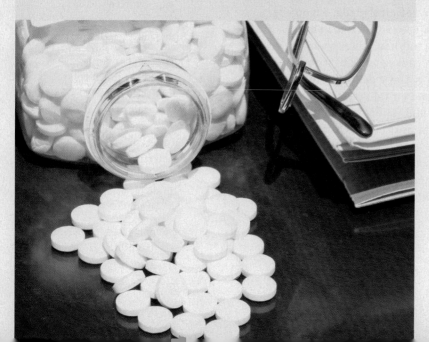

He will grab you and throw you
out of your tent;
he will tear you away from the
land of the living.   *Selah*
[6]Those who do right will see this
and fear God.
They will laugh at you and say,
[7]"Look what happened to the man
who did not depend on God
but depended on his money.
He grew strong by his evil
plans."

[8]But I am like an olive tree
growing in God's Temple.
I trust God's love
forever and ever.
[9]God, I will thank you forever for
what you have done.
With those who worship you, I
will trust you because you
are good.

The Unbelieving Fool

For the director of music. By mahalath. A maskil of David.

53 Fools say to themselves,
"There is no God."
Fools are evil and do terrible
things;
none of them does anything good.

[2]God looked down from heaven on
all people
to see if anyone was wise,
if anyone was looking to God for
help.
[3]But all have turned away.
Together, everyone has become
evil;
none of them does anything good.
Not a single person.

[4]Don't the wicked understand?
They destroy my people as if
they were eating bread.
They do not ask God for help.
[5]The wicked are filled with terror

Q: HOW DO I KNOW THAT THE BIBLE IS BELIEVABLE?

A: The Bible contains hundreds of prophecies that were fulfilled in detail. For example, Old Testament prophets gave over three hundred specific prophecies about the coming Messiah. These prophecies were perfectly fulfilled by Jesus Christ hundreds of years later. Archaeological discoveries have confirmed people's names, historical events, and geographical details exactly as they are recorded in the Bible. Compared to other ancient writings, the Bible has been remarkably well-protected and preserved over time. Many early manuscripts of the New Testament still exist, and a comparison of the texts shows them to be remarkably consistent.

WISE WORDS

Avoid the Comparison Trap

It's far too easy to look at someone else's life and make judgments about what their life is really like. You may look at a person's material wealth—whether it's a car, home, or designer clothes—and assume that the person is wealthy. But the Bible reminds us that sometimes these people are just putting on a show. Proverbs 12:9 says, "A person who is not important but has a servant is better off than someone who acts important but has no food." Don't allow yourself to become envious over what another person "seems" to own—it may not be as much as you think! And after all, external riches and beauty are not really what impresses God anyway. God cares about your heart!

where there had been nothing
to fear.
God will scatter the bones of
your enemies.
You will defeat them,
because God has rejected them.

⁶I pray that victory will come to
Israel from Mount
Zion!
May God bring them back.
Then the people of Jacob will
rejoice,
and the people of Israel will be
glad.

A Prayer for Help

For the director of music. With stringed instruments. A maskil of David when the Ziphites went to Saul and said, "We think David is hiding among our people."

54 God, save me because of
who you are.
By your strength show that I am
innocent.

²Hear my prayer, God;
listen to what I say.
³Strangers turn against me,
and cruel people want to kill me.
They do not care about God.
Selah

⁴See, God will help me;
the Lord will support me.
⁵Let my enemies be punished with
their own evil.
Destroy them because you are
loyal to me.

⁶I will offer a sacrifice as a special
gift to you.
I will thank you, Lord, because
you are good.
⁷You have saved me from all my
troubles,
and I have seen my enemies
defeated.

A Prayer About a False Friend

For the director of music. With stringed instruments. A maskil of David.

55 God, listen to my prayer
and do not ignore my
cry for help.
²Pay attention to me and answer me.
I am troubled and upset
³by what the enemy says
and how the wicked look at me.
They bring troubles down on me,
and in anger they attack me.

⁴I am frightened inside;
the terror of death has attacked
me.
⁵I am scared and shaking,
and terror grips me.
⁶I said, "I wish I had wings like a
dove.
Then I would fly away and rest.
⁷I would wander far away
and stay in the desert. *Selah*
⁸I would hurry to my place of escape,
far away from the wind and
storm."

⁹Lord, destroy and confuse their
words,
because I see violence and
fighting in the city.

Making Love Last

About half of all marriages in America end in divorce. For second marriages, the statistics are even more depressing. Sadly, the numbers are about the same among Christians as the rest of society. Why do some marriages make it while others fail? Is there a secret to making love last? Perhaps the single greatest factor in successful marriages is communication. Couples who learn to share their needs, emotions, and even their grievances in a constructive, loving way are able to overcome the obstacles that might spell doom for other couples. Conflicts in marriage are a given, but if viewed as an opportunity to learn more about your spouse, they can actually be a doorway to deeper intimacy within the marriage.

¹⁰Day and night they are all around
its walls,
and evil and trouble are
everywhere inside.
¹¹Destruction is everywhere in the
city;
trouble and lying never leave its
streets.

¹²It was not an enemy insulting me.
I could stand that.
It was not someone who hated me.
I could hide from him.
¹³But it is you, a person like me,
my companion and good friend.
¹⁴We had a good friendship
and walked together to God's
Temple.

¹⁵Let death take away my enemies.
Let them die while they are still
young
because evil lives with them.
¹⁶But I will call to God for help,
and the LORD will save me.
¹⁷Morning, noon, and night I am
troubled and upset,
but he will listen to me.
¹⁸Many are against me,
but he keeps me safe in battle.
¹⁹God who lives forever
will hear me and punish them.
Selah

But they will not change;
they do not fear God.

²⁰The one who was my friend attacks
his friends
and breaks his promises.
²¹His words are slippery like butter,
but war is in his heart.
His words are smoother than oil,
but they cut like knives.

²²Give your worries to the LORD,
and he will take care of you.
He will never let good people
down.
²³But, God, you will bring down
the wicked to the grave.
Murderers and liars will live
only half a lifetime.
But I will trust in you.

MONEY

Giving Out of Abundance

If you've spent much time in church, you've probably heard of "tithing," the Old Testament concept that required God's people to offer him a portion of their crops. While people still use the term today, God's new agreement with his people does not outline specific giving requirements. But it does call for a radical attitude of sacrificial living and giving. Instead of wondering how *much* to give, ask yourself, "How much *can* I give?" God wants our giving to be Spirit-led and generous, never coerced or reluctant. Second Corinthians 9:7 sums it up well: "Each of you should give as you have decided in your heart to give. You should not be sad when you give...[or] feel forced to give. God loves the person who gives happily."

Consider the poor widow's sacrifice in Luke 21:1–4. While she had only two small coins to offer, Jesus honored her gift by saying that she actually gave *more* than the wealthy did because she "'gave all she had to live on'" (verse 4). Giving in this way, with joyful abandon and sacrificial love, shows God that he is your first priority. It's not so much about the amount, it's about having a grateful heart that says, "God, you have blessed me lavishly, and I choose to give cheerfully and sacrificially out of that abundance." As God prompts you, consider being more generous with everything he has given you—time, talents, abilities, *and* finances.

Trusting God for Help

For the director of music. To the tune of "The Dove in the Distant Oak." A miktam of David when the Philistines captured him in Gath.

56 God, be merciful to me
because people are
chasing me;
the battle has pressed me all day
long.
²My enemies have chased me all day;
there are many proud people
fighting me.
³When I am afraid,
I will trust you.
⁴I praise God for his word.
I trust God, so I am not afraid.
What can human beings do to me?

⁵All day long they twist my words;
all their evil plans are against me.
⁶They wait. They hide.
They watch my steps,
hoping to kill me.
⁷God, do not let them escape;

punish the foreign nations in
your anger.
⁸You have recorded my troubles.
You have kept a list of my tears.
Aren't they in your records?

⁹On the day I call for help, my
enemies will be defeated.
I know that God is on my side.

BE STILL & KNOW

¹⁰I praise God for his word to me;
I praise the LORD for his word.
¹¹I trust in God. I will not be afraid.
What can people do to me?

¹²God, I must keep my promises to you.
I will give you my offerings to
thank you,
¹³because you have saved me from
death.
You have kept me from being
defeated.
So I will walk with God
in light among the living.

A Prayer in Troubled Times

For the director of music. To the tune of "Do Not Destroy." A miktam of David when he escaped from Saul in the cave.

57 Be merciful to me, God;
be merciful to me
because I come to you for
protection.
Let me hide under the shadow of
your wings
until the trouble has passed.

²I cry out to God Most High,
to the God who does everything
for me.
³He sends help from heaven and
saves me.
He punishes those who chase
me. *Selah*
God sends me his love and truth.

⁴Enemies, like lions, are all around me;
I must lie down among them.
Their teeth are like spears and
arrows,
their tongues as sharp as swords.
⁵God is supreme over the skies;
his majesty covers the earth.

'Fess Up

If you accidentally bump into someone, it's polite to say, "I'm sorry." When you purposely hurt someone, "I'm sorry" is not enough. You need to confess what you did and humbly ask, "Will you forgive me?" When you pray, it's also important to spill your guts to God. Tell him everything you have done wrong, and express your genuine remorse for the ways you have hurt him and others. Then ask him to forgive you. In Psalm 32, David says that confessing sins to God replaces feelings of guilt with true happiness and security. Clearing the slate with God melts away the burdens of separation and shame, and the best part is that God promises not to remember what you did to hurt him.

⁶They set a trap for me.
    I am very worried.
They dug a pit in my path,
    but they fell into it themselves.
                                    Selah

⁷My heart is steady, God; my heart is
        steady.
    I will sing and praise you.
⁸Wake up, my soul.
    Wake up, harp and lyre!
    I will wake up the dawn.
⁹Lord, I will praise you among the
        nations;
    I will sing songs of praise about
        you to all the nations.
¹⁰Your great love reaches to the skies,
    your truth to the clouds.
¹¹God, you are supreme above the skies.
    Let your glory be over all the
        earth.

Unfair Judges

*For the director of music. To the tune of "Do Not
Destroy." A miktam of David.*

58 Do you rulers really say
        what is right?
    Do you judge people fairly?
²No, in your heart you plan evil;
    you think up violent crimes in
        the land.
³From birth, evil people turn away
        from God;
    they wander off and tell lies as
        soon as they are born.
⁴They are like poisonous snakes,
    like deaf cobras that stop up
        their ears
⁵so they cannot hear the music of
        the snake charmer
    no matter how well he
        plays.

⁶God, break the teeth in their
        mouths!
    Tear out the fangs of those
        lions, Lord!
⁷Let them disappear like water that
        flows away.
    Let them be cut short like a
        broken arrow.
⁸Let them be like snails that melt as
        they move.

Let them be like a child born
    dead who never saw the sun.
⁹His anger will blow them away
        alive
    faster than burning thorns can
        heat a pot.
¹⁰Good people will be glad when they
        see him get even.
    They will wash their feet in the
        blood of the wicked.
¹¹Then people will say,
    "There really are rewards for
        doing what is right.
    There really is a God who judges
        the world."

A Prayer for Protection

*For the director of music. To the tune of "Do Not
Destroy." A miktam of David when Saul sent men to
watch David's house to kill him.*

59 God, save me from my
        enemies.
    Protect me from those who
        come against me.
²Save me from those who do evil
    and from murderers.

³Look, they are waiting to ambush
        me.
    Cruel people attack me,
    but I have not sinned or done
        wrong, Lord.

⁴I have done nothing wrong, but
    they are ready to attack me.
    Wake up to help me, and look.
⁵You are the Lord God All-Powerful,
    the God of Israel.
    Arise and punish those people.
    Do not give those traitors any
        mercy.   *Selah*

⁶They come back at night.
    Like dogs they growl and roam
        around the city.
⁷Notice what comes from their
        mouths.
    Insults come from their lips,
    because they say, "Who's
        listening?"
⁸But, Lord, you laugh at them;
    you make fun of all of them.

⁹God, my strength, I am looking to
        you,
    because God is my defender.
¹⁰My God loves me, and he goes in
        front of me.
    He will help me defeat my
        enemies.

BIBLE Women & Men

David

What if David was your best friend's husband? He had an impressive pedigree, great favor, enormous responsibility, and a charming way about him. But he also made some very poor choices! He cheated with a married woman and made sure her husband was killed so he could have her. Although he wouldn't find favor in your eyes, God offered him love and forgiveness. David loved God in return and praised him during prosperity *and* through the aftermath of his poor choices. He cried out to God for mercy, leaving a legacy that shows us how to do the same.

What's the POINT?

Psalm 56:12

Just what does it mean to give an offering? Does God really need your money? No, God made everything and owns everything. He really doesn't *need* anything from you. But he wants your love, your grateful heart, and your respect, which you can show by giving to him with a cheerful attitude. Offerings are not so much about money as they are about attitude. An offering is simply something you give because you want to thank someone for all he or she has done for you. You can give an offering of your time by spending an extra hour in prayer, reading your Bible, or helping someone in need. You can give an offering of your talent by singing a solo in a choir, mentoring someone, or sewing new clothes for a child who needs them. And, yes, you can give an offering of your money and your possessions. Does God need your old car? No, but maybe a single parent needs it more than you need the money you could get from selling it. The key to an offering is not so much what you give but the attitude behind giving it. Give joyfully, excitedly, as an expression of your gratitude. When you give in order to bless someone, you will also be blessed.

11Lord, our protector, do not kill
  them, or my people will
  forget.
  With your power scatter them
  and defeat them.
12They sin by what they say;
  they sin with their words.
  They curse and tell lies,
  so let their pride trap them.
13Destroy them in your anger;
  destroy them completely!
  Then they will know
  that God rules over Israel
  and to the ends of the earth.

Selah

14They come back at night.
  Like dogs they growl
  and roam around the city.
15They wander about looking for
  food,
  and they howl if they do not
  find enough.
16But I will sing about your strength.
  In the morning I will sing about
  your love.
  You are my defender,
  my place of safety in times of
  trouble.
17God, my strength, I will sing praises
  to you.
  God, my defender, you are the
  God who loves me.

A Prayer After a Defeat

For the director of music. To the tune of "Lily of the Agreement." A miktam of David. For teaching. When David fought the Arameans of Northwest Mesopotamia and Zobah, and when Joab returned and defeated twelve thousand Edomites at the Valley of Salt.

60 God, you have rejected us
  and scattered us.
  You have been angry, but please
  come back to us.
2You made the earth shake and
  crack.
  Heal its breaks because it is
  shaking.
3You have given your people
  trouble.
  You made us unable to walk
  straight, like people drunk
  with wine.

Beauty BECOMES HER

Softer Hands

If your hands and nails need a quick refresher, warm a cup of milk to a comfortable temperature. Soak your hands in the milk for five minutes to strengthen, soften, and hydrate your nails and skin. Psalm 108:1 says, "God, my heart is steady. I will sing and praise you with all my being." Milk may strengthen and soften your hands, but the presence of God will strengthen and soften your heart. Take every opportunity to soak your life in his presence.

⁴You have raised a banner to gather
    those who fear you.
  Now they can stand up against
    the enemy.   *Selah*

⁵Answer us and save us by your
    power
  so the people you love will be
    rescued.

⁶God has said from his Temple,
  "When I win, I will divide
    Shechem
  and measure off the Valley of
    Succoth.
⁷Gilead and Manasseh are mine.
  Ephraim is like my helmet.
  Judah holds my royal scepter.
⁸Moab is like my washbowl.

  I throw my sandals at Edom.
  I shout at Philistia."

⁹Who will bring me to the strong,
    walled city?
  Who will lead me to Edom?
¹⁰God, surely you have rejected us;
  you do not go out with our
    armies.
¹¹Help us fight the enemy.
  Human help is useless,
¹²but we can win with God's help.
  He will defeat our enemies.

A Prayer for Protection

For the director of music. With stringed instruments. Of David.

61 God, hear my cry;
      listen to my prayer.

²I call to you from the ends of the
    earth
  when I am afraid.
  Carry me away to a high
    mountain.
³You have been my protection,
  like a strong tower against my
    enemies.

⁴Let me live in your Holy Tent
    forever.
  Let me find safety in the shelter
    of your wings.   *Selah*

⁵God, you have heard my
    promises.
  You have given me what belongs
    to those who fear you.

⁶Give the king a long life;
  let him live many years.
⁷Let him rule in the presence of God
    forever.
  Protect him with your love and
    truth.
⁸Then I will praise your name
    forever,
  and every day I will keep my
    promises.

Trust Only in God

For the director of music. For Jeduthun. A psalm of David.

62 I find rest in God;
      only he can save me.
²He is my rock and my salvation.
  He is my defender;
  I will not be defeated.

WHAT'S IN A word?

Psalm 59:6 "Dogs" In ancient times, dogs were considered to be semi-wild and dangerous scavengers. They weren't the cute, fluffy pets of our time!

³How long will you attack someone?
 Will all of you kill that person?
 Who is like a leaning wall, like a
  fence ready to fall?
⁴They are planning to make that
  person fall.
 They enjoy telling lies.
 With their mouths they bless,
  but in their hearts they curse.

Selah

⁵I find rest in God;
 only he gives me hope.
⁶He is my rock and my salvation.
 He is my defender;
 I will not be defeated.
⁷My honor and salvation come from
  God.
 He is my mighty rock and my
  protection.

⁸People, trust God all the time.
 Tell him all your problems,
 because God is our protection.

Selah

⁹The least of people are only a
  breath,
 and even the greatest are just a
  lie.
 On the scales, they weigh nothing;
  together they are only a breath.
¹⁰Do not trust in force.
 Stealing is of no use.
 Even if you gain more riches,
  don't put your trust in them.

¹¹God has said this,
 and I have heard it over and
  over:
 God is strong.
¹²The Lord is loving.
 You reward people for what they
  have done.

Wishing to Be Near God

A psalm of David when he was in the desert of Judah.

63 God, you are my God.
 I search for you.
 I thirst for you
  like someone in a dry, empty
  land
  where there is no water.

²I have seen you in the Temple
 and have seen your strength and
  glory.
³Because your love is better than life,
 I will praise you.
⁴I will praise you as long as I live.
 I will lift up my hands in prayer
  to your name.
⁵I will be content as if I had eaten
  the best foods.
 My lips will sing, and my mouth
  will praise you.

⁶I remember you while I'm lying in
  bed;
 I think about you through the
  night.
⁷You are my help.
 Because of your protection, I
  sing.
⁸I stay close to you;
 you support me with your right
  hand.

⁹Some people are trying to kill me,
 but they will go down to the
  grave.
¹⁰They will be killed with swords
 and eaten by wild dogs.
¹¹But the king will rejoice in his God.
 All who make promises in his
  name will praise him,
 but the mouths of liars will be
  shut.

A Prayer Against Enemies

For the director of music. A psalm of David.

64 God, listen to my
  complaint.
 I am afraid of my enemies;
 protect my life from them.
²Hide me from those who plan
  wicked things,
 from that gang who does evil.
³They sharpen their tongues like
  swords
 and shoot bitter words like
  arrows.
⁴From their hiding places they shoot
  at innocent people;
 they shoot suddenly and are not
  afraid.

5They encourage each other to do
wrong.
They talk about setting traps,
thinking no one will see them.
6They plan wicked things and say,
"We have a perfect plan."
The mind of human beings is
hard to understand.

7But God will shoot them with
arrows;
they will suddenly be struck down.
8Their own words will be used
against them.
All who see them will shake
their heads.
9Then everyone will fear God.
They will tell what God has
done,
and they will learn from what he
has done.
10Good people will be happy in the
LORD
and will find protection in him.
Let everyone who is honest
praise the LORD.

A Hymn of Thanksgiving

For the director of music. A psalm of David. A song.

65 God, you will be praised
in Jerusalem.
We will keep our promises to you.
2You hear our prayers.

WHAT'S IN A
word?

Psalm 61:4 "Shelter of your
wings" The psalmists loved
to use this analogy. Just
as the wings of a mama bird
offer refuge, protection,
and defense for her
chicks, God shields us and
offers a warm embrace of
security.

All people will come to you.
3Our guilt overwhelms us,
but you forgive our sins.
4Happy are the people you choose
and invite to stay in your court.
We are filled with good things in
your house,
your holy Temple.

5You answer us in amazing ways,
God our Savior.
People everywhere on the earth
and beyond the sea trust you.
6You made the mountains by your
strength;
you are dressed in power.
7You stopped the roaring seas,
the roaring waves,
and the uproar of the nations.
8Even those people at the ends of
the earth fear your miracles.
You are praised from where the
sun rises to where it sets.

9You take care of the land and water
it;
you make it very fertile.
The rivers of God are full of water.
Grain grows because you make it
grow.
10You send rain to the plowed fields;
you fill the rows with water.
You soften the ground with rain,
and then you bless it with crops.
11You give the year a good harvest,
and you load the wagons with
many crops.
12The desert is covered with grass
and the hills with happiness.
13The pastures are full of flocks,
and the valleys are covered with
grain.
Everything shouts and sings for
joy.

Praise God for What He Has Done

For the director of music. A song. A psalm.

66 Everything on earth,
shout with joy to God!
2Sing about his glory!
Make his praise glorious!

WISE
WORDS

The Tortoise and the Hare

Have you ever noticed all
the get-rich-quick schemes
advertised in newspapers
and magazines, as well as
on television and the Internet? They seem to be everywhere! While the path to
wealth varies with each
offer, they lure people in by
promising that in no time
participants will be bringing
home a big check, literally
rolling in the dough. They
may sound promising, but if
it was really that easy, don't
you think everyone would be
following the same formula?
Proverbs 13:11 says, "Money
that comes easily disap-
pears quickly, but money
that is gathered little by little will grow." This verse
highlights an important
principle: Slow and steady
wins the race every time.

3Say to God, "Your works are
amazing!
Because your power is great,
your enemies fall before you.
4All the earth worships you
and sings praises to you.
They sing praises to your name."
Selah

What's the
POINT?

Psalm 63:8

Sometimes when people you love are out of sight, they really are out of mind. In today's busy world, it is usually easier to have a close relationship with people you see and interact with every day than to maintain closeness with someone you see only once in a great while. You may have a deep love for someone who lives far away, but because you are not together very often, your relationship can't help but become a little...well, distant. Instant messaging, e-mail, and phone calls can help bridge the gap, but nothing beats having a friend right by your side. David knew that staying close to God was the key to a great relationship with him. He constantly cried out to the Lord, talking with him, begging him, waiting to hear from him, singing to him, and praising his name. When he stayed in close proximity to God and kept the lines of communication wide open, seeking God's advice through his Word and talking to him frequently, he could sense God's love and support. When he let the relationship drift, he quickly made mistakes and slid into sin. Seek God every day. Stay close to him. It's the only way to keep the relationship vibrant and strong.

5 Come and see what God has done,
  the amazing things he has done
    for people.
6 He turned the sea into dry land.
  The people crossed the river on
    foot.
  So let us rejoice because of what
    he did.
7 He rules forever with his power.
  He keeps his eye on the nations,
  so people should not turn
    against him.   *Selah*

8 You people, praise our God;
  loudly sing his praise.
9 He protects our lives
  and does not let us be defeated.
10 God, you have tested us;
  you have purified us like silver.
11 You let us be trapped
  and put a heavy load on us.
12 You let our enemies walk on our
    heads.
  We went through fire and flood,
  but you brought us to a place
    with good things.

13 I will come to your Temple with
    burnt offerings.
  I will give you what I promised,
14   things I promised when I was in
    trouble.
15 I will bring you offerings of fat
    animals,
  and I will offer sheep, bulls, and
    goats.   *Selah*

16 All of you who fear God, come and
    listen,
  and I will tell you what he has
    done for me.
17 I cried out to him with my mouth
  and praised him with my
    tongue.
18 If I had known of any sin in my
    heart,
  the Lord would not have
    listened to me.
19 But God has listened;
  he has heard my prayer.
20 Praise God,
  who did not ignore my prayer
  or hold back his love from me.

Everyone Should Praise God

For the director of music. With stringed instruments. A psalm. A song.

67 God, have mercy on us
and bless us
and show us your kindness   *Selah*
²so the world will learn your ways,
and all nations will learn that
you can save.

³God, the people should praise you;
all people should praise you.
⁴The nations should be glad and sing
because you judge people
fairly.
You guide all the nations on
earth.   *Selah*
⁵God, the people should praise you;
all people should praise you.

⁶The land has given its crops.
God, our God, blesses us.
⁷God blesses us
so people all over the earth will
fear him.

Praise God Who Saved the Nation

For the director of music. A psalm of David. A song.

68 Let God rise up and
scatter his enemies;
let those who hate him run away
from him.
²Blow them away as smoke
is driven away by the wind.
As wax melts before a fire,
let the wicked be destroyed
before God.
³But those who do right should be
glad
and should rejoice before God;
they should be happy and glad.

⁴Sing to God; sing praises to his
name.
Prepare the way for him
who rides through the desert,
whose name is the LORD.
Rejoice before him.
⁵God is in his holy Temple.
He is a father to orphans,
and he defends the widows.
⁶God gives the lonely a home.
He leads prisoners out with joy,
but those who turn against God
will live in a dry land.

⁷God, you led your people out
when you marched through the
desert.   *Selah*

Seven ways to...

Practice Personal Safety in Your Car

1. Don't park in dark or isolated places.

2. Have someone walk you to your car, especially at night.

3. Have your keys in your hand, ready to unlock the door.

4. When walking to your car, try to walk in well-lit, open spaces.

5. After you get in your car, immediately lock the doors.

6. Avoid ATMs in unfamiliar or remote locations.

7. Carry a cell phone in case of emergency.

MODERN Worship

Listen to Your Heart

David writes in Psalm 27:8 that his heart told him to worship the Lord, so he did. Do you listen to your own heart? When that still, small voice speaks, do you obey? God does speak to the human heart—not the actual organ, but a person's emotions—particularly when the intellect refuses to respond. In worship, be open to allowing the Lord to work in this way. Worship with your heart. As Charles Spurgeon said, "God is to be praised with the voice, and the heart should go there with in holy exultation."

how techno-savvy are you?

CHECK THE STATEMENTS THAT BEST DESCRIBE YOU:

❑ Your primary means of written communication is e-mail.

❑ You instant message on a regular basis.

❑ You feel comfortable doing research on-line.

❑ You own an iPod.

❑ You're the first among your friends to buy and use new technology.

❑ You have sent a text message from your cell phone.

❑ You have used your cell phone to take and send a photo.

❑ You have traded in your VHS collection for DVDs.

❑ When something goes wrong with your computer, you try to fix it yourself.

❑ You know the difference between a Mac and a PC.

❑ You know how to operate a digital camera.

❑ You have purchased or sold something on eBay.

❑ You have played Xbox or PlayStation in the last three months.

❑ You have filed your taxes on-line.

❑ You own a computer *and* know its processing speed.

1-5 CHECKS: YOU'RE NOT VERY TECHNO-SAVVY. You hear a lot of terms thrown around about computers, cell phones, and other devices, but they all seem foreign. New technology makes you a bit uncomfortable, and you have other interests you'd rather spend your time and money on.

6-10 CHECKS: YOU'RE SOMEWHAT TECHNO-SAVVY. You embrace technology when it benefits you, but you aren't convinced you need the latest and greatest devices. You have friends, family members, and coworkers who are willing to show you new products and have convinced you to make a few purchases. Sometimes you're hesitant to take the plunge, but as long as someone stays around long enough to show you how the product works, you'll be okay.

11-15 CHECKS: YOU'RE TOTALLY TECHNO-SAVVY. You are comfortable with all kinds of devices and love what they can do for you. You like owning or knowing about new products as soon as they're on the market. Whether it's a new program, game, or device, you aren't afraid to figure it out on your own.

{ fun FACTS }

25% of men and 45% of women are on a diet on any given day.

(www.womensissues.about.com)

Balancing Act

⁸The ground shook
   and the sky poured down rain
before God, the God of Mount
      Sinai,
      before God, the God of Israel.
⁹God, you sent much rain;
   you refreshed your tired land.
¹⁰Your people settled there.
   God, in your goodness
   you took care of the poor.

¹¹The Lord gave the command,
   and a great army told the news:
¹²"Kings and their armies run away.
   In camp they divide the wealth
      taken in war.
¹³Those who stayed by the campfires
   will share the riches taken in
      battle."
¹⁴The Almighty scattered kings
   like snow on Mount Zalmon.

¹⁵The mountains of Bashan are high;
   the mountains of Bashan have
      many peaks.
¹⁶Why do you mountains with many
      peaks look with envy
   on the mountain that God chose
      for his home?
   The LORD will live there forever.
¹⁷God comes with millions of
      chariots;
   the Lord comes from Mount
      Sinai to his holy place.
¹⁸When you went up to the heights,
   you led a parade of captives.
   You received gifts from the
      people,
even from those who turned
      against you.
   And the LORD God will live
      there.

¹⁹Praise the Lord, God our Savior,
   who helps us every day.   *Selah*
²⁰Our God is a God who saves us;
   the LORD God saves us from
      death.

²¹God will crush his enemies' heads,
   the hairy skulls of those who
      continue to sin.
²²The Lord said, "I will bring the
      enemy back from Bashan;
   I will bring them back from the
      depths of the sea.
²³Then you can stick your feet in
      their blood,
   and your dogs can lick their
      share."

²⁴God, people have seen your victory
      march;
   God my King marched into the
      holy place.
²⁵The singers are in front and the
      instruments are behind.
   In the middle are the girls with
      the tambourines.
²⁶Praise God in the meeting place;
   praise the LORD in the gathering
      of Israel.
²⁷There is the smallest tribe,
      Benjamin, leading them.
   And there are the leaders of
      Judah with their group.
   There also are the leaders of
      Zebulun and of Naphtali.

²⁸God, order up your power;
   show the mighty power you have
      used for us before.
²⁹Kings will bring their wealth to
      you,
   to your Temple in Jerusalem.

Food Fight

When your stomach rumbles, it's time to eat. When your spirit rumbles, it's time to put down the popcorn and open up God's Word. Food can be like a comfortable old friend, always there to comfort you when you're having a bad day, to reward you when you're having a great day, or to fill that empty spot when you're longing for an unidentified *something* inside. It can often be difficult to determine if you need physical fuel or a spiritual feast for your heart and soul. Spiritual and emotional hunger pangs are just as real as your physical appetite, but trying to fill those desires with food will never fully satisfy. The next time you are angry, hurting, lonely, or bored, pray before opening the pantry. Ask God to satisfy your true hunger, and let his Word fill you up.

What's the POINT?

Psalm 66:2

Whether you could pass as a lead soprano with the Metropolitan Opera or sound more like the foghorn on an ocean liner, the Bible says you should sing to God. All through the psalms that King David wrote, he urges people to sing praises. In fact, the words "sing" and "praise" appear some fifty times, along with variations of the same idea, such as "cried out to him with my mouth" (Psalm 66:17) and "Shout to God with joy" (Psalm 47:1). Part of loving, praising, and thanking God is doing it out loud. Why? Because he deserves it, for one thing, and he also tells us to in Scripture. You should be naturally overflowing with joy and gratitude for the good things he has done for you all through your life. Even on a bad day, you still have a lot to be grateful for! If you allowed yourself to really express your joy, you wouldn't keep quiet about God, just like you wouldn't keep quiet about a huge sale at Nordstrom's or free latte day at Starbucks. Wouldn't you run around practically singing the good news to all your friends? Sure you would. And we have so much more to celebrate than some free coffee! So sing to God. Sing often. To his ears, you sound absolutely perfect.

---

30 Punish Egypt, the beast in the tall grass along the river.
Punish the leaders of nations, those bulls among the cows.
Defeated, they will bring you their silver.
Scatter those nations that love war.
31 Messengers will come from Egypt; the people of Cush will pray to God.

32 Kingdoms of the earth, sing to God;
sing praises to the Lord.   *Selah*
33 Sing to the one who rides through the skies, which are from long ago.
He speaks with a thundering voice.
34 Announce that God is powerful.
He rules over Israel,
and his power is in the skies.
35 God, you are wonderful in your Temple.
The God of Israel gives his people strength and power.

Praise God!

A Cry for Help

For the director of music. To the tune of "Lilies." A psalm of David.

69 God, save me,
because the water has risen to my neck.
2 I'm sinking down into the mud,
and there is nothing to stand on.
I am in deep water,
and the flood covers me.
3 I am tired from calling for help;
my throat is sore.
My eyes are tired from waiting for God to help me.
4 There are more people who hate me for no reason than hairs on my head;
powerful enemies want to destroy me for no reason.
They make me pay back what I did not steal.

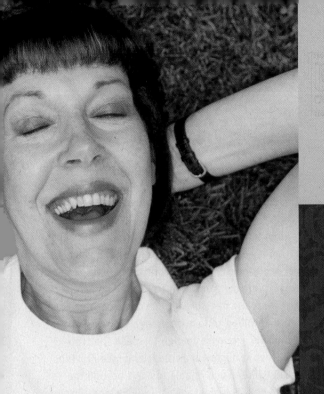

Blending a Family

TALIE'S STORY

When I met my husband, it was love at first sight. We had prayed to find each other and knew without a doubt it was the right fit. After a year of dating, our relationship led us right down the aisle and out the chapel doors to live happily every after. Well, not exactly. We actually walked down the aisle with five children between us—three of his and two of mine. Two years later, we added one of "ours" to the bunch. We also brought along the baggage of two failed marriages, battered and bruised hearts, trust issues, a custody battle, and former spouses who ranged from cordial to hostile.

I found out quickly that being a stepfamily is hard—really, really hard. No one told me that trying to love my stepdaughters would make their mother feel displaced. My stepfamily made me lean on God like I never had before—for patience, for self-confidence, for peace, for justice, for wisdom, and for the strength and energy to manage

> NO ONE TOLD ME THAT TRYING TO LOVE MY STEPDAUGHTERS WOULD MAKE THEIR MOTHER FEEL DISPLACED.

six children. And that's just for starters. Trying to live and love together as a stepfamily literally drove my husband and me to our knees and developed in us the daily habit of praying together beside our bed.

My breakthrough came when I realized that my children and stepchildren were God's dearly loved children and that each circumstance was a piece of his plan. When a situation seemed hopeless, I often repeated Romans 8:28: "We know that in everything God works for the good of those who love him." That verse says "everything"— no exceptions. God is always in control, even when things seem out of control. What a relief! Ten years later, our stepfamily has adjusted, and our children are thriving. I look back on those early years and see that the toughest time of my life did work for my good because it was during that time that my faith grew like never before.

RELATIONSHIPS

Wounds from a Friend

It's one thing when a stranger hurts you, but it's an entirely different wound when a friend causes it. Psalm 55 is David's lament about the betrayal of a friend. Verses 12-14 are especially poignant. David essentially says this: "Hey, I could have taken it from my enemy. But this was my *friend*, man. And that really hurt." While genuine betrayal is excruciating, loving confrontation from a friend can *feel* like betrayal if her words touch on something you're unwilling to face or change. However, a friend who is honest enough to speak the truth—even when it hurts—is a true friend (see Proverbs 27:6, 17). When you're able to move beyond the hurt to hear the message, you will be a better person for it.

⁵God, you know what I have done wrong;
    I cannot hide my guilt from you.
⁶Lord GOD All-Powerful,
    do not let those who hope in you
        be ashamed because of me.
God of Israel,
    do not let your worshipers be
        disgraced because of me.
⁷For you, I carry this shame,
    and my face is covered with
        disgrace.
⁸I am like a stranger to my closest
        relatives
    and a foreigner to my mother's
        children.
⁹My strong love for your Temple
        completely controls me.
    When people insult you, it hurts
        me.
¹⁰When I cry and fast,
    they make fun of me.
¹¹When I wear clothes of sadness,
    they joke about me.
¹²They make fun of me in public
        places,
    and the drunkards make up
        songs about me.

¹³But I pray to you, LORD, for favor.
God, because of your great love,
        answer me.
    You are truly able to save.
¹⁴Pull me from the mud,
    and do not let me sink.
Save me from those who hate me
    and from the deep water.
¹⁵Do not let the flood drown me
    or the deep water swallow me
    or the grave close its mouth over
        me.
¹⁶LORD, answer me because your love
        is so good.
    Because of your great kindness,
        turn to me.
¹⁷Do not hide from me, your servant.
    I am in trouble. Hurry to help me!
¹⁸Come near and save me;
    rescue me from my enemies.

¹⁹You see my shame and disgrace.
    You know all my enemies and
        what they have said.
²⁰Insults have broken my heart
    and left me weak.
I looked for sympathy, but there
        was none;
    I found no one to comfort me.

²¹They put poison in my food
    and gave me vinegar to drink.
²²Let their own feasts cause their
        ruin;
    let their feasts trap them and
        pay them back.
²³Let their eyes be closed so they
        cannot see
    and their backs be forever weak
        from troubles.
²⁴Pour your anger out on them;
    let your anger catch up with
        them.
²⁵May their place be empty;
    leave no one to live in their tents.
²⁶They chase after those you have
        hurt,
    and they talk about the pain of
        those you have wounded.
²⁷Charge them with crime after
        crime,
    and do not let them have
        anything good.
²⁸Wipe their names from the book of
        life,
    and do not list them with those
        who do what is right.

29I am sad and hurting.
God, save me and protect me.

30I will praise God in a song
and will honor him by giving
thanks.
31That will please the LORD more
than offering him cattle,
more than sacrificing a bull with
horns and hoofs.
32Poor people will see this and be
glad.
Be encouraged, you who worship
God.
33The LORD listens to those in
need
and does not look down on
captives.

34Heaven and earth should praise
him,
the seas and everything in them.
35God will save Jerusalem
and rebuild the cities of Judah.
Then people will live there and own
the land.
36 The descendants of his servants
will inherit that land,
and those who love him will live
there.

A Cry for God to Help Quickly

*For the director of music. A psalm of David. To help
people remember.*

70 God, come quickly and
save me.
LORD, hurry to help me.
2Let those who are trying to kill me
be ashamed and disgraced.
Let those who want to hurt me
run away in disgrace.
3Let those who make fun of me
stop because of their shame.
4But let all those who worship you
rejoice and be glad.
Let those who love your salvation
always say, "Praise the greatness
of God."
5I am poor and helpless;
God, hurry to me.
You help me and save me.
LORD, do not wait.

An Old Person's Prayer

71 In you, LORD, is my
protection.
Never let me be ashamed.
2Because you do what is right, save
and rescue me;
listen to me and save me.
3Be my place of safety
where I can always come.
Give the command to save me,
because you are my rock and my
strong, walled city.
4My God, save me from the power of
the wicked
and from the hold of evil and
cruel people.
5LORD, you are my hope.
LORD, I have trusted you since I
was young.
6I have depended on you since I was
born;
you helped me even on the day
of my birth.
I will always praise you.

7I am an example to many people,
because you are my strong
protection.
8I am always praising you;
all day long I honor you.
9Do not reject me when I am old;
do not leave me when my
strength is gone.
10My enemies make plans against
me,
and they meet together to kill
me.
11They say, "God has left him.
Go after him and take him,
because no one will save him."

12God, don't be far off.
My God, hurry to help me.
13Let those who accuse me
be ashamed and destroyed.
Let those who are trying to hurt
me
be covered with shame and
disgrace.

Q: WHO WROTE THE BIBLE?

A: The Bible was written over a period of around sixteen hundred years by about forty different people, including prominent Bible characters like Moses, Paul, and David. Christians refer to the Bible as the Word of God because even though God did not physically pen the Bible, he *inspired* the authors to write his love letter to humankind. The amazing thing is that all the authors, spread over so much time, were unified in their message of a loving God who wants to redeem sinful people. Their unity shows that the Bible has one primary author, and that author is God.

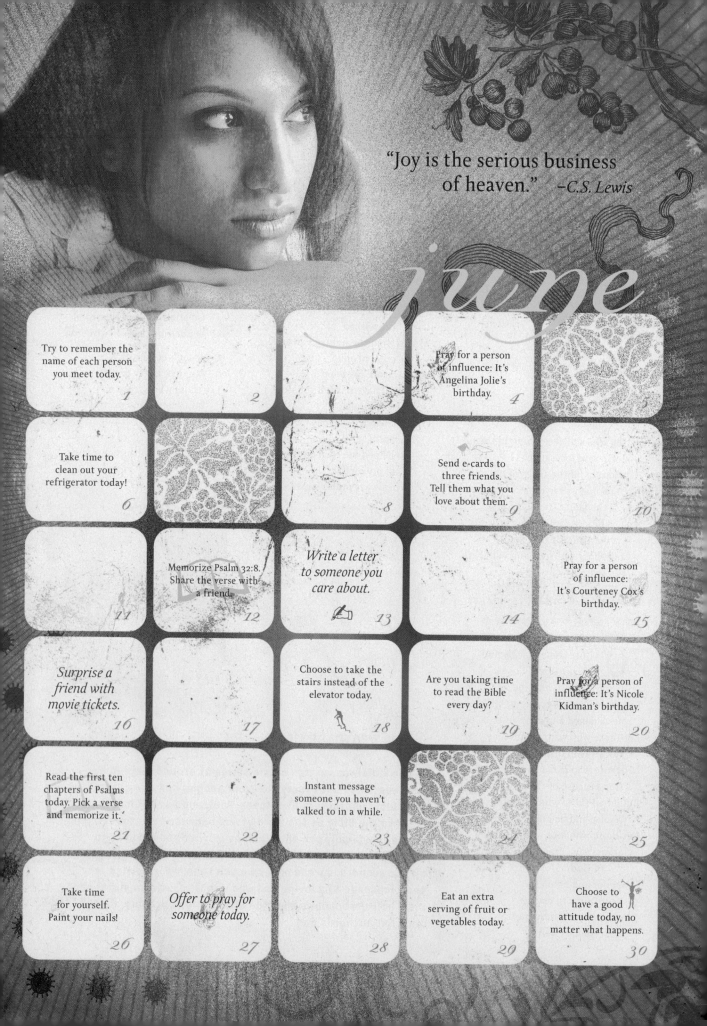

"Joy is the serious business
of heaven."   –*C.S. Lewis*

june

Try to remember the name of each person you meet today. *1*	*2*	*3*	Pray for a person of influence: It's Angelina Jolie's birthday. *4*	*5*
Take time to clean out your refrigerator today! *6*	*7*	*8*	Send e-cards to three friends. Tell them what you love about them. *9*	*10*
11	Memorize Psalm 32:8. Share the verse with a friend. *12*	*Write a letter to someone you care about.* *13*	*14*	Pray for a person of influence: It's Courteney Cox's birthday. *15*
Surprise a friend with movie tickets. *16*	*17*	Choose to take the stairs instead of the elevator today. *18*	Are you taking time to read the Bible every day? *19*	Pray for a person of influence: It's Nicole Kidman's birthday. *20*
Read the first ten chapters of Psalms today. Pick a verse and memorize it. *21*	*22*	Instant message someone you haven't talked to in a while. *23*	*24*	*25*
Take time for yourself. Paint your nails! *26*	*Offer to pray for someone today.* *27*	*28*	Eat an extra serving of fruit or vegetables today. *29*	Choose to have a good attitude today, no matter what happens. *30*

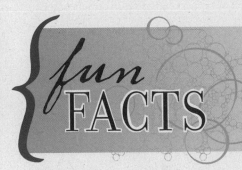

¹⁴But I will always have hope
   and will praise you more and
      more.
¹⁵I will tell how you do what is right.
   I will tell about your salvation all
      day long,
   even though it is more than I
      can tell.
¹⁶I will come and tell about your
      powerful works, Lord GOD.
   I will remind people that only
      you do what is right.

¹⁷God, you have taught me since I was
      young.
   To this day I tell about the
      miracles you do.
¹⁸Even though I am old and gray,
   do not leave me, God.
   I will tell the children about your
      power;
   I will tell those who live after me
      about your might.

¹⁹God, your justice reaches to the
      skies.
   You have done great things;
   God, there is no one like you.
²⁰You have given me many troubles
      and bad times,
   but you will give me life again.
   When I am almost dead,
      you will keep me alive.
²¹You will make me greater than ever,
   and you will comfort me again.

²²I will praise you with the harp.
   I trust you, my God.
   I will sing to you with the lyre,
      Holy One of Israel.
²³I will shout for joy when I sing
      praises to you.
   You have saved me.

²⁴I will tell about your justice all day
      long.
   And those who want to hurt me
      will be ashamed and disgraced.

A Prayer for the King

Of Solomon.

72 God, give the king your
         good judgment
   and the king's son your
      goodness.
²Help him judge your people
      fairly
   and decide what is right for the
      poor.
³Let there be peace on the
      mountains
   and goodness on the hills for
      the people.
⁴Help him be fair to the poor
   and save the needy
   and punish those who hurt
      them.

⁵May they respect you as long as the
      sun shines
   and as long as the moon glows.
⁶Let him be like rain on the grass,
   like showers that water the
      earth.
⁷Let goodness be plentiful while he
      lives.
   Let peace continue as long as
      there is a moon.

⁸Let his kingdom go from sea to sea,
   and from the Euphrates River to
      the ends of the earth.
⁹Let the people of the desert bow
      down to him,
   and make his enemies lick the
      dust.

¹⁰Let the kings of Tarshish and the
      faraway lands
   bring him gifts.
   Let the kings of Sheba and Seba
      bring their presents to him.
¹¹Let all kings bow down to him
   and all nations serve him.

¹²He will help the poor when they cry
      out
   and will save the needy when no
      one else will help.
¹³He will be kind to the weak and
      poor,
   and he will save their lives.
¹⁴He will save them from cruel people
      who try to hurt them,
   because their lives are precious
      to him.

¹⁵Long live the king!
   Let him receive gold from
      Sheba.
   Let people always pray for him
      and bless him all day long.
¹⁶Let the fields grow plenty of grain
   and the hills be covered with
      crops.
   Let the land be as fertile as
      Lebanon,
   and let the cities grow like the
      grass in a field.
¹⁷Let the king be famous forever;
   let him be remembered as long
      as the sun shines.
   Let the nations be blessed because
      of him,
   and may they all bless him.

WHAT'S IN A word?

Psalm 72:20 "David" means "beloved." It's an appropriate description of the shepherd-boy-turned-king who had a rich, vibrant relationship with God through all the ups and downs of his life.

What's the POINT?

Psalm 71:17

No matter how you were raised, you may have instinctively sensed the presence and reality of God when you were a child. Children often connect with God, talk to him, and find it easy to have a relationship with him without much guidance from parents or teachers. God has a way of making himself very real to children. In fact, God may have revealed himself to you even when you were very young. In the New Testament Gospels of Mark and Luke, Jesus talks to his followers about their need to become like children in order to enter the kingdom of heaven (see Mark 10:15 and Luke 18:17). Why does he make that point? Because children have no preconceived notions, no inflated sense of self-worth, and no demands or expectations that must be met. They aren't worried about what people think about them, and they usually don't overanalyze everything. Children simply come into God's presence with wonder and joyful abandon. Have you ever watched children sing to God? Their little faces light up with delight, and they have a time of worship on their own level. When was the last time you humbled yourself and just had a good time with God? Try it—your gift of love will honor God when you do.

[18]Praise the LORD God, the God of Israel,
who alone does such miracles.
[19]Praise his glorious name forever.
Let his glory fill the whole world.

Amen and amen.

[20]This ends the prayers of David son of Jesse.

BOOK 3

Should the Wicked Be Rich?

A psalm of Asaph.

73 God is truly good to Israel,
to those who have pure hearts.
[2]But I had almost stopped believing;
I had almost lost my faith
[3]because I was jealous of proud people.
I saw wicked people doing well.

[4]They are not suffering;
they are healthy and strong.
[5]They don't have troubles like the rest of us;
they don't have problems like other people.
[6]They wear pride like a necklace
and put on violence as their clothing.
[7]They are looking for profits
and do not control their selfish desires.
[8]They make fun of others and speak evil;
proudly they speak of hurting others.
[9]They brag to the sky.
They say that they own the earth.
[10]So their people turn to them
and give them whatever they want.
[11]They say, "How can God know?
What does God Most High know?"
[12]These people are wicked,
always at ease, and getting richer.

¹³So why have I kept my heart pure?
    Why have I kept my hands from
        doing wrong?
¹⁴I have suffered all day long;
    I have been punished every
        morning.
¹⁵God, if I had decided to talk like
    this,
    I would have let your people
        down.
¹⁶I tried to understand all this,
    but it was too hard for me to see
¹⁷until I went to the Temple of God.
    Then I understood what will
        happen to them.
¹⁸You have put them in danger;
    you cause them to be
        destroyed.
¹⁹They are destroyed in a moment;
    they are swept away by terrors.
²⁰It will be like waking from a
    dream.
    Lord, when you rise up, they will
        disappear.

²¹When my heart was sad
    and I was angry,
²²I was senseless and stupid.
    I acted like an animal toward
        you.
²³But I am always with you;
    you have held my hand.
²⁴You guide me with your advice,
    and later you will receive me in
        honor.
²⁵I have no one in heaven but you;
    I want nothing on earth besides
        you.
²⁶My body and my mind may become
    weak,
    but God is my strength.
    He is mine forever.

²⁷Those who are far from God will
    die;
    you destroy those who are
        unfaithful.
²⁸But I am close to God, and that is
    good.
    The Lord GOD is my protection.
    I will tell all that you have
        done.

A Nation in Trouble Prays

A maskil of Asaph.

74 God, why have you
        rejected us for so long?
    Why are you angry with us, the
        sheep of your pasture?
²Remember the people you bought
    long ago.
    You saved us, and we are your
        very own.
    After all, you live on Mount Zion.
³Make your way through these old
    ruins;

the enemy wrecked everything
    in the Temple.
⁴Those who were against you
    shouted in your meeting
        place
    and raised their flags there.
⁵They came with axes raised
    as if to cut down a forest of
        trees.
⁶They smashed the carved panels
    with their axes and hatchets.
⁷They burned your Temple to the
    ground;

Become INVOLVED

YMCA

Though YMCA programs differ from one community to another, each program is committed to helping families in the local area. The YMCA in your city or county may have facilities with a gymnasium, pool, child-care center, and fitness center. It may have a wide variety of programs for everyone to enjoy, or it may be a storefront operation delivering community-based projects like job training or youth development. It may be a camp, or it may be a satellite program in a local school. It may be all of the above!

Across the country, nearly eighteen million members come together at more than twenty-four hundred local YMCA associations. As a YMCA volunteer, you can help those members through leading an exercise class, reading to preschoolers, coaching a basketball team, providing goods for a bake sale, greeting people at the front desk, working in the office, drumming up donations for an auction, serving as a role model for young people, helping out at a special event, or joining a committee to work on a neighborhood problem. The YMCA volunteers help connect members of their community with the resources they need. To be part of that link, check out www.ymca.net.

they have made the place where you live unclean.

⁸They thought, "We will completely crush them!"

They burned every place where God was worshiped in the land.

⁹We do not see any signs.

There are no more prophets, and no one knows how long this will last.

¹⁰God, how much longer will the enemy make fun of you?

Will they insult you forever?

¹¹Why do you hold back your power?

Bring your power out in the open and destroy them!

¹²God, you have been our king for a long time.

You bring salvation to the earth.

¹³You split open the sea by your power

and broke the heads of the sea monster.

¹⁴You smashed the heads of the monster Leviathan

and gave it to the desert creatures as food.

¹⁵You opened up the springs and streams

and made the flowing rivers run dry.

¹⁶Both the day and the night are yours;

you made the sun and the moon.

¹⁷You set all the limits on the earth;

you created summer and winter.

¹⁸LORD, remember how the enemy insulted you.

Remember how those foolish people made fun of you.

¹⁹Do not give us, your doves, to those wild animals.

Never forget your poor people.

²⁰Remember the agreement you made with us,

because violence fills every dark corner of this land.

²¹Do not let your suffering people be disgraced.

Let the poor and helpless praise you.

²²God, arise and defend yourself.

Remember the insults that come from those foolish people all day long.

²³Don't forget what your enemies said;

don't forget their roar as they rise against you always.

God the Judge

For the director of music. To the tune of "Do Not Destroy." A psalm of Asaph. A song.

75

God, we thank you;
        we thank you because
            you are near.
    We tell about the miracles you
        do.

²You say, "I set the time for trial,
    and I will judge fairly.
³The earth with all its people may shake,
    but I am the one who holds it steady.   *Selah*
⁴I say to those who are proud, 'Don't brag,'
    and to the wicked, 'Don't show your power.
⁵Don't try to use your power against heaven.
    Don't be stubborn.' "

⁶No one from the east or the west
    or the desert can judge you.
⁷God is the judge;
    he judges one person as guilty
        and another as innocent.
⁸The LORD holds a cup of anger in his hand;
    it is full of wine mixed with spices.
He pours it out even to the last drop,
    and the wicked drink it all.

⁹I will tell about this forever;
    I will sing praise to the God of Jacob.

Life Issues

Getting through Grief

Divorce, death, the loss of a dream—all of these can plunge you into despair and make you unsure of what to do next. Be assured that God has not left you, even when life seems most unfair. In Matthew 28:20, Jesus said, "I will be with you always," and Matthew 5:4 says that those who grieve are blessed, for God will comfort them. Grief may not feel like a blessing, but it can bring you closer to God as you cling to him like a lifeboat in the midst of stormy seas. You will probably experience the emotional ups and downs that go with grief—from anger to denial to depression—but he is with you. Hang on to his love and the love of those around you as you ride out the storm. God will keep you afloat.

¹⁰He will take all power away from
the wicked,
but the power of good people
will grow.

The God Who Always Wins

*For the director of music. With stringed instruments. A
psalm of Asaph. A song.*

76 People in Judah know
God;
his fame is great in Israel.
²His Tent is in Jerusalem;
his home is on Mount Zion.
³There God broke the flaming
arrows,
the shields, the swords, and the
weapons of war.   *Selah*

⁴God, how wonderful you are!
You are more splendid than the
hills full of animals.
⁵The brave soldiers were stripped
as they lay asleep in death.
Not one warrior
had the strength to stop it.
⁶God of Jacob, when you spoke
strongly,
horses and riders fell dead.
⁷You are feared;
no one can stand against you
when you are angry.
⁸From heaven you gave the
decision,
and the earth was afraid and
silent.
⁹God, you stood up to judge
and to save the needy people of
the earth.   *Selah*
¹⁰People praise you for your anger
against evil.
Those who live through your
anger are stopped from
doing more evil.

¹¹Make and keep your promises to the
LORD your God.
From all around, gifts should
come to the God we worship.
¹²God breaks the spirits of great
leaders;
the kings on earth fear him.

Remembering God's Help

*For the director of music. For Jeduthun. A psalm of
Asaph.*

77 I cry out to God;
I call to God, and he
will hear me.
²I look for the Lord on the day of
trouble.
All night long I reach out my
hands,
but I cannot be comforted.
³When I remember God, I become
upset;
when I think, I become afraid.
      Selah

⁴You keep my eyes from closing.
I am too upset to say anything.
⁵I keep thinking about the old days,
the years of long ago.
⁶At night I remember my songs.
I think and I ask myself:
⁷"Will the Lord reject us forever?
Will he never be kind to us
again?
⁸Is his love gone forever?
Has he stopped speaking for all
time?
⁹Has God forgotten mercy?
Is he too angry to pity us?"
      Selah
¹⁰Then I say, "This is what makes me
sad:
For years the power of God Most
High was with us."

¹¹I remember what the LORD did;
I remember the miracles you did
long ago.
¹²I think about all the things you did
and consider your deeds.

¹³God, your ways are holy.
No god is as great as our God.
¹⁴You are the God who does miracles;
you have shown people your
power.
¹⁵By your power you have saved your
people,
the descendants of Jacob and
Joseph.   *Selah*

¹⁶God, the waters saw you;

WISE WORDS

Good Parenting Requires Discipline

Any good parent knows that disciplining a child isn't easy. It's much easier to say yes than to set boundaries and enforce them. Consistency is difficult! But good parenting requires that you discipline your children lovingly and consistently. Proverbs 13:24-25 says, "If you do not punish your children, you don't love them, but if you love your children, you will correct them." That's one reason why God's discipline is actually a sign of his love. It's because of his devotion to you that he sets boundaries to prevent you from hurting yourself and others. The next time you become aware of something you've done wrong, remember to seek God's forgiveness and accept his great love for you!

they saw you and became afraid;
the deep waters shook with fear.
¹⁷The clouds poured down their rain.
The sky thundered.
Your lightning flashed back and
forth like arrows.

¹⁸Your thunder sounded in the
    whirlwind.
  Lightning lit up the world.
  The earth trembled and shook.
¹⁹You made a way through the sea
    and paths through the deep
      waters,
  but your footprints were not
    seen.
²⁰You led your people like a flock
  by using Moses and Aaron.

God Saved Israel from Egypt

A maskil of Asaph.

78 My people, listen to my
      teaching;
  listen to what I say.
²I will speak using stories;
  I will tell secret things from
    long ago.
³We have heard them and known
  them

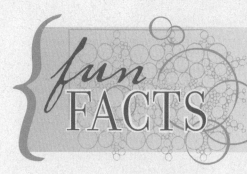

by what our ancestors have told
  us.
⁴We will not keep them from our
    children;
  we will tell those who come later
    about the praises of the LORD.
  We will tell about his power
    and the miracles he has done.

⁵The LORD made an agreement with
    Jacob
  and gave the teachings to
    Israel,

which he commanded our ancestors
    to teach to their children.
⁶Then their children would know
    them,
  even their children not yet born.
  And they would tell their
    children.
⁷So they would all trust God
  and would not forget what he
    had done
  but would obey his commands.
⁸They would not be like their
    ancestors
  who were stubborn and
    disobedient.
  Their hearts were not loyal to
    God,
  and they were not true to him.

⁹The men of Ephraim had bows for
    weapons,
  but they ran away on the day of
    battle.
¹⁰They didn't keep their agreement
    with God
  and refused to live by his
    teachings.
¹¹They forgot what he had done
  and the miracles he had shown
    them.
¹²He did miracles while their
    ancestors watched,
  in the fields of Zoan in Egypt.
¹³He divided the Red Sea and led
    them through.
  He made the water stand up like
    a wall.
¹⁴He led them with a cloud by day
  and by the light of a fire by
    night.
¹⁵He split the rocks in the desert
  and gave them more than

**Q: I'M AFRAID TO RELOCATE TO TAKE A NEW JOB. ARE
THERE VERSES THAT CAN GUIDE ME IN MAKING THE RIGHT
DECISION?**

A: Joshua 1:9 is a good one! It says: "Don't be afraid, because
the Lord your God will be with you everywhere you go." There
are many verses in the Bible directing believers not to be
afraid. If you have prayed about the move, believe it is the
right choice, and people you trust concur with your decision,
take the plunge! Remember that few things in life have to be
permanent. If you relocate and the move doesn't work out, you
can always move back!

enough water, as if from the deep ocean.

[16] He brought streams out of the rock
and caused water to flow down like rivers.

[17] But the people continued to sin against him;
in the desert they turned against God Most High.

[18] They decided to test God
by asking for the food they wanted.

[19] Then they spoke against God,
saying, "Can God prepare food in the desert?

[20] When he hit the rock, water poured out
and rivers flowed down.
But can he give us bread also?
Will he provide his people with meat?"

[21] When the LORD heard them, he was very angry.
His anger was like fire to the people of Jacob;
his anger grew against the people of Israel.

[22] They had not believed God
and had not trusted him to save them.

[23] But he gave a command to the clouds above
and opened the doors of heaven.

[24] He rained manna down on them to eat;
he gave them grain from heaven.

[25] So they ate the bread of angels.
He sent them all the food they could eat.

[26] He sent the east wind from heaven
and led the south wind by his power.

[27] He rained meat on them like dust.
The birds were as many as the sand of the sea.

[28] He made the birds fall inside the camp,
all around the tents.

[29] So the people ate and became very full.

God had given them what they wanted.

[30] While they were still eating,
and while the food was still in their mouths,

[31] God became angry with them.
He killed some of the healthiest of them;
he struck down the best young men of Israel.

[32] But they kept on sinning;
they did not believe even with the miracles.

[33] So he ended their days without meaning
and their years in terror.

[34] Anytime he killed them, they would look to him for help;
they would come back to God and follow him.

[35] They would remember that God was their Rock,
that God Most High had saved them.

[36] But their words were false,
and their tongues lied to him.

[37] Their hearts were not really loyal to God;
they did not keep his agreement.

[38] Still God was merciful.
He forgave their sins
and did not destroy them.

Many times he held back his anger
and did not stir up all his anger.

[39] He remembered that they were only human,
like a wind that blows and does not come back.

[40] They turned against God so often in the desert
and grieved him there.

[41] Again and again they tested God
and brought pain to the Holy One of Israel.

[42] They did not remember his power
or the time he saved them from the enemy.

[43] They forgot the signs he did in Egypt
and his wonders in the fields of Zoan.

[44] He turned their rivers to blood
so no one could drink the water.

[45] He sent flies that bit the people.
He sent frogs that destroyed them.

[46] He gave their crops to grasshoppers

BIBLE Women & Men

Priscilla

Some people work hard, and they're remembered for it. Take Priscilla, for instance. In Romans 16:3, Paul says this industrious woman and her husband, Aquila, worked with him "in Jesus Christ" and even saved his life. This tent-making couple is mentioned six times in the New Testament, and four of the references mention Priscilla first. She was a faithful woman who served God and supported her husband as he did God's work. God used her faithfulness for a very important task—to help build the Ephesian and Corinthian churches, two of the first congregations of Christ-followers.

Love

Open-Handed Love

"I just feel smothered." More than one relationship has ended over this familiar quandary. When you find someone that you care about—that you might want to spend the rest of your life with—it's normal to want to hold on for dear life! But just as God holds his children loosely—giving us free will and an intellect for decision-making—we should hold those we love with open hands. Men are even warned about women who are too aggressive and needy (Ecclesiastes 7:26). If you find yourself clinging too tightly to a relationship, reread 1 Corinthians 13—a refresher course on how real love conducts itself.

and what they worked for to
  locusts.
47He destroyed their vines with hail
  and their sycamore trees with
  sleet.
48He killed their animals with hail
  and their cattle with lightning.
49He showed them his hot anger.
  He sent his strong anger against
  them,
  his destroying angels.
50He found a way to show his anger.
  He did not keep them from dying
  but let them die by a terrible
  disease.
51God killed all the firstborn sons in
  Egypt,
  the oldest son of each family of
  Ham.ⁿ
52But God led his people out like
  sheep
  and he guided them like a flock
  through the desert.
53He led them to safety so they had
  nothing to fear,
  but their enemies drowned in
  the sea.
54So God brought them to his holy
  land,
  to the mountain country he took
  with his own power.
55He forced out the other nations,
  and he had his people inherit
  the land.
  He let the tribes of Israel settle
  there in tents.
56But they tested God
  and turned against God Most
  High;
  they did not keep his rules.
57They turned away and were disloyal
  just like their ancestors.
  They were like a crooked bow
  that does not shoot straight.
58They made God angry by building
  places to worship gods;
  they made him jealous with
  their idols.
59When God heard them, he became
  very angry

and rejected the people of Israel
  completely.
60He left his dwelling at Shiloh,
  the Tent where he lived among
  the people.
61He let the Ark, his power, be
  captured;
  he let the Ark, his glory, be
  taken by enemies.
62He let his people be killed;
  he was very angry with his
  children.
63The young men died by fire,
  and the young women had no
  one to marry.
64Their priests fell by the sword,
  but their widows were not
  allowed to cry.
65Then the Lord got up as if he had
  been asleep;
  he awoke like a man who had
  been drunk with wine.
66He struck down his enemies
  and disgraced them forever.
67But God rejected the family of
  Joseph;
  he did not choose the tribe of
  Ephraim.
68Instead, he chose the tribe of
  Judah
  and Mount Zion, which he
  loves.
69And he built his Temple high like
  the mountains.
  Like the earth, he built it to last
  forever.
70He chose David to be his servant
  and took him from the sheep
  pens.
71He brought him from tending the
  sheep
  so he could lead the flock, the
  people of Jacob,
  his own people, the people of
  Israel.
72And David led them with an
  innocent heart
  and guided them with skillful
  hands.

➡ 78:51 Ham The people in Egypt were descendants of Ham, one of Noah's sons. See Genesis 10:6.

The Nation Cries for Jerusalem

A psalm of Asaph.

79 God, nations have come against your chosen people.
They have ruined your holy Temple.
They have turned Jerusalem into ruins.
[2]They have given the bodies of your servants as food to the wild birds.
They have given the bodies of those who worship you to the wild animals.
[3]They have spilled blood like water all around Jerusalem.
No one was left to bury the dead.
[4]We are a joke to the other nations; they laugh and make fun of us.

[5]LORD, how long will this last?
Will you be angry forever?
How long will your jealousy burn like a fire?
[6]Be angry with the nations that do not know you
and with the kingdoms that do not honor you.
[7]They have gobbled up the people of Jacob
and destroyed their land.
[8]Don't punish us for our past sins.
Show your mercy to us soon, because we are helpless!
[9]God our Savior, help us
so people will praise you.
Save us and forgive our sins
so people will honor you.
[10]Why should the nations say, "Where is their God?"
Tell the other nations in our presence
that you punish those who kill your servants.
[11]Hear the moans of the prisoners.
Use your great power
to save those sentenced to die.

[12]Repay those around us seven times over
for their insults to you, Lord.

[13]We are your people, the sheep of your flock.
We will thank you always;
forever and ever we will praise you.

A Prayer to Bring Israel Back

For the director of music. To the tune of "Lilies of the Agreement." A psalm of Asaph.

80 Shepherd of Israel, listen to us.
You lead the people of Joseph like a flock.
You sit on your throne between the gold creatures with wings.
Show your greatness [2]to the people of Ephraim, Benjamin, and Manasseh.
Use your strength,
and come to save us.

[3]God, take us back.
Show us your kindness so we can be saved.

[4]LORD God All-Powerful,
how long will you be angry at the prayers of your people?
[5]You have fed your people with tears;
you have made them drink many tears.
[6]You made those around us fight over us,
and our enemies make fun of us.

[7]God All-Powerful, take us back.
Show us your kindness so we can be saved.

[8]You brought us out of Egypt as if we were a vine.
You forced out other nations
and planted us in the land.
[9]You cleared the ground for us.
Like a vine, we took root and filled the land.

BE STILL & KNOW

Popcorn Prayers

It's important to set aside time every day for focused prayer, but God also loves to hear "popcorn prayers," those mini-prayers that pop into your head throughout the day. You can tell him "Good morning" in the car on the way to work, ask him for help when you have to face your boss, praise him when you take a quick break, thank him for your lunch, and ask him to remind you to pick up the dry cleaning on the way home! Nothing is too small to talk to God about. He wants to be intimately involved in your day, and he loves it when you keep the conversation going (see 1 Thessalonians 5:17).

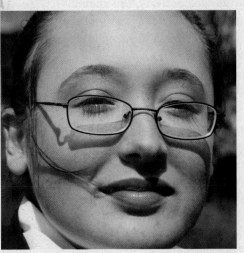

MONEY

Uncovering Identity Theft

It's estimated that every seventy-nine seconds, someone's identity is stolen. Identity thieves can use a person's name, social security number, birth date, credit card number, and other key information to commit fraud and other crimes. In a short time, someone who is pretending to be you can ruin your credit report and reputation. It can take a long time to clean up the mess. People who have experienced identity theft have been refused loans, denied admission to schools, and even arrested for crimes they didn't commit! That is why it's so important to regularly check your credit report to make sure there isn't any unauthorized activity. You should also avoid giving out your social security number whenever possible. Offer a driver's license instead. Shred all of your mail, including junk mail—and especially credit or bank statements and anything that lists your personal information. Be wary of solicitors who ask for personal information.

If you think you have been a victim of identity theft, the Federal Trade Commission (FTC) advises that you contact the three major credit bureaus— www.equifax.com, www.experian.com, and www.transunion.com—and place a fraud alert on your file. Close any accounts you think the thief may have used. File a police report as well as a complaint with the FTC. You *can* defend yourself.

---

¹⁰We covered the mountains with our
    shade.
  We had limbs like the mighty
    cedar tree.
¹¹Our branches reached the
    Mediterranean Sea,
  and our shoots went to the
    Euphrates River.

¹²So why did you pull down our
    walls?
  Now everyone who passes by
    steals from us.
¹³Like wild pigs they walk over us;
  like wild animals they feed on
    us.

¹⁴God All-Powerful, come back.
  Look down from heaven and see.
  Take care of us, your vine.
¹⁵   You planted this shoot with your
    own hands
  and strengthened this child.
¹⁶Now it is cut down and burned with
    fire;
  you destroyed us by your angry
    looks.
¹⁷With your hand,
  strengthen the one you have
    chosen for yourself.
¹⁸Then we will not turn away from
    you.
  Give us life again, and we will
    call to you for help.

¹⁹Lord God All-Powerful, take us
    back.
  Show us your kindness so we can
    be saved.

A Song for a Holiday

For the director of music. By the gittith. A psalm of Asaph.

81 Sing for joy to God, our
    strength;
  shout out loud to the God of
    Jacob.
²Begin the music. Play the
    tambourines.
  Play pleasant music on the harps
    and lyres.
³Blow the trumpet at the time of the
    New Moon,

when the moon is full, when our
feast begins.
⁴This is the law for Israel;
it is the command of the God of
Jacob.
⁵He gave this rule to the people of
Joseph
when they went out of the land
of Egypt.

I heard a language I did not know,
saying:
⁶"I took the load off their shoulders;
I let them put down their
baskets.
⁷When you were in trouble, you
called, and I saved you.
I answered you with thunder.
I tested you at the waters of
Meribah.   *Selah*

⁸My people, listen. I am warning you.
Israel, please listen to me!
⁹You must not have foreign gods;
you must not worship any false
god.
¹⁰I, the LORD, am your God,
who brought you out of Egypt.
Open your mouth and I will feed
you.

¹¹"But my people did not listen to me;
Israel did not want me.
¹²So I let them go their stubborn way
and follow their own advice.
¹³I wish my people would listen to
me;
I wish Israel would live my way.
¹⁴Then I would quickly defeat their
enemies
and turn my hand against their
foes.

¹⁵Those who hate the LORD would
bow before him.
Their punishment would
continue forever.
¹⁶But I would give you the finest
wheat
and fill you with honey from the
rocks."

A Cry for Justice

A psalm of Asaph.

82 God is in charge of the
great meeting;
he judges among the "gods."
²He says, "How long will you defend
evil people?
How long will you show greater
kindness to the wicked?   *Selah*

³Defend the weak and the orphans;
defend the rights of the poor
and suffering.
⁴Save the weak and helpless;
free them from the power of the
wicked.

⁵"You know nothing. You don't
understand.
You walk in the dark,
while the world is falling apart.
⁶I said, 'You are "gods."
You are all sons of God Most
High.'
⁷But you will die like any other
person;
you will fall like all the leaders."

⁸God, come and judge the earth,
because you own all the
nations.

WISE WORDS

Anger Can Get the Best of You

When was the last time you got really mad? What made you so angry? It's easy to get upset and stressed over the littlest things, but the Bible challenges us to remain even-tempered and cool-headed. Proverbs 14:17 says, "Someone with a quick temper does foolish things, but someone with understanding remains calm." It's a challenge to remain calm all the time, but it's in your best interest to do so. A hot temper can go a long way toward destroying your relationships with others and your testimony. If you have a tendency to get angry, pause and pray before responding to difficult situations. Ask God for the grace and peace that only he can give you!

A Prayer Against the Enemies

A song. A psalm of Asaph.

83 God, do not keep quiet;
God, do not be silent
or still.
²Your enemies are making noises;

those who hate you are getting
ready to attack.
³They are making secret plans
against your people;
they plot against those you love.
⁴They say, "Come, let's destroy them
as a nation.

Then no one will ever remember
the name 'Israel.' "
⁵They are united in their plan.
These have made an agreement
against you:
⁶the families of Edom and the
Ishmaelites,
Moab and the Hagrites,
⁷the people of Byblos, Ammon,
Amalek,
Philistia, and Tyre.
⁸Even Assyria has joined them

to help Ammon and Moab, the
descendants of Lot.   Selah
⁹God, do to them what you did to
Midian,
what you did to Sisera and Jabin
at the Kishon River.
¹⁰They died at Endor,
and their bodies rotted on the
ground.
¹¹Do to their important leaders what
you did to Oreb and Zeeb.
Do to their princes what you did
to Zebah and Zalmunna.
¹²They said, "Let's take for ourselves
the pasturelands that belong to
God."
¹³My God, make them like tumbleweed,
like chaff blown away by the
wind.
¹⁴Be like a fire that burns a forest
or like flames that blaze
through the hills.
¹⁵Chase them with your storm,
and frighten them with your
wind.
¹⁶Cover them with shame.
Then people will look for you,
LORD.
¹⁷Make them afraid and ashamed
forever.
Disgrace them and destroy them.
¹⁸Then they will know that you are
the LORD,
that only you are God Most High
over all the earth.

HEALTH
Healthy Habits

Although you don't often hear this message from our culture, you are so much more than what you weigh! God loves you no matter what size you wear, but that is not a license for unhealthy living. In 1 Corinthians, Paul says, "Your body is a temple for the Holy Spirit who is in you....So honor God with your bodies" (6:19–20). Choosing healthy foods, exercising on a regular basis, and drinking lots of water are three ways you can make sure your body stays strong. These guidelines will not only help you stay in shape but also give you the energy you need to serve and bless others. When you discipline yourself to live a healthy lifestyle, God is pleased!

Wishing to Be in the Temple

For the director of music. On the gittith. A psalm of the sons of Korah.

84 LORD All-Powerful,
how lovely is your
Temple!
²I want more than anything
to be in the courtyards of the
LORD's Temple.
My whole being wants
to be with the living God.
³The sparrows have found a home,
and the swallows have nests.
They raise their young near your
altars,

Beauty BECOMES HER

Lash Out

When you're putting on makeup, the final touch should be your eyelashes. Before applying mascara, use an eyelash curler to give your lashes extra lift. Next, apply a little powder to your lashes to help the mascara stay in place longer. Finally, apply two coats of mascara to your upper lashes and a single coat to your lower ones. Your eyes will look great! And remember to keep your eyes wide open, always on the lookout for the ways God is working in your life and in the lives of those around you. As Psalm 119:18 says, "Open my eyes to see the miracles in your teachings."

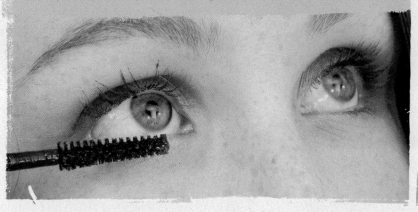

happy are the people who trust
    you!

A Prayer for the Nation

For the director of music. A psalm of the sons of Korah.

85 Lord, you have been kind
    to your land;
you brought back the people of
    Jacob.

Q: I'VE BEEN CONSIDERING PLASTIC SURGERY. DOES THE BIBLE SAY ANYTHING ABOUT IT?

A: The Bible does not talk about plastic surgery directly, but it does talk about your body (see 1 Corinthians 6:19). Scriptures abound on the issue of vanity or pride leading to a person's downfall. If you have a medical problem or a defect that affects your quality of life, surgery may be the right option. However, undergoing surgery solely for the sake of becoming more attractive is an unnecessary medical risk. Ask God to help you determine if you need surgery and to help you see yourself as beautiful—the way God made you.

Lord All-Powerful, my King and
    my God.
⁴Happy are the people who live at
    your Temple;
    they are always praising you.
            Selah

⁵Happy are those whose strength
    comes from you,
    who want to travel to Jerusalem.
⁶As they pass through the Valley of
    Baca,
    they make it like a spring.
    The autumn rains fill it with
        pools of water.
⁷The people get stronger as they go,
    and everyone meets with God in
        Jerusalem.
⁸Lord God All-Powerful, hear my
    prayer;

God of Jacob, listen to me.   *Selah*
⁹God, look at our shield;
    be kind to your appointed king.

¹⁰One day in the courtyards of your
    Temple is better
    than a thousand days anywhere
        else.
I would rather be a doorkeeper in
    the Temple of my God
    than live in the homes of the
        wicked.
¹¹The Lord God is like a sun and shield;
    the Lord gives us kindness and
        honor.
He does not hold back anything
    good
    from those whose lives are
        innocent.
¹²Lord All-Powerful,

What's the POINT?

Psalm 84:1-2

Are you excited when you go to church each week? Do you go to church at all? In these verses, the psalmist can hardly contain his excitement over going to the temple, the place where the Jews gathered to worship God. He couldn't wait to get there and spend time praising and worshiping God. In your relationship with God, where is the excitement? Are you thrilled to meet others who love him, or are you still sitting on the fence, trying to decide what you really believe and how you will express it in your actions and throughout your life? There is great value in going to a place that is designated as a house of worship, a place to meet God in a setting where there is music, prayer, and teaching. You honor God with your desire to praise him and thank him publicly. You also get a chance to step out of your routine and focus on your relationship with him. What's more, you receive the support and benefit of joining with others who have likewise made it their priority to connect with God. Like the psalmist, you should be excited that you have an opportunity to be a part of a worship experience with others who also love God.

²You forgave the guilt of the people
   and covered all their sins.   *Selah*
³You stopped all your anger;
   you turned back from your
      strong anger.

⁴God our Savior, bring us back again.
   Stop being angry with us.
⁵Will you be angry with us forever?
   Will you stay angry from now
      on?
⁶Won't you give us life again?
   Your people would rejoice in
      you.
⁷Lord, show us your love,
   and save us.

⁸I will listen to God the Lord.
   He has ordered peace for those
      who worship him.
   Don't let them go back to
      foolishness.
⁹God will soon save those who
      respect him,
   and his glory will be seen in our
      land.
¹⁰Love and truth belong to God's
      people;
   goodness and peace will be
      theirs.
¹¹On earth people will be loyal to
      God,
   and God's goodness will shine
      down from heaven.
¹²The Lord will give his goodness,
   and the land will give its crops.
¹³Goodness will go before God
   and prepare the way for him.

A Cry for Help

A prayer of David.

86 Lord, listen to me and
      answer me.
   I am poor and helpless.
²Protect me, because I worship you.
   My God, save me, your servant
      who trusts in you.
³Lord, have mercy on me,
   because I have called to you all
      day.
⁴Give happiness to me, your
      servant,

because I give my life to you,
Lord.
[5]Lord, you are kind and forgiving
and have great love for those
who call to you.
[6]LORD, hear my prayer,
and listen when I ask for mercy.
[7]I call to you in times of trouble,
because you will answer me.

[8]Lord, there is no god like you
and no works like yours.
[9]Lord, all the nations you have made
will come and worship you.
They will honor you.
[10]You are great and you do miracles.
Only you are God.
[11]LORD, teach me what you want me
to do,
and I will live by your truth.
Teach me to respect you completely.
[12]Lord, my God, I will praise you with
all my heart,
and I will honor your name
forever.
[13]You have great love for me.
You have saved me from death.

[14]God, proud people are attacking
me;
a gang of cruel people is trying
to kill me.
They do not respect you.
[15]But, Lord, you are a God who shows
mercy and is kind.
You don't become angry
quickly.
You have great love and
faithfulness.
[16]Turn to me and have mercy.

WHAT'S IN A word?

Psalm 84:6 "Valley of Baca"
means "valley of weeping" and
symbolizes the difficult por-
tions of a spiritual journey or
pilgrimage.

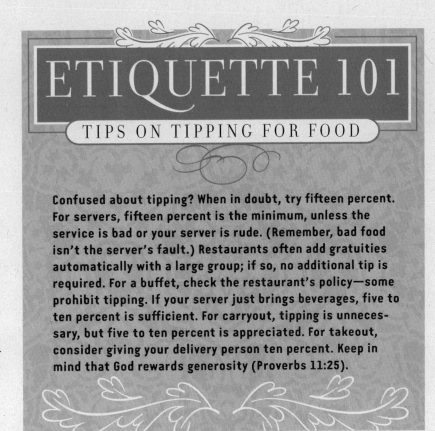

ETIQUETTE 101

TIPS ON TIPPING FOR FOOD

Confused about tipping? When in doubt, try fifteen percent. For servers, fifteen percent is the minimum, unless the service is bad or your server is rude. (Remember, bad food isn't the server's fault.) Restaurants often add gratuities automatically with a large group; if so, no additional tip is required. For a buffet, check the restaurant's policy—some prohibit tipping. If your server just brings beverages, five to ten percent is sufficient. For carryout, tipping is unnecessary, but five to ten percent is appreciated. For takeout, consider giving your delivery person ten percent. Keep in mind that God rewards generosity (Proverbs 11:25).

Give me, your servant, strength.
Save me, the son of your female
servant.
[17]Show me a sign of your goodness.
When my enemies look, they will
be ashamed.
You, LORD, have helped me and
comforted me.

God Loves Jerusalem

A song. A psalm of the sons of Korah.

87 The LORD built Jerusalem
on the holy mountain.
[2] He loves its gates more than any
other place in Israel.
[3]City of God,
wonderful things are said about
you.   *Selah*
[4]God says, "I will put Egypt and
Babylonia
on the list of nations that know
me.
People from Philistia, Tyre, and
Cush
will be born there."

[5]They will say about Jerusalem,
"This one and that one were
born there.
God Most High will strengthen
her."
[6]The LORD will keep a list of the
nations.
He will note, "This person was
born there."   *Selah*

[7]They will dance and sing,
"All good things come from
Jerusalem."

A Sad Complaint

A song. A psalm of the sons of Korah. For the director of music. By the mahalath leannoth. A maskil of Heman the Ezrahite.

88 LORD, you are the God
who saves me.
I cry out to you day and night.
[2]Receive my prayer,
and listen to my cry.

[3]My life is full of troubles,
and I am nearly dead.

⁴They think I am on the way to my
    grave.
    I am like a man with no
        strength.
⁵I have been left as dead,
    like a body lying in a grave

24/7 God

**Think about time zones.
Right now, it may be 8:15
A.M. in New York City but
only 5:15 A.M. in Los Ange-
les. Now consider the In-
ternational Date Line. It
could be Monday in
Chicago and Tuesday in
Tokyo. But no matter what
time it is or where in the
world you are, God is still
God, and someone is al-
ways worshiping him!
Psalm 65:8 tells us that
the Lord is "praised from
where the sun rises to
where it sets." Morning,
noon, and night, God's
people worship him world-
wide!**

**A Cornell University study
found that 37% of phone
calls involve deceptions,
compared to only 14% of
e-mails.**

(Reader's Digest)

whom you don't remember
        anymore,
    cut off from your care.
⁶You have brought me close to death;
    I am almost in the dark place of
        the dead.
⁷You have been very angry with me;
    all your waves crush me.   *Selah*
⁸You have taken my friends away
        from me
    and have made them hate me.
I am trapped and cannot escape.
⁹   My eyes are weak from crying.
LORD, I have prayed to you every
        day;
    I have lifted my hands in prayer
        to you.

¹⁰Do you show your miracles for the
        dead?
    Do their spirits rise up and
        praise you?   *Selah*
¹¹Will your love be told in the
        grave?
    Will your loyalty be told in the
        place of death?
¹²Will your miracles be known in the
        dark grave?
    Will your goodness be known in
        the land of forgetfulness?
¹³But, LORD, I have called out to you
        for help;
    every morning I pray to you.
¹⁴LORD, why do you reject me?
    Why do you hide from me?
¹⁵I have been weak and dying since I
        was young.
    I suffer from your terrors, and I
        am helpless.
¹⁶You have been angry with me,

and your terrors have destroyed
        me.
¹⁷They surround me daily like a flood;
    they are all around me.
¹⁸You have taken away my loved ones
        and friends.
    Darkness is my only friend.

A Song About God's Loyalty

A maskil of Ethan the Ezrahite.

89   I will always sing about
        the LORD's love;
    I will tell of his loyalty from now
        on.
²I will say, "Your love continues
        forever;
    your loyalty goes on and on like
        the sky."
³You said, "I made an agreement
        with the man of my choice;
    I made a promise to my servant
        David.
⁴I told him, 'I will make your family
        continue forever.
    Your kingdom will go on and on.'"
                            Selah

⁵LORD, the heavens praise you for
        your miracles
    and for your loyalty in the
        meeting of your holy ones.
⁶Who in heaven is equal to the LORD?
    None of the angels is like the
        LORD.
⁷When the holy ones meet, it is God
        they fear.
    He is more frightening than all
        who surround him.
⁸LORD God All-Powerful, who is like
        you?

LORD, you are powerful and
completely trustworthy.
[9]You rule the mighty sea
and calm the stormy waves.
[10]You crushed the sea monster
Rahab;
by your power you scattered
your enemies.

[11]The skies and the earth belong to
you.
You made the world and
everything in it.
[12]You created the north and the
south.
Mount Tabor and Mount
Hermon sing for joy at your
name.
[13]Your arm has great power.
Your hand is strong; your right
hand is lifted up.
[14]Your kingdom is built on what is
right and fair.
Love and truth are in all you do.

[15]Happy are the people who know
how to praise you.
LORD, let them live in the light
of your presence.
[16]In your name they rejoice
and continually praise your
goodness.
[17]You are their glorious strength,
and in your kindness you honor
our king.
[18]Our king, our shield, belongs to the
LORD,
to the Holy One of Israel.

[19]Once, in a vision, you spoke
to those who worship you.
You said, "I have given strength to a
warrior;
I have raised up a young man
from my people.
[20]I have found my servant David;
I appointed him by pouring holy
oil on him.
[21]I will steady him with my hand
and strengthen him with my
arm.

[22]No enemy will make him give
forced payments,
and wicked people will not
defeat him.
[23]I will crush his enemies in front of
him;
I will defeat those who hate him.
[24]My loyalty and love will be with
him.
Through me he will be strong.
[25]I will give him power over the sea
and control over the rivers.
[26]He will say to me, 'You are my
father,

my God, the Rock, my Savior.'
[27]I will make him my firstborn son,
the greatest king on earth.
[28]My love will watch over him forever,
and my agreement with him will
never end.
[29]I will make his family continue,
and his kingdom will last as long
as the skies.

[30]"If his descendants reject my
teachings
and do not follow my laws,

Become INVOLVED

Become a Donor

Are you seventeen or older, weigh at least 110 pounds, enjoy good health, and have an hour to spare? If so, you can help save as many as three lives by donating a single pint of blood. According to the American Red Cross, blood is needed every two seconds for emergencies and for people who have diseases such as sickle cell anemia, cancer, and blood disorders. Nearly five million people receive blood transfusions each year, and some need regular transfusions to live.

If you can't donate, you can still get involved by volunteering at a blood drive. Volunteers serve refreshments in the canteen area, help first-time donors feel more comfortable by offering a smile and kind words, and thank donors for making a difference. You can also sponsor a blood drive at the place where you worship, work, or play.

The American Red Cross is a great place to gather information. You can register as a donor and find local blood drives by visiting www.givelife.org or calling 1-800-GIVELIFE. If you are willing to give blood, you may also want to consider becoming a bone marrow donor to help children and adults overcome cancer, leukemia, and other diseases. Visit www.marrow.org for more information.

july

1 Pray for a person of influence: It's Liv Tyler's birthday.

2

3

4 It's Independence Day. Pray for our nation's leaders.

5 Get honest with God in your prayer time. Tell him what is really on your mind.

6

7 *Don't forget to wear sunscreen.*

8

9 Pray for a person of influence: It's Tom Hanks's birthday.

10 Pray for a person of influence: It's Jessica Simpson's birthday.

11

12 Look for ways to honor the Sabbath this week.

13 Pray for a person of influence: Harrison Ford is having a birthday today.

14

15

16

17 *Go for a long walk. Pray along the way.*

18

19 Read the book of Ecclesiastes. Tell a friend what you learned.

20 Pray for persecuted Christians around the world.

21

22

23 Invite people over for lunch after church this Sunday.

24

25

26 Pray for a person of influence: It's Sandra Bullock's birthday.

27

28

29 *Write a letter to God. Fill it with your prayers.*

30 Pray for a person of influence: It's Arnold Schwarzenegger's birthday.

31 Ask a parent or grandparent to share stories from his or her childhood.

"The greatest gift we can give to one another is our prayers."
–Anonymous

³¹if they ignore my demands
   and disobey my commands,
³²then I will punish their sins with a
      rod
   and their wrongs with a whip.
³³But I will not hold back my love
      from David,
   nor will I stop being loyal.
³⁴I will not break my agreement
   nor change what I have said.
³⁵I have promised by my holiness,
   I will not lie to David.
³⁶His family will go on forever.
   His kingdom will last before me
      like the sun.
³⁷It will continue forever, like the
      moon,
   like a dependable witness in the
      sky."   *Selah*

³⁸But now you have refused and
      rejected your appointed
      king.
   You have been angry with him.
³⁹You have abandoned the agreement
      with your servant
   and thrown his crown to the
      ground.
⁴⁰You have torn down all his city
      walls;
   you have turned his strong cities
      into ruins.
⁴¹Everyone who passes by steals from
      him.
   His neighbors insult him.
⁴²You have given strength to his
      enemies
   and have made them all happy.
⁴³You have made his sword useless;
   you did not help him stand in
      battle.
⁴⁴You have kept him from winning

and have thrown his throne to
      the ground.
⁴⁵You have cut his life short
   and covered him with shame.
                                    Selah

⁴⁶Lord, how long will this go on?
   Will you ignore us forever?
   How long will your anger burn
      like a fire?
⁴⁷Remember how short my life is.
   Why did you create us? For
      nothing?
⁴⁸What person alive will not die?
   Who can escape the grave? *Selah*

⁴⁹Lord, where is your love from times
      past,
   which in your loyalty you
      promised to David?
⁵⁰Lord, remember how they insulted
      your servant;
   remember how I have suffered
      the insults of the nations.
⁵¹Lord, remember how your enemies
      insulted you
   and how they insulted your
      appointed king wherever he
      went.

⁵²Praise the Lord forever!
                  Amen and amen.

BOOK 4

God Is Eternal, and We Are Not

A prayer of Moses, the man of God.

90 Lord, you have been our
      home
   since the beginning.
²Before the mountains were born

and before you created the earth
      and the world,
you are God.
   You have always been, and you
      will always be.

³You turn people back into dust.
   You say, "Go back into dust,
      human beings."
⁴To you, a thousand years
   is like the passing of a day,
   or like a few hours in the night.

WISE WORDS

Honor the Least of These

Even without realizing it, you can find yourself looking down on others—especially people you perceive to have less money, status, education, or basic social skills. But God isn't concerned or impressed with the superficial labels we apply to people. He wants you to honor everyone in what you say and do. In fact, God takes it personally when you don't treat others well! Proverbs 14:31 says, "Whoever mistreats the poor insults their Maker, but whoever is kind to the needy honors God." So the next time you encounter someone you're tempted to look down on, look for ways to honor and esteem that person instead. In doing so, you'll be honoring God.

5 While people sleep, you take their lives.
They are like grass that grows up in the morning.
6 In the morning they are fresh and new,
but by evening they dry up and die.

7 We are destroyed by your anger;
we are terrified by your hot anger.
8 You have put the evil we have done right in front of you;
you clearly see our secret sins.
9 All our days pass while you are angry.
Our years end with a moan.
10 Our lifetime is seventy years
or, if we are strong, eighty years.
But the years are full of hard work and pain.
They pass quickly, and then we are gone.

11 Who knows the full power of your anger?
Your anger is as great as our fear of you should be.
12 Teach us how short our lives really are
so that we may be wise.

13 Lord, how long before you return
and show kindness to your servants?
14 Fill us with your love every morning.
Then we will sing and rejoice all our lives.
15 We have seen years of trouble.
Now give us as much joy as you gave us sorrow.
16 Show your servants the wonderful things you do;
show your greatness to their children.
17 Lord our God, treat us well.
Give us success in what we do;
yes, give us success in what we do.

Safe in the Lord

91

Those who go to God Most High for safety
will be protected by the Almighty.
2 I will say to the Lord, "You are my place of safety and protection.
You are my God and I trust you."

3 God will save you from hidden traps
and from deadly diseases.
4 He will cover you with his feathers,
and under his wings you can hide.
His truth will be your shield and protection.
5 You will not fear any danger by night
or an arrow during the day.
6 You will not be afraid of diseases that come in the dark
or sickness that strikes at noon.
7 At your side one thousand people may die,
or even ten thousand right beside you,
but you will not be hurt.
8 You will only watch
and see the wicked punished.

9 The Lord is your protection;
you have made God Most High your place of safety.
10 Nothing bad will happen to you;
no disaster will come to your home.
11 He has put his angels in charge of you
to watch over you wherever you go.
12 They will catch you in their hands
so that you will not hit your foot on a rock.
13 You will walk on lions and cobras;
you will step on strong lions and snakes.

14 The Lord says, "Whoever loves me, I will save.
I will protect those who know me.
15 They will call to me, and I will answer them.
I will be with them in trouble;
I will rescue them and honor them.
16 I will give them a long, full life,
and they will see how I can save."

RELATIONSHIPS

Sticking It Out at Work

Your boss has been a total jerk lately. While you love your work, it seems like nothing you do is good enough, and she's making your life miserable. If you feel like quitting, check out Ecclesiastes 10:4: "Don't leave your job just because your boss is angry with you. Remaining calm solves great problems." If you enjoy what you do and are generally satisfied with your workplace, it would be a mistake to allow one bad relationship to taint your entire job or interfere with your daily tasks. It may be tempting to jump ship, but perhaps you can work through the interpersonal issues with your boss. And you wouldn't want to leave on bad terms—you'll need a reference for your *next* job!

Thanksgiving for God's Goodness

A psalm. A song for the Sabbath day.

92 It is good to praise you, LORD,
   to sing praises to God Most High.
²It is good to tell of your love in the morning
   and of your loyalty at night.
³It is good to praise you with the ten-stringed lyre
   and with the soft-sounding harp.

⁴LORD, you have made me happy by what you have done;
   I will sing for joy about what your hands have done.
⁵LORD, you have done such great things!
   How deep are your thoughts!
⁶Stupid people don't know these things,
   and fools don't understand.
⁷Wicked people grow like the grass.
   Evil people seem to do well,
but they will be destroyed forever.
⁸But, LORD, you will be honored forever.

⁹LORD, surely your enemies,
   surely your enemies will be destroyed,
   and all who do evil will be scattered.
¹⁰But you have made me as strong as an ox.
   You have poured fine oils on me.
¹¹When I looked, I saw my enemies;
   I heard the cries of those who are against me.

¹²But good people will grow like palm trees;
   they will be tall like the cedars of Lebanon.
¹³Like trees planted in the Temple of the LORD,
   they will grow strong in the courtyards of our God.
¹⁴When they are old, they will still produce fruit;
   they will be healthy and fresh.
¹⁵They will say that the LORD is good.
He is my Rock, and there is no wrong in him.

The Majesty of the Lord

93 The LORD is king. He is clothed in majesty.
   The LORD is clothed in majesty
   and armed with strength.
   The world is set,
   and it cannot be moved.
²LORD, your kingdom was set up long ago;
   you are everlasting.

WHAT'S IN A word?

Psalm 91:14 "Love" in this particular verse means to "hold close" or "hug tightly." It communicates the idea of someone who clings to a genuine, intimate relationship with God.

A Rough Breakup

ANITA'S STORY

The Bible says "You are not the same as those who do not believe. So do not join yourselves to them" (2 Corinthians 6:14). But a number of years ago I began dating someone who did not base his life on Christian values. Though I knew in my mind and in my heart that it was wrong to date him, I did not want to walk away from the relationship. For three years we dated, argued over religion, cried together, but still continued dating.

My parents voiced their concerns, but I ignored them. I was stubborn. Eventually I grew weary of the lack of peace in my life. The verse from 2 Corinthians kept coming up in my Bible studies. I felt as if God was reminding me of the heartache to come if I didn't end the relationship.

I began to pray for a miracle because I knew I couldn't end it in my own strength. The answer came one December evening. Rusty's father called him and,

> THOUGH I KNEW IN MY MIND AND IN MY HEART THAT IT WAS WRONG TO DATE HIM, I DID NOT WANT TO WALK AWAY FROM THE RELATIONSHIP.

with no real explanation, told him he had to end the relationship immediately. I knew this was the miracle I had hoped for, but it still hurt. Throughout that period of my life, God made himself real by reminding me that nothing could separate me from his love. Romans 8:38–39 says, "Yes, I am sure that neither death, nor life, nor angels, nor ruling spirits, nothing now, nothing in the future, no powers, nothing above us, nothing below us, nor anything else in the whole world will ever be able to separate us from the love of God that is in Christ Jesus our Lord."

Even though I was hurting from the breakup, God used this verse to remind me that his love for me was eternal and unchanging. Rusty and I still run into each other on occasion, but he is now nothing more than a reminder to guard my heart. God is my true love, and he is the one in control of my life.

Q: I LOVE TO SHOP! IS THERE ANYTHING WRONG WITH THAT?

A: Anything done in excess can become greed or gluttony, whether it is eating, drinking, or shopping too much. Is your shopping cutting in to the time you spend with others? Is it jeopardizing your financial stability? Is it hurting anyone else? Are you relying on it as an emotional crutch instead of going to God? Based on these guidelines, if you still feel okay about your shopping habit, consider using this passion as a ministry. Instead of just filling up your own closets, give what you purchase to those in need. Now that's a win-win situation!

³LORD, the seas raise,
    the seas raise their voice.
    The seas raise up their
        pounding waves.
⁴The sound of the water is loud;
    the ocean waves are powerful,
    but the LORD above is much
        greater.
⁵LORD, your laws will stand forever.
    Your Temple will be holy
        forevermore.

God Will Pay Back His Enemies

94
The LORD is a God who
    punishes.
God, show your greatness and
    punish!
²Rise up, Judge of the earth,
    and give the proud what they
        deserve.

³How long will the wicked be happy?
    How long, LORD?

⁴They are full of proud words;
    those who do evil brag about
        what they have done.
⁵LORD, they crush your people
    and make your children suffer.
⁶They kill widows and foreigners
    and murder orphans.
⁷They say, "The LORD doesn't see;
    the God of Jacob doesn't notice."

⁸You stupid ones among the people,
    pay attention.
    You fools, when will you
        understand?
⁹Can't the creator of ears hear?
    Can't the maker of eyes see?
¹⁰Won't the one who corrects nations
        punish you?
    Doesn't the teacher of people
        know everything?

¹¹The LORD knows what people think.
    He knows their thoughts are
        just a puff of wind.

¹²LORD, those you correct are happy;
    you teach them from your law.
¹³You give them rest from times of
        trouble
    until a pit is dug for the
        wicked.
¹⁴The LORD won't leave his people
    nor give up his children.
¹⁵Judgment will again be fair,
    and all who are honest will
        follow it.

¹⁶Who will help me fight against the
        wicked?
    Who will stand with me against
        those who do evil?
¹⁷If the LORD had not helped me,
    I would have died in a minute.
¹⁸I said, "I am about to fall,"
    but, LORD, your love kept me
        safe.
¹⁹I was very worried,
    but you comforted me and made
        me happy.

²⁰Crooked leaders cannot be your
        friends.
    They use the law to cause
        suffering.
²¹They join forces against people who
        do right
    and sentence to death the
        innocent.

WHAT'S IN A word?

Psalm 92:6 "Fools" The idea of being foolish in the Bible means more than just making an unwise decision from time to time. A fool is someone who ignores God and is morally and spiritually insensitive.

Balancing Act

Finding Fellowship

Life can be so full, can't it? You hurry out the door in the morning, work or run errands all day, get home, find something to eat, straighten up the house, spend a little time with roommates or your family, and then it's off to bed so you can start the whole thing again the next day. Right? Weekends are packed with those errands, activities, and events you couldn't fit in during the week. Somewhere in your busy routine, it's important to build in time for fellowship with those who share a common faith. You need to meet with friends who can hold you accountable and encourage you in your relationship with God. Fellowship is vitally important to your spiritual health. It's good for your emotional health, too. Spending time with others who also love Christ is one of the best time investments you can make.

²²But the LORD is my defender;
my God is the rock of my
protection.
²³God will pay them back for their
sins
and will destroy them for their
evil.
The LORD our God will destroy
them.

A Call to Praise and Obedience

95 Come, let's sing for joy to
the LORD.
Let's shout praises to the Rock
who saves us.
²Let's come to him with
thanksgiving.
Let's sing songs to him,
³because the LORD is the great
God,
the great King over all gods.
⁴The deepest places on earth are
his,
and the highest mountains
belong to him.
⁵The sea is his because he made it,
and he created the land with his
own hands.

⁶Come, let's worship him and bow
down.
Let's kneel before the LORD
who made us,

⁷because he is our God
and we are the people he takes
care of,
the sheep that he tends.

Today listen to what he says:
⁸ "Do not be stubborn, as your
ancestors were at Meribah,
as they were that day at Massah
in the desert.
⁹There your ancestors tested me
and tried me even though they
saw what I did.
¹⁰I was angry with those people for
forty years.
I said, 'They are not loyal to me
and have not understood my
ways.'
¹¹I was angry and made a promise,
'They will never enter my rest.'"

Praise for the Lord's Glory

96 Sing to the LORD a new
song;
sing to the LORD, all the earth.
²Sing to the LORD and praise his
name;
every day tell how he saves us.
³Tell the nations of his glory;

BIBLE Women & Men

Lot's Wife

Do you know people who have a lot of head knowledge about God, but it doesn't seem to connect with their hearts? Meet Lot's wife. Before God judged the city of Sodom, he instructed her family to run and not look back. But Lot's wife couldn't do that. She knew of God and his power, but her heart remained back in Sodom. She looked back at the sinful city and turned into a pillar of salt. Jesus told his followers to "Remember Lot's wife," encouraging them to look ahead with anticipation to what God has in store (Luke 17:32).

WHAT'S IN A word?

Psalm 95:8 "Meribah" means "rebellion." While Meribah was a real place, the name also served as a reminder to the Israelites of their ancestors' rebellion in Numbers 14.

tell all peoples the miracles he does,

⁴because the LORD is great; he
should be praised at all
times.
He should be honored more
than all the gods,
⁵because all the gods of the nations
are only idols,
but the LORD made the heavens.
⁶The LORD has glory and majesty;
he has power and beauty in his
Temple.

⁷Praise the LORD, all nations on
earth;
praise the LORD's glory and
power.
⁸Praise the glory of the LORD's name.
Bring an offering and come into
his Temple courtyards.
⁹Worship the LORD because he is
holy.
Tremble before him, everyone
on earth.
¹⁰Tell the nations, "The LORD is king."
The earth is set, and it cannot
be moved.
He will judge the people fairly.
¹¹Let the skies rejoice and the earth
be glad;
let the sea and everything in it
shout.
¹² Let the fields and everything in
them rejoice.
Then all the trees of the forest will
sing for joy
¹³ before the LORD, because he is
coming.

He is coming to judge the world;
he will judge the world with
fairness
and the peoples with truth.

A Hymn About the Lord's Power

97 The LORD is king. Let the
earth rejoice;
faraway lands should be glad.
²Thick, dark clouds surround him.
His kingdom is built on what is
right and fair.
³A fire goes before him
and burns up his enemies all
around.
⁴His lightning lights up the world;
when the people see it, they
tremble.
⁵The mountains melt like wax before
the LORD,
before the Lord of all the earth.
⁶The heavens tell about his
goodness,
and all the people see his glory.

⁷Those who worship idols should be
ashamed;
they brag about their gods.
All the gods should worship the
LORD.
⁸When Jerusalem hears this, she is
glad,
and the towns of Judah rejoice.
They are happy because of your
judgments, LORD.
⁹You are the LORD Most High over all
the earth;
you are supreme over all gods.

¹⁰People who love the LORD hate evil.
The LORD watches over those
who follow him
and frees them from the power
of the wicked.
¹¹Light shines on those who do right;
joy belongs to those who are
honest.
¹²Rejoice in the LORD, you who do
right.
Praise his holy name.

The Lord of Power and Justice

A psalm.

98 Sing to the LORD a new
song,
because he has done miracles.
By his right hand and holy arm
he has won the victory.

WISE WORDS

Use Your Secret Weapon

Did you know you have a secret weapon? You do, and it's packed with power! Each word you choose to speak is like a secret weapon, capable of great good or terrible harm. Whether you realize it or not, your words have a tremendous influence on those around you. Kind and gracious words bring healing and life to others, but negative and destructive words bring others down. Proverbs 15:4 is very clear about the power of words that are full of grace and love: "As a tree gives fruit, healing words give life, but dishonest words crush the spirit." Look for ways to use your secret weapon—your words—to bring healing and life to those around you.

What's the POINT?

Psalm 96:8

Do certain names carry particular connotations for you? Think of some of your friends' names. Do any of them sound romantic, cool, or unusual? Names can reveal a lot about a person, particularly in the Bible because names often reflected a life-defining experience or personality trait. Most likely, your own name was specifically chosen for you, given to you in love. One of the ways you can praise God is by reflecting on his various names. Throughout the Bible, God reveals his characteristics through the names he is called. The triune God—meaning that he is Father, Son, and Holy Spirit—has a variety of names throughout the Old and New Testaments. You can praise God for being a provider, as he was when he provided a ram to be sacrificed instead of Abraham's son (Genesis 22). You can praise him for being "I am" because he has always been and will always be, just as he told Moses in Exodus 3:14. You can praise him for being your Savior (Psalm 18:2, Luke 1:69, and many others). You can praise him for being Immanuel, which means "God is with us" (Isaiah 7:14). Praising God by using his names teaches you a great deal about him and reminds you of his remarkable characteristics. Learn God's names, and learn to praise him in a whole new way.

²The LORD has made known his
power to save;
he has shown the other nations
his victory for his people.
³He has remembered his love
and his loyalty to the people of
Israel.
All the ends of the earth have seen
God's power to save.

⁴Shout with joy to the LORD, all the
earth;
burst into songs and make music.
⁵Make music to the LORD with harps,
with harps and the sound of
singing.
⁶Blow the trumpets and the sheep's
horns;
shout for joy to the LORD the
King.

⁷Let the sea and everything in it
shout;
let the world and everyone in it
sing.
⁸Let the rivers clap their hands;
let the mountains sing together
for joy.
⁹Let them sing before the LORD,
because he is coming to judge
the world.
He will judge the world fairly;
he will judge the peoples with
fairness.

The Lord, the Fair and Holy King

99 The LORD is king.
Let the peoples shake
with fear.
He sits between the gold creatures
with wings.
Let the earth shake.
²The LORD in Jerusalem is great;
he is supreme over all the
peoples.
³Let them praise your name;
it is great, holy and to be feared.

⁴The King is powerful and loves
justice.
LORD, you made things fair;
you have done what is fair and
right

how happy are you at work?

1. WHEN YOU THINK ABOUT GOING TO WORK, YOU FEEL:

☐ A. Frustrated that you have to go to "that place" again.

☐ B. Glad you have a job, but wonder if there's something better suited for you.

☐ C. Excited about the projects you're working on and the people you work with.

2. WHEN YOU THINK ABOUT THE MAJORITY OF YOUR COWORKERS, YOU FEEL:

☐ A. Depressed.

☐ B. Grateful that you get to work with such great people.

☐ C. Content.

3. WHEN YOU THINK ABOUT WHAT YOU CONTRIBUTE TO YOUR PLACE OF EMPLOYMENT, YOU:

☐ A. Feel you're making a difference.

☐ B. Believe anyone could do your job.

☐ C. Wish someone else *would* do your job.

4. IF YOU COULD SWITCH TO A DIFFERENT JOB THAT HAD THE SAME HOURS, PAY, AND A SIMILAR WORKLOAD, YOU WOULD ACCEPT THE POSITION:

☐ A. Right away.

☐ B. In a few months.

☐ C. In a few years—maybe.

5. WHEN YOU THINK ABOUT YOUR BOSS, YOU FEEL:

☐ A. Angry and upset.

☐ B. Indifferent.

☐ C. Appreciative.

6. YOU FIND OUT YOUR BOSS IS SENDING YOU TO A THREE-DAY SEMINAR LATER IN THE WEEK. YOU'RE EXCITED BECAUSE:

☐ A. You feel like you've just escaped from Alcatraz.

☐ B. It will provide a great opportunity to find a new employer.

☐ C. It will allow you to learn more and be a better employee.

7. NUMBER OF SHORT BREAKS YOU TAKE EACH DAY:

☐ A. 1 – 2

☐ B. 3 – 4

☐ C. 5 or more.

Scoring:

1. A=1, B=2, C=3	4. A=1, B=2, C=3	7. A=3, B=2, C=1
2. A=1, B=3, C=2	5. A=1, B=2, C=3	
3. A=3, B=2, C=1	6. A=1, B=1, C=3	

IF YOU SCORED 8 OR LOWER, YOU ARE DEFINITELY UNHAPPY AT WORK. Your job takes more from you than it gives, and you should probably begin looking for a new job right away.

IF YOU SCORED 9-17, YOU MAY BE DISCONTENT WITH PARTS OF YOUR JOB, BUT you've also found enough reasons to postpone looking for a new one. You may like your boss, your coworkers, or much of what you do, but the pieces haven't come together to provide a truly satisfying experience. You may want to prayerfully consider changing jobs or looking for ways to improve your situation.

IF YOU SCORED 18 OR HIGHER, YOU ARE RELATIVELY HAPPY WITH YOUR JOB. You know it's not perfect, but you have found enough redeeming qualities to keep you engaged in your work. You want to stay put for now.

for the people of Jacob.
[5]Praise the LORD our God,
and worship at the Temple, his
footstool.
He is holy.

[6]Moses and Aaron were among his
priests,
and Samuel was among his
worshipers.
They called to the LORD,
and he answered them.
[7]He spoke to them from the pillar of
cloud.
They kept the rules and laws he
gave them.

[8]LORD our God, you answered them.
You showed them that you are a
forgiving God,
but you punished them for their
wrongs.
[9]Praise the LORD our God,
and worship at his holy
mountain,

because the LORD our God is
holy.

A Call to Praise the Lord

A psalm of thanks.

100
Shout to the LORD,
all the earth.
[2] Serve the LORD with joy;
come before him with singing.
[3]Know that the LORD is God.
He made us, and we belong to
him;
we are his people, the sheep he
tends.

[4]Come into his city with songs of
thanksgiving
and into his courtyards with
songs of praise.
Thank him and praise his name.
[5]The LORD is good. His love is
forever,
and his loyalty goes on and on.

A Promise to Rule Well

A psalm of David.

101
I will sing of your
love and fairness;
LORD, I will sing praises to you.
[2]I will be careful to live an innocent
life.
When will you come to me?

I will live an innocent life in my
house.
[3] I will not look at anything wicked.
I hate those who turn against you;
they will not be found near me.
[4]Let those who want to do wrong
stay away from me;
I will have nothing to do with
evil.
[5]If anyone secretly says things
against his neighbor,
I will stop him.
I will not allow people
to be proud and look down on
others.

[6]I will look for trustworthy people
so I can live with them in the
land.
Only those who live innocent lives
will be my servants.
[7]No one who is dishonest will live in
my house;
no liars will stay around me.
[8]Every morning I will destroy the
wicked in the land.
I will rid the LORD's city of
people who do evil.

A Cry for Help

*A prayer of a person who is suffering when he is
discouraged and tells the LORD his complaints.*

102
LORD, listen to my
prayer;
let my cry for help come to you.
[2]Do not hide from me
in my time of trouble.
Pay attention to me.
When I cry for help, answer me
quickly.

[3]My life is passing away like smoke,
and my bones are burned up
with fire.

Life Issues

People-Pleasing

Many women fall into the trap of being people-pleasers, fearing that the earth will stop spinning if they disappoint someone. Although the urge to be everything to everyone is tempting, it's an impossible goal! If saying yes to a request will overextend you or is not what God wants you to do, you should say no even if it irritates the person you are refusing. That may feel uncomfortable, but the discomfort does not mean you are wrong or should give in. Establishing healthy boundaries, which Jesus modeled in Luke 5:15–16, gives you balance and peace. Even when the crowds pressed in, waiting to hear his words and feel his healing touch, Jesus frequently slipped away to be alone and pray. Not exactly the behavior you'd expect from the keynote speaker, but Jesus showed that his priority was pleasing his Father, not the crowds. Follow his example in your life!

⁴My heart is like grass
  that has been cut and dried.
  I forget to eat.
⁵Because of my grief,
  my skin hangs on my bones.
⁶I am like a desert owl,
  like an owl living among the
    ruins.
⁷I lie awake.
  I am like a lonely bird on a
    housetop.
⁸All day long enemies insult me;
  those who make fun of me use
    my name as a curse.
⁹I eat ashes for food,
  and my tears fall into my drinks.
¹⁰Because of your great anger,
  you have picked me up and
    thrown me away.
¹¹My days are like a passing shadow;
  I am like dried grass.

¹²But, LORD, you rule forever,
  and your fame goes on and on.
¹³You will come and have mercy on
    Jerusalem,
  because the time has now come
    to be kind to her;
  the right time has come.
¹⁴Your servants love even her stones;
  they even care about her dust.
¹⁵Nations will fear the name of the
    LORD,
  and all the kings on earth will
    honor you.
¹⁶The LORD will rebuild Jerusalem;
  there his glory will be seen.
¹⁷He will answer the prayers of the
    needy;
  he will not reject their prayers.

¹⁸Write these things for the future
  so that people who are not yet
    born will praise the LORD.
¹⁹The LORD looked down from his
    holy place above;
  from heaven he looked down at
    the earth.
²⁰He heard the moans of the prisoners,
  and he freed those sentenced to
    die.
²¹The name of the LORD will be heard
    in Jerusalem;
  his praise will be heard there.

²²People will come together,
  and kingdoms will serve the LORD.
²³God has made me tired of living;
  he has cut short my life.
²⁴So I said, "My God, do not take me
    in the middle of my life.
  Your years go on and on.
²⁵In the beginning you made the
    earth,
  and your hands made the skies.
²⁶They will be destroyed, but you will
    remain.

What—or Who—Do You Love?

Even if you haven't consciously ranked your priorities in life, you can glean a lot from perusing your calendar and checkbook. What are the top five things you consistently invest your time, energy, and money in? How you allocate your money and schedule your time says a lot about your heart. Reading, sports, the arts, hobbies—these may be worthy pursuits, but we shouldn't allow them to rule our lives. The pleasures of this life are fleeting and can distract us from what really matters (see Proverbs 21:17). Ultimately, our priorities should reflect that familiar Sunday school acronym, JOY: 1) Jesus, 2) Others, and 3) You. When you put God first in your life, everything else falls into place.

They will all wear out like
clothes.
And, like clothes, you will change
them
and throw them away.
²⁷But you never change,
and your life will never end.
²⁸Our children will live in your
presence,
and their children will remain
with you."

Praise to the Lord of Love

Of David.

103 All that I am, praise
the LORD;
everything in me, praise his holy
name.
²My whole being, praise the LORD
and do not forget all his
kindnesses.
³He forgives all my sins
and heals all my diseases.

⁴He saves my life from the grave
and loads me with love and
mercy.
⁵He satisfies me with good things
and makes me young again, like
the eagle.

⁶The LORD does what is right and
fair
for all who are wronged by
others.
⁷He showed his ways to Moses
and his deeds to the people of
Israel.
⁸The LORD shows mercy and is kind.
He does not become angry
quickly, and he has great
love.
⁹He will not always accuse us,
and he will not be angry forever.
¹⁰He has not punished us as our sins
should be punished;
he has not repaid us for the evil
we have done.
¹¹As high as the sky is above the earth,
so great is his love for those who
respect him.
¹²He has taken our sins away from
us
as far as the east is from west.
¹³The LORD has mercy on those who
respect him,
as a father has mercy on his
children.
¹⁴He knows how we were made;
he remembers that we are dust.

¹⁵Human life is like grass;
we grow like a flower in the
field.
¹⁶After the wind blows, the flower is
gone,
and there is no sign of where it
was.
¹⁷But the LORD's love for those who
respect him
continues forever and ever,
and his goodness continues to
their grandchildren
¹⁸and to those who keep his
agreement
and who remember to obey his
orders.

¹⁹The LORD has set his throne in
heaven,
and his kingdom rules over
everything.
²⁰You who are his angels, praise the
LORD.
You are the mighty warriors who
do what he says
and who obey his voice.
²¹You, his armies, praise the LORD;
you are his servants who do
what he wants.
²²Everything the LORD has made
should praise him in all the
places he rules.
My whole being, praise the
LORD.

BE STILL & KNOW

Sounds of Silence

When God wanted to make his presence real to the prophet Elijah in a powerful way (see 1 Kings 19), he sent a massive wind that actually caused the mountains to crumble and rocks to fall. Then he sent an earthquake and a huge fire. As loud and impressive as those natural phenomena were, the Bible says that the Lord was not in those things. Instead, God wrapped himself in a "quiet, gentle sound" to communicate with Elijah. It's crucial to a vibrant prayer life to turn off all the noise, go somewhere in solitude, and spend time in silence as often as you can. When you immerse yourself in silence, like Elijah, you just might hear the sound of God.

WHAT'S IN A word?

Psalm 102:6 "Desert owl" The psalmist describes himself as a "desert owl" to communicate the idea that he feels isolated, alone, and vulnerable.

Praise to God Who Made the World

104

My whole being, praise the LORD.
LORD my God, you are very great.
You are clothed with glory and majesty;
2 you wear light like a robe.
You stretch out the skies like a tent.
3 You build your room above the clouds.
You make the clouds your chariot,
and you ride on the wings of the wind.
4 You make the winds your messengers,
and flames of fire are your servants.

5 You built the earth on its foundations
so it can never be moved.
6 You covered the earth with oceans;
the water was above the mountains.
7 But at your command, the water rushed away.
When you thundered your orders, it hurried away.
8 The mountains rose; the valleys sank.
The water went to the places you made for it.
9 You set borders for the seas that they cannot cross,
so water will never cover the earth again.

10 You make springs pour into the ravines;
they flow between the mountains.
11 They water all the wild animals;
the wild donkeys come there to drink.
12 Wild birds make nests by the water;
they sing among the tree branches.
13 You water the mountains from above.
The earth is full of the things you made.
14 You make the grass for cattle
and vegetables for the people.
You make food grow from the earth.
15 You give us wine that makes happy hearts
and olive oil that makes our faces shine.
You give us bread that gives us strength.
16 The LORD's trees have plenty of water;
they are the cedars of Lebanon, which he planted.
17 The birds make their nests there;
the stork's home is in the fir trees.
18 The high mountains belong to the wild goats.
The rocks are hiding places for the badgers.

19 You made the moon to mark the seasons,
and the sun always knows when to set.
20 You make it dark, and it becomes night.
Then all the wild animals creep around.
21 The lions roar as they attack.
They look to God for food.
22 When the sun rises, they leave
and go back to their dens to lie down.
23 Then people go to work
and work until evening.

24 LORD, you have made many things;
with your wisdom you made them all.
The earth is full of your riches.

Q&A

Q: WHY DO INNOCENT PEOPLE SUFFER?

A: One reason innocent people suffer is that we live in a fallen world. Some suffering is unexplainable; some is a result of poor choices with serious consequences. When Adam and Eve turned their backs on God, nature revolted, too. His perfect creation became flawed. Disease entered in, and the earth was cursed. Despite all this, it is often during times of suffering that our hearts are drawn closest to God. The simple truth is that we live in an unjust world that is kept intact while God patiently waits to be reunited with his children.

25 Look at the sea, so big and wide,
with creatures large and small that cannot be counted.
26 Ships travel over the ocean,
and there is the sea monster Leviathan,
which you made to play there.

27 All these things depend on you

Defining Worship

"Worship" is a word we use a lot in Christian circles, but do we really understand what it means? *Random House Webster's Unabridged Dictionary* lists ten definitions for "worship," half of them nouns and half verbs. The most prevalent distinctions among these definitions relate to the words "adore" and "revere." That means that worship is anything—anything!—we do to show adoration and reverence for God. Think outside the box to determine distinct ways you can worship the Lord with your specific talents and abilities.

to give them their food at the right time.
²⁸When you give it to them, they gather it up.
When you open your hand, they are filled with good food.
²⁹When you turn away from them, they become frightened.
When you take away their breath, they die and turn to dust.
³⁰When you breathe on them, they are created, and you make the land new again.

³¹May the glory of the LORD be forever.
May the LORD enjoy what he has made.
³²He just looks at the earth, and it shakes.
He touches the mountains, and they smoke.

³³I will sing to the LORD all my life; I will sing praises to my God as long as I live.
³⁴May my thoughts please him; I am happy in the LORD.
³⁵Let sinners be destroyed from the earth, and let the wicked live no longer.

My whole being, praise the LORD.
Praise the LORD.

God's Love for Israel

105 Give thanks to the LORD and pray to him.
Tell the nations what he has done.
²Sing to him; sing praises to him.
Tell about all his miracles.
³Be glad that you are his; let those who seek the LORD be happy.
⁴Depend on the LORD and his strength; always go to him for help.
⁵Remember the miracles he has done; remember his wonders and his decisions.
⁶You are descendants of his servant Abraham,

the children of Jacob, his chosen people.
⁷He is the LORD our God.
His laws are for all the world.

⁸He will keep his agreement forever; he will keep his promises always.
⁹He will keep the agreement he made with Abraham and the promise he made to Isaac.
¹⁰He made it a law for the people of Jacob;
he made it an agreement with Israel to last forever.
¹¹The LORD said, "I will give you the land of Canaan, and it will belong to you."

¹²Then God's people were few in number.
They were strangers in the land.
¹³They went from one nation to another, from one kingdom to another.
¹⁴But the LORD did not let anyone hurt them;
he warned kings not to harm them.
¹⁵He said, "Don't touch my chosen people, and don't harm my prophets."

¹⁶God ordered a time of hunger in the land, and he destroyed all the food.

WHAT'S IN A word?

Psalm 104:3 "Your room above the clouds" is a poetic description of the heavenly dwelling place of God. Psalm 104 demonstrates that God's ways are higher than our ways. He is worthy of honor and praise!

Beauty BECOMES HER

The Health–Beauty Link

Taking better care of your body will naturally improve your appearance as well. Your skin, eyes, teeth, weight, and energy level will all benefit. There is also a mental component of well-being that is evident in your smile, alertness, and responsiveness. Whether you realize it or not, health and beauty are vitally linked together. In the same way, following God's commands will affect your ability to live a successful life. As Proverbs 3:1–2 tells us, "Do not forget my teaching, but keep my commands in mind. Then you will live a long time, and your life will be successful."

24 The LORD made his people grow in
number,
and he made them stronger than
their enemies.
25 He caused the Egyptians to hate his
people
and to make plans against his
servants.
26 Then he sent his servant Moses,
and Aaron, whom he had chosen.
27 They did many signs among the
Egyptians
and worked wonders in Egypt.
28 The LORD sent darkness and made
the land dark,
but the Egyptians turned
against what he said.
29 So he changed their water into
blood
and made their fish die.
30 Then their country was filled with
frogs,
even in the bedrooms of their
rulers.
31 The LORD spoke and flies came,
and gnats were everywhere in
the country.
32 He made hail fall like rain
and sent lightning through
their land.
33 He struck down their grapevines
and fig trees,
and he destroyed every tree in
the country.
34 He spoke and grasshoppers came;
the locusts were too many to
count.
35 They ate all the plants in the
land
and everything the earth
produced.

17 Then he sent a man ahead of
them—
Joseph, who was sold as a
slave.
18 They put chains around his feet
and an iron ring around his
neck.
19 Then the time he had spoken of
came,
and the LORD's words proved
that Joseph was right.
20 The king of Egypt sent for Joseph
and freed him;
the ruler of the people set him
free.
21 He made him the master of his
house;
Joseph was in charge of his
riches.

22 He could order the princes as he
wished.
He taught the older men to be
wise.
23 Then his father Israel came to
Egypt;
Jacob[n] lived in Egypt.[n]

fun FACTS

Women make up nearly 52% of all Internet users.

(Shop.org)

105:23 Jacob Also called Israel.   **105:23 Egypt** Literally, "the land of Ham." Also in verse 27. The people in Egypt were descendants of Ham, one of Noah's sons. See Genesis 10:6.

³⁶The LORD also killed all the
firstborn sons in the land,
the oldest son of each family.

³⁷Then he brought his people out,
and they carried with them
silver and gold.
Not one of his people stumbled.

HEALTH
Letting Go

When people hurt us emotionally or mentally—whether intentional or not—the pain often manifests itself in our physical bodies. Psalm 42:10 describes this phenomenon in the following way: "My enemies' insults make me feel as if my bones were broken. They are always saying, 'Where is your God?'" An unkind word or response can actually make us ache inside or feel nauseated. That's one reason God asks us to forgive others: letting go of that pain is not only for their benefit but also for our own. By pardoning others for their mistakes and wrongdoings, we find personal freedom and the keys to healthy living in every area.

³⁸The Egyptians were glad when they
left,
because the Egyptians were
afraid of them.
³⁹The LORD covered them with a
cloud
and lit up the night with fire.
⁴⁰When they asked, he brought them
quail
and filled them with bread from
heaven.

⁴¹God split the rock, and water
flowed out;
it ran like a river through the
desert.
⁴²He remembered his holy promise
to his servant Abraham.

⁴³So God brought his people out with
joy,
his chosen ones with singing.
⁴⁴He gave them lands of other
nations,
so they received what others
had worked for.
⁴⁵This was so they would keep his
orders
and obey his teachings.

Praise the LORD!

Israel's Failure to Trust God

106
Praise the LORD!

Thank the LORD because he is good.
His love continues forever.
²No one can tell all the mighty
things the LORD has done;
no one can speak all his
praise.
³Happy are those who do right,
who do what is fair at all times.

⁴LORD, remember me when you are
kind to your people;
help me when you save them.
⁵Let me see the good things you do
for your chosen people.
Let me be happy along with your
happy nation;
let me join your own people in
praising you.

⁶We have sinned just as our
ancestors did.
We have done wrong; we have
done evil.
⁷Our ancestors in Egypt
did not learn from your
miracles.
They did not remember all your
kindnesses,
so they turned against you at
the Red Sea.

⁸But the LORD saved them for his
  own sake,
    to show his great power.
⁹He commanded the Red Sea, and it
  dried up.
    He led them through the deep
    sea as if it were a desert.
¹⁰He saved them from those who
  hated them.
    He saved them from their
    enemies,
¹¹and the water covered their foes.
    Not one of them escaped.
¹²Then the people believed what the
  LORD said,
    and they sang praises to him.

¹³But they quickly forgot what he had
  done;
    they did not wait for his advice.
¹⁴They became greedy for food in the
  desert,
    and they tested God there.
¹⁵So he gave them what they wanted,
    but he also sent a terrible
    disease among them.

and worshiped a metal statue.
²⁰They exchanged their glorious God
  for a statue of a bull that eats
  grass.
²¹They forgot the God who saved
  them,
    who had done great things in
    Egypt,
²²who had done miracles in Egypt"
    and amazing things by the Red
    Sea.
²³So God said he would destroy them.
    But Moses, his chosen one, stood
    before him
    and stopped God's anger from
    destroying them.

²⁴Then they refused to go into the
  beautiful land of Canaan;
    they did not believe what God
    promised.
²⁵They grumbled in their tents
    and did not obey the LORD.
²⁶So he swore to them
    that they would die in the
    desert.

WISE WORDS

Contentment Begins Now

It's easy to look at another woman and think she has a picture-perfect life, especially when it appears that her bank account is a little healthier than yours is. But money doesn't buy happiness or contentment, and it certainly isn't the answer to every problem in life. Proverbs 17:1 says, "It is better to eat a dry crust of bread in peace than to have a feast where there is quarreling." In other words, sometimes less is more. Material wealth will never buy the things that really matter—like peace, joy, love, and faithfulness. Don't postpone contentment until you have a nicer car, the newest gadget, or a big promotion—make the choice today to be content right where you are!

fun FACTS

It's estimated that 28 million Americans have osteoporosis, but less than 15% know they do.

(Bottom Line)

¹⁶The people in the camp were
  jealous of Moses
    and of Aaron, the holy priest of
    the LORD.
¹⁷Then the ground opened up and
  swallowed Dathan
    and closed over Abiram's
    group.
¹⁸A fire burned among their
  followers,
    and flames burned up the
    wicked.

¹⁹The people made a gold calf at
  Mount Sinai

²⁷He said their children would be
  killed by other nations
    and that they would be scattered
    among other countries.

²⁸They joined in worshiping Baal at
  Peor
    and ate meat that had been
    sacrificed to lifeless statues.
²⁹They made the LORD angry by what
  they did,
    so many people became sick
    with a terrible disease.
³⁰But Phinehas prayed to the LORD,
    and the disease stopped.

³¹Phinehas did what was right,
    and it will be remembered from
    now on.
³²The people also made the LORD
    angry at Meribah,

and Moses was in trouble
    because of them.
[33]The people turned against the
    Spirit of God,
  so Moses spoke without
    stopping to think.

[34]The people did not destroy the
    other nations
  as the LORD had told them to do.
[35]Instead, they mixed with the other
    nations
  and learned their customs.

[36]They worshiped other nations'
    idols
  and were trapped by them.
[37]They even killed their sons and
    daughters
  as sacrifices to demons.
[38]They killed innocent people,
  their own sons and daughters,
  as sacrifices to the idols of Canaan.
  So the land was made unholy by
    their blood.
[39]The people became unholy by their
    sins;

they were unfaithful to God in
    what they did.
[40]So the LORD became angry with his
    people
  and hated his own children.
[41]He handed them over to other
    nations
  and let their enemies rule over
    them.
[42]Their enemies were cruel to them
  and kept them under their
    power.
[43]The LORD saved his people many
    times,
  but they continued to turn
    against him.
  So they became even more
    wicked.

[44]But God saw their misery
  when he heard their cry.
[45]He remembered his agreement
    with them,
  and he felt sorry for them
    because of his great love.
[46]He caused them to be pitied
  by those who held them
    captive.

[47]LORD our God, save us
  and bring us back from other
    nations.
  Then we will thank you
    and will gladly praise you.

[48]Praise the LORD, the God of Israel.
  He always was and always will be.
  Let all the people say, "Amen!"

Praise the LORD!

BOOK 5

God Saves from Many Dangers

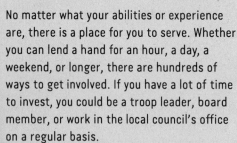

107 Thank the LORD
    because he is good.
  His love continues forever.
[2]That is what those whom the LORD
    has saved should say.
  He has saved them from the
    enemy
[3]and has gathered them from other
    lands,

Become INVOLVED

Girl Scouts of America

For more than ninety years, men and women have mentored girls through the Girl Scouts of the USA. Girl Scouts offers programs that build practical skills, encourage responsibility, and promote the development of strong leadership and decision-making skills.

No matter what your abilities or experience are, there is a place for you to serve. Whether you can lend a hand for an hour, a day, a weekend, or longer, there are hundreds of ways to get involved. If you have a lot of time to invest, you could be a troop leader, board member, or work in the local council's office on a regular basis.

Opportunities with smaller time commitments also abound. You could teach a workshop about your hobby or passion, help girls explore possible careers, or suggest service projects to benefit the community. You could be a public relations consultant and communicate with the local media about your troop's events, activities, and projects. You could even put your computer skills to work designing a troop's Web site.

If you want to instill confidence in girls and help them realize their full potential, the Girl Scouts is the organization for you. For more information, visit www.girlscouts.org.

from east and west, north and
south.

⁴Some people had wandered in the
desert lands.
They found no city in which to
live.
⁵They were hungry and thirsty,
and they were discouraged.
⁶In their misery they cried out to the
LORD,
and he saved them from their
troubles.
⁷He led them on a straight road
to a city where they could
live.
⁸Let them give thanks to the LORD
for his love
and for the miracles he does for
people.
⁹He satisfies the thirsty
and fills up the hungry.

¹⁰Some sat in gloom and darkness;
they were prisoners suffering in
chains.
¹¹They had turned against the words
of God
and had refused the advice of
God Most High.
¹²So he broke their pride by hard
work.
They stumbled, and no one
helped.
¹³In their misery they cried out to the
LORD,
and he saved them from their
troubles.
¹⁴He brought them out of their
gloom and darkness
and broke their chains.
¹⁵Let them give thanks to the LORD
for his love
and for the miracles he does for
people.
¹⁶He breaks down bronze gates
and cuts apart iron bars.

¹⁷Some fools turned against God
and suffered for the evil they
did.
¹⁸They refused to eat anything,
so they almost died.

MONEY

The Dark Side of Bankruptcy

Bankruptcy is a last resort for people who have bor-
rowed too much money and can't pay it back. Two
common forms of bankruptcy are Chapter 7 and
Chapter 11. Under Chapter 7, every possession (with
the possible exception of a home) is sold in order to
pay back the creditors. The debt—other than student loans, child support, alimony, income taxes,
and fines—are permanently erased. Chapter 11 is
less severe. Instead of selling everything, the consumer repays as much of the debt as possible over a
three- to five-year period with the help of a cus-
tomized repayment plan.

Some people look at bankruptcy as an easy way out,
but this isn't the case. Bankruptcy is expensive.
Attorney fees and court costs add up, and they
won't disappear. Not only does bankruptcy damage
your credit history, it can also take a heavy toll on
your relationships and quality of life. In addition,
bankruptcy does nothing to solve spending problems. If you are in the habit of spending more than
you make, bankruptcy won't fix the core problem—
overspending. That's why almost half of all people
who file for bankruptcy do it again six years later,
as soon as the law allows. If at all possible, you
should avoid bankruptcy, not just because it hurts
your credit rating but also because it hurts you.

ETIQUETTE 101

HOW FRIENDLY IS FRIENDLY ENOUGH?

In the age of iPods and PDAs, it's easy to tune out the world around you. But to maintain a civilized society, personal interaction is still essential. Most commuters on public transportation expect to ride in silence, so conversation should be by mutual consent. (Few people appreciate a "Chatty Cathy." See Proverbs 9:13–15.) In elevators, offer brief hellos, and if you are closest to the panel, ask other riders for floor numbers. Likewise, on sidewalks and in stores, simple niceties—"Excuse me," "Thank you," and so forth—are sufficient. Never underestimate the power of a friendly smile.

¹⁹In their misery they cried out to
the LORD,
and he saved them from their
troubles.
²⁰God gave the command and healed
them,
so they were saved from
dying.
²¹Let them give thanks to the LORD
for his love
and for the miracles he does for
people.
²²Let them offer sacrifices to thank
him.
With joy they should tell what
he has done.

²³Others went out to sea in ships
and did business on the great
oceans.
²⁴They saw what the LORD could do,
the miracles he did in the deep
oceans.
²⁵He spoke, and a storm came up,
which blew up high waves.
²⁶The ships were tossed as high as
the sky and fell low to the
depths.
The storm was so bad that they
lost their courage.
²⁷They stumbled and fell like people
who were drunk.
They did not know what to do.
²⁸In their misery they cried out to
the LORD,
and he saved them from their
troubles.
²⁹He stilled the storm
and calmed the waves.
³⁰They were happy that it was quiet,
and God guided them to the
port they wanted.
³¹Let them give thanks to the LORD
for his love
and for the miracles he does for
people.
³²Let them praise his greatness in
the meeting of the people;
let them praise him in the
meeting of the elders.

³³He changed rivers into a desert
and springs of water into dry
ground.
³⁴He made fertile land salty,
because the people there did evil.
³⁵He changed the desert into pools of
water
and dry ground into springs of
water.
³⁶He had the hungry settle there
so they could build a city in
which to live.
³⁷They planted seeds in the fields
and vineyards,
and they had a good harvest.
³⁸God blessed them, and they grew in
number.
Their cattle did not become
fewer.

³⁹Because of disaster, troubles, and
sadness,
their families grew smaller and
weaker.
⁴⁰He showed he was displeased with
their leaders
and made them wander in a
pathless desert.
⁴¹But he lifted the poor out of their
suffering
and made their families grow
like flocks of sheep.
⁴²Good people see this and are happy,
but the wicked say nothing.

WHAT'S IN A word?

Psalm 107:33 "Rivers into a desert" illustrates God's power over nature to accomplish his will. Whether he turns rivers into a desert or dry ground into springs of water (verse 35), God knows what lessons we need to learn and the best way for us to learn them. Trust his timing and his plan!

43Whoever is wise will remember
these things
and will think about the love of
the Lord.

A Prayer for Victory

A song. A psalm of David.

108 God, my heart is
steady.
I will sing and praise you with
all my being.
2Wake up, harp and lyre!
I will wake up the dawn.
3Lord, I will praise you among the
nations;
I will sing songs of praise about
you to all the nations.
4Your great love reaches to the
skies,
your truth to the heavens.
5God, you are supreme above the skies.
Let your glory be over all the
earth.

6Answer us and save us by your
power
so the people you love will be
rescued.
7God has said from his Temple,
"When I win, I will divide
Shechem
and measure off the Valley of
Succoth.
8Gilead and Manasseh are mine.
Ephraim is like my helmet.
Judah holds my royal scepter.
9Moab is like my washbowl.
I throw my sandals at Edom.
I shout at Philistia."

10Who will bring me to the strong,
walled city?
Who will lead me to Edom?
11God, surely you have rejected us;
you do not go out with our
armies.
12Help us fight the enemy.
Human help is useless,

Q: THE BIBLE SAYS I AM SUPPOSED TO HONOR MY PARENTS, BUT ONE OF THEM WAS ABUSIVE TO ME. HOW CAN I POSSIBLY HONOR THAT PARENT?

A: You can honor your abusive parent through forgiveness, even if the parent is not repentant. Pray for your parent, and ask the Lord to transform your attitude and actions. By obeying God's word and honoring your parents (Exodus 20:12), you can rest assured that you are pleasing God, regardless of your parent's behavior. This road of forgiveness is not an easy one to walk, but God will be right by your side. Lean on him for your strength.

Seven ways to...

Study the Bible

1. Ask God to open your eyes and heart before you begin reading.

2. Read whole chapters and books for an overview of Scripture.

3. Read and re-read smaller passages for more depth.

4. Pick a verse to memorize this week.

5. Make notes on what a passage reveals about God.

6. Underline or circle meaningful verses.

7. Use colored pencils or markers to highlight different themes.

13but we can win with God's help.
He will defeat our enemies.

A Prayer Against an Enemy

For the director of music. A psalm of David.

109 God, I praise you.
Do not be silent.

august

Clean out your e-mail folders. 1	Don't forget to practice personal safety, especially when you're traveling alone. 2	3	4	*Get outside and go for a walk today.* 5
National Fresh Breath Day. Don't forget to brush, floss, and use mouthwash. 6	7	Pray for a person of influence: Scott Stapp, formerly of Creed, is having a birthday. 8	9	Read Psalm 128. Make a list of God's blessings in your life. 10
11	Spot check your financial situation. Do you need to make any changes? 12	13	Pray for a person of influence: It's Halle Berry's birthday. 14	Take a nap on your next day off. Rest is good for you. 15
Pray for a person of influence: It's Madonna's birthday. 16	Don't forget the importance of a smile. 17	18	Pray for a person of influence: It's Matthew Perry's birthday. 19	20
21	22	Look for ways to share your faith at work. 23	*Clean your car today.* 24	Pray for a person of influence: Sean Connery is having a birthday. 25
Go through your clothes and donate what you seldom wear. 26	27	28	Instead of watching television one night this week, spend an extra hour with God. 29	30
Look at the sky tonight. Reflect on God's majesty. 31				

"I didn't find my friends; the good God gave them to me."
–Ralph Waldo Emerson

Life Issues

Friendship

Do you have good friends? Friends that stick by you in any circumstance and strengthen your faith? If you see yourself as a loner, are too busy to find friends, or only have friends who do not share your spiritual beliefs, you are missing out on fellowship. Proverbs 18:24 describes a real friend as one who is "more loyal than a brother." In order for God to fill your life with friends who can give wise counsel, bless you, and love you with Christ's love, you need to put yourself in places where you can meet them. Sounds simple, right? Make time for Sunday school, singles' groups, or a women's Bible study where you can get to know other women who also want to be plugged in to fellowship and friendship. Take the initiative and introduce yourself, and give the group more than one try. The effort could result in lifelong Christian friendships.

²Wicked people and liars have
   spoken against me;
   they have told lies about me.
³They have said hateful things about
   me
   and attack me for no reason.
⁴They attacked me, even though I
   loved them
   and prayed for them.
⁵I was good to them, but they repay
   me with evil.
   I loved them, but they hate me
   in return.

⁶They say about me, "Have an evil
   person work against him,
   and let an accuser stand against
   him.
⁷When he is judged, let him be
   found guilty,
   and let even his prayers show his
   guilt.
⁸Let his life be cut short,
   and let another man replace him
   as leader.
⁹Let his children become orphans

and his wife a widow.
¹⁰Make his children wander around,
   begging for food.
   Let them be forced out of the
   ruins in which they live.
¹¹Let the people to whom he owes
   money take everything he
   owns,

Solomon

When God told Solomon he would give him whatever he asked for, Solomon hit the jackpot! He asked for wisdom, and that choice pleased God so much that he gave Solomon all the rest, too. In the early days of his reign, Solomon was a man of God to be admired. Then, Solomon seemed to let his greatness go to his head. For a wise man, he made some pretty unwise moves that ultimately cost him his kingdom. Solomon serves as a reminder that we need to always obey God in every way, no matter how powerful we think we are.

and let strangers steal
   everything he has worked
   for.
¹²Let no one show him love
   or have mercy on his orphaned
   children.
¹³Let all his descendants die
   and be forgotten by those who
   live after him.
¹⁴LORD, remember how wicked his
   ancestors were,
   and don't let the sins of his
   mother be wiped out.
¹⁵LORD, always remember their sins.
   Then make people forget about
   them completely.

¹⁶"He did not remember to be loving.
   He hurt the poor, the needy, and
   those who were sad
   until they were nearly dead.
¹⁷He loved to put curses on others,
   so let those same curses fall on
   him.
   He did not like to bless others,
   so do not let good things
   happen to him.
¹⁸He cursed others as often as he
   wore clothes.

**BIBLE
*Women
& Men***

Cursing others filled his body
and his life,
like drinking water and using
olive oil.

¹⁹So let curses cover him like clothes
and wrap around him like a
belt."

²⁰May the LORD do these things to
those who accuse me,

WISE WORDS

Stay Humble

Although humility should characterize every Christian's life, pride has a way of creeping in unannounced if we let it get a foothold. Pride can manifest itself in our actions, thoughts, responses to others, and the way we carry ourselves. Any time we place greater value on ourselves than others, we become vulnerable to the sin of pride. Then we're venturing into dangerous territory. Proverbs 18:12 says, "Proud people will be ruined, but the humble will be honored." In other words, God tears down the proud, but he lifts up the humble. It definitely takes conscious effort to place others first, but God wants us to walk in humility in our relationships with others and with him.

Q: MY HUSBAND IS NOT A CHRISTIAN. HOW CAN I GET HIM TO BECOME A BELIEVER?

A: Only God can work on your husband's heart, so that means your responsibility is to live your life in a way that honors Christ's presence in your life. Pray for your husband and demonstrate how God has changed your heart by loving and serving your husband to the very best of your ability. As you grow spiritually and become more like Christ, you will naturally exhibit more "love, joy, peace, patience, kindness, goodness, faithfulness, gentleness, [and] self-control" (Galatians 5:22–23). Even if your husband doesn't express it right away, he'll notice the changes in you.

to those who speak evil against
me.

²¹But you, Lord GOD,
be kind to me so others will
know you are good.
Because your love is good, save
me.

²²I am poor and helpless
and very sad.

²³I am dying like an evening
shadow;
I am shaken off like a locust.

²⁴My knees are weak from fasting,
and I have grown thin.

²⁵My enemies insult me;
they look at me and shake their
heads.

²⁶LORD my God, help me;
because you are loving, save
me.

²⁷Then they will know that your
power has done this;
they will know that you have
done it, LORD.

²⁸They may curse me, but you bless
me.
They may attack me, but they
will be disgraced.
Then I, your servant, will be
glad.

²⁹Let those who accuse me be
disgraced
and covered with shame like a
coat.

³⁰I will thank the LORD very much;
I will praise him in front of
many people.

³¹He defends the helpless
and saves them from those who
accuse them.

The Lord Appoints a King

A psalm of David.

110 The LORD said to my Lord,
"Sit by me at my right side
  until I put your enemies under
  your control."
[2]The LORD will enlarge your
  kingdom beyond
  Jerusalem,
and you will rule over your
  enemies.
[3]Your people will join you on your
  day of battle.
You have been dressed in
  holiness from birth;
you have the freshness of a
  child.

[4]The LORD has made a promise
  and will not change his mind.
He said, "You are a priest forever,
  a priest like Melchizedek."

[5]The Lord is beside you to help
  you.
When he becomes angry, he will
  crush kings.

[6]He will judge those nations, filling
  them with dead bodies;
he will defeat rulers all over the
  world.
[7]The king will drink from the brook
  on the way.
Then he will be strengthened.

Praise the Lord's Goodness

111 Praise the LORD!

I will thank the LORD with all my
  heart
  in the meeting of his good
  people.
[2]The LORD does great things;
  those who enjoy them seek
  them.
[3]What he does is glorious and
  splendid,
  and his goodness continues
  forever.
[4]His miracles are unforgettable.
  The LORD is kind and merciful.
[5]He gives food to those who fear
  him.
  He remembers his agreement
  forever.

[6]He has shown his people his power
  when he gave them the lands of
  other nations.

[7]Everything he does is good and fair;
  all his orders can be trusted.
[8]They will continue forever.
  They were made true and right.
[9]He sets his people free.
  He made his agreement
  everlasting.
  He is holy and wonderful.

[10]Wisdom begins with respect for the
  LORD;
  those who obey his orders have
  good understanding.
  He should be praised forever.

Honest People Are Blessed

112 Praise the LORD!

Happy are those who respect the
  LORD,
  who want what he commands.
[2]Their descendants will be powerful
  in the land;
  the children of honest people
  will be blessed.

RELATIONSHIPS

Insecurity

Song of Songs is perhaps the greatest love story
ever told, full of passion and ecstasy. But what you
may have missed is an issue almost all women
struggle with: insecurity. In the opening chapter,
the woman isn't bragging about her great tan—
she's expressing an intimate concern about how
she looks (verse 6). Body image isn't a modern
issue—Adam and Eve became acutely aware and
ashamed of their naked bodies after sin entered
the picture (see Genesis 3:7-10). If insecurity is
hindering your ability to express love in a relationship, understand that physical beauty is only one
element of attraction. (There's something especially attractive about confidence!) You are a magnificent creation of a loving God; if you know that
in your heart, it will show in your life.

Balancing Act

We Need to Talk

There is a time to talk and a time to close your mouth. Studies show that women need to speak ten- to twenty-thousand words per day, so keeping your mouth shut may be easier *said* than done (get it?). It's not that talking is a bad thing. Talking helps you communicate, resolve differences, express your needs, and connect with others. However, too much talking tempts others to tune you out—and gives you precious little opportunity to really listen. Psalm 46:10 says it's important to be quiet and know that God is God. The point is that you might miss God's answer when he speaks to you if you are too busy running your mouth instead of listening. Next time you get alone with God, try being quiet and waiting for what he has to say.

³Their houses will be full of wealth and riches,
  and their goodness will continue forever.
⁴A light shines in the dark for honest people,
  for those who are merciful and kind and good.
⁵It is good to be merciful and generous.
  Those who are fair in their business
⁶will never be defeated.
  Good people will always be remembered.
⁷They won't be afraid of bad news;
  their hearts are steady because they trust the LORD.
⁸They are confident and will not be afraid;
  they will look down on their enemies.
⁹They give freely to the poor.
  The things they do are right and will continue forever.
  They will be given great honor.
¹⁰The wicked will see this and become angry;
  they will grind their teeth in anger and then disappear.
  The wishes of the wicked will come to nothing.

Praise for the Lord's Kindness

113 Praise the LORD!

Praise him, you servants of the LORD;
  praise the name of the LORD.
²The LORD's name should be praised now and forever.
³The LORD's name should be praised from where the sun rises to where it sets.
⁴The LORD is supreme over all the nations;
  his glory reaches to the skies.

⁵No one is like the LORD our God,
  who rules from heaven,
⁶who bends down to look
  at the skies and the earth.
⁷The LORD lifts the poor from the dirt
  and takes the helpless from the ashes.
⁸He seats them with princes,
  the princes of his people.
⁹He gives children to the woman who has none
  and makes her a happy mother.

Praise the LORD!

God Brought Israel from Egypt

114 When the Israelites went out of Egypt,
  the people of Jacob left that foreign country.
²Then Judah became God's holy place;
  Israel became the land he ruled.

³The Red Sea looked and ran away;
  the Jordan River turned back.
⁴The mountains danced like sheep
  and the hills like little lambs.
⁵Sea, why did you run away?
  Jordan, why did you turn back?
⁶Mountains, why did you dance like sheep?
  Hills, why did you dance like little lambs?

⁷Earth, shake with fear before the Lord,
  before the God of Jacob.
⁸He turned a rock into a pool of water,
  a hard rock into a spring of water.

The One True God

115 It does not belong to us, LORD.
  The glory belongs to you
  because of your love and loyalty.

²Why do the nations ask,
  "Where is their God?"
³Our God is in heaven.
  He does what he pleases.
⁴Their idols are made of silver and gold,
  the work of human hands.
⁵They have mouths, but they cannot speak.
  They have eyes, but they cannot see.

⁶They have ears, but they cannot
   hear.
   They have noses, but they
   cannot smell.
⁷They have hands, but they cannot
   feel.
   They have feet, but they cannot
   walk.
   No sounds come from their
   throats.
⁸People who make idols will be like
   them,
   and so will those who trust
   them.
⁹Family of Israel, trust the LORD;
   he is your helper and your
   protection.
¹⁰Family of Aaron, trust the LORD;
   he is your helper and your
   protection.
¹¹You who respect the LORD should
   trust him;
   he is your helper and your
   protection.

but he gave the earth to people.
¹⁷Dead people do not praise the LORD;
   those in the grave are silent.
¹⁸But we will praise the LORD
   now and forever.

Praise the LORD!

Thanksgiving for Escaping Death

116 I love the LORD,
   because he listens
   to my prayers
   for help.
²He paid attention to me,
   so I will call to him for help as
   long as I live.
³The ropes of death bound me,
   and the fear of the grave took
   hold of me.
   I was troubled and sad.
⁴Then I called out the name of the
   LORD.
   I said, "Please, LORD, save me!"

Thirst for God

"As a deer thirsts for streams of water, so I thirst for you, God" (Psalm 42:1). We sing this verse in a popular worship song, but are we living with a genuine thirst for more of God in our lives? It seems like a strange thing to pray for—"More thirst, please, Lord!"—and yet that's exactly what we should want. Ask God to give you a sincere thirst for him; then allow him to fill your soul from the spring of living water (see John 4:13).

A study of Americans ages 30 to 60 found that 45% of men and 25% of women snore.

(AARP)

¹²The LORD remembers us and will
   bless us.
   He will bless the family of Israel;
   he will bless the family of Aaron.
¹³The LORD will bless those who
   respect him,
   from the smallest to the
   greatest.
¹⁴May the LORD give you success,
   and may he give you and your
   children success.
¹⁵May you be blessed by the LORD,
   who made heaven and earth.

¹⁶Heaven belongs to the LORD,

⁵The LORD is kind and does what is
   right;
   our God is merciful.
⁶The LORD watches over the foolish;
   when I was helpless, he saved me.
⁷I said to myself, "Relax,
   because the LORD takes care of
   you."
⁸Lord, you saved me from death.
   You stopped my eyes from
   crying;
   you kept me from being
   defeated.
⁹So I will walk with the LORD
   in the land of the living.

¹⁰I believed, so I said,
   "I am completely ruined."
¹¹In my distress I said,
   "All people are liars."

¹²What can I give the LORD
   for all the good things he has
   given to me?

¹³I will lift up the cup of salvation,
   and I will pray to the LORD.
¹⁴I will give the LORD what I promised
   in front of all his people.

¹⁵The death of one that belongs to
      the LORD
   is precious in his sight.
¹⁶LORD, I am your servant;
   I am your servant and the son of
      your female servant.
   You have freed me from my chains.
¹⁷I will give you an offering to show
      thanks to you,

and I will pray to the LORD.
¹⁸I will give the LORD what I
      promised
   in front of all his people,
¹⁹in the Temple courtyards
   in Jerusalem.

Praise the LORD!

A Hymn of Praise

117
All you nations,
   praise the LORD.
All you people, praise him

because the LORD loves us very much,
   and his truth is everlasting.

Praise the LORD!

Thanksgiving for Victory

118
Thank the LORD
   because he is good.
His love continues forever.
²Let the people of Israel say,
   "His love continues forever."
³Let the family of Aaron say,
   "His love continues forever."
⁴Let those who respect the LORD say,
   "His love continues forever."

⁵I was in trouble, so I called to the
      LORD.
   The LORD answered me and set
      me free.
⁶I will not be afraid, because the
      LORD is with me.
   People can't do anything to me.
⁷The LORD is with me to help me,
   so I will see my enemies
      defeated.
⁸It is better to trust the LORD
   than to trust people.
⁹It is better to trust the LORD
   than to trust princes.

¹⁰All the nations surrounded me,
   but I defeated them in the name
      of the LORD.
¹¹They surrounded me on every side,
   but with the LORD's power I
      defeated them.
¹²They surrounded me like a swarm
      of bees,
   but they died as quickly as
      thorns burn.
   By the LORD's power, I defeated
      them.
¹³They chased me until I was almost
      defeated,
   but the LORD helped me.
¹⁴The LORD gives me strength and a
      song.
   He has saved me.

¹⁵Shouts of joy and victory
   come from the tents of those
      who do right:

Love

Trust God's Love

A trustworthy friend is a blessing we all hope to have. But trust doesn't come easily; it's earned by consistent honorable behavior. If you have been hurt or betrayed, it's easy to lose your trust in just about everyone. We all make mistakes. We fail. We disappoint. But God's love never disappoints! Psalm 59:9-10 says, "God, my strength, I am looking to you, because God is my defender. My God loves me, and he goes in front of me. He will help me defeat my enemies." God is our protector, caregiver, and constant companion. Listen to David's instruction—coming from personal experience, no doubt—in Psalm 62:8: "People, trust God all the time. Tell him all your problems, because God is our protection."

"The LORD has done powerful
things."
[16]The power of the LORD has won the
victory;
with his power the LORD has
done mighty things.

[17]I will not die, but live,
and I will tell what the LORD has
done.
[18]The LORD has taught me a hard
lesson,
but he did not let me die.

[19]Open for me the Temple gates.
Then I will come in and thank
the LORD.

With branches in your hands, join
the feast.
Come to the corners of the altar.
[28]You are my God, and I will thank
you;
you are my God, and I will praise
your greatness.
[29]Thank the LORD because he is good.
His love continues forever.

The Word of God

119 Happy are those who
live pure lives,
who follow the LORD's teachings.
[2]Happy are those who keep his
rules,

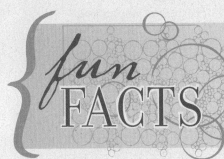

**35% of Americans say
they have been through a
breakup at least once in
the past 10 years.**

(Market Facts)

[20]This is the LORD's gate;
only those who are good may
enter through it.
[21]LORD, I thank you for answering me.
You have saved me.

[22]The stone that the builders
rejected
became the cornerstone.
[23]The LORD did this,
and it is wonderful to us.
[24]This is the day that the LORD has
made.
Let us rejoice and be glad today!

[25]Please, LORD, save us;
please, LORD, give us success.
[26]God bless the one who comes in the
name of the LORD.
We bless all of you from the
Temple of the LORD.
[27]The LORD is God,
and he has shown kindness to
us.

who try to obey him with their
whole heart.
[3]They don't do what is wrong;
they follow his ways.
[4]LORD, you gave your orders
to be obeyed completely.
[5]I wish I were more loyal
in obeying your demands.
[6]Then I would not be ashamed
when I study your commands.
[7]When I learned that your laws are
fair,
I praised you with an honest
heart.
[8]I will obey your demands,
so please don't ever leave me.
[9]How can a young person live a pure
life?
By obeying your word.
[10]With all my heart I try to obey you.
Don't let me break your
commands.
[11]I have taken your words to heart

WISE WORDS

God Keeps the Master Plan

Did you envision every detail
of your wedding before you
knew the groom or choose a
nursery theme long before a
positive pregnancy test an-
nounced the news? If so,
you're not alone! Though
some women plan more
than others do, it is not uncommon to spend time day-
dreaming and planning for
the future. No matter your
plans, it's important to remember that God is ulti-
mately in control. Proverbs
19:21 says, "People can
make all kinds of plans, but
only the LORD's plan will
happen." That's why it's so
important to ask God to
align your desires and plans
with his. You can trust him
to work out all the details
because his master plan is
better than you could ever
imagine.

so I would not sin against you.
[12]LORD, you should be praised.
Teach me your demands.
[13]My lips will tell about
all the laws you have spoken.
[14]I enjoy living by your rules
as people enjoy great riches.

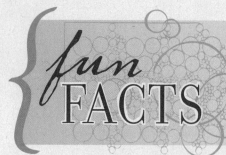

fun FACTS

84% of rape victims never file a police report.

(Oprah.com)

¹⁵I think about your orders
  and study your ways.
¹⁶I enjoy obeying your demands,
  and I will not forget your
  word.

¹⁷Do good to me, your servant, so I
  can live,
  so I can obey your word.
¹⁸Open my eyes to see
  the miracles in your teachings.
¹⁹I am a stranger on earth.
  Do not hide your commands
  from me.
²⁰I wear myself out with desire
  for your laws all the time.
²¹You scold proud people;
  those who ignore your
  commands are cursed.
²²Don't let me be insulted and hated
  because I keep your rules.
²³Even if princes speak against me,
  I, your servant, will think about
  your demands.
²⁴Your rules give me pleasure;
  they give me good advice.

²⁵I am about to die.
  Give me life, as you have
  promised.
²⁶I told you about my life, and you
  answered me.
  Teach me your demands.
²⁷Help me understand your
  orders.
  Then I will think about your
  miracles.
²⁸I am sad and tired.
  Make me strong again as you
  have promised.
²⁹Don't let me be dishonest;
  have mercy on me by helping
  me obey your teachings.

³⁰I have chosen the way of truth;
  I have obeyed your laws.
³¹I hold on to your rules.
  LORD, do not let me be
  disgraced.
³²I will quickly obey your commands,
  because you have made me
  happy.

³³LORD, teach me your demands,
  and I will keep them until the
  end.
³⁴Help me understand, so I can keep
  your teachings,
  obeying them with all my heart.

³⁵Lead me in the path of your
  commands,
  because that makes me happy.
³⁶Make me want to keep your rules
  instead of wishing for riches.
³⁷Keep me from looking at worthless
  things.
  Let me live by your word.
³⁸Keep your promise to me, your
  servant,
  so you will be respected.
³⁹Take away the shame I fear,
  because your laws are good.
⁴⁰How I want to follow your
  orders.
  Give me life because of your
  goodness.

⁴¹LORD, show me your love,
  and save me as you have
  promised.

BE STILL & KNOW

How Jesus Prayed

Although his words in Matthew 6:9–13 are commonly referred to as the Lord's Prayer, Jesus' real intent was to give his followers a template for their own prayer lives. In his introduction, Jesus illustrates that God is as intimate and close as he is awe-inspiring and divine. This sets the stage for the second section in which Jesus expresses his desire for God to reign on earth and accomplish his will as he does in heaven. Only then does Jesus petition God with his requests. He asks God for the fulfillment of physical needs, forgiveness of sins, and deliverance from Satan's temptations. Now that's the perfect primer for prayer!

Surviving Singleness

ERIN'S STORY

I have known many people who always wanted to be married. Many of my closest female friends had already picked out their wedding gowns, flowers, and bridesmaids by the time they were sixteen. I was amazed that they could describe their weddings in such detail even when there weren't any grooms on the horizon.

As for me, I knew I wanted to get married, but I also knew there was a lot I wanted to do before I settled down. I spent most of my twenties enjoying my singleness and all the freedom that came with it. I traveled, spent time with friends, and put in extra time at work. I enjoyed church and looked for ways to grow in my relationship with God—through prayer, fellowship, and study. I was so busy loving God, my friends, and my life that I almost forgot that I was single—until I turned 27. I don't know what happened, but suddenly I realized that I was alone. I suddenly *felt* alone.

> I REMEMBER FEELING AWKWARD ABOUT MY SINGLENESS AT DINNER PARTIES I ATTENDED.

I remember feeling awkward about my singleness at dinner parties I attended. I grew tired of people asking if there was someone special in my life. I spent time in prayer, struggling with God—asking him why he hadn't brought anyone into my life. It was during this time that I stumbled upon Isaiah 43:1-2: "Don't be afraid, because I have saved you. I have called you by name, and you are mine. When you pass through the waters, I will be with you." While this passage is an exchange between God and Israel, I felt like God was speaking directly to me. It was a powerful reminder that God had not forgotten me or abandoned me.

I clung to that verse for several years until I met the godly man who eventually became my husband. Even to this day, that verse serves as a reminder that God is always faithful and can sustain us through anything—no matter how big or small the challenge may be.

What's the
POINT?

Psalm 119:45

Can you really experience freedom if you have to follow rules and live within boundaries? Even though this sounds paradoxical, the answer is absolutely yes. For example, studies show that if an unfenced playground is close to a busy street, most children will play in the middle of the playground, far away from the street. They do not even go close to the sides or enjoy any part of the play area except the part that feels the safest. However, if a fence is put around the outside of the playground, children will run and play throughout the whole area, even right up to the fence. The boundary actually gives them the freedom of knowing they are safe. It expands their world. Your life with God is no different. Like the children on the playground, you feel freer inside when you follow his rules because you know that the rules are designed to keep you safe. Sure, there are boundaries, but those limitations allow you more room to experience all of life. When God gives a command for you to follow, it's not because he wants to put a damper on your fun. Instead, he wants you to choose a life that is healthy, free, and whole.

⁴²I have an answer for people who
    insult me,
    because I trust what you say.
⁴³Never keep me from speaking your
    truth,
    because I depend on your fair
    laws.
⁴⁴I will obey your teachings
    forever and ever.
⁴⁵So I will live in freedom,
    because I want to follow your
    orders.
⁴⁶I will discuss your rules with kings
    and will not be ashamed.
⁴⁷I enjoy obeying your commands,
    which I love.
⁴⁸I praise your commands, which I
    love,
    and I think about your demands.

⁴⁹Remember your promise to me,
    your servant;
    it gives me hope.
⁵⁰When I suffer, this comforts me:
    Your promise gives me life.
⁵¹Proud people always make fun of
    me,
    but I do not reject your
    teachings.
⁵²I remember your laws from long
    ago,
    and they comfort me, LORD.
⁵³I become angry with wicked people
    who do not keep your teachings.
⁵⁴I sing about your demands
    wherever I live.
⁵⁵LORD, I remember you at night,
    and I will obey your teachings.
⁵⁶This is what I do:
    I follow your orders.

⁵⁷LORD, you are my share in life;
    I have promised to obey your
    words.
⁵⁸I prayed to you with all my heart.
    Have mercy on me as you have
    promised.
⁵⁹I thought about my life,
    and I decided to follow your
    rules.
⁶⁰I hurried and did not wait
    to obey your commands.

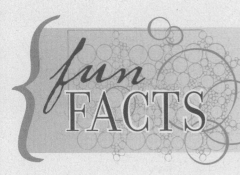

fun FACTS

The average adult Internet user receives 155 unsolicited e-mail messages every week.

(Kiplinger's)

61 Wicked people have tied me up,
 but I have not forgotten your teachings.
62 In the middle of the night, I get up to thank you
 because your laws are right.
63 I am a friend to everyone who fears you,
 to anyone who obeys your orders.
64 LORD, your love fills the earth.
 Teach me your demands.

65 You have done good things for your servant,
 as you have promised, LORD.
66 Teach me wisdom and knowledge
 because I trust your commands.
67 Before I suffered, I did wrong,
 but now I obey your word.
68 You are good, and you do what is good.
 Teach me your demands.
69 Proud people have made up lies about me,
 but I will follow your orders with all my heart.
70 Those people have no feelings,
 but I love your teachings.
71 It was good for me to suffer
 so I would learn your demands.
72 Your teachings are worth more to me
 than thousands of pieces of gold and silver.

73 You made me and formed me with your hands.
 Give me understanding so I can learn your commands.
74 Let those who respect you rejoice when they see me,
 because I put my hope in your word.
75 LORD, I know that your laws are right
 and that it was right for you to punish me.
76 Comfort me with your love,
 as you promised me, your servant.
77 Have mercy on me so that I may live.
 I love your teachings.
78 Make proud people ashamed because they lied about me.

But I will think about your orders.
79 Let those who respect you return to me,
 those who know your rules.
80 Let me obey your demands perfectly
 so I will not be ashamed.

81 I am weak from waiting for you to save me,
 but I hope in your word.
82 My eyes are tired from looking for your promise.
 When will you comfort me?
83 Even though I am like a wine bag going up in smoke,
 I do not forget your demands.
84 How long will I live?
 When will you judge those who are hurting me?
85 Proud people have dug pits to trap me.
 They have nothing to do with your teachings.

Q: IF I ASKED GOD TO FORGIVE ME FOR MY SINS, DO I STILL HAVE TO TELL SOMEONE ELSE WHAT I DID WRONG?

A: James 5:16 says, "Confess your sins to each other and pray for each other so God can heal you." If your sin affected others, you need to confess to them and make amends. If you believe your sin affected only you, it is still cleansing to confess to someone you trust and have accountability in that area of temptation. God has forgiven you, even if you do not tell another soul. However, his Word instructs us to let others in on it.

⁸⁶All of your commands can be
trusted.
Liars are hurting me. Help me!
⁸⁷They have almost put me in the
grave,
but I have not rejected your
orders.
⁸⁸Give me life by your love
so I can obey your rules.

⁸⁹LORD, your word is everlasting;
it continues forever in heaven.
⁹⁰Your loyalty will go on and on;
you made the earth, and it still
stands.
⁹¹All things continue to this day
because of your laws,

because all things serve you.
⁹²If I had not loved your teachings,
I would have died from my
sufferings.
⁹³I will never forget your orders,
because you have given me life
by them.
⁹⁴I am yours. Save me.
I want to obey your orders.
⁹⁵Wicked people are waiting to
destroy me,
but I will think about your rules.
⁹⁶Everything I see has its limits,
but your commands have none.

⁹⁷How I love your teachings!
I think about them all day long.
⁹⁸Your commands make me wiser
than my enemies,
because they are mine forever.

⁹⁹I am wiser than all my teachers,
because I think about your
rules.
¹⁰⁰I have more understanding than
the elders,
because I follow your orders.
¹⁰¹I have avoided every evil way
so I could obey your word.
¹⁰²I haven't walked away from your
laws,
because you yourself are my
teacher.
¹⁰³Your promises are sweet to me,
sweeter than honey in my
mouth!
¹⁰⁴Your orders give me
understanding,
so I hate lying ways.

¹⁰⁵Your word is like a lamp for my
feet
and a light for my path.
¹⁰⁶I will do what I have promised
and obey your fair laws.
¹⁰⁷I have suffered for a long time.
LORD, give me life by your word.
¹⁰⁸LORD, accept my willing praise
and teach me your laws.
¹⁰⁹My life is always in danger,
but I haven't forgotten your
teachings.
¹¹⁰Wicked people have set a trap for
me,
but I haven't strayed from your
orders.
¹¹¹I will follow your rules forever,
because they make me happy.
¹¹²I will try to do what you demand
forever, until the end.
¹¹³I hate disloyal people,
but I love your teachings.
¹¹⁴You are my hiding place and my
shield;
I hope in your word.
¹¹⁵Get away from me, you who do evil,
so I can keep my God's
commands.
¹¹⁶Support me as you promised so I
can live.
Don't let me be embarrassed
because of my hopes.
¹¹⁷Help me, and I will be saved.

Beauty BECOMES HER

Puffiness

If you have puffiness around your eyes, consider applying cool cucumber or potato slices for about five to fifteen minutes. If neither is available, you can use cool, damp teabags after making a pitcher of tea. Unfortunately, it's not just the area around our eyes that can get puffed up. Our hearts can become puffed up with pride. Proverbs 29:23 says, "Pride will ruin people, but those who are humble will be honored." Have you done a heart check recently? Don't let pride get the best of you.

I will always respect your demands.
118You reject those who ignore your demands,
because their lies mislead them.
119You throw away the wicked of the world like trash.
So I will love your rules.
120I shake in fear of you;
I respect your laws.

121I have done what is fair and right.
Don't leave me to those who wrong me.
122Promise that you will help me, your servant.
Don't let proud people wrong me.
123My eyes are tired from looking for your salvation
and for your good promise.
124Show your love to me, your servant,
and teach me your demands.
125I am your servant. Give me wisdom so I can understand your rules.
126LORD, it is time for you to do something,
because people have disobeyed your teachings.
127I love your commands more than the purest gold.
128I respect all your orders,
so I hate lying ways.

129Your rules are wonderful.
That is why I keep them.
130Learning your words gives wisdom and understanding for the foolish.
131I am nearly out of breath.
I really want to learn your commands.
132Look at me and have mercy on me
as you do for those who love you.
133Guide my steps as you promised;
don't let any sin control me.
134Save me from harmful people
so I can obey your orders.
135Show your kindness to me, your servant.
Teach me your demands.
136Tears stream from my eyes,
because people do not obey your teachings.

137LORD, you do what is right,
and your laws are fair.
138The rules you commanded are right
and completely trustworthy.
139I am so upset I am worn out,
because my enemies have forgotten your words.
140Your promises are proven,
so I, your servant, love them.
141I am unimportant and hated,
but I have not forgotten your orders.
142Your goodness continues forever,
and your teachings are true.
143I have had troubles and misery,
but I love your commands.
144Your rules are always good.
Help me understand so I can live.

145LORD, I call to you with all my heart.
Answer me, and I will keep your demands.

Become INVOLVED

Salvation Army

The Salvation Army began more than 140 years ago when London minister William Booth gave up his pulpit and decided to take the gospel message to the streets. The Salvation Army's mission is "to preach the gospel of Jesus Christ and to meet human needs in his name without discrimination." Today, the Salvation Army is an evangelical movement accomplishing its mission in more than a hundred countries around the world. The Salvation Army has a variety of programs, including disaster relief, addiction rehabilitation, women's ministries, medical clinics, and a crusade against human trafficking.

The Salvation Army provides volunteer opportunities to serve the poor, the homeless, and the hungry by working in local food kitchens and thrift shops, ringing the donation bell during the Christmas season, or donating items to the organization's many thrift stores. If you want to donate large items, such as furniture, that need to be picked up, call 1-800-95-TRUCK or visit www.satruck.com.

From improving the lives of the December 2004 tsunami victims to helping homeless hurricane victims in Florida, the Salvation Army is fulfilling its mission to be an advocate for needy people all over the globe. To join this army of volunteers, check out www.salvationarmy.org.

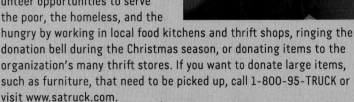

¹⁴⁶I call to you.
> Save me so I can obey your
> rules.

¹⁴⁷I wake up early in the morning and
> cry out.
> I hope in your word.

¹⁴⁸I stay awake all night
> so I can think about your
> promises.

¹⁴⁹Listen to me because of your love;
> LORD, give me life by your laws.

¹⁵⁰Those who love evil are near,
> but they are far from your
> teachings.

¹⁵¹But, LORD, you are also near,
> and all your commands are true.

¹⁵²Long ago I learned from your rules
> that you made them to continue
> forever.

¹⁵³See my suffering and rescue me,
> because I have not forgotten your
> teachings.

¹⁵⁴Argue my case and save me.
> Let me live by your promises.

¹⁵⁵Wicked people are far from being
> saved,
> because they do not want your
> demands.

¹⁵⁶LORD, you are very kind;
> give me life by your laws.

¹⁵⁷Many enemies are after me,
> but I have not rejected your rules.

¹⁵⁸I see those traitors, and I hate them,
> because they do not obey what
> you say.

¹⁵⁹See how I love your orders.
> LORD, give me life by your love.

¹⁶⁰Your words are true from the start,
> and all your laws will be fair
> forever.

¹⁶¹Leaders attack me for no reason,
> but I fear your law in my heart.

¹⁶²I am as happy over your promises
> as if I had found a great treasure.

¹⁶³I hate and despise lies,
> but I love your teachings.

¹⁶⁴Seven times a day I praise you
> for your fair laws.

¹⁶⁵Those who love your teachings will
> find true peace,
> and nothing will defeat them.

¹⁶⁶I am waiting for you to save me,
> LORD.
> I will obey your commands.

¹⁶⁷I obey your rules,
> and I love them very much.

¹⁶⁸I obey your orders and rules,
> because you know everything I
> do.

¹⁶⁹Hear my cry to you, LORD.
> Let your word help me
> understand.

¹⁷⁰Listen to my prayer;
> save me as you promised.

¹⁷¹Let me speak your praise,
> because you have taught me
> your demands.

¹⁷²Let me sing about your promises,
> because all your commands are
> fair.

¹⁷³Give me your helping hand,
> because I have chosen your
> commands.

HEALTH
Recovery from Sexual Abuse

If you've experienced the tragedy of sexual abuse, you need to know that God wants to comfort and heal you. He is a compassionate God whose desire is for you to be wholly restored. Psalm 147:3 describes God's empowering work in this way: "He heals the brokenhearted and bandages their wounds." No matter how deep your hurts or how long you've carried this burden, God sees your broken heart and wants to make you well. Nothing is impossible for him. Allow God to draw close to you, and trust that he is capable of more than you can imagine or expect.

[174]I want you to save me, LORD.
 I love your teachings.
[175]Let me live so I can praise you,
 and let your laws help me.
[176]I have wandered like a lost sheep.
 Look for your servant, because I
 have not forgotten your
 commands.

A Prayer of Someone Far from Home

A psalm for going up to worship.

120 When I was in trouble,
 I called to the LORD,
 and he answered me.
[2]LORD, save me from liars
 and from those who plan evil.

[3]You who plan evil, what will God do
 to you?
 How will he punish you?
[4]He will punish you with the sharp
 arrows of a warrior
 and with burning coals of wood.

[5]How terrible it is for me to live in
 the land of Meshech,
 to live among the people of Kedar.
[6]I have lived too long
 with people who hate peace.
[7]When I talk peace,
 they want war.

The Lord Guards His People

A song for going up to worship.

121 I look up to the hills,
 but where does my
 help come from?
[2]My help comes from the LORD,
 who made heaven and earth.

[3]He will not let you be defeated.
 He who guards you never sleeps.
[4]He who guards Israel
 never rests or sleeps.
[5]The LORD guards you.
 The LORD is the shade that
 protects you from the sun.
[6]The sun cannot hurt you during the
 day,
 and the moon cannot hurt you
 at night.

[7]The LORD will protect you from all
 dangers;
 he will guard your life.
[8]The LORD will guard you as you
 come and go,
 both now and forever.

Happy People in Jerusalem

A song for going up to worship. Of David.

122 I was happy when
 they said to me,
 "Let's go to the Temple of the
 LORD."
[2]Jerusalem, we are standing
 at your gates.

[3]Jerusalem is built as a city
 with the buildings close
 together.
[4]The tribes go up there,
 the tribes who belong to the
 LORD.
 It is the rule in Israel
 to praise the LORD at Jerusalem.
[5]There the descendants of David
 set their thrones to judge the
 people.

[6]Pray for peace in Jerusalem:
 "May those who love her be safe.
[7]May there be peace within her walls
 and safety within her strong
 towers."
[8]To help my relatives and friends,
 I say, "Let Jerusalem have peace."
[9]For the sake of the Temple of the
 LORD our God,
 I wish good for her.

A Prayer for Mercy

A song for going up to worship.

123 LORD, I look upward
 to you,
 you who live in heaven.
[2]Slaves depend on their masters,
 and a female servant depends on
 her mistress.
 In the same way, we depend on the
 LORD our God;
 we wait for him to show us
 mercy.

[3]Have mercy on us, LORD. Have mercy
 on us,
 because we have been
 insulted.
[4]We have suffered many insults from
 lazy people
 and much cruelty from the
 proud.

7 Seven ways to...

Enjoy Your Friends

1. Organize a theme party—try an 80s bash or a Hawaiian luau.

2. Watch a funny movie together.

3. Have a cookout and play Frisbee.

4. Go on a camping trip.

5. Start a book club.

6. Scrapbook together.

7. Spend an evening playing board games or cards.

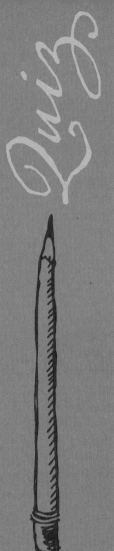

is he a
player?

You've found someone you think is too good to be true. He might be your prince, or he might turn out to be a toad. Look at the questions below to see if they describe him.

1. IS HE OVERLY KIND AND ATTENTIVE WHEN IT'S JUST THE TWO OF YOU BUT IGNORES YOU IN FRONT OF HIS FRIENDS?

❑ A. Yes. ❑ B. No.

2. DOES HE MAKE SPECIFIC PLANS WITH YOU AND THEN SUDDENLY CANCEL WHEN SOMETHING ELSE COMES UP?

❑ A. Yes. ❑ B. No.

3. DOES HE HAVE A REPUTATION FOR DATING SEVERAL WOMEN AT ONCE?

❑ A. Yes. ❑ B. No.

4. DO HIS PROMISES TO CALL YOU TYPICALLY FALL THROUGH?

❑ A. Yes. ❑ B. No.

5. WHEN YOU GO OUT IN A GROUP, DOES HE TALK TO THE OTHER WOMEN MORE THAN HE TALKS TO YOU?

❑ A. Yes. ❑ B. No.

6. DOES HE SHY AWAY FROM REFERRING TO YOU AS HIS GIRLFRIEND, EVEN THOUGH YOU'VE BEEN "DATING" FOR SEVERAL MONTHS?

❑ A. Yes. ❑ B. No.

7. DOES HE GO THROUGH PERIODS OF DISCONNECT WHEN HE WON'T CALL OR SEE YOU FOR DAYS OR EVEN WEEKS AT A TIME?

❑ A. Yes. ❑ B. No.

8. HAS HE BROKEN DATES WITH YOU AT THE LAST MINUTE?

❑ A. Yes. ❑ B. No.

9. DOES HE TRY TO KEEP YOUR RELATIONSHIP A SECRET FROM OTHER PEOPLE?

❑ A. Yes. ❑ B. No.

10. DOES HE PUSH YOU TO GO FURTHER PHYSICALLY THAN YOU WANT TO GO?

❑ A. Yes. ❑ B. No.

IF YOU ANSWERED **YES** TO FOUR OR MORE QUESTIONS, YOU PROBABLY HAVE A "PLAYER" ON YOUR HANDS.

You may ask, "What's a player, and what's the big deal anyway?" A player is someone who is "playing" with your heart. Whether it's intentional or not, he's a tease. Although he seems to like you, he's not ready to make a commitment. You should be concerned because you are probably going to get hurt. You may be investing a lot in this relationship, but you won't get much in return. He's not worth it. Protect your heart and get rid of this guy!

Life Issues

Stealing

Are you a thief? Of course not! You may steal things without realizing it, though. If you consistently run late, you are stealing other people's time. Ouch! If you take home notepads, pens, and office supplies without permission, you are stealing from your employer. If you slip in a coupon that has expired, switch a price tag, or illegally download music from the Internet, you are stealing. Same goes for fudging on your time card. We all know that taking something that isn't ours is not the right thing to do. But sometimes we feel entitled to the things we take, not realizing that what we're doing is no different from picking up a shirt at Saks and stuffing it in our purse. Remember that God gave very clear instructions: "You must not steal" (Exodus 20:15).

The Lord Saves His People

A song for going up to worship. Of David.

124 What if the LORD had not been on our side?
(Let Israel repeat this.)
²What if the LORD had not been on our side
when we were attacked?
³When they were angry with us,
they would have swallowed us alive.
⁴They would have been like a flood drowning us;
they would have poured over us like a river.
⁵ They would have swept us away like a mighty stream.

⁶Praise the LORD,
who did not let them chew us up.
⁷We escaped like a bird
from the hunter's trap.
The trap broke,
and we escaped.

⁸Our help comes from the LORD,
who made heaven and earth.

God Protects Those Who Trust Him

A song for going up to worship.

125 Those who trust the LORD are like Mount Zion,
which sits unmoved forever.
²As the mountains surround Jerusalem,
the LORD surrounds his people now and forever.

³The wicked will not rule
over those who do right.
If they did, the people who do right
might use their power to do evil.

⁴LORD, be good to those who are good,
whose hearts are honest.
⁵But, LORD, when you remove those who do evil,
also remove those who stop following you.

Let there be peace in Israel.

Lord, Bring Your People Back

A song for going up to worship.

126 When the LORD brought the prisoners back to Jerusalem,
it seemed as if we were dreaming.
²Then we were filled with laughter,
and we sang happy songs.
Then the other nations said,
"The LORD has done great things for them."
³The LORD has done great things for us,
and we are very glad.

⁴LORD, return our prisoners again,
as you bring streams to the desert.
⁵Those who cry as they plant crops
will sing at harvest time.
⁶Those who cry
as they carry out the seeds
will return singing
and carrying bundles of grain.

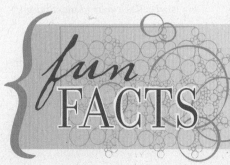

fun FACTS

The majority of fashion models are thinner than 98% of American women.
(www.womensissues.about.com)

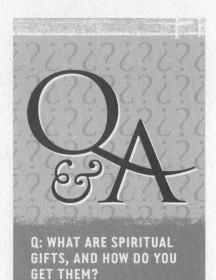

Q: WHAT ARE SPIRITUAL GIFTS, AND HOW DO YOU GET THEM?

A: Congratulations! You already have them. God created you with special abilities and talents to help others and fulfill his purpose for your life. "We all have different gifts, each of which came because of the grace God gave us" (Romans 12:6). Spiritual gifts are detailed in Romans 12, 1 Corinthians 12, and Ephesians 4 and include teaching, serving, giving, and evangelizing, to name a few. There are many spiritual gifts "quizzes" available on-line and through churches that can help you discover what your gifts are if you aren't sure.

the guards are watching for nothing.

²It is no use for you to get up early
and stay up late,
working for a living.
The LORD gives sleep to those he loves.

³Children are a gift from the LORD;
babies are a reward.

⁴Children who are born to a young man
are like arrows in the hand of a warrior.

⁵Happy is the man
who has his bag full of arrows.
They will not be defeated
when they fight their enemies
at the city gate.

The Happy Home

A song for going up to worship.

128 Happy are those who respect the LORD and obey him.

²You will enjoy what you work for,
and you will be blessed with good things.

³Your wife will give you many children,
like a vine that produces much fruit.
Your children will bring you much good,
like olive branches that produce many olives.

⁴This is how the man who respects the LORD
will be blessed.

⁵May the LORD bless you from Mount Zion;
may you enjoy the good things of Jerusalem all your life.

⁶May you see your grandchildren.

Let there be peace in Israel.

A Prayer Against the Enemies

A song for going up to worship.

129 They have treated me badly all my life.
(Let Israel repeat this.)

²They have treated me badly all my life,
but they have not defeated me.

³Like farmers plowing, they plowed over my back,
making long wounds.

⁴But the LORD does what is right;
he has set me free from those wicked people.

⁵Let those who hate Jerusalem
be turned back in shame.

⁶Let them be like the grass on the roof
that dries up before it has grown.

⁷There is not enough of it to fill a hand
or to make into a bundle to fill one's arms.

⁸Let those who pass by them not say,
"May the LORD bless you.
We bless you by the power of the LORD."

A Prayer for Mercy

A song for going up to worship.

130 LORD, I am in great trouble,
so I call out to you.

²Lord, hear my voice;
listen to my prayer for help.

³LORD, if you punished people for all their sins,
no one would be left, Lord.

⁴But you forgive us,
so you are respected.

WHAT'S IN A word?

Psalm 127:4 "Arrows" In ancient times, having a "full quiver" of arrows enhanced a warrior's strength. Likewise, having many children was considered a source of strength and a sign of God's blessing!

All Good Things Come from God

A song for going up to worship. Of Solomon.

127 If the LORD doesn't build the house,
the builders are working for nothing.
If the LORD doesn't guard the city,

"Character is what you are in the dark."
—D.L. Moody

september

This month honors Hispanic culture and heritage. *1*	*Labor Day* is the first Monday of September. Take a day off and relax. *2*	*3*	Pray for a person of influence: It's Beyoncé Knowles's birthday. *4*	*Pray for our troops today.* *5*
The first Sunday after Labor Day is *National Grandparents Day.* Call a grandparent! *6*	*Treat yourself to fresh flowers today.* *7*	*8*	Pray for a person of influence: Adam Sandler is having a birthday today. *9*	*10*
Pray for all those who lost loved ones during the September 11 attacks. *11*	*12*	*Send a card to your oldest living relative.* *13*	Don't forget to water your plants! *14*	*15*
Sit outside for an hour and enjoy God's creation. *16*	*17*	Rent a comedy and spend time laughing with your friends or family. *18*	Read Job 38—39. Share with someone what it teaches you about God. *19*	*20*
Pray for a person of influence: It's Faith Hill's birthday. *21*	*22*	Plan a fall getaway weekend with some girlfriends. *23*	Give yourself a facial. It's important to take care of your skin. *24*	Pray for a person of influence: It's Will Smith's birthday. *25*
26	Memorize a scripture verse from the back of this Bible. *27*	Pray for a person of influence: It's Gwyneth Paltrow's birthday. *28*	*29*	*30*

MONEY

Finding Contentment

How much is enough? That's a tough question for most people to answer. Just when you think you have enough, you realize there's something bigger, better, or brighter that you could have. Contentment can be hard to find, especially in a consumer-oriented culture. That's one reason why it's so important to realize that contentment is a choice. One of the quickest ways to discover contentment is to stop thinking about what you don't have and begin being grateful for what you do have! Make a list of the things in your life that you're thankful for—you may be surprised how many there are!

The Bible offers a healthy perspective on money and material possessions. Proverbs 30:8–9 says, "Don't make me either rich or poor; just give me enough food for each day. If I have too much, I might reject you and say, 'I don't know the Lord.' If I am poor, I might steal and disgrace the name of my God." Finding balance in this area of contentment will help keep your heart honest and pleasing to God. Remember that you can choose to enjoy life where you are right now rather than spending your life waiting for the next stage—whether it's marriage, having a baby, or even the next raise. Choose contentment today!

⁵I wait for the LORD to help me,
and I trust his word.
⁶I wait for the Lord to help me
more than night watchmen wait
for the dawn,
more than night watchmen wait
for the dawn.

⁷People of Israel, put your hope in
the LORD
because he is loving
and able to save.
⁸He will save Israel
from all their sins.

Childlike Trust in the Lord

A song for going up to worship. Of David.

131 LORD, my heart is not
proud;
I don't look down on others.
I don't do great things,
and I can't do miracles.
²But I am calm and quiet,
like a baby with its mother.
I am at peace, like a baby with
its mother.

³People of Israel, put your hope in
the LORD
now and forever.

In Praise of the Temple

A song for going up to worship.

132 LORD, remember
David
and all his suffering.
²He made an oath to the LORD,
a promise to the Mighty God of
Jacob.
³He said, "I will not go home to my
house,
or lie down on my bed,
⁴or close my eyes,
or let myself sleep
⁵until I find a place for the LORD.
I want to provide a home for the
Mighty God of Jacob."

⁶We heard about the Ark in
Bethlehem.
We found it at Kiriath Jearim.
⁷Let's go to the LORD's house.
Let's worship at his footstool.

⁸Rise, LORD, and come to your
  resting place;
  come with the Ark that shows
  your strength.
⁹May your priests do what is right.
  May your people sing for joy.

¹⁰For the sake of your servant David,
  do not reject your appointed
  king.
¹¹The LORD made a promise to David,
  a sure promise that he will not
  take back.
  He promised, "I will make one of
  your descendants
  rule as king after you.
¹²If your sons keep my agreement
  and the rules that I teach them,
  then their sons after them will rule
  on your throne forever and
  ever."

¹³The LORD has chosen Jerusalem;
  he wants it for his home.
¹⁴He says, "This is my resting place
  forever.
  Here is where I want to stay.
¹⁵I will bless her with plenty;
  I will fill her poor with food.
¹⁶I will cover her priests with
  salvation,
  and those who worship me will
  really sing for joy.

¹⁷"I will make a king come from the
  family of David.
  I will provide my appointed one
  descendants to rule after
  him.
¹⁸I will cover his enemies with
  shame,
  but his crown will shine."

The Love of God's People

A song for going up to worship. Of David.

133

It is good and pleasant
when God's people
live together in
peace!
²It is like perfumed oil poured on
  the priest's head
  and running down his beard.
  It ran down Aaron's beard

and on to the collar of his robes.
³It is like the dew of Mount Hermon
  falling on the hills of Jerusalem.
  There the LORD gives his blessing
  of life forever.

Temple Guards, Praise the Lord

A song for going up to worship.

134

Praise the LORD, all
you servants of the
LORD,
  you who serve at night in the
  Temple of the LORD.
²Raise your hands in the Temple
  and praise the LORD.

³May the LORD bless you from Mount
  Zion,
  he who made heaven and earth.

The Lord Saves, Idols Do Not

135

Praise the LORD!

Praise the name of the LORD;
  praise him, you servants of the
  LORD,
²you who stand in the LORD's Temple
  and in the Temple courtyards.
³Praise the LORD, because he is good;
  sing praises to him, because it is
  pleasant.

⁴The LORD has chosen the people of
  Jacob for himself;
  he has chosen the people of
  Israel for his very own.
⁵I know that the LORD is great.
  Our Lord is greater than all the
  gods.
⁶The LORD does what he pleases,
  in heaven and on earth,
  in the seas and the deep oceans.
⁷He brings the clouds from the ends
  of the earth.
  He sends the lightning with the
  rain.
  He brings out the wind from his
  storehouses.

⁸He destroyed the firstborn sons in
  Egypt

Testify!

We worship God because of who he is, but we should also praise him for what he has done. Psalm 66 is all about the excellent works of our Father. In verse 16, the psalmist begins to testify: "Come and listen, and I will tell you what he has done for me." Has the Lord done something for you? Testify! Has he healed you? Testify! Has he brought you through the valley? Testify! Has he saved you from an enemy? Testify! God's amazing works in your life will encourage other people, so don't be silent about his goodness.

Balancing Act

Tolerance versus Toeing the Line

There's a fine line between tolerating sin and holding others accountable for their actions. But sometimes it's tough to tell the difference. What do you do when a friend tells you she's having an affair? What do you do when one of your friends comes out of the closet? What's a girl to do? First, get on your knees and pray. Then, love your friends and listen, but don't get caught up in their dramas. Speak the truth in love and remember that God never lowers his standards to fit the circumstances. He always expects his followers to bring their circumstances up to his standards.

the firstborn of both people and animals.
⁹He did many signs and miracles in Egypt
against the king and his servants.
¹⁰He defeated many nations
and killed powerful kings:
¹¹Sihon king of the Amorites,
Og king of Bashan,
and all the kings of Canaan.
¹²Then he gave their land as a gift,
a gift to his people, the Israelites.

¹³Lord, your name is everlasting;
Lord, you will be remembered forever.
¹⁴The Lord defends his people
and has mercy on his servants.

¹⁵The idols of other nations are made of silver and gold,
the work of human hands.
¹⁶They have mouths, but they cannot speak.
They have eyes, but they cannot see.
¹⁷They have ears, but they cannot hear.
They have no breath in their mouths.
¹⁸People who make idols will be like them,
and so will those who trust them.

¹⁹Family of Israel, praise the Lord.
Family of Aaron, praise the Lord.
²⁰Family of Levi, praise the Lord.
You who respect the Lord should praise him.
²¹You people of Jerusalem, praise the Lord on Mount Zion.
Praise the Lord!

God's Love Continues Forever

136 Give thanks to the Lord because he is good.
His love continues forever.
²Give thanks to the God of gods.
His love continues forever.
³Give thanks to the Lord of lords.
His love continues forever.

⁴Only he can do great miracles.
His love continues forever.
⁵With his wisdom he made the skies.
His love continues forever.
⁶He spread out the earth on the seas.
His love continues forever.
⁷He made the sun and the moon.
His love continues forever.
⁸He made the sun to rule the day.
His love continues forever.
⁹He made the moon and stars to rule the night.
His love continues forever.

¹⁰He killed the firstborn sons of the Egyptians.
His love continues forever.
¹¹He brought the people of Israel out of Egypt.
His love continues forever.
¹²He did it with his great power and strength.
His love continues forever.
¹³He parted the water of the Red Sea.
His love continues forever.
¹⁴He brought the Israelites through the middle of it.
His love continues forever.
¹⁵But the king of Egypt and his army drowned in the Red Sea.
His love continues forever.

¹⁶He led his people through the desert.
His love continues forever.
¹⁷He defeated great kings.
His love continues forever.
¹⁸He killed powerful kings.

WHAT'S IN A word?

Psalm 133:2 "Perfumed oil" was used to anoint priests in ancient times as a symbol of God's blessing.

RELATIONSHIPS

Overstaying Your Welcome

You've heard it said: "Fish and houseguests stink after three days." There's truth in that statement, but you don't even have to be a houseguest to be an annoyance—you could just be a meddlesome neighbor (see Proverbs 25:17). The point is, everyone likes to hang out with friends, but even the best of friends need a break from one another. If you find that you're always the one who extends lunch invitations, if she rarely returns your phone calls, or if your e-mails are mysteriously getting lost in transit, perhaps you're being a little overbearing and need to give your friend some time to herself. It may be difficult at first, but it could ultimately save your friendship.

His love continues forever.
19He defeated Sihon king of the
Amorites.
His love continues forever.
20He defeated Og king of Bashan.
His love continues forever.
21He gave their land as a gift.
His love continues forever.
22It was a gift to his servants, the
Israelites.
His love continues forever.

23He remembered us when we were
in trouble.
His love continues forever.
24He freed us from our enemies.
His love continues forever.
25He gives food to every living
creature.
His love continues forever.

26Give thanks to the God of heaven.
His love continues forever.

Israelites in Captivity

137 By the rivers in
Babylon we sat and
cried
when we remembered Jerusalem.

2On the poplar trees nearby
we hung our harps.
3Those who captured us asked us to
sing;
our enemies wanted happy
songs.
They said, "Sing us a song about
Jerusalem!"
4But we cannot sing songs about the
LORD
while we are in this foreign
country!
5Jerusalem, if I forget you,
let my right hand lose its skill.
6Let my tongue stick to the roof of
my mouth
if I do not remember you,
if I do not think about Jerusalem
as my greatest joy.
7LORD, remember what the Edomites
did
on the day Jerusalem fell.
They said, "Tear it down!
Tear it down to its foundations!"
8People of Babylon, you will be
destroyed.
The people who pay you back for

what you did to us will be
happy.
9They will grab your babies
and throw them against the
rocks.

A Hymn of Thanksgiving

A psalm of David.

138 LORD, I will thank you
with all my heart;
I will sing to you before the gods.
2I will bow down facing your holy
Temple,
and I will thank you for your
love and loyalty.
You have made your name and your
word
greater than anything.
3On the day I called to you, you
answered me.
You made me strong and brave.

4LORD, let all the kings of the earth
praise you
when they hear the words you
speak.
5They will sing about what the LORD
has done,

because the LORD's glory is
great.

[6]Though the LORD is supreme,
he takes care of those who are
humble,
but he stays away from the
proud.
[7]LORD, even when I have trouble all
around me,
you will keep me alive.
When my enemies are angry,
you will reach down and save me
by your power.
[8]LORD, you do everything for me.

LORD, your love continues forever.
Do not leave us, whom you made.

God Knows Everything

For the director of music. A psalm of David.

139 LORD, you have
examined me
and know all about me.
[2]You know when I sit down and when
I get up.
You know my thoughts before I
think them.
[3]You know where I go and where I lie
down.

You know everything I do.
[4]LORD, even before I say a word,
you already know it.
[5]You are all around me—in front and
in back—
and have put your hand on me.
[6]Your knowledge is amazing to me;
it is more than I can understand.

[7]Where can I go to get away from
your Spirit?
Where can I run from you?
[8]If I go up to the heavens, you are
there.
If I lie down in the grave, you are
there.
[9]If I rise with the sun in the east
and settle in the west beyond
the sea,
[10]even there you would guide me.
With your right hand you would
hold me.

[11]I could say, "The darkness will hide
me.
Let the light around me turn
into night."
[12]But even the darkness is not dark to
you.
The night is as light as the
day;
darkness and light are the same
to you.

[13]You made my whole being;
you formed me in my mother's
body.
[14]I praise you because you made me
in an amazing and
wonderful way.
What you have done is
wonderful.
I know this very well.
[15]You saw my bones being formed
as I took shape in my mother's
body.
When I was put together there,
[16] you saw my body as it was
formed.
All the days planned for me
were written in your book
before I was one day old.

Unconditional Love

Unconditional love. It's something we talk about a lot—we may even claim to have it for a spouse—but it's rarely seen among humans. Do you really have unconditional love for your family? What if they cut off all communication and denied that you were related to them? How about your spouse? What if he did something to betray your trust? The only one who has consistently shown unconditional love is God. Even when we deny him, he continues to love. And when we serve other gods and idols, he still loves us. Granted, the Lord will save the just and punish the wicked, but his greatest desire is to love and be loved by his children. Read Psalm 36:5-7 and rest in his unconditional love!

¹⁷God, your thoughts are precious to
me.
They are so many!
¹⁸If I could count them,
they would be more than all the
grains of sand.
When I wake up,
I am still with you.

¹⁹God, I wish you would kill the
wicked!
Get away from me, you
murderers!
²⁰They say evil things about you.
Your enemies use your name
thoughtlessly.
²¹LORD, I hate those who hate you;
I hate those who rise up against
you.
²²I feel only hate for them;
they are my enemies.

²³God, examine me and know my
heart;
test me and know my anxious
thoughts.
²⁴See if there is any bad thing in me.
Lead me on the road to
everlasting life.

A Prayer for Protection

For the director of music. A psalm of David.

140 LORD, rescue me
from evil people;
protect me from cruel people
²who make evil plans,
who always start fights.
³They make their tongues sharp as a
snake's;
their words are like snake
poison.   *Selah*

⁴LORD, guard me from the power of
wicked people;
protect me from cruel people
who plan to trip me up.
⁵The proud hid a trap for me.
They spread out a net beside the
road;
they set traps for me.   *Selah*

⁶I said to the LORD, "You are my
God."

What's the POINT?

Psalm 139:14–16

Did you know that God knew you while you were still growing inside your mother's body? It's true. King David writes that God saw your bones and body being formed before you were born. That means God knows you inside and out, and he has a plan for your life that he envisioned since the beginning of time. Hard to fathom, isn't it? A God who has an entire world to run knows exactly how many hairs you have on your head, what you will eat for breakfast tomorrow, and how many breaths you have left to breathe. God knows more about you than you know about yourself, and he loves you more than you will ever know. Just remember that a God who knows you that intimately is a God who can be your closest, most trusted companion. He is the one you want to go to for good advice, the one who can counsel you through the toughest of times. Although you can only see today, God sees all the way down the road of your life and will encourage you to hang in there when the going gets rough. He is your proud father, and you are his child. And you always will be *his*.

ETIQUETTE 101
CELL PHONE ETIQUETTE

Many people today have a mobile phone, but not everyone uses good cell phone manners. Here are a few tips. Choose the least annoying ring tone possible. (Was Beethoven's Fifth *really* meant to be enjoyed in high-pitched electronic beeps?) When phoning in public, keep your voice down. Avoid answering your phone in a restaurant, during a meeting, or mid-conversation with someone else. Taking calls in those situations is just plain rude! If it's an emergency, the caller will keep trying. Always silence your ringer at concerts, the theater, and, of course, church.

Lord, listen to my prayer for help.
7 Lord God, my mighty savior, you protect me in battle.
8 Lord, do not give the wicked what they want.
Don't let their plans succeed, or they will become proud.

Selah

9 Those around me have planned trouble.
Now let it come to them.
10 Let burning coals fall on them.
Throw them into the fire or into pits from which they cannot escape.
11 Don't let liars settle in the land.
Let evil quickly hunt down cruel people.
12 I know the Lord will get justice for the poor and will defend the needy in court.
13 Good people will praise his name;

honest people will live in his presence.

A Prayer Not to Sin

A psalm of David.

141 Lord, I call to you.
Come quickly.
Listen to me when I call to you.
2 Let my prayer be like incense placed before you,
and my praise like the evening sacrifice.

3 Lord, help me control my tongue;
help me be careful about what I say.
4 Take away my desire to do evil or to join others in doing wrong.
Don't let me eat tasty food with those who do evil.
5 If a good person punished me, that would be kind.
If he corrected me, that would be like perfumed oil on my head.

I shouldn't refuse it.
But I pray against those who do evil.
6 Let their leaders be thrown down the cliffs.
Then people will know that I have spoken correctly:
7 "The ground is plowed and broken up.
In the same way, our bones have been scattered at the grave."

8 God, I look to you for help.
I trust in you, Lord. Don't let me die.
9 Protect me from the traps they set for me and from the net that evil people have spread.
10 Let the wicked fall into their own nets, but let me pass by safely.

A Prayer for Safety

A maskil of David when he was in the cave. A prayer.

142 I cry out to the Lord;
I pray to the Lord for mercy.
2 I pour out my problems to him;
I tell him my troubles.
3 When I am afraid, you, Lord, know the way out.
In the path where I walk, a trap is hidden for me.
4 Look around me and see.
No one cares about me.
I have no place of safety;
no one cares if I live.

WHAT'S IN A WORD?

Psalm 139:23 "Examine me" is an honest prayer asking God to examine us and reveal areas where our lives don't line up with his teachings.

What's the POINT?

⁵LORD, I cry out to you.
    I say, "You are my protection.
    You are all I want in this life."
⁶Listen to my cry,
    because I am helpless.
Save me from those who are
    chasing me,
    because they are too strong for
    me.
⁷Free me from my prison,
    and then I will praise your name.
Then good people will surround me,
    because you have taken care of
    me.

A Prayer Not to Be Killed

A psalm of David.

143
LORD, hear my prayer;
    listen to my cry for
    mercy.
Answer me
    because you are loyal and good.
²Don't judge me, your servant,
    because no one alive is right
    before you.
³My enemies are chasing me;
    they crushed me to the ground.
They made me live in darkness
    like those long dead.
⁴I am afraid;
    my courage is gone.

⁵I remember what happened long
    ago;
    I consider everything you have
    done.
    I think about all you have made.
⁶I lift my hands to you in prayer.
    As a dry land needs rain, I thirst
    for you.   *Selah*

⁷LORD, answer me quickly,
    because I am getting weak.
Don't turn away from me,
    or I will be like those who are
    dead.
⁸Tell me in the morning about your
    love,
    because I trust you.
Show me what I should do,
    because my prayers go up to
    you.

Psalm 141:3

It is so hard not to talk. Just try it for twenty-four hours. Even if it sounds easy, you probably couldn't stick to it. Women tend to be born talkers, but the tongue can get you into deep trouble. One of the toughest self-disciplines to develop is the ability to tame the tongue. Proverbs 10:19 says, "If you talk a lot, you are sure to sin; if you are wise, you will keep quiet." Easy to *say*, extremely difficult to do. The only answer is to ask for God's help. When you talk too much, you annoy those around you (at the very least). Even worse, your tongue can injure others through gossip, rumors, stories, lies, and innuendos. When you throw out harsh words in anger toward someone you love deeply, the words stick in their hearts and minds long after the fight is over. By talking all the time, you also lose opportunities to enjoy the fine art of listening. If you tend to talk a lot, you could be missing what's really going on in other people's lives, severely limiting the depth of your relationships. So pause the next time you're tempted to open your mouth, and take a moment to open up your ears. You just might be surprised at what you discover about yourself and those around you!

Q: IS IT WRONG TO LISTEN TO MUSIC THAT ISN'T CHRISTIAN MUSIC?

A: The Bible doesn't mention types of music, but there are guidelines you can follow. If you like a certain band or song, find out about the members and what the lyrics say, and decide if those elements line up with your beliefs. If a particular band or CD has a negative impact on you, try replacing it with some contemporary Christian music that can strengthen your faith and encourage you. The change may seem difficult at first, but you'll probably notice a positive change in your attitude and demeanor because of the switch.

⁹LORD, save me from my enemies;
   I hide in you.
¹⁰Teach me to do what you want,
   because you are my God.
Let your good Spirit
   lead me on level ground.

¹¹LORD, let me live
   so people will praise you.
In your goodness
   save me from my troubles.
¹²In your love defeat my enemies.
   Destroy all those who trouble me,
   because I am your servant.

A Prayer for Victory

Of David.

144 Praise the LORD, my Rock,
   who trains me for war,
   who trains me for battle.
²He protects me like a strong, walled city, and he loves me.

He is my defender and my Savior,
   my shield and my protection.
   He helps me keep my people under control.
³LORD, why are people important to you?
   Why do you even think about human beings?
⁴People are like a breath;
   their lives are like passing shadows.

⁵LORD, tear open the sky and come down.
   Touch the mountains so they will smoke.
⁶Send the lightning and scatter my enemies.
   Shoot your arrows and force them away.
⁷Reach down from above.
   Save me and rescue me out of this sea of enemies,

from these foreigners.
⁸They are liars;
   they are dishonest.

⁹God, I will sing a new song to you;
   I will play to you on the ten-stringed harp.
¹⁰You give victory to kings.
   You save your servant David from cruel swords.
¹¹Save me, rescue me from these foreigners.
   They are liars; they are dishonest.

¹²Let our sons in their youth grow like plants.
   Let our daughters be like the decorated stones in the Temple.
¹³Let our barns be filled with crops of all kinds.
   Let our sheep in the fields have thousands and tens of thousands of lambs.
¹⁴ Let our cattle be strong.
Let no one break in.
   Let there be no war,
   no screams in our streets.

¹⁵Happy are those who are like this;
   happy are the people whose God is the LORD.

Praise to God the King

A psalm of praise. Of David.

145 I praise your greatness, my God the King;
   I will praise you forever and ever.
²I will praise you every day;
   I will praise you forever and ever.
³The LORD is great and worthy of our praise;
   no one can understand how great he is.

⁴Parents will tell their children what you have done.
   They will retell your mighty acts,
⁵wonderful majesty, and glory.

And I will think about your
miracles.
[6] They will tell about the amazing
things you do,
and I will tell how great you are.
[7] They will remember your great
goodness
and will sing about your fairness.

[8] The LORD is kind and shows mercy.
He does not become angry
quickly but is full of love.
[9] The LORD is good to everyone;
he is merciful to all he has made.
[10] LORD, everything you have made
will praise you;
those who belong to you will
bless you.
[11] They will tell about the glory of
your kingdom
and will speak about your power.
[12] Then everyone will know the
mighty things you do
and the glory and majesty of
your kingdom.
[13] Your kingdom will go on and on,
and you will rule forever.

The LORD will keep all his promises;
he is loyal to all he has made.
[14] The LORD helps those who have
been defeated
and takes care of those who are
in trouble.
[15] All living things look to you for
food,
and you give it to them at the
right time.

WHAT'S IN A word?

Psalm 145:1 "Greatness" is one
of God's most amazing qualities. Recognizing his greatness
will humble you and put your
importance in perspective.

[16] You open your hand,
and you satisfy all living things.

[17] Everything the LORD does is right.
He is loyal to all he has made.
[18] The LORD is close to everyone who
prays to him,
to all who truly pray to him.
[19] He gives those who respect him
what they want.
He listens when they cry, and he
saves them.
[20] The LORD protects everyone who
loves him,
but he will destroy the wicked.

[21] I will praise the LORD.
Let everyone praise his holy
name forever.

Praise God Who Helps the Weak

146

Praise the LORD!

My whole being, praise the LORD.
[2] I will praise the LORD all my life;
I will sing praises to my God as
long as I live.

[3] Do not put your trust in princes
or other people, who cannot
save you.
[4] When people die, they are buried.
Then all of their plans come to
an end.
[5] Happy are those who are helped by
the God of Jacob.
Their hope is in the LORD their
God.
[6] He made heaven and earth,
the sea and everything in it.
He remains loyal forever.
[7] He does what is fair for those who
have been wronged.
He gives food to the hungry.
The LORD sets the prisoners free.
[8]   The LORD gives sight to the blind.
The LORD lifts up people who are in
trouble.
The LORD loves those who do
right.
[9] The LORD protects the foreigners.
He defends the orphans and
widows,

WISE WORDS

Beware of Greed

If you're not careful, greed
can control your life! Greed
capitalizes on feelings of
discontent, telling you that
you deserve much more. So
you begin to feed your desires, and before you know
it, your appetite for stuff is
out of control. The problem
with greed is that it de-
ceives you into believing
that this world's wealth will
eventually satisfy the hole
in your heart if you just get
that "one more thing."
Proverbs 23:4 says, "Don't
wear yourself out trying to
get rich; be wise enough to
control yourself." The Bible
is quick to point out that
wealth is fleeting—it can
vanish in the blink of an
eye. Don't spend your life
running after things that
will not satisfy. Beware of
greed!

but he blocks the way of the
wicked.
[10] The LORD will be King forever.
Jerusalem, your God is everlasting.

Praise the LORD!

WISE WORDS

Don't Be Lazy

In our fast-paced world, it's easy to overdo it with too many activities. But some people respond to the overwhelming number of options by doing nothing at all. Rather than get involved, they choose to take the easy way out. In doing so, they become moochers: people who live off the hard work of others. Proverbs has strong words for lazy people. In fact, Proverbs 21:25 says, "Lazy people's desire for sleep will kill them, because they refuse to work. All day long they wish for more, but good people give without holding back." In other words, laziness is a choice that God does not reward. The good news is that it's never too late to develop a healthy work ethic.

Praise God Who Helps His People

147
Praise the LORD!

It is good to sing praises to our
God;
  it is good and pleasant to praise
  him.

²The LORD rebuilds Jerusalem;
  he brings back the captured
  Israelites.
³He heals the brokenhearted
  and bandages their wounds.

⁴He counts the stars
  and names each one.
⁵Our Lord is great and very
  powerful.
  There is no limit to what he knows.
⁶The LORD defends the humble,
  but he throws the wicked to the
  ground.

⁷Sing praises to the LORD;
  praise our God with harps.
⁸He fills the sky with clouds
  and sends rain to the earth
  and makes grass grow on the
  hills.
⁹He gives food to cattle
  and to the little birds that call.

¹⁰He is not impressed with the
  strength of a horse
  or with human might.
¹¹The LORD is pleased with those who
  respect him,
  with those who trust his love.

¹²Jerusalem, praise the LORD;
  Jerusalem, praise your God.
¹³He makes your city gates strong
  and blesses your children
  inside.
¹⁴He brings peace to your country
  and fills you with the finest
  grain.

¹⁵He gives a command to the earth,
  and it quickly obeys him.
¹⁶He spreads the snow like wool
  and scatters the frost like ashes.
¹⁷He throws down hail like rocks.
  No one can stand the cold he
  sends.
¹⁸Then he gives a command, and it
  melts.
  He sends the breezes, and the
  waters flow.

¹⁹He gave his word to Jacob,
  his laws and demands to Israel.
²⁰He didn't do this for any other
  nation.
  They don't know his laws.

Praise the LORD!

The World Should Praise the Lord

148
Praise the LORD!

Praise the LORD from the skies.
  Praise him high above the earth.
²Praise him, all you angels.
  Praise him, all you armies of
  heaven.
³Praise him, sun and moon.
  Praise him, all you shining stars.
⁴Praise him, highest heavens
  and you waters above the sky.
⁵Let them praise the LORD,
  because they were created by his
  command.
⁶He put them in place forever and
  ever;

  he made a law that will never
  change.

⁷Praise the LORD from the earth,
  you large sea animals and all the
  oceans,
⁸lightning and hail, snow and mist,
  and stormy winds that obey him,
⁹mountains and all hills,
  fruit trees and all cedars,
¹⁰wild animals and all cattle,
  crawling animals and birds,
¹¹kings of the earth and all nations,
  princes and all rulers of the
  earth,
¹²young men and women,
  old people and children.

¹³Praise the LORD,
  because he alone is great.
  He is more wonderful than
  heaven and earth.
¹⁴God has given his people a king.
  He should be praised by all who
  belong to him;
  he should be praised by the
  Israelites, the people closest
  to his heart.

Praise the LORD!

Stories of SURVIVAL

Battling Eating Disorders
VERONICA'S STORY

While average-sized, my mother always struggled with her weight. She was quick to try every fad diet that came along, and somehow we all ended up on the same diet with her. I can still vividly remember the grapefruit diet, cabbage soup diet, protein diet, and eating some wholesome "cookies" that tasted a lot like dog biscuits.

When I went off to college, I immediately put on the "Freshman Fifteen," packing on an extra fifteen pounds in the first six months. My clothes didn't fit, and I felt terrible about myself. That's when my struggle with eating disorders really began. In addition to some of the yo-yo dieting tricks I had learned from my mother, I began throwing up, starving myself, and exercising for hours on end in order to maintain my weight. I became obsessed over food and my appearance. That obsession began affecting my relationships as I tried to keep my unhealthy habits a secret.

> I SAT ON THE BATHROOM FLOOR AND CRIED OUT TO GOD. I HAD COME TO THE END OF MY SELF.

After throwing up five times in one day, I sat on the bathroom floor and cried out to God. I had come to the end of my self. I needed him to save me from this destructive pattern. I prayed and cried for some time, and then an unmistakable sense of peace came over me. I grabbed my Bible and began reading. It seemed as if everything I read touched on my struggle. I remember reading 1 Corinthians 6:19, which says, "You should know that your body is a temple for the Holy Spirit who is in you." I realized that my eating disorder was not only destroying my body but was also dishonoring to God.

Over the next few months, I began battling the eating disorder through prayer, memorizing Scripture, and asking some friends to hold me accountable. By God's grace, I was able to develop healthy eating and exercise patterns. Although I still struggle from time to time, God continues to give me the strength and courage I need to be victorious over the eating disorder.

Praise the God of Israel

149

Praise the LORD!

Sing a new song to the LORD;
  sing his praise in the meeting of
    his people.

²Let the Israelites be happy because
    of God, their Maker.
  Let the people of Jerusalem
    rejoice because of their King.
³They should praise him with
    dancing.
  They should sing praises to him
    with tambourines and harps.
⁴The LORD is pleased with his
    people;
  he saves the humble.
⁵Let those who worship him rejoice
    in his glory.
  Let them sing for joy even in
    bed!

⁶Let them shout his praise
  with their two-edged swords in
    their hands.
⁷They will punish the nations
  and defeat the people.
⁸They will put those kings in
    chains
  and those important men in
    iron bands.
⁹They will punish them as God has
    written.

God is honored by all who
  worship him.

Praise the LORD!

Praise the Lord with Music

150

Praise the LORD!

Praise God in his Temple;
  praise him in his mighty heaven.
²Praise him for his strength;
  praise him for his greatness.
³Praise him with trumpet blasts;
  praise him with harps and
    lyres.

⁴Praise him with tambourines and
    dancing;
  praise him with stringed
    instruments and flutes.
⁵Praise him with loud cymbals;
  praise him with crashing cymbals.
⁶Let everything that breathes praise
    the LORD.

Praise the LORD!

BIBLE Women & Men

Moses

When you have to do things you don't want to do, do you complain or proceed with a big smile? Moses was initially reluctant when God told him to speak to the Pharaoh of Egypt about setting the Israelites free from slavery. Moses told God to send his brother Aaron, because Aaron was a better public speaker. God sent Aaron—but he sent Moses, too. When we balk at God's plan, we may think we have escaped, but we're actually postponing the blessings and lessons God has in store. Our lives always go better when we follow his plan.

notes

Proverbs

The book of Proverbs is about one thing: wisdom. It's a book that promises to help you understand how to live wisely, be self-controlled, and do what is honest, right, and fair. The book of Proverbs promises to help readers make wiser choices (Proverbs 1:4) and get to know God better (Proverbs 2:5). Those are pretty big promises, and this book delivers on them.

Although you could read Proverbs like a how-to guide for life, it is more than just a collection of quick tips; Proverbs provides a core of knowledge and experience that God says we must have if we are going to bring him honor and joy.

Written largely by King Solomon, the book is filled with practical wisdom on all kinds of topics, including personal relationships, finances, and success. Proverbs provides guidance on how to get along with family members, neighbors, and friends. You'll also learn how to manage your finances and your attitude about money. And it draws a clear line between those who live wisely and those who live foolishly.

With this book, you don't have to learn all of your lessons the hard way. Even if you've made poor choices in the past, the guidance found in Proverbs will help you begin to make godly choices. Consider the book of Proverbs a timeless course in wisdom that will transform your life now and prepare you for the years to come. This book will change your life—if you read it, believe it, and live it!

The Importance of Proverbs

1 These are the wise words of Solomon son of David, king of Israel.
^{2}They teach wisdom and self-control; they will help you understand wise words.
^{3}They will teach you how to be wise and self-controlled and will teach you to do what is honest and fair and right.
^{4}They make the uneducated wise and give knowledge and sense to the young.
^{5}Wise people can also listen and learn; even they can find good advice in these words.
^{6}Then anyone can understand wise words and stories, the words of the wise and their riddles.

^{7}Knowledge begins with respect for the LORD, but fools hate wisdom and discipline.

Warnings Against Evil

^{8}My child, listen to your father's teaching and do not forget your mother's advice.
^{9}Their teaching will be like flowers in your hair or a necklace around your neck.

^{10}My child, if sinners try to lead you into sin, do not follow them.

"As a tree produces fruit, wisdom gives life to those who use it, and everyone who uses it will be happy."

BOOKS & MUSIC

BOOKS

KNOWING GOD

by J.I. Packer

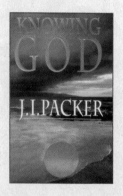

The title gives this book away, as *Knowing God* is a crash course in theology—that is, the study of God. If your goal is to know God, J.I. Packer suggests that your first step is to begin to learn about him. And the best way to do that is to study the Bible. He examines numerous passages detailing why you should study God, his characteristics, and our relationship to God as his created beings. *Knowing God* covers topics such as God's sovereignty, the Trinity, and even God's wrath to give you a better understanding of his character, attributes, and actions.

MORE THAN A CARPENTER

by Josh McDowell

If you've ever wondered whether Jesus really was the Savior of mankind or want to be able to more easily explain why you believe in him, *More Than a Carpenter* is a classic that provides the answers. Written by a former skeptic of Christianity, Josh McDowell deals head-on with the question of whether Jesus was God's Son by proposing that Jesus must have been a) a lunatic, b) a liar, or c) exactly who he said he was. By examining the evidence and applying logic and reasoning, McDowell concludes that Jesus lived up to all of his claims.

MUSIC

LIVING ROOM SESSIONS

by Chris Rice

Whether you're looking for the perfect musical backdrop for a quiet evening in or an intimate dinner party, Chris Rice's *Living Room Sessions* is the choice for you. This album is a bit of a departure for Rice, having made a name for himself with his witty, sometimes goofy pop songs. However, this departure is worth taking—*Living Room Sessions* is comfort food for the soul with piano versions of classic hymns and Rice himself tickling the ivories beautifully. Relax to "All Creatures of Our God and King," "Great Is Thy Faithfulness," and ten more classics of the church.

> *"Jesus must have been a) a lunatic, b) a liar, or c) exactly who he said he was."*

¹¹They will say, "Come with us.
Let's ambush and kill someone;
let's attack some innocent
people just for fun.
¹²Let's swallow them alive, as death
does;
let's swallow them whole, as the
grave does.
¹³We will take all kinds of valuable
things
and fill our houses with stolen
goods.
¹⁴Come join us,
and we will share with you
stolen goods."
¹⁵My child, do not go along with them;
do not do what they do.
¹⁶They are eager to do evil
and are quick to kill.
¹⁷It is useless to spread out a net
right where the birds can see it.
¹⁸But sinners will fall into their own
traps;
they will only catch themselves!
¹⁹All greedy people end up this
way;
greed kills selfish people.

Wisdom Speaks

²⁰Wisdom is like a woman shouting
in the street;
she raises her voice in the city
squares.
²¹She cries out in the noisy street
and shouts at the city gates:
²²"You fools, how long will you be
foolish?
How long will you make fun of
wisdom
and hate knowledge?
²³If only you had listened when I
corrected you,
I would have told you what's in
my heart;
I would have told you what I am
thinking.
²⁴I called, but you refused to listen;
I held out my hand, but you paid
no attention.
²⁵You did not follow my advice
and did not listen when I
corrected you.

²⁶So I will laugh when you are in
trouble.
I will make fun when disaster
strikes you,
²⁷when disaster comes over you like a
storm,
when trouble strikes you like a
whirlwind,
when pain and trouble
overwhelm you.

²⁸"Then you will call to me,
but I will not answer.
You will look for me,
but you will not find me.
²⁹It is because you rejected
knowledge
and did not choose to respect
the Lord.
³⁰You did not accept my advice,
and you rejected my correction.
³¹So you will get what you deserve;
you will get what you planned
for others.

³²Fools will die because they refuse
to listen;
they will be destroyed because
they do not care.
³³But those who listen to me will live
in safety
and be at peace, without fear of
injury."

Rewards of Wisdom

2 My child, listen to what I say
and remember what I
command you.
²Listen carefully to wisdom;
set your mind on understanding.
³Cry out for wisdom,
and beg for understanding.
⁴Search for it like silver,
and hunt for it like hidden
treasure.

BE STILL & KNOW

When God Answers

You may be in the habit of praying when you need things, and tough times may drive you to your knees. But what do you do when God answers your prayers—when he actually gives you what you have been begging for? Do you head out merrily on your way, or do you remember to stop in your tracks and praise him for how good he is to you? Your

grateful heart should spill over with joy and thanksgiving when God answers your prayers, whether they are big or small requests. Then you should spread the good news of what God has done for you. Your enthusiasm will be contagious!

october

October is Clergy Appreciation Month. Do something nice for your pastor and youth leader. *1*	*2*	*Bake a cake from scratch today!* *3*	Pray for a person of influence: It's Alicia Silverstone's birthday. *4*	*5*
Read one of the books featured in the book reviews in this Bible. *6*	*Try memorizing your favorite psalm.* *7*	Collect fall leaves and use them to make your own artwork. *8*	*9*	Take one hour today to do something you truly love. *10*
Try to spend some extra time with family this month! *11*	*12*	*13*	Send a letter of appreciation to a former teacher. *14*	Pray for a person of influence: Jaci Velasquez is having a birthday. *15*
16	*17*	Spend an evening with your family without turning on the TV. *18*	*19*	Pull out your high school yearbook. Stroll down memory lane. *20*
21	It's Breast Cancer Awareness Month. Make time to schedule a mammogram. *22*	Think about what you'd say if someone asked you why you believe in God. *23*	Take care of your feet. Give yourself a pedicure. *24*	*25*
Pray for a person of influence: It's Hillary Rodham Clinton's birthday. *26*	*Visit a lonely elderly person today.* *27*	Pray for a person of influence: It's Julia Roberts's birthday. *28*	*29*	Standard time kicks in the last Sunday of October. Turn your clocks back one hour at 2 A.M.! *30*
It's *Halloween.* Research All Hallows Eve. *31*				

"It takes a long time to grow an old friend."

–John Leonard

What's the POINT?

5 Then you will understand respect for the LORD,
and you will find that you know God.
6 Only the LORD gives wisdom;
he gives knowledge and understanding.
7 He stores up wisdom for those who are honest.
Like a shield he protects the innocent.
8 He makes sure that justice is done,
and he protects those who are loyal to him.

9 Then you will understand what is honest and fair
and what is the good and right thing to do.
10 Wisdom will come into your mind,
and knowledge will be pleasing to you.
11 Good sense will protect you;
understanding will guard you.
12 It will keep you from the wicked,
from those whose words are bad,
13 who don't do what is right
but what is evil.
14 They enjoy doing wrong
and are happy to do what is crooked and evil.
15 What they do is wrong,
and their ways are dishonest.

16 It will save you from the unfaithful wife
who tries to lead you into adultery with pleasing words.
17 She leaves the husband she married when she was young.
She ignores the promise she made before God.
18 Her house is on the way to death;
those who took that path are now all dead.
19 No one who goes to her comes back
or walks the path of life again.

20 But wisdom will help you be good
and do what is right.
21 Those who are honest will live in the land,

Proverbs 3:27

When you see a need, do you go out of your way to offer assistance? Are you known for your generosity and giving spirit? Whenever you can, God expects you to offer help to anyone who needs it. That means you have to be aware of what's happening around you, sensitive to other people, and creative in finding ways to lend a hand. If you see someone on the side of the road by a broken-down car, you may not want to stop because of concern for your own safety, but you can help by using your cell phone to call the police. You may not want to hand out money to someone who is begging because you are concerned that you will only feed an alcohol or drug addiction, but you can carry gift certificates for nearby restaurants to give the person or offer the address of a nearby shelter. Maybe you will never do giant things like give away a million dollars or build a school in a foreign country, but God has given you special abilities to do some unique things of your own right where you are. And every time you help someone he loves, you are doing something wonderful in his eyes.

and those who are innocent will
    remain in it.
²²But the wicked will be removed
    from the land,
    and the unfaithful will be
    thrown out of it.

Advice to Children

3 My child, do not forget my
    teaching,
    but keep my commands in mind.
²Then you will live a long time,
    and your life will be successful.

³Don't ever forget kindness and
    truth.
    Wear them like a necklace.
    Write them on your heart as if
    on a tablet.
⁴Then you will be respected
    and will please both God and
    people.

⁵Trust the LORD with all your heart,
    and don't depend on your own
    understanding.
⁶Remember the LORD in all you do,
    and he will give you success.

⁷Don't depend on your own wisdom.
    Respect the LORD and refuse to
    do wrong.
⁸Then your body will be healthy,
    and your bones will be strong.

⁹Honor the LORD with your wealth
    and the firstfruits from all your
    crops.
¹⁰Then your barns will be full,
    and your wine barrels will
    overflow with new wine.

¹¹My child, do not reject the LORD's
    discipline,
    and don't get angry when he
    corrects you.
¹²The LORD corrects those he loves,
    just as parents correct the child
    they delight in.

¹³Happy is the person who finds
    wisdom,
    the one who gets
    understanding.
¹⁴Wisdom is worth more than silver;
    it brings more profit than gold.
¹⁵Wisdom is more precious than
    rubies;
    nothing you could want is equal
    to it.
¹⁶With her right hand wisdom offers
    you a long life,
    and with her left hand she gives
    you riches and honor.

¹⁷Wisdom will make your life pleasant
    and will bring you peace.
¹⁸As a tree produces fruit, wisdom
    gives life to those who use it,
    and everyone who uses it will be
    happy.

¹⁹The LORD made the earth, using his
    wisdom.
    He set the sky in place, using his
    understanding.
²⁰With his knowledge, he made
    springs flow into rivers
    and the clouds drop rain on the
    earth.

²¹My child, hold on to wisdom and
    good sense.
    Don't let them out of your sight.
²²They will give you life
    and beauty like a necklace
    around your neck.
²³Then you will go your way in safety,
    and you will not get hurt.
²⁴When you lie down, you won't be
    afraid;
    when you lie down, you will
    sleep in peace.
²⁵You won't be afraid of sudden
    trouble;
    you won't fear the ruin that
    comes to the wicked,
²⁶because the LORD will keep you safe.
    He will keep you from being
    trapped.

²⁷Whenever you are able,
    do good to people who need
    help.
²⁸If you have what your neighbor
    asks for,
    don't say, "Come back later.
    I will give it to you tomorrow."
²⁹Don't make plans to hurt your
    neighbor
    who lives nearby and trusts you.
³⁰Don't accuse a person for no good
    reason;
    don't accuse someone who has
    not harmed you.

³¹Don't be jealous of those who use
    violence,
    and don't choose to be like
    them.

BIBLE Women & Men

Sapphira

You can't hide anything from God. Sapphira tried, and it cost her her life. She and her husband, Ananias, sold a piece of land. They were entitled to keep the profits, but they decided to give some of the money to their church. They led people to believe that they were giving God all of their profits from the sale, but they actually kept some back for themselves. They gave, but they also lied. When their lies were exposed, Ananias and Sapphira fell down and died. The moral of their story? Don't try to fool God—it never works.

What's the POINT?

³²The LORD hates those who do wrong,
    but he is a friend to those who
    are honest.
³³The LORD will curse the evil
    person's house,
    but he will bless the home of
    those who do right.
³⁴The LORD laughs at those who
    laugh at him,
    but he gives grace to those who
    are not proud.
³⁵Wise people will receive honor,
    but fools will be disgraced.

Wisdom Is Important

4 My children, listen to your
    father's teaching;
    pay attention so you will
    understand.
²What I am telling you is good,
    so do not forget what I teach you.
³When I was a young boy in my
    father's house
    and like an only child to my
    mother,
⁴my father taught me and said,
    "Hold on to my words with all
    your heart.
    Keep my commands and you will
    live.
⁵Get wisdom and understanding.
    Don't forget or ignore my words.
⁶Hold on to wisdom, and it will take
    care of you.
    Love it, and it will keep you safe.
⁷Wisdom is the most important
    thing; so get wisdom.
    If it costs everything you have,
    get understanding.
⁸Treasure wisdom, and it will make
    you great;
    hold on to it, and it will bring
    you honor.
⁹It will be like flowers in your hair
    and like a beautiful crown on
    your head."

¹⁰My child, listen and accept what I
    say.
    Then you will have a long life.
¹¹I am guiding you in the way of
    wisdom,

Proverbs 4:23

What do you think about when you lie in bed at night? Are you a worrier? Do you fantasize, allowing your mind to go places you know it has no business going? How about during the day? What are those things that are constantly running through your mind? This verse says very clearly that your thoughts rule your life. That can be comforting or downright scary! If you are constantly thinking negative thoughts about yourself, your job, or those around you, your pessimistic outlook will affect your actions, your outcomes, and your relationships. If you approach everything you do expecting failure, telling yourself that you'll never be successful at anything, you are very likely to prove yourself right. Your many negative thoughts have created a self-fulfilling prophecy. On the flip side, the Bible says that you can "capture every thought and make it give up and obey Christ" (2 Corinthians 10:5). By doing this, you can have more joy, more enthusiasm, and more self-confidence. The next time a negative thought enters your mind, chase it away by praying, repeating a Bible verse you have learned, getting up and doing something else, or singing praises. You'll be a much healthier person—mentally, emotionally, and spiritually.

and I am leading you on the
    right path.
¹²Nothing will hold you back;
    you will not be overwhelmed.
¹³Always remember what you have
    been taught,
    and don't let go of it.
Keep all that you have learned;
    it is the most important thing in
    life.
¹⁴Don't follow the ways of the wicked;
    don't do what evil people do.
¹⁵Avoid their ways, and don't follow
    them.
Stay away from them and keep
    on going,

¹⁶because they cannot sleep until
    they do evil.
They cannot rest until they
    harm someone.
¹⁷They feast on wickedness and
    cruelty
    as if they were eating bread and
    drinking wine.
¹⁸The way of the good person is like
    the light of dawn,
    growing brighter and brighter
    until full daylight.
¹⁹But the wicked walk around in the
    dark;
    they can't even see what makes
    them stumble.
²⁰My child, pay attention to my
    words;

listen closely to what I say.
²¹Don't ever forget my words;
    keep them always in mind.
²²They are the key to life for those
    who find them;
    they bring health to the whole
    body.
²³Be careful what you think,
    because your thoughts run your
    life.
²⁴Don't use your mouth to tell lies;
    don't ever say things that are
    not true.
²⁵Keep your eyes focused on what is
    right,
    and look straight ahead to what
    is good.
²⁶Be careful what you do,
    and always do what is right.
²⁷Don't turn off the road of
    goodness;
    keep away from evil paths.

Warning About Adultery

5 My son, pay attention to my
    wisdom;
    listen to my words of
    understanding.
²Be careful to use good sense,
    and watch what you say.
³The words of another man's wife
    may seem sweet as honey;
    they may be as smooth as olive
    oil.
⁴But in the end she will bring you
    sorrow,
    causing you pain like a
    two-edged sword.
⁵She is on the way to death;
    her steps are headed straight to
    the grave.
⁶She gives little thought to life.
    She doesn't even know that her
    ways are wrong.

⁷Now, my sons, listen to me,
    and don't ignore what I say.
⁸Stay away from such a woman.
    Don't even go near the door of
    her house,
⁹or you will give your riches to
    others,

Beauty BECOMES HER

A Whiter Smile

**According to a spring 2004 survey by
the American Dental Association, the number one
question among patients had to do with teeth-whitening
procedures. A variety of options are available, ranging
from at-home kits to in-office procedures. But whether
or not you choose to whiten your teeth, it's what comes
out of your mouth that is important. Ecclesiastes 3:7
says, "There is a time to be silent and a time to speak."
Remember to choose your words carefully and use
discretion in your everyday speech.**

and the best years of your life
will be given to someone
cruel.
¹⁰Strangers will enjoy your wealth,
and what you worked so hard for
will go to someone else.
¹¹You will groan at the end of your
life
when your health is gone.
¹²Then you will say, "I hated being
told what to do!
I would not listen to correction!
¹³I would not listen to my teachers
or pay attention to my
instructors.
¹⁴I came close to being completely
ruined
in front of a whole group of
people."

¹⁵Be faithful to your own wife,
just as you drink water from
your own well.
¹⁶Don't pour your water in the
streets;
don't give your love to just any
woman.
¹⁷These things are yours alone
and shouldn't be shared with
strangers.
¹⁸Be happy with the wife you married
when you were young.
She gives you joy, as your
fountain gives you water.
¹⁹She is as lovely and graceful as a deer.
Let her love always make you
happy;
let her love always hold you
captive.
²⁰My son, don't be held captive by a
woman who takes part in
adultery.
Don't fondle a woman who is not
your wife.
²¹The LORD sees everything you do,
and he watches where you go.
²²An evil man will be caught in his
wicked ways;
the ropes of his sins will tie him
up.
²³He will die because he does not
control himself,

and he will be held captive by
his foolishness.

Dangers of Being Foolish

6 My child, be careful about
giving a guarantee for
somebody else's loan,
about promising to pay what
someone else owes.
²You might get trapped by what you
say;
you might be caught by your
own words.
³My child, if you have done this and
are under your neighbor's
control,
here is how to get free.
Don't be proud. Go to your
neighbor

and beg to be free from your
promise.
⁴Don't go to sleep
or even rest your eyes,
⁵but free yourself like a deer
running from a hunter,
like a bird flying away from a
trapper.

⁶Go watch the ants, you lazy person.
Watch what they do and be wise.
⁷Ants have no commander,
no leader or ruler,
⁸but they store up food in the
summer
and gather their supplies at
harvest.
⁹How long will you lie there, you lazy
person?
When will you get up from
sleeping?

¹⁰You sleep a little; you take a nap.
You fold your hands and lie
down to rest.
¹¹So you will be as poor as if you had
been robbed;
you will have as little as if you
had been held up.

¹²Some people are wicked and no
good.
They go around telling lies,
¹³winking with their eyes, tapping
with their feet,
and making signs with their
fingers.
¹⁴They make evil plans in their hearts
and are always starting
arguments.
¹⁵So trouble will strike them in an
instant;

**Only 2% of female rape
victims will ever see their
rapist spend a day in jail.**

(Oprah.com)

suddenly they will be so hurt no
one can help them.

¹⁶There are six things the LORD hates.
There are seven things he
cannot stand:
¹⁷ a proud look,
a lying tongue,
hands that kill innocent people,
¹⁸ a mind that thinks up evil plans,
feet that are quick to do evil,
¹⁹ a witness who lies,
and someone who starts
arguments among families.

Warning About Adultery

²⁰My son, keep your father's
commands,
and don't forget your mother's
teaching.
²¹Keep their words in mind forever

as though you had them tied
around your neck.
22They will guide you when you walk.
They will guard you when you
sleep.
They will speak to you when you
are awake.
23These commands are like a lamp;
this teaching is like a light.
And the correction that comes
from them
will help you have life.
24They will keep you from sinful
women
and from the pleasing words of
another man's unfaithful
wife.
25Don't desire her because she is
beautiful.
Don't let her capture you by the
way she looks at you.
26A prostitute will treat you like a
loaf of bread,
and a woman who takes part in
adultery may cost you your
life.

27You cannot carry hot coals against
your chest
without burning your clothes,
28and you cannot walk on hot
coals
without burning your feet.
29The same is true if you have sexual
relations with another man's
wife.
Anyone who does so will be
punished.

30People don't hate a thief
when he steals because he is
hungry.
31But if he is caught, he must pay
back seven times what he
stole,
and it may cost him everything
he owns.
32A man who takes part in adultery
has no sense;
he will destroy himself.
33He will be beaten up and disgraced,
and his shame will never go
away.

34Jealousy makes a husband very
angry,
and he will have no pity when he
gets revenge.
35He will accept no payment for the
wrong;
he will take no amount of
money.

The Woman of Adultery

7 My son, remember what I say,
and treasure my commands.
2Obey my commands, and you will
live.
Guard my teachings as you
would your own eyes.
3Remind yourself of them;
write them on your heart as if
on a tablet.
4Treat wisdom as a sister,
and make understanding your
closest friend.
5Wisdom and understanding will
keep you away from
adultery,
away from the unfaithful wife
and her pleasing words.

6Once while I was at the window of
my house
I looked out through the
shutters
7and saw some foolish, young men.
I noticed one of them had no
wisdom.
8He was walking down the street
near the corner
on the road leading to her house.
9It was the twilight of the evening;
the darkness of the night was
just beginning.
10Then the woman approached him,
dressed like a prostitute
and planning to trick him.
11She was loud and stubborn
and never stayed at home.
12She was always out in the streets or
in the city squares,
waiting around on the corners
of the streets.
13She grabbed him and kissed him.
Without shame she said to him,

Life Issues

To Quit or Not to Quit

Although they may not admit it, many women think that
quitting a task or job is practically a sin. Have you ever felt
that way? There are different seasons in life (see
Ecclesiastes 3:1–8), and sometimes it's time to let a job go.
If you feel it's time to quit a job because the atmosphere is
damaging or another opportunity has arisen—or out of obedience to God—don't be afraid to let go. Give your employer
time to find someone new. Offer to train the new person, and
thank your boss for the opportunities the job offered you.
Leave on the best terms possible, but don't be afraid to
leave. If you have sought the Lord in prayer and believe his
answer is clear, leave in good conscience and see what he
has in store for you next.

¹⁴"I made my fellowship offering and
took some of the meat
home.
Today I have kept my special
promises.
¹⁵So I have come out to meet you;
I have been looking for you and
have found you.
¹⁶I have covered my bed
with colored sheets from
Egypt.
¹⁷I have made my bed smell sweet
with myrrh, aloes, and
cinnamon.
¹⁸Come, let's make love until
morning.
Let's enjoy each other's love.
¹⁹My husband is not home;
he has gone on a long trip.
²⁰He took a lot of money with him
and won't be home for weeks."
²¹By her clever words she made him
give in;
by her pleasing words she led
him into doing wrong.
²²All at once he followed her,
like an ox led to the butcher,
like a deer caught in a trap
²³   and shot through the liver with
an arrow.
Like a bird caught in a trap,
he didn't know what he did
would kill him.

²⁴Now, my sons, listen to me;
pay attention to what I say.
²⁵Don't let yourself be tricked by
such a woman;
don't go where she leads you.
²⁶She has ruined many good men,
and many have died because of
her.
²⁷Her house is on the road to death,
the road that leads down to the
grave.

Listen to Wisdom

8 Wisdom calls to you like
someone shouting;
understanding raises her
voice.
²On the hilltops along the road

and at the crossroads, she stands
calling.
³Beside the city gates,
at the entrances into the city,
she calls out:
⁴"Listen, everyone, I'm calling out to
you;
I am shouting to all people.
⁵You who are uneducated, seek
wisdom.
You who are foolish, get
understanding.
⁶Listen, because I have important
things to say,
and what I tell you is right.
⁷What I say is true,
I refuse to speak evil.
⁸Everything I say is honest;
nothing I say is crooked or
false.
⁹People with good sense know what I
say is true;
and those with knowledge know
my words are right.
¹⁰Choose my teachings instead of
silver,
and knowledge rather than the
finest gold.
¹¹Wisdom is more precious than
rubies.
Nothing you could want is equal
to it.

¹²"I am wisdom, and I have good
judgment.
I also have knowledge and good
sense.
¹³If you respect the LORD, you will
also hate evil.
I hate pride and bragging,
evil ways and lies.
¹⁴I have good sense and advice,
and I have understanding and
power.
¹⁵I help kings to govern
and rulers to make fair laws.
¹⁶Princes use me to lead,
and so do all important people
who judge fairly.
¹⁷I love those who love me,
and those who seek me find me.
¹⁸Riches and honor are mine to give.

WISE WORDS

Maintain a Godly Attitude

How do you respond when bad things happen to bad people? Sometimes it's hard not to feel pleased or a bit self-righteous. But Proverbs 24:17-18 makes it clear that a superiority complex isn't pleasing to God: "Don't be happy when your enemy is defeated; don't be glad when he is overwhelmed. The Lord will notice and be displeased. He may not be angry with them anymore." God is not looking for a high five from you when you see people earning what you think they deserve. You are not their judge, and the energy you spend gloating gives you less time to devote to positive, godly pursuits. Focus on your own relationship with God, and let him deal with everyone else.

So are wealth and lasting
success.
¹⁹What I give is better than the finest
gold,
better than the purest silver.
²⁰I do what is right
and follow the path of justice.

21I give wealth to those who love me,
  filling their houses with
  treasures.

22"I, wisdom, was with the LORD when
  he began his work,
  long before he made anything
  else.
23I was created in the very beginning,
  even before the world began.
24I was born before there were
  oceans,
  or springs overflowing with
  water,
25before the hills were there,
  before the mountains were put
  in place.
26God had not made the earth or
  fields,
  not even the first dust of the
  earth.
27I was there when God put the skies
  in place,
  when he stretched the horizon
  over the oceans,
28when he made the clouds above
  and put the deep underground
  springs in place.
29I was there when he ordered the
  sea
  not to go beyond the borders he
  had set.
  I was there when he laid the earth's
  foundation.
30   I was like a child by his side.
  I was delighted every day,

enjoying his presence all the
  time,
31enjoying the whole world,
  and delighted with all its people.

32"Now, my children, listen to me,
  because those who follow my
  ways are happy.
33Listen to my teaching, and you will
  be wise;
  do not ignore it.
34Happy are those who listen to me,
  watching at my door every day,
  waiting at my open doorway.
35Those who find me find life,
  and the LORD will be pleased
  with them.
36Those who do not find me hurt
  themselves.
  Those who hate me love death."

Being Wise or Foolish

9 Wisdom has built her house;
  she has made its seven
  columns.
2She has prepared her food and
  wine;
  she has set her table.
3She has sent out her servant girls,
  and she calls out from the
  highest place in the city.
4She says to those who are
  uneducated,
  "Come in here, you foolish
  people!
5Come and eat my food
  and drink the wine I have
  prepared.
6Stop your foolish ways, and you will
  live;
  take the road of understanding.

7"If you correct someone who makes
  fun of wisdom, you will be
  insulted.
  If you correct an evil person, you
  will get hurt.
8Do not correct those who make fun
  of wisdom, or they will hate
  you.
  But correct the wise, and they
  will love you.

9Teach the wise, and they will
  become even wiser;
  teach good people, and they will
  learn even more.

10"Wisdom begins with respect for
  the LORD,
  and understanding begins with
  knowing the Holy One.
11If you live wisely, you will live a long
  time;
  wisdom will add years to your
  life.
12The wise person is rewarded by
  wisdom,
  but whoever makes fun of
  wisdom will suffer for it."

13Foolishness is like a loud woman;
  she does not have wisdom or
  knowledge.
14She sits at the door of her house
  at the highest place in the city.
15She calls out to those who are
  passing by,
  who are going along, minding
  their own business.
16She says to those who are
  uneducated,
  "Come in here, you foolish
  people!
17Stolen water is sweeter,
  and food eaten in secret tastes
  better."
18But these people don't know that
  everyone who goes there dies,
  that her guests end up deep in
  the grave.

The Wise Words of Solomon

10 These are the wise words
  of Solomon:
Wise children make their father
  happy,
  but foolish children make their
  mother sad.

2Riches gotten by doing wrong have
  no value,
  but right living will save you
  from death.

3The LORD does not let good people
  go hungry,

WHAT'S IN A word?

Proverbs 9:1 "Seven columns"
The number seven represents
completeness throughout the
Bible. "Seven columns" doesn't
refer to architecture but
rather indicates that the
"house" of wisdom was complete and well-built.

but he keeps evil people from getting what they want.

⁴A lazy person will end up poor, but a hard worker will become rich.

⁵Those who gather crops on time are wise, but those who sleep through the harvest are a disgrace.

⁶Good people will have rich blessings, but the wicked will be overwhelmed by violence.

⁷Good people will be remembered as a blessing, but evil people will soon be forgotten.

⁸The wise do what they are told, but a talkative fool will be ruined.

⁹The honest person will live in safety, but the dishonest will be caught.

¹⁰A wink may get you into trouble, and foolish talk will lead to your ruin.

¹¹The words of a good person give life, like a fountain of water, but the words of the wicked contain nothing but violence.

¹²Hatred stirs up trouble, but love forgives all wrongs.

¹³Wise people speak with understanding, but people without wisdom should be punished.

¹⁴The wise don't tell everything they know, but the foolish talk too much and are ruined.

¹⁵Having lots of money protects the rich, but having no money destroys the poor.

¹⁶Good people are rewarded with life,

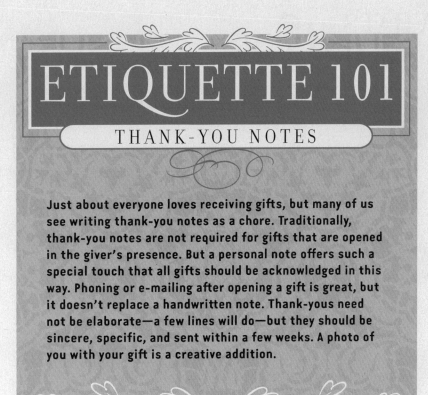

ETIQUETTE 101

THANK-YOU NOTES

Just about everyone loves receiving gifts, but many of us see writing thank-you notes as a chore. Traditionally, thank-you notes are not required for gifts that are opened in the giver's presence. But a personal note offers such a special touch that all gifts should be acknowledged in this way. Phoning or e-mailing after opening a gift is great, but it doesn't replace a handwritten note. Thank-yous need not be elaborate—a few lines will do—but they should be sincere, specific, and sent within a few weeks. A photo of you with your gift is a creative addition.

but evil people are paid with punishment.

¹⁷Whoever accepts correction is on the way to life, but whoever ignores correction will lead others away from life.

¹⁸Whoever hides hate is a liar. Whoever tells lies is a fool.

¹⁹If you talk a lot, you are sure to sin; if you are wise, you will keep quiet.

²⁰The words of a good person are like pure silver, but an evil person's thoughts are worth very little.

²¹Good people's words will help many others, but fools will die because they don't have wisdom.

²²The Lord's blessing brings wealth, and no sorrow comes with it.

²³A foolish person enjoys doing wrong, but a person with understanding enjoys doing what is wise.

²⁴Evil people will get what they fear most, but good people will get what they want most.

²⁵A storm will blow the evil person away, but a good person will always be safe.

²⁶A lazy person affects the one he works for like vinegar on the teeth or smoke in the eyes.

²⁷Whoever respects the Lord will have a long life, but the life of an evil person will be cut short.

²⁸A good person can look forward to happiness,

WHAT'S IN A word?

Proverbs 11:22 "A gold ring in a pig's snout" would obviously be a ridiculous sight! But this analogy was even more outrageous to the ancient Israelites because they considered pigs to be unclean and disgusting.

but an evil person can expect nothing.

29The LORD will protect good people
but will ruin those who do evil.

30Good people will always be safe,
but evil people will not remain in the land.

31A good person says wise things,
but a liar's tongue will be stopped.

32Good people know the right thing to say,
but evil people only tell lies.

11 The LORD hates dishonest scales,
but he is pleased with honest weights.

2Pride leads only to shame;
it is wise to be humble.

3Good people will be guided by honesty;
dishonesty will destroy those who are not trustworthy.

4Riches will not help when it's time to die,
but right living will save you from death.

5The goodness of the innocent makes life easier,
but the wicked will be destroyed by their wickedness.

6Doing right brings freedom to honest people,
but those who are not trustworthy will be caught by their own desires.

7When the wicked die, hope dies with them;

their hope in riches will come to nothing.

8The good person is saved from trouble;
it comes to the wicked instead.

9With words an evil person can destroy a neighbor,
but a good person will escape by being resourceful.

10When good people succeed, the city is happy.
When evil people die, there are shouts of joy.

11Good people bless and build up their city,
but the wicked can destroy it with their words.

12People without good sense find fault with their neighbors,
but those with understanding keep quiet.

13Gossips can't keep secrets,
but a trustworthy person can.

14Without leadership a nation falls,
but lots of good advice will save it.

15Whoever guarantees to pay somebody else's loan will suffer.
It is safer to avoid such promises.

16A kind woman gets respect,
but cruel men get only wealth.

17Kind people do themselves a favor,
but cruel people bring trouble on themselves.

18An evil person really earns nothing,
but a good person will surely be rewarded.

19Those who are truly good will live,
but those who chase after evil will die.

20The LORD hates those with evil hearts
but is pleased with those who are innocent.

21Evil people will certainly be punished,
but those who do right will be set free.

22A beautiful woman without good sense
is like a gold ring in a pig's snout.

23Those who do right only wish for good,
but the wicked can expect to be defeated by God's anger.

24Some people give much but get back even more.
Others don't give what they should and end up poor.

25Whoever gives to others will get richer;
those who help others will themselves be helped.

26People curse those who keep all the grain,
but they bless the one who is willing to sell it.

27Whoever looks for good will find kindness,
but whoever looks for evil will find trouble.

28Those who trust in riches will be ruined,
but a good person will be healthy like a green leaf.

29Whoever brings trouble to his family
will be left with nothing but the wind.
A fool will be a servant to the wise.

30A good person gives life to others;
the wise person teaches others how to live.

³¹Good people will be rewarded on
earth,
and the wicked and the sinners
will be punished.

12 Anyone who loves learning
accepts correction,
but a person who hates being
corrected is stupid.

²The LORD is pleased with a good
person,
but he will punish anyone who
plans evil.

³Doing evil brings no safety at all,
but a good person has safety and
security.

⁴A good wife is like a crown for her
husband,
but a disgraceful wife is like a
disease in his bones.

⁵The plans that good people make
are fair,
but the advice of the wicked will
trick you.

⁶The wicked talk about killing
people,
but the words of good people
will save them.

⁷Wicked people die and they are no
more,
but a good person's family
continues.

⁸The wisdom of the wise wins
praise,
but there is no respect for the
stupid.

⁹A person who is not important but
has a servant is better off
than someone who acts
important but has no food.

¹⁰Good people take care of their
animals,
but even the kindest acts of the
wicked are cruel.

¹¹Those who work their land will
have plenty of food,
but the one who chases empty
dreams is not wise.

¹²The wicked want what other evil
people have stolen,
but good people want to give
what they have to others.

¹³Evil people are trapped by their evil
talk,
but good people stay out of
trouble.

¹⁴People will be rewarded for what
they say,
and they will also be rewarded
for what they do.

¹⁵Fools think they are doing right,
but the wise listen to advice.

¹⁶Fools quickly show that they are
upset,
but the wise ignore insults.

¹⁷An honest witness tells the truth,
but a dishonest witness tells lies.

¹⁸Careless words stab like a sword,
but wise words bring healing.

¹⁹Truth will continue forever,
but lies are only for a moment.

Become INVOLVED

Mercy Ships

Mercy Ships have set sail around the world since 1978, transporting doctors and surgeons to provide free medical care and operations to more than 5.5 million people. The newest ship in the fleet, the Africa

Mercy, will be the world's largest non-governmental hospital ship when renovations are completed. Mercy Ships volunteers help run the ship, manage public relations, cook, clean, and assist doctors on short-term mission trips of two weeks or long-term assignments for up to a full year.

The ships sail to foreign countries, and volunteer doctors and surgeons perform operations such as cleft lip and palate reconstruction, cataract removal, and orthopedic and facial reconstruction. Medical teams and volunteers have treated more than 300,000 people in village medical clinics, performed 110,000 dental treatments, and educated more than 5,500 local health care and professional workers, who in turn have trained hundreds of thousands in primary health care.

Mercy Ships also deliver medical equipment, hospital supplies, and medicine to countries in need. Volunteers help change lives by working to dig water wells, construct orphanages, and build clinics. If you can't hop on board, consider visiting a ship that docks near you and donate supplies or money. For more information, stop by www.mercyships.org.

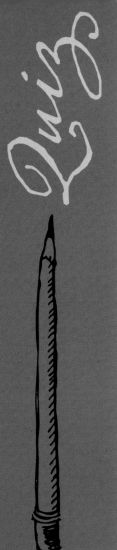

are you overcommitted?

1. HOW OFTEN DO YOU "DOUBLE BOOK" YOURSELF (COMMIT TO BEING IN TWO PLACES AT ONCE)?

❑ A. Once every few months.

❑ B. Once every few weeks.

❑ C. Once every few days.

2. WHEN WAS THE LAST TIME YOU SPENT A FULL DAY DOING ABSOLUTELY NOTHING?

❑ A. A few days ago.

❑ B. A few weeks ago.

❑ C. A few months ago.

3. YOU EAT THE MAJORITY OF YOUR MEALS:

❑ A. At home—you take time to prepare each meal.

❑ B. In restaurants—you don't have time to go grocery shopping.

❑ C. In your car—you have to eat on your way to the next activity, event, or meeting.

4. WHEN YOU HAVE DOWNTIME, YOU TEND TO:

❑ A. Kick back and enjoy relaxing.

❑ B. Think about all the things you need to do.

❑ C. Use the time to get more things done.

5. WHEN YOU'RE ASKED TO BE INVOLVED IN A NEW ACTIVITY OR PROJECT OUTSIDE OF WORK, YOU:

❑ A. Ask detailed questions and consider how it will affect your schedule before committing.

❑ B. Make sure you have an open slot in your schedule and agree to do it.

❑ C. Say yes without checking your schedule.

MOSTLY A'S: YOU EASILY AVOID OVERCOMMITTING YOURSELF! You know how to keep track of your schedule and give yourself enough downtime so you can take care of yourself and those around you. You have learned how to say no, and you use that skill wisely. Many women could learn from you!

MOSTLY B'S: DESPITE YOUR BEST EFFORTS, you can't help but overcommit yourself from time to time. You know you should decline, but you want to be a part of what's going on and believe people need your help. As a result, you live much of your life on the go, even though you secretly want to slow down.

MOSTLY C'S: YOU ARE COMPLETELY OVERCOMMITTED. Some days you aren't sure whether you're coming or going because you're involved in so many different projects and activities. You tend to live in constant motion, and your diet—among other things—suffers as a result. You know you need to eat better and take more time for yourself, but you can't because there's so much going on. It's time to learn to say no and come to terms with the fact that you can't do everything.

²⁰Those who plan evil are full of lies,
but those who plan peace are
happy.

²¹No harm comes to a good person,
but an evil person's life is full of
trouble.

²²The Lord hates those who tell lies
but is pleased with those who
keep their promises.

²³Wise people keep what they know
to themselves,
but fools can't keep from showing
how foolish they are.

²⁴Hard workers will become leaders,
but those who are lazy will be
slaves.

²⁵Worry is a heavy load,
but a kind word cheers you up.

²⁶Good people take advice from their
friends,
but an evil person is easily led to
do wrong.

²⁷The lazy catch no food to cook,
but a hard worker will have
great wealth.

²⁸Doing what is right is the way to
life,
but there is another way that
leads to death.

13 Wise children take their
parents' advice,
but whoever makes fun of
wisdom won't listen to
correction.

²People will be rewarded for what
they say,
but those who can't be trusted
want only violence.

³Those who are careful about what
they say protect their lives,
but whoever speaks without
thinking will be ruined.

⁴The lazy will not get what they want,
but those who work hard will.

⁵Good people hate what is false,
but the wicked do shameful and
disgraceful things.

MONEY

Making the Grade

Your credit rating is like a report card of your financial history. It includes information about your loans, past payment history, debt, and overall financial stability. You may not think your credit rating is a big deal, but it is important. Every time you want to take out a loan—whether it's for a home, a car, or your education—your credit rating is taken into consideration. But it's not just loan officers who check your scores. Insurance agencies look up your numbers, too. The rates you pay for everything from life insurance to homeowner's insurance can be affected. One of the most important numbers on your credit report is your credit score, a number between 300 and 850 that rates your overall financial history. While late payments and uncollectible accounts will bring your score down, you may be surprised to discover that factors like *not* having a credit card can actually lower your credit score, too.

If you haven't already, consider contacting one or all of the three major credit bureaus—www.equifax.com, www.experian.com, or www.trans-union.com—to ask for a copy of your credit report. Sometimes the reports and scores will vary, so it's worthwhile to check out all three. In the process, you may also discover incorrect information on your report, including accounts that you never opened. By identifying and disputing any misinformation with the credit bureau, you'll begin to build a better credit rating immediately.

⁶Doing what is right protects the
honest person,
but doing evil ruins the sinner.

⁷Some people pretend to be rich but
really have nothing.
Others pretend to be poor but
really are wealthy.

⁸The rich may have to pay a ransom
for their lives,
but the poor will face no such
danger.

⁹Good people can look forward to a
bright future,
but the future of the wicked is
like a flame going out.

¹⁰Pride only leads to arguments,
but those who take advice are
wise.

¹¹Money that comes easily disappears
quickly,
but money that is gathered little
by little will grow.

¹²It is sad not to get what you hoped
for.
But wishes that come true are
like eating fruit from the
tree of life.

¹³Those who reject what they are
taught will pay for it,
but those who obey what they
are told will be rewarded.

¹⁴The teaching of a wise person gives
life.
It is like a fountain that can save
people from death.

¹⁵People with good understanding
will be well liked,
but the lives of those who are
not trustworthy are hard.

¹⁶Every wise person acts with good
sense,
but fools show how foolish they
are.

¹⁷A wicked messenger brings nothing
but trouble,
but a trustworthy one makes
everything right.

¹⁸A person who refuses correction
will end up poor and
disgraced,
but the one who accepts
correction will be honored.

¹⁹It is so good when wishes come
true,
but fools hate to stop doing
evil.

²⁰Spend time with the wise and you
will become wise,
but the friends of fools will
suffer.

²¹Trouble always comes to sinners,
but good people enjoy
success.

²²Good people leave their wealth to
their grandchildren,

HEALTH
Seasonal Affective Disorder

If you struggle with symptoms of depression during the
winter months, you may be suffering from Seasonal Affec-
tive Disorder (SAD). Doctors believe the seasonal variation in
light affects the internal clocks of some people more drastically than others. Symptoms include common signs of depression, such as reluctance to get out of bed, craving for
sugary and starchy snacks, excessive eating, and with-
drawal. As days grow longer in the spring, the signs of depression disappear. We all experience periods of sadness,
but if your down times consistently occur during the winter,
you may want to seek help from a doctor. Even during down
times, it's important to remember that God has not left you.
Psalm 69:33 says, "The Lord listens to those in need and
does not look down on captives." Remember that God will always be by your side, no matter what the seasons bring.

but a sinner's wealth is stored
up for good people.

²³A poor person's field might
produce plenty of food,
but others often steal it away.

²⁴If you do not punish your children,
you don't love them,
but if you love your children,
you will correct them.

²⁵Good people have enough to eat,
but the wicked will go hungry.

14 A wise woman strengthens
her family,
but a foolish woman destroys
hers by what she does.

²People who live good lives respect
the LORD,
but those who live evil lives
don't.

³Fools will be punished for their
proud words,
but the words of the wise will
protect them.

⁴When there are no oxen, no food is
in the barn.
But with a strong ox, much
grain can be grown.

⁵A truthful witness does not lie,
but a false witness tells nothing
but lies.

⁶Those who make fun of wisdom
look for it and do not find it,
but knowledge comes easily to
those with understanding.

⁷Stay away from fools,
because they can't teach you
anything.

⁸A wise person will understand what
to do,
but a foolish person is
dishonest.

⁹Fools don't care if they sin,
but honest people work at being
right.

¹⁰No one else can know your sadness,
and strangers cannot share your
joy.

¹¹The wicked person's house will be
destroyed,
but a good person's tent will
still be standing.

¹²Some people think they are doing
right,
but in the end it leads to
death.

¹³Someone who is laughing may be
sad inside,
and joy may end in sadness.

¹⁴Evil people will be paid back for
their evil ways,
and good people will be
rewarded for their good
ones.

¹⁵Fools will believe anything,
but the wise think about what
they do.

¹⁶Wise people are careful and stay out
of trouble,
but fools are careless and quick
to act.

¹⁷Someone with a quick temper does
foolish things,
but someone with understanding
remains calm.

¹⁸Fools are rewarded with nothing
but more foolishness,
but the wise are rewarded with
knowledge.

¹⁹Evil people will bow down to those
who are good;
the wicked will bow down at the
door of those who do
right.

²⁰The poor are rejected, even by
their neighbors,
but the rich have many friends.

²¹It is a sin to hate your neighbor,
but being kind to the needy
brings happiness.

²²Those who make evil plans will be
ruined,
but those who plan to do good
will be loved and trusted.

Seven ways to...

Share Your Faith

1. Offer to pray with someone.

2. Exhibit peace and joy, and others will want it.

3. Get to know the Bible so you can share its truth.

4. Ask for forgiveness when you've done something wrong or hurt someone.

5. Remember that your life is its own sermon.

6. Maintain consistent standards.

7. Tell others about your journey of faith.

²³Those who work hard make a
profit,
but those who only talk will be
poor.

²⁴Wise people are rewarded with
wealth,
but fools only get more
foolishness.

What's the POINT?

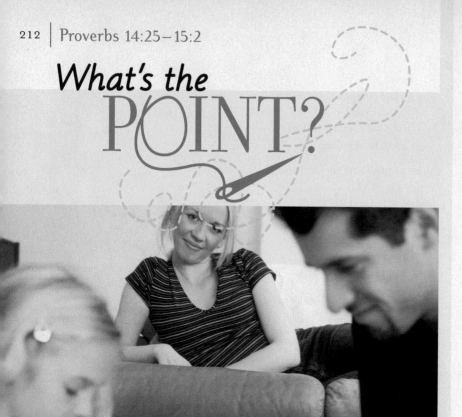

Proverbs 14:1

When you honor your parents, spend time with your children, or encourage your spouse, you are strengthening your family. Did you know that when you do those things, God calls you "wise"? It's true, and a wise woman is one who will choose her words and actions carefully, knowing that her influence will not only preserve and strengthen her family but also enable it to become a living example to the rest of the world of a family who lives for God. When you argue with your husband, yell at your children, or disrespect your mother or father, you eat away at the foundation of love that holds your entire family together. Guard your family carefully, not just from what can come in from the outside to hurt you but also from the damage you can do from within. Harsh words from someone you hardly know don't cut nearly as deeply as an insult from someone you love. That is why you should aim to keep your words, thoughts, and actions positive and encouraging, no matter how frustrating a family member can be. In doing so, you'll help grow a healthy and prosperous family. And when you succeed, you'll be able to call yourself a wise woman.

²⁵A truthful witness saves lives,
but a false witness is a traitor.

²⁶Those who respect the LORD will
have security,
and their children will be
protected.

²⁷Respect for the LORD gives life.
It is like a fountain that can save
people from death.

²⁸A king is honored when he has
many people to rule,
but a prince is ruined if he has
none.

²⁹Patient people have great
understanding,
but people with quick tempers
show their foolishness.

³⁰Peace of mind means a healthy
body,
but jealousy will rot your
bones.

³¹Whoever mistreats the poor insults
their Maker,
but whoever is kind to the needy
honors God.

³²The wicked are ruined by their own
evil,
but those who do right are
protected even in death.

³³Wisdom lives in those with
understanding,
and even fools recognize it.

³⁴Doing what is right makes a nation
great,
but sin will bring disgrace to
any people.

³⁵A king is pleased with a wise
servant,
but he will become angry with
one who causes him shame.

15 A gentle answer will calm
a person's anger,
but an unkind answer will cause
more anger.

²Wise people use knowledge when
they speak,
but fools pour out foolishness.

³The LORD's eyes see everything;
   he watches both evil and good
   people.

⁴As a tree gives fruit, healing words
   give life,
   but dishonest words crush the
   spirit.

⁵Fools reject their parents' correction,
   but anyone who accepts
   correction is wise.

⁶Much wealth is in the houses of
   good people,
   but evil people get nothing but
   trouble.

⁷Wise people use their words to
   spread knowledge,
   but there is no knowledge in the
   thoughts of fools.

⁸The LORD hates the sacrifice that
   the wicked offer,
   but he likes the prayers of
   honest people.

⁹The LORD hates what evil people do,
   but he loves those who do what
   is right.

¹⁰The person who quits doing what is
   right will be punished,
   and the one who hates to be
   corrected will die.

¹¹The LORD knows what is happening
   in the world of the dead,
   so he surely knows the thoughts
   of the living.

¹²Those who make fun of wisdom
   don't like to be corrected;
   they will not ask the wise for
   advice.

¹³Happiness makes a person smile,
   but sadness can break a person's
   spirit.

¹⁴People with understanding want
   more knowledge,
   but fools just want more
   foolishness.

¹⁵Every day is hard for those who
   suffer,
   but a happy heart is like a
   continual feast.

¹⁶It is better to be poor and respect
   the LORD
   than to be wealthy and have
   much trouble.

¹⁷It is better to eat vegetables with
   those who love you
   than to eat meat with those who
   hate you.

¹⁸People with quick tempers cause
   trouble,
   but those who control their
   tempers stop a quarrel.

¹⁹A lazy person's life is like a patch of
   thorns,
   but an honest person's life is
   like a smooth highway.

²⁰Wise children make their father
   happy,
   but foolish children disrespect
   their mother.

²¹A person without wisdom enjoys
   being foolish,
   but someone with understanding
   does what is right.

²²Plans fail without good advice,
   but they succeed with the advice
   of many others.

²³People enjoy giving good advice.
   Saying the right word at the
   right time is so pleasing.

²⁴Wise people's lives get better and
   better.
   They avoid whatever would
   cause their death.

²⁵The LORD will tear down the proud
   person's house,
   but he will protect the widow's
   property.

Q: THERE ARE SOME PEOPLE I JUST CAN'T STAND. HOW CAN I POSSIBLY LOVE EVERYONE?

A: If you think love is based on your feelings, it will be impossible for you to love everyone all the time. However, when you realize that love is based on your actions, not your emotions, loving others becomes an act of your will. With God's help, you can act lovingly toward every person you meet, even those who frustrate you the most! Ask God for grace in dealing with difficult people, and ask him to reveal to you his love for them. Seeing people through God's eyes makes the decision to love so much easier.

²⁶The Lord hates evil thoughts
but is pleased with kind
words.

²⁷Greedy people bring trouble to
their families,
but the person who can't be paid
to do wrong will live.

²⁸Good people think before they
answer,
but the wicked simply pour out
evil.

²⁹The Lord does not listen to the
wicked,
but he hears the prayers of
those who do right.

³⁰Good news makes you feel better.
Your happiness will show in your
eyes.

³¹If you listen to correction to
improve your life,
you will live among the wise.

³²Those who refuse correction hate
themselves,
but those who accept correction
gain understanding.

³³Respect for the Lord will teach you
wisdom.
If you want to be honored, you
must be humble.

16 People may make plans in
their minds,
but only the Lord can make
them come true.

²You may believe you are doing
right,
but the Lord will judge your
reasons.

³Depend on the Lord in whatever
you do,
and your plans will succeed.

⁴The Lord makes everything go as
he pleases.
He has even prepared a day of
disaster for evil people.

⁵The Lord hates those who are
proud.
They will surely be punished.

⁶Love and truth bring forgiveness of
sin.
By respecting the Lord you will
avoid evil.

⁷When people live so that they
please the Lord,
even their enemies will make
peace with them.

⁸It is better to be poor and right
than to be wealthy and
dishonest.

⁹People may make plans in their
minds,
but the Lord decides what they
will do.

¹⁰The words of a king are like a
message from God,
so his decisions should be fair.

¹¹The Lord wants honest balances
and scales;
all the weights are his work.

¹²Kings hate those who do wrong,
because governments only
continue if they are fair.

¹³Kings like honest people;
they value someone who speaks
the truth.

¹⁴An angry king can put someone to
death,
so a wise person will try to make
him happy.

¹⁵A smiling king can give people life;
his kindness is like a spring
shower.

¹⁶It is better to get wisdom than gold,
and to choose understanding
rather than silver!

¹⁷Good people stay away from
evil.
By watching what they do, they
protect their lives.

¹⁸Pride leads to destruction;
a proud attitude brings ruin.

¹⁹It is better to be humble and be
with those who suffer
than to share stolen property
with the proud.

²⁰Whoever listens to what is taught
will succeed,
and whoever trusts the Lord
will be happy.

²¹The wise are known for their
understanding.
Their pleasant words make them
better teachers.

²²Understanding is like a fountain
which gives life to those
who use it,
but foolishness brings
punishment to fools.

²³Wise people's minds tell them what
to say,
and that helps them be better
teachers.

²⁴Pleasant words are like a
honeycomb,
making people happy and healthy.

²⁵Some people think they are doing
right,
but in the end it leads to death.

²⁶The workers' hunger helps them,
because their desire to eat
makes them work.

²⁷Useless people make evil plans,

WHAT'S IN A word?

Proverbs 16:24 "Honeycomb" was used as a sweetener and was considered a healthy food in biblical times. This verse says that pleasant words are like honey—sweet to the soul and soothing to the body. With so much potential at stake, choose your words carefully!

What's the
POINT?

and their words are like a
burning fire.

²⁸A useless person causes trouble,
and a gossip ruins friendships.

²⁹Cruel people trick their neighbors
and lead them to do wrong.

³⁰Someone who winks is planning
evil,
and the one who grins is
planning something
wrong.

³¹Gray hair is like a crown of honor;
it is earned by living a good
life.

³²Patience is better than strength.
Controlling your temper is
better than capturing a
city.

³³People throw lots to make a
decision,
but the answer comes from the
LORD.

17 It is better to eat a dry
crust of bread in peace
than to have a feast where there
is quarreling.

²A wise servant will rule over the
master's disgraceful child
and will even inherit a share of
what the master leaves his
children.

³A hot furnace tests silver and gold,
but the LORD tests hearts.

⁴Evil people listen to evil words.
Liars pay attention to cruel
words.

⁵Whoever mistreats the poor insults
their Maker;
whoever enjoys someone's trouble
will be punished.

⁶Old people are proud of their
grandchildren,
and children are proud of their
parents.

⁷Fools should not be proud,
and rulers should not be liars.

Proverbs 15:1

It's amazing how quickly a tiny spark can start an enormous fire. A little boy playing with a box of matches never dreamed he would cause a forest to go up in flames. A man who decided to burn a pile of debris in his yard had no idea that one little flame would escape, spread like crazy, and race across the field to nearly burn down the neighbor's house. Anger escalates just like wildfire, especially if you add volume to it. Have you ever had one of those arguments with someone over something absolutely ridiculous, like which kind of peanut butter to buy, only to end up in a shouting match about anything and everything else? Both of you yell louder and louder to get your point across, but neither one of you is actually listening. The next time someone raises his voice at you, whisper gently in return. That person is likely to be so surprised that he stops in mid-shout. If nothing else, he will have to quiet down to hear what you just said. Responding to anger with anger starts an emotional wildfire. Like a blast of cold water, kindness and gentleness can quickly put out the flames.

8Some people think they can pay
others to do anything they
ask.
They think it will work every time.

9Whoever forgives someone's sin
makes a friend,
but gossiping about the sin
breaks up friendships.

10A wise person will learn more from
a warning
than a fool will learn from a
hundred lashings.

11Disobedient people look only for
trouble,
so a cruel messenger will be sent
against them.

12It is better to meet a bear robbed of
her cubs
than to meet a fool doing foolish
things.

13Whoever gives evil in return for
good
will always have trouble at home.

14Starting a quarrel is like a leak in a
dam,

and a brother helps in time of
trouble.

18It is not wise to promise
to pay what your neighbor owes.

19Whoever loves to argue loves to sin.
Whoever brags a lot is asking for
trouble.

20A person with an evil heart will
find no success,
and the person whose words are
evil will get into trouble.

21It is sad to have a foolish child;
there is no joy in being the
parent of a fool.

22A happy heart is like good
medicine,
but a broken spirit drains your
strength.

23When the wicked accept money to
do wrong
there can be no justice.

24The person with understanding is
always looking for wisdom,
but the mind of a fool wanders
everywhere.

WHAT'S IN A word?

Proverbs 18:18 "Throwing lots"
was a biblical method of decision-making. It was believed
that the lots represented
God's perfect and sovereign
will.

28Even fools seem to be wise if they
keep quiet;
if they don't speak, they appear
to understand.

18 Unfriendly people are
selfish
and hate all good sense.

2Fools do not want to understand
anything.
They only want to tell others
what they think.

3Do something evil, and people
won't like you.
Do something shameful, and
they will make fun of you.

4Spoken words can be like deep
water,
but wisdom is like a flowing
stream.

5It is not good to honor the wicked
or to be unfair to the innocent.

6The words of fools start quarrels.
They make people want to beat
them.

7The words of fools will ruin them;
their own words will trap them.

8The words of a gossip are like tasty
bits of food.
People like to gobble them up.

9A person who doesn't work hard
is just like someone who
destroys things.

10The LORD is like a strong tower;
those who do right can run to
him for safety.

fun FACTS

so stop it before a fight breaks
out.

15The LORD hates both of these
things:
freeing the guilty and punishing
the innocent.

16It won't do a fool any good to try to
buy wisdom,
because he doesn't have the
ability to be wise.

17A friend loves you all the time,

25Foolish children make their father
sad
and cause their mother great
sorrow.

26It is not good to punish the
innocent
or to beat leaders for being
honest.

27The wise say very little,
and those with understanding
stay calm.

¹¹Rich people trust their wealth to
protect them.
They think it is like the high
walls of a city.

¹²Proud people will be ruined,
but the humble will be honored.

¹³Anyone who answers without
listening
is foolish and confused.

¹⁴The will to live can get you through
sickness,
but no one can live with a
broken spirit.

¹⁵The mind of a person with
understanding gets
knowledge;
the wise person listens to learn
more.

¹⁶Taking gifts to important people
will help get you in to see them.

¹⁷The person who tells one side of a
story seems right,
until someone else comes and
asks questions.

¹⁸Throwing lots can settle arguments
and keep the two sides from
fighting.

¹⁹A brother who has been insulted is
harder to win back than a
walled city,
and arguments separate people
like the barred gates of a
palace.

²⁰People will be rewarded for what
they say;
they will be rewarded by how
they speak.

²¹What you say can mean life or
death.
Those who speak with care will
be rewarded.

²²When a man finds a wife, he finds
something good.
It shows that the LORD is pleased
with him.

²³The poor beg for mercy,
but the rich give rude answers.

²⁴Some friends may ruin you,
but a real friend will be more
loyal than a brother.

19 It is better to be poor and
honest
than to be foolish and tell lies.

²Enthusiasm without knowledge is
not good.
If you act too quickly, you might
make a mistake.

³People's own foolishness ruins their
lives,
but in their minds they blame
the LORD.

⁴Wealthy people are always finding
more friends,
but the poor lose all theirs.

⁵A witness who lies will not go free;
liars will never escape.

⁶Many people want to please a
leader,
and everyone is friends with
those who give gifts.

⁷Poor people's relatives avoid them;
even their friends stay far away.
They run after them, begging,
but they are gone.

⁸Those who get wisdom do
themselves a favor,
and those who love learning will
succeed.

⁹A witness who lies will not go free,
liars will die.

¹⁰A fool should not live in luxury.
A slave should not rule over
princes.

¹¹The wise are patient;
they will be honored if they
ignore insults.

¹²An angry king is like a roaring lion,
but his kindness is like the dew
on the grass.

¹³A foolish child brings disaster to a
father,
and a quarreling wife is like
dripping water.

WISE WORDS

Do What You Say

Do you ever promise to do something with the best of intentions but neglect to follow through? If so, you're not alone! However, the Bible calls us to keep our word even when it's inconvenient or difficult. Proverbs 25:14 says, "People who brag about gifts they never give are like clouds and wind that give no rain." If you promise to do something and don't do it, you may be hurting your relationships and reputation even more than you realize! The next time you're about to promise to do something, pause and weigh the consequences. If you have the time and resources, get involved. But if you don't, save your promise for a time when you can honor your commitment.

¹⁴Houses and wealth are inherited
from parents,
but a wise wife is a gift from the
LORD.

¹⁵Lazy people sleep a lot,
and idle people will go hungry.

¹⁶Those who obey the commands
protect themselves,

but those who are careless will die.

¹⁷Being kind to the poor is like lending to the LORD;
he will reward you for what you have done.

¹⁸Correct your children while there is still hope;
do not let them destroy themselves.

¹⁹People with quick tempers will have to pay for it.
If you help them out once, you will have to do it again.

²⁰Listen to advice and accept correction,
and in the end you will be wise.

²¹People can make all kinds of plans,
but only the LORD's plan will happen.

²²People want others to be loyal,
so it is better to be poor than to be a liar.

²³Those who respect the LORD will live
and be satisfied, unbothered by trouble.

²⁴Though the lazy person puts his hand in the dish,
he won't lift the food to his mouth.

²⁵Whip those who make fun of wisdom, and perhaps foolish people will gain some wisdom.

Correct those with understanding, and they will gain knowledge.

²⁶A child who robs his father and sends away his mother
brings shame and disgrace on himself.

²⁷Don't stop listening to correction, my child,
or you will forget what you have already learned.

²⁸An evil witness makes fun of fairness,
and wicked people love what is evil.

²⁹People who make fun of wisdom will be punished,

and the backs of foolish people will be beaten.

20 Wine and beer make people loud and uncontrolled;
it is not wise to get drunk on them.

²An angry king is like a roaring lion.
Making him angry may cost you your life.

³Foolish people are always fighting,
but avoiding quarrels will bring you honor.

⁴Lazy farmers don't plow when they should;
they expect a harvest, but there is none.

⁵People's thoughts can be like a deep well,

but someone with understanding can find the wisdom there.

⁶Many people claim to be loyal,
but it is hard to find a trustworthy person.

⁷The good people who live honest lives
will be a blessing to their children.

⁸When a king sits on his throne to judge,
he knows evil when he sees it.

⁹No one can say, "I am innocent;
I have never done anything wrong."

¹⁰The LORD hates both these things:
dishonest weights and dishonest measures.

¹¹Even children are known by their behavior;
their actions show if they are innocent and good.

¹²The LORD has made both these things:
ears to hear and eyes to see.

¹³If you love to sleep, you will be poor.
If you stay awake, you will have plenty of food.

¹⁴Buyers say, "This is bad. It's no good."
Then they go away and brag about what they bought.

¹⁵There is gold and plenty of rubies,
but only a few people speak with knowledge.

¹⁶Take the coat of someone who promises to pay a stranger's debts,
and keep it until he pays what the stranger owes.

¹⁷Stolen food may taste sweet at first,
but later it will feel like a mouth full of gravel.

fun FACTS

Heart disease is the number one killer of women, taking more than ten times as many lives as cancer every year.

(The Well Spring Journal)

Stories of SURVIVAL

A Family Member's Murder

JENNA'S STORY

I was outside my home when I heard the sirens. I remember being curious, but it wasn't until I got a call asking what was happening at my brother's house around the corner that I began to put the pieces together. When I arrived there, my oldest brother broke the news: My brother and his wife had been murdered.

An eighteen-year-old confessed to committing the murders for kicks. He had started dabbling in the occult years before. His tragic story ended just after his arrest when he committed suicide. Looking back, it amazes me to see how the Holy Spirit intervened on my family's behalf. God replaced our anger with a supernatural compassion for this troubled young man.

My brother and his wife were Christians, so we knew they were with the Lord. But my family also knew that we were facing a trial of our faith. We trusted the Lord, and he proved himself faithful. My father quoted 1 Corinthians 13:12: "Now we see a dim reflection, as if we were looking into a mirror, but then we shall see clearly." Things were very dim during that time, but we knew one day it would all become clear.

The tragedy opened doors to share Christ with people who were hurting and confused. Several of our friends lost loved ones in the weeks that followed, and we found 2 Corinthians 1:4 to be a source of hope: "He comforts us every time we have trouble, so when others have trouble, we can comfort them with the same comfort God gives us."

Our pain continues to provide a platform for us to share about God's enabling strength and love. Nothing within us was strong enough to get through that trial; it was simply the grace of a loving and merciful God. I've experienced firsthand that God gives us what we need, just at the time we need it.

> THINGS WERE VERY DIM DURING THAT TIME, BUT WE KNEW ONE DAY IT WOULD ALL BECOME CLEAR.

Balancing Act

Media Madness

With the rise of iPods, BlackBerrys, TiVo, and Wi-Fi, it's hard to disconnect from all the high-tech distractions and turn your attention back to the real life that is going on all around you. If you're constantly answering your cell phone during meals or checking for new e-mail around the clock, chances are you're running on technology overload. Take time to pull the plug on all your electronic devices and go for a walk outside. Notice the birds and the trees, the colors and odors of the great outdoors. Hang up the phone and greet your neighbor. Make eye contact with those you meet and give them a smile. Give your body a media break so you can recharge your batteries.

18 Get advice if you want your plans to work.
  If you go to war, get the advice of others.

19 Gossips can't keep secrets,
  so avoid people who talk too much.

20 Those who curse their father or mother
  will be like a light going out in darkness.

21 Wealth inherited quickly in the beginning
  will do you no good in the end.

22 Don't say, "I'll pay you back for the wrong you did."
  Wait for the LORD, and he will make things right.

23 The LORD hates dishonest weights,
  and dishonest scales do not please him.

24 The LORD decides what a person will do;
  no one understands what his life is all about.

25 It's dangerous to promise something to God too quickly.
  After you've thought about it, it may be too late.

26 A wise king sorts out the evil people,
  and he punishes them as they deserve.

27 The LORD looks deep inside people
  and searches through their thoughts.

28 Loyalty and truth keep a king in power;
  he continues to rule if he is loyal.

29 The young glory in their strength,
  and the old are honored for their gray hair.

30 Hard punishment will get rid of evil,
  and whippings can change an evil heart.

21 The LORD can control a king's mind as he controls a river;
  he can direct it as he pleases.

2 You may believe you are doing right,
  but the LORD judges your reasons.

3 Doing what is right and fair
  is more important to the LORD than sacrifices.

4 Proud looks, proud thoughts,
  and evil actions are sin.

5 The plans of hard-working people earn a profit,
  but those who act too quickly become poor.

6 Wealth that comes from telling lies
  vanishes like a mist and leads to death.

7 The violence of the wicked will destroy them,
  because they refuse to do what is right.

8 Guilty people live dishonest lives,
  but honest people do right.

9 It is better to live in a corner on the roof[n]
  than inside the house with a quarreling wife.

10 Evil people only want to harm others.
  Their neighbors get no mercy from them.

11 If you punish those who make fun of wisdom, a foolish person may gain some wisdom.
  But if you teach the wise, they will get knowledge.

12 God, who is always right, watches the house of the wicked
  and brings ruin on every evil person.

13 Whoever ignores the poor when they cry for help

21:9 roof In Bible times houses were built with flat roofs. The roof was used for drying things such as flax and fruit. And it was used as an extra room, as a place for worship, and as a cool place to sleep in the summer.

will also cry for help and not be
answered.

14A secret gift will calm an angry
person;
a present given in secrecy will
quiet great anger.

15When justice is done, good people
are happy,
but evil people are ruined.

16Whoever does not use good sense
will end up among the dead.

17Whoever loves pleasure will become
poor;
whoever loves wine and perfume
will never be rich.

18Wicked people will suffer instead of
good people,
and those who cannot be trusted
will suffer instead of those
who do right.

19It is better to live alone in the
desert
than with a quarreling and
complaining wife.

20Wise people's houses are full of the
best foods and olive oil,
but fools waste everything they
have.

21Whoever tries to live right and be
loyal
finds life, success, and honor.

22A wise person can defeat a city full
of warriors
and tear down the defenses they
trust in.

23Those who are careful about what
they say
keep themselves out of trouble.

24People who act with stubborn pride
are called "proud," "bragger,"
and "mocker."

25Lazy people's desire for sleep will
kill them,
because they refuse to work.

26All day long they wish for more,
but good people give without
holding back.

27The LORD hates sacrifices brought
by evil people,
particularly when they offer
them for the wrong reasons.

28A lying witness will be forgotten,
but a truthful witness will speak
on.

29Wicked people are stubborn,
but good people think carefully
about what they do.

30There is no wisdom,
understanding, or advice
that can succeed against the LORD.

31You can get the horses ready for
battle,
but it is the LORD who gives the
victory.

22 Being respected is more
important than having
great riches.
To be well thought of is better than
silver or gold.

2The rich and the poor are alike
in that the LORD made them all.

3The wise see danger ahead and
avoid it,
but fools keep going and get
into trouble.

4Respecting the LORD and not being
proud
will bring you wealth, honor,
and life.

5Evil people's lives are like paths
covered with thorns and
traps.

People who guard themselves
don't have such
problems.

6Train children to live the right
way,
and when they are old, they will
not stray from it.

7The rich rule over the poor,
and borrowers are servants to
lenders.

8Those who plan evil will receive
trouble.
Their cruel anger will come to
an end.

9Generous people will be
blessed,
because they share their food
with the poor.

10Get rid of the one who makes fun
of wisdom.
Then fighting, quarrels, and
insults will stop.

11Whoever loves pure thoughts and
kind words
will have even the king as a
friend.

12The LORD guards knowledge,
but he destroys false words.

13The lazy person says, "There's a lion
outside!
I might get killed out in the
street!"

14The words of an unfaithful wife are
like a deep trap.

"Our life is a gift from God.
What we do with that life
is our gift to God."
–Anonymous

november

This month honors Native American heritage and culture. **1**	Invite a friend to attend a Bible study with you. **2**	**3**	**4**	*Plan for a restful Sabbath this week.* **5**
6	**7**	The second week of November is World Kindness Week. Do something kind every day! **8**	**9**	*Lift some weights to get in shape.* **10**
Veterans Day. Thank someone who served in the military for their service. **11**	**12**	**13**	**14**	Consider sponsoring a child through www.compassion.com. **15**
Memorize a verse from Proverbs today. **16**	This is Good Nutrition Month. Try eating a salad with dinner every night. **17**	Track down a hard-to-find item on eBay for a friend. **18**	Pray for a person of influence: It's Meg Ryan's birthday. **19**	**20**
Thanksgiving is the fourth Thursday in November. **21**	Pray for a person of influence: It's Jamie Lee Curtis's birthday. **22**	Get ready for Thanksgiving by writing down five things you are thankful for. **23**	**24**	Pray for a person of influence: Amy Grant is having a birthday. **25**
Try writing your own psalm. Offer it as a form of written praise to God. **26**	**27**	**28**	Take your dog for a long walk. If you don't have a dog, go with a friend. **29**	Pray for a person of influence: It's Clay Aiken's birthday. **30**

Those who make the LORD angry
will get caught by them.

¹⁵Every child is full of foolishness,
but punishment can get rid of it.

¹⁶Whoever gets rich by mistreating
the poor,
and gives presents to the
wealthy, will become poor.

Other Wise Sayings

¹⁷Listen carefully to what wise people
say;
pay attention to what I am
teaching you.
¹⁸It will be good to keep these things
in mind
so that you are ready to repeat
them.
¹⁹I am teaching them to you now
so that you will put your trust in
the LORD.
²⁰I have written thirty sayings for you,
which give knowledge and good
advice.
²¹I am teaching you true and reliable
words

so that you can give true
answers to anyone who asks.

²²Do not abuse poor people because
they are poor,
and do not take away the rights
of the needy in court.
²³The LORD will defend them in court
and will take the life of those
who take away their rights.

²⁴Don't make friends with
quick-tempered people
or spend time with those who
have bad tempers.
²⁵If you do, you will be like them.
Then you will be in real
danger.

²⁶Don't promise to pay what someone
else owes,
and don't guarantee anyone's loan.
²⁷If you cannot pay the loan,
your own bed may be taken
right out from under you.

²⁸Don't move an old stone that marks
a border,
because those stones were set
up by your ancestors.

²⁹Do you see people skilled in their
work?
They will work for kings, not for
ordinary people.

23 If you sit down to eat
with a ruler,
notice the food that is in front
of you.
²Control yourself
if you have a big appetite.
³Don't be greedy for his fine foods,
because that food might be a
trick.
⁴Don't wear yourself out trying to
get rich;
be wise enough to control
yourself.
⁵Wealth can vanish in the wink of an
eye.
It can seem to grow wings
and fly away like an eagle.

⁶Don't eat the food of selfish people;
don't be greedy for their fine
foods.
⁷Selfish people are always worrying
about how much the food costs.
They tell you, "Eat and drink,"

RELATIONSHIPS

Revenge Isn't Always Sweet

When you broke up with your last boyfriend, it got a little ugly. Words were said, feelings were hurt, and now you can't even think about him without fuming. But have you gone so far as to wish bad things for him? If so, Proverbs 24:17-18 offers a reality check for you: just because *you're* mad at him doesn't mean that God is. And God is definitely not pleased when we seek revenge or take things into our own hands. Read Romans 12:19-21 to grasp God's way of dealing with an enemy. While you're there, check out the preface to that passage on handling people who hurt us: "Do your best to live in peace with everyone" (verse 18). That goes for the ex-boyfriend, too!

but they don't really mean it.
⁸You will throw up the little you
have eaten,
and you will have wasted your
kind words.

⁹Don't speak to fools;
they will only ignore your wise
words.

¹⁰Don't move an old stone that marks
a border,
and don't take fields that belong
to orphans.
¹¹God, their defender, is strong;
he will take their side against
you.

¹²Remember what you are taught,
and listen carefully to words of
knowledge.

According to a recent
study, men have an aver-
age of $2,742 in credit
card debt, whereas
women average $2,522.

¹³Don't fail to punish children.
If you spank them, they won't
die.
¹⁴If you spank them,
you will save them from death.

¹⁵My child, if you are wise,
then I will be happy.
¹⁶I will be so pleased
if you speak what is right.

¹⁷Don't envy sinners,
but always respect the LORD.
¹⁸Then you will have hope for the
future,
and your wishes will come true.

¹⁹Listen, my child, and be wise.
Keep your mind on what is right.
²⁰Don't drink too much wine
or eat too much food.

²¹Those who drink and eat too much
become poor.
They sleep too much and end up
wearing rags.

²²Listen to your father, who gave you
life,
and do not forget your mother
when she is old.
²³Learn the truth and never reject it.
Get wisdom, self-control, and
understanding.
²⁴The father of a good child is very
happy;
parents who have wise children
are glad because of them.
²⁵Make your father and mother
happy;
give your mother a reason to be
glad.

²⁶My son, pay attention to me,
and watch closely what I do.
²⁷A prostitute is as dangerous as a
deep pit,
and an unfaithful wife is like a
narrow well.
²⁸They ambush you like robbers
and cause many men to be
unfaithful to their wives.

²⁹Who has trouble? Who has pain?
Who fights? Who complains?
Who has unnecessary bruises?
Who has bloodshot eyes?
³⁰It is people who drink too much
wine,
who try out all different kinds
of strong drinks.
³¹Don't stare at the wine when it is
red,

when it sparkles in the cup,
when it goes down smoothly.
³²Later it bites like a snake
with poison in its fangs.
³³Your eyes will see strange sights,
and your mind will be confused.
³⁴You will feel dizzy as if you're in a
storm on the ocean,
as if you're on top of a ship's sails.
³⁵You will think, "They hit me, but
I'm not hurt.
They beat me up, but I don't
remember it.
I wish I could wake up.
Then I would get another
drink."

24 Don't envy evil people
or try to be friends
with them.
²Their minds are always planning
violence,
and they always talk about
making trouble.

³It takes wisdom to have a good
family,
and it takes understanding to
make it strong.
⁴It takes knowledge to fill a home
with rare and beautiful treasures.

⁵Wise people have great power,
and those with knowledge have
great strength.
⁶So you need advice when you go to
war.
If you have lots of good advice,
you will win.

⁷Foolish people cannot understand
wisdom.
They have nothing to say in a
discussion.

⁸Whoever makes evil plans
will be known as a troublemaker.
⁹Making foolish plans is sinful,
and making fun of wisdom is
hateful.

¹⁰If you give up when trouble comes,
it shows that you are weak.

¹¹Save those who are being led to
their death;

rescue those who are about to be killed.
[12]If you say, "We don't know anything about this,"
God, who knows what's in your mind, will notice.
He is watching you, and he will know.
He will reward each person for what he has done.

[13]My child, eat honey because it is good.
Honey from the honeycomb tastes sweet.
[14]In the same way, wisdom is pleasing to you.
If you find it, you have hope for the future,
and your wishes will come true.

[15]Don't be wicked and attack a good family's house;
don't rob the place where they live.
[16]Even though good people may be bothered by trouble seven times, they are never defeated,
but the wicked are overwhelmed by trouble.

[17]Don't be happy when your enemy is defeated;
don't be glad when he is overwhelmed.
[18]The LORD will notice and be displeased.
He may not be angry with them anymore.

[19]Don't envy evil people,
and don't be jealous of the wicked.
[20]An evil person has nothing to hope for;
the wicked will die like a flame that is put out.

[21]My child, respect the LORD and the king.
Don't join those people who refuse to obey them.
[22]The LORD and the king will quickly destroy such people.
Those two can cause great disaster!

More Words of Wisdom

[23]These are also sayings of the wise:
It is not good to take sides when you are the judge.
[24]Don't tell the wicked that they are innocent;
people will curse you, and nations will hate you.
[25]But things will go well if you punish the guilty,
and you will receive rich blessings.

[26]An honest answer is as pleasing as a kiss on the lips.

[27]First, finish your outside work and prepare your fields.
After that, you can build your house.

[28]Don't testify against your neighbor for no good reason.
Don't say things that are false.
[29]Don't say, "I'll get even;
I'll do to him what he did to me."

[30]I passed by a lazy person's field and by the vineyard of someone with no sense.
[31]Thorns had grown up everywhere.
The ground was covered with weeds,
and the stone walls had fallen down.
[32]I thought about what I had seen;
I learned this lesson from what I saw.
[33]You sleep a little; you take a nap.
You fold your hands and lie down to rest.
[34]Soon you will be as poor as if you had been robbed;
you will have as little as if you had been held up.

More Wise Sayings of Solomon

25 These are more wise sayings of Solomon, copied by the men of Hezekiah king of Judah.

Loving the Poor

Perhaps you have served food in a soup kitchen, collected non-perishable items for the needy, or donated your used clothing to a charitable organization. These are all great ways to demonstrate love to the poor. But have you ever befriended someone who is less fortunate than yourself? Have you ever taken the time to treat a needy person as simply a *person*? Too often, we show our love in material ways and fail to offer the compassion and esteem that all of God's children deserve. By all means, continue to do all you can to meet physical and financial needs. But don't forget to love them on a personal level as well.

BIBLE
Women & Men

Abraham

God called Abraham to change his name, leave his family, and go wherever God said. Abraham must have had incredible faith to do that—to leave all he knew and head out. Could you leave everything behind to follow God? Later, Abraham's faith was so strong that he was willing to put his son Isaac on an altar of sacrifice. God spared Isaac's life and sent a ram as a sacrifice in his place. Because of Abraham's faith and obedience, his descendants became great nations that still exist today.

²God is honored for what he keeps secret.
Kings are honored for what they can discover.

³No one can measure the height of the skies or the depth of the earth.
So also no one can understand the mind of a king.

⁴Remove the scum from the silver, so the silver can be used by the silversmith.
⁵Remove wicked people from the king's presence;
then his government will be honest and last a long time.

⁶Don't brag to the king and act as if you are great.
⁷It is better for him to give you a higher position
than to bring you down in front of the prince.

Because of something you have seen,
⁸ do not quickly take someone to court.
What will you do later
when your neighbor proves you wrong?

⁹If you have an argument with your neighbor,
don't tell other people what was said.
¹⁰Whoever hears it might shame you, and you might not ever be respected again.

¹¹The right word spoken at the right time
is as beautiful as gold apples in a silver bowl.

¹²A wise warning to someone who will listen
is as valuable as gold earrings or fine gold jewelry.

¹³Trustworthy messengers refresh those who send them,
like the coolness of snow in the summertime.

¹⁴People who brag about gifts they never give
are like clouds and wind that give no rain.

¹⁵With patience you can convince a ruler,
and a gentle word can get through to the hard-headed.

¹⁶If you find honey, don't eat too much,
or it will make you throw up.
¹⁷Don't go to your neighbor's house too often;
too much of you will make him hate you.

¹⁸When you lie about your neighbors, it hurts them as much as a club, a sword, or a sharp arrow.

¹⁹Trusting unfaithful people when you are in trouble
is like eating with a broken tooth or walking with a crippled foot.

²⁰Singing songs to someone who is sad
is like taking away his coat on a cold day
or pouring vinegar on soda.

²¹If your enemy is hungry, feed him. If he is thirsty, give him a drink.
²²Doing this will be like pouring burning coals on his head,
and the LORD will reward you.

²³As the north wind brings rain, telling gossip brings angry looks.

²⁴It is better to live in a corner on the roof[n]
than inside the house with a quarreling wife.

²⁵Good news from a faraway place is like a cool drink when you are tired.

²⁶A good person who gives in to evil
is like a muddy spring or a dirty well.

²⁷It is not good to eat too much honey, nor does it bring you honor to brag about yourself.

²⁸Those who do not control themselves
are like a city whose walls are broken down.

26

It shouldn't snow in summer or rain at harvest.
Neither should a foolish person ever be honored.

25:24 **roof** In Bible times houses were built with flat roofs. The roof was used for drying things such as flax and fruit. And it was used as an extra room, as a place for worship, and as a cool place to sleep in the summer.

²Curses will not harm someone who
is innocent;
they are like sparrows or
swallows that fly around and
never land.

³Whips are for horses, and harnesses
are for donkeys,
so paddles are good for fools.

⁴Don't answer fools when they speak
foolishly,
or you will be just like them.

⁵Answer fools when they speak
foolishly,
or they will think they are really
wise.

⁶Sending a message by a foolish
person
is like cutting off your feet or
drinking poison.

⁷A wise saying spoken by a fool
is as useless as the legs of a
crippled person.

⁸Giving honor to a foolish person
is like tying a stone in a
slingshot.

⁹A wise saying spoken by a fool
is like a thorn stuck in the hand
of a drunk.

¹⁰Hiring a foolish person or anyone
just passing by
is like an archer shooting at just
anything.

¹¹A fool who repeats his foolishness
is like a dog that goes back
to what it has thrown
up.

¹²There is more hope for a foolish
person
than for those who think they
are wise.

¹³The lazy person says, "There's a lion
in the road!
There's a lion in the streets!"

¹⁴Like a door turning back and forth
on its hinges,
the lazy person turns over and
over in bed.

¹⁵Lazy people may put their hands in
the dish,
but they are too tired to lift the
food to their mouths.

¹⁶The lazy person thinks he is wiser
than seven people who give
sensible answers.

¹⁷Interfering in someone else's
quarrel as you pass by
is like grabbing a dog by the
ears.

¹⁸Like a madman shooting
deadly, burning arrows
¹⁹is the one who tricks a neighbor
and then says, "I was just
joking."

²⁰Without wood, a fire will go out,
and without gossip, quarreling
will stop.

²¹Just as charcoal and wood keep a
fire going,
a quarrelsome person keeps an
argument going.

²²The words of a gossip are like tasty
bits of food;
people like to gobble them up.

²³Kind words from a wicked mind
are like a shiny coating on a clay
pot.

²⁴Those who hate you may try to fool
you with their words,
but in their minds they are
planning evil.

²⁵People's words may be kind, but
don't believe them,
because their minds are full of
evil thoughts.

²⁶Lies can hide hate,
but the evil will be plain to
everyone.

²⁷Whoever digs a pit for others will
fall into it.
Whoever tries to roll a boulder
down on others will be
crushed by it.

²⁸Liars hate the people they hurt,
and false praise can ruin others.

27 Don't brag about
tomorrow;
you don't know what may
happen then.

²Don't praise yourself. Let someone
else do it.
Let the praise come from a
stranger and not from your
own mouth.

³Stone is heavy, and sand is weighty,
but a complaining fool is worse
than either.

⁴Anger is cruel and destroys like a
flood,
but no one can put up with
jealousy!

⁵It is better to correct someone
openly
than to have love and not show
it.

⁶The slap of a friend can be trusted
to help you,
but the kisses of an enemy are
nothing but lies.

⁷When you are full, not even honey
tastes good,
but when you are hungry, even
something bitter tastes
sweet.

⁸A person who leaves his home
is like a bird that leaves its nest.

WHAT'S IN A word?

Proverbs 26:17 "Grabbing a dog by the ears" is never a good idea because the dog will probably get angry and try to bite you! In the same way, it's not wise to get involved in someone else's disputes.

Life Issues

Betrayal

Your best friend steals your boyfriend. Your parents divorce after thirty years. Your husband is sleeping with another woman. Betrayal can quickly lead to bitterness and a hardened heart. Revenge would seem so sweet, but Christ calls believers to do what seems to be impossible—forgive. Jesus faced the ultimate betrayal when one of his closest followers, Judas, "sold" him to Roman soldiers for thirty pieces of silver. Jesus could have become enraged, fought the soldiers, or lashed out verbally out of bitterness and hatred. Yet among his last words while dying on the cross were pleas to God to forgive those who had nailed him there (Luke 23:34). In Matthew 5:38—41, Jesus instructs his followers to bend over backwards to accommodate those who hurt us. Why? Because it's God's job to determine the consequences for wrong behavior, not yours. Ask him to handle it, and you will find peace.

⁹The sweet smell of perfume and oils
    is pleasant,
  and so is good advice from a
    friend.

¹⁰Don't forget your friend or your
    parent's friend.
  Don't always go to your family
    for help when trouble comes.
  A neighbor close by is better
    than a family far away.

¹¹Be wise, my child, and make me
    happy.
  Then I can respond to any insult.

¹²The wise see danger ahead and
    avoid it,
  but fools keep going and get
    into trouble.

¹³Take the coat of someone who
    promises to pay a stranger's
    loan,
  and keep it until he pays what
    the stranger owes.

¹⁴If you loudly greet your neighbor
    early in the morning,
  he will think of it as a
    curse.

¹⁵A quarreling wife is as bothersome
    as a continual dripping on a
    rainy day.

¹⁶Stopping her is like stopping the
    wind
  or trying to grab oil in your
    hand.

¹⁷As iron sharpens iron,
  so people can improve each
    other.

¹⁸Whoever tends a fig tree gets to eat
    its fruit,
  and whoever takes care of his
    master will receive honor.

¹⁹As water reflects your face,
  so your mind shows what kind of
    person you are.

²⁰People will never stop dying and
    being destroyed,
  and they will never stop wanting
    more than they have.

²¹A hot furnace tests silver and gold,
  and people are tested by the
    praise they receive.

²²Even if you ground up a foolish
    person like grain in a bowl,
  you couldn't remove the
    foolishness.

²³Be sure you know how your sheep
    are doing,
  and pay attention to the
    condition of your cattle.

²⁴Riches will not go on forever,
  nor do governments go on
    forever.

²⁵Bring in the hay, and let the new
    grass appear.
  Gather the grass from the hills.

²⁶Make clothes from the lambs'
    wool,
  and sell some goats to buy a
    field.

²⁷There will be plenty of goat's
    milk
  to feed you and your family
  and to make your servant girls
    healthy.

28 Evil people run even
    though no one is
    chasing them,
  but good people are as brave as a
    lion.

²When a country is lawless, it has
    one ruler after another;
  but when it is led by a leader
    with understanding and
    knowledge, it continues
    strong.

³Rulers who mistreat the poor
  are like a hard rain that destroys
    the crops.

⁴Those who disobey what they have
    been taught praise the
    wicked,
  but those who obey what they

have been taught are against them.

⁵Evil people do not understand justice,
but those who follow the Lord understand it completely.

⁶It is better to be poor and innocent than to be rich and wicked.

⁷Children who obey what they have been taught are wise,
but friends of troublemakers disgrace their parents.

⁸Some people get rich by overcharging others,
but their wealth will be given to those who are kind to the poor.

⁹If you refuse to obey what you have been taught,
your prayers will not be heard.

¹⁰Those who lead good people to do wrong
will be ruined by their own evil,
but the innocent will be rewarded with good things.

¹¹Rich people may think they are wise,
but the poor with understanding will prove them wrong.

¹²When good people triumph, there is great happiness,
but when the wicked get control, everybody hides.

¹³If you hide your sins, you will not succeed.
If you confess and reject them, you will receive mercy.

¹⁴Those who are always respectful will be happy,
but those who are stubborn will get into trouble.

¹⁵A wicked ruler is as dangerous to poor people
as a roaring lion or a charging bear.

¹⁶A ruler without wisdom will be cruel,
but the one who refuses to take dishonest money will rule a long time.

¹⁷Don't help those who are guilty of murder;
let them run until they die.

¹⁸Innocent people will be kept safe,
but those who are dishonest will suddenly be ruined.

¹⁹Those who work their land will have plenty of food,
but the ones who chase empty dreams instead will end up poor.

²⁰A truthful person will have many blessings,
but those eager to get rich will be punished.

²¹It is not good for a judge to take sides,
but some will sin for only a piece of bread.

²²Selfish people are in a hurry to get rich
and do not realize they soon will be poor.

²³Those who correct others will later be liked
more than those who give false praise.

²⁴Whoever robs father or mother
and says, "It's not wrong,"
is just like someone who destroys things.

²⁵A greedy person causes trouble,
but the one who trusts the Lord will succeed.

²⁶Those who trust in themselves are foolish,
but those who live wisely will be kept safe.

²⁷Whoever gives to the poor will have everything he needs,
but the one who ignores the poor will receive many curses.

²⁸When the wicked get control, everybody hides,
but when they die, good people do well.

29 Whoever is stubborn after being corrected many times
will suddenly be hurt beyond cure.

²When good people do well, everyone is happy,
but when evil people rule, everyone groans.

³Those who love wisdom make their parents happy,
but friends of prostitutes waste their money.

⁴If a king is fair, he makes his country strong,
but if he takes gifts dishonestly, he tears his country down.

⁵Those who give false praise to their neighbors
are setting a trap for them.

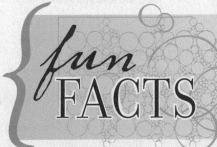

⁶Evil people are trapped by their
own sin,
but good people can sing and be
happy.

⁷Good people care about justice for
the poor,
but the wicked are not
concerned.

⁸People who make fun of wisdom
cause trouble in a city,
but wise people calm anger
down.

⁹When a wise person takes a foolish
person to court,
the fool only shouts or laughs,
and there is no peace.

¹⁰Murderers hate an honest person
and try to kill those who do
right.

¹¹Foolish people lose their tempers,
but wise people control
theirs.

¹²If a ruler pays attention to lies,
all his officers will become
wicked.

¹³The poor person and the cruel
person are alike
in that the LORD gave eyes to
both of them.

¹⁴If a king judges poor people fairly,
his government will continue
forever.

¹⁵Correction and punishment make
children wise,
but those left alone will disgrace
their mother.

¹⁶When there are many wicked
people, there is much sin,
but those who do right will see
them destroyed.

¹⁷Correct your children, and you will
be proud;
they will give you satisfaction.

¹⁸Where there is no word from God,
people are uncontrolled,
but those who obey what they
have been taught are happy.

¹⁹Words alone cannot correct a
servant,
because even if they understand,
they won't respond.

²⁰Do you see people who speak too
quickly?
There is more hope for a foolish
person than for them.

²¹If you spoil your servants when
they are young,
they will bring you grief later on.

²²An angry person causes trouble;
a person with a quick temper
sins a lot.

²³Pride will ruin people,
but those who are humble will
be honored.

²⁴Partners of thieves are their own
worst enemies.
If they have to testify in court,
they are afraid to say
anything.

²⁵Being afraid of people can get you
into trouble,
but if you trust the LORD, you
will be safe.

²⁶Many people want to speak to a
ruler,
but justice comes only from the
LORD.

²⁷Good people hate those who are
dishonest,
and the wicked hate those who
are honest.

Wise Words from Agur

30 These are the words of Agur
son of Jakeh.
This is his message to Ithiel and
Ucal:

²"I am the most stupid person there
is,
and I have no understanding.
³I have not learned to be wise,
and I don't know much about
God, the Holy One.
⁴Who has gone up to heaven and
come back down?
Who can hold the wind in his
hand?
Who can gather up the waters in
his coat?

Who has set in place the ends of
the earth?
What is his name or his son's name?
Tell me, if you know!

5"Every word of God is true.
He guards those who come to
him for safety.
6Do not add to his words,
or he will correct you and prove
you are a liar.

7"I ask two things from you, LORD.
Don't refuse me before I die.
8Keep me from lying and being
dishonest.
And don't make me either rich
or poor;
just give me enough food for
each day.
9If I have too much, I might reject
you
and say, 'I don't know the LORD.'
If I am poor, I might steal
and disgrace the name of my
God.

10"Do not say bad things about
servants to their masters,
or they will curse you, and you
will suffer for it.

11"Some people curse their fathers
and do not bless their mothers.
12Some people think they are pure,
but they are not really free from
evil.
13Some people have such a proud
look!
They look down on others.
14Some people have teeth like swords;
their jaws seem full of knives.
They want to remove the poor from
the earth
and the needy from the land.

15"Greed has two daughters
named 'Give' and 'Give.'
There are three things that are
never satisfied,
really four that never say, 'I've
had enough!':
16the cemetery, the childless mother,

MONEY

The Art of Budgeting

If you don't know whether your money is coming or going, you are not alone! Many people struggle to keep up with their finances. The good news is that basic budgeting isn't complicated. Anyone—including you—can do it. It begins with getting in the habit of saving your receipts. If it's too much trouble to keep all those little slips of paper, then buy a small notebook and write down your purchases for an entire week. You might be surprised how much those Frappuccinos are costing you! Once you've recorded everything for seven days, continue that habit for the next three weeks. After that first month, you'll have a good idea of exactly where your hard-earned money is going each month. Don't forget to add in your fixed expenses, such as rent, electricity, car insurance, and health insurance. Now compare that figure with your income after taxes. If you're spending more than you earn, it's time to make a change and cut back in some areas.

Once you've gotten a handle on your finances, you can occasionally take a month to spot-check your expenses in one category, such as food, entertainment, or car expenses. Simply record your purchases like you did in the beginning of the budgeting process to make sure you're still on target with your financial goals.

the land that never gets enough
rain,
and fire that never says, 'I've had
enough!'

¹⁷"If you make fun of your father
and refuse to obey your
mother,

WISE WORDS

Trust God's Word

Did you know that everything God says is true—100 percent accurate? His Word is pure and holy, standing the test of time and circumstances. In addition, 2 Timothy 3:16-17 says that the Bible is God-inspired and provides everything needed to live a godly life. Proverbs 30:5 says, "Every word of God is true. He guards those who come to him for safety." Not only is God's Word reliable and trustworthy, it is a shield for those who draw close to him. You can rely on the Bible as your source of strength, guidance, and assurance of God's love for you. His Word is a solid foundation that you can stand on—no matter what you're facing.

the birds of the valley will peck out
your eyes,
and the vultures will eat
them.

¹⁸"There are three things that are too
hard for me,
really four I don't understand:
¹⁹the way an eagle flies in the sky,
the way a snake slides over a
rock,
the way a ship sails on the sea,
and the way a man and a woman
fall in love.

²⁰"This is the way of a woman who
takes part in adultery:
She acts as if she had eaten and
washed her face;
she says, 'I haven't done
anything wrong.'

²¹"There are three things that make
the earth tremble,
really four it cannot stand:
²²a servant who becomes a king,
a foolish person who has plenty
to eat,
²³a hated woman who gets married,
and a maid who replaces her
mistress.

²⁴"There are four things on earth
that are small,
but they are very wise:
²⁵Ants are not very strong,
but they store up food in the
summer.
²⁶Rock badgers are not very
powerful,
but they can live among the
rocks.
²⁷Locusts have no king,
but they all go forward in
formation.
²⁸Lizards can be caught in the hand,
but they are found even in
kings' palaces.

²⁹"There are three things that strut
proudly,
really four that walk as if they
were important:
³⁰a lion, the proudest animal,

which is strong and runs from
nothing,
³¹a rooster, a male goat,
and a king when his army is
around him.

³²"If you have been foolish and proud,
or if you have planned evil, shut
your mouth.
³³Just as stirring milk makes butter,
and twisting noses makes them
bleed,
so stirring up anger causes
trouble."

Wise Words of King Lemuel

31 These are the words of King Lemuel, the message his mother taught him:
²"My son, I gave birth to you.
You are the son I prayed for.
³Don't waste your strength on
women
or your time on those who ruin
kings.

⁴"Kings should not drink wine,
Lemuel,
and rulers should not desire beer.
⁵If they drink, they might forget the
law
and keep the needy from getting
their rights.
⁶Give beer to people who are dying
and wine to those who are sad.
⁷Let them drink and forget their
need
and remember their misery no
more.

⁸"Speak up for those who cannot
speak for themselves;
defend the rights of all those
who have nothing.
⁹Speak up and judge fairly,
and defend the rights of the
poor and needy."

The Good Wife

¹⁰It is hard to find a good wife,
because she is worth more than
rubies.
¹¹Her husband trusts her completely.

With her, he has everything he needs.

[12] She does him good and not harm for as long as she lives.

[13] She looks for wool and flax and likes to work with her hands.

[14] She is like a trader's ship, bringing food from far away.

[15] She gets up while it is still dark and prepares food for her family and feeds her servant girls.

[16] She inspects a field and buys it. With money she earned, she plants a vineyard.

[17] She does her work with energy, and her arms are strong.

[18] She knows that what she makes is good. Her lamp burns late into the night.

[19] She makes thread with her hands and weaves her own cloth.

[20] She welcomes the poor and helps the needy.

[21] She does not worry about her family when it snows, because they all have fine clothes to keep them warm.

[22] She makes coverings for herself; her clothes are made of linen and other expensive material.

[23] Her husband is known at the city meetings, where he makes decisions as one of the leaders of the land.

[24] She makes linen clothes and sells them and provides belts to the merchants.

[25] She is strong and is respected by the people. She looks forward to the future with joy.

[26] She speaks wise words and teaches others to be kind.

[27] She watches over her family and never wastes her time.

[28] Her children speak well of her. Her husband also praises her,

[29] saying, "There are many fine women,

but you are better than all of them."

[30] Charm can fool you, and beauty can trick you, but a woman who respects the LORD should be praised.

[31] Give her the reward she has earned; she should be praised in public for what she has done.

BE STILL & KNOW

The Position of Prayer

There is no "right" position for prayer. While getting on your knees is a great way to focus and show humility, it's not necessary. You can talk to God with your eyes open (although shutting them may help you concentrate only on him). You can pray silently or out loud, in a crowd or by yourself. Like Moses in Exodus 9:29, some people like to

raise their hands to God when they pray; others may prefer to simply fold their hands and bow their heads right where they are. Whether you're kneeling, lying in bed, or flat on your face before God, be assured that he is always listening, no matter what position or location you choose.

Ecclesiastes

The meaning of life has been discussed and debated for centuries. The book of Ecclesiastes concludes the matter with one solid answer: Our existence is futile apart from God.

At first glance, the book of Ecclesiastes may seem a little strange or even misplaced. Some have even called it cynical and fatalistic because it focuses so much on the emptiness and meaninglessness of life. But if you keep reading to the end, you will find the book's compelling conclusion: "Now, everything has been heard, so I give my final advice: Honor God and obey his commands, because this is all people must do" (Ecclesiastes 12:13).

What's particularly interesting about Ecclesiastes is the author's unique perspective on affluence and power. As the king of Israel, King Solomon had experienced unprecedented wealth and fame, extraordinary wisdom, and the power to obtain any of the world's pleasures. Yet, at the end of his life, he realized that none of those endeavors had brought him the satisfaction he sought because his priorities had been out of balance. Truly, the human soul longs for something more. Only a thriving, intimate relationship with God will satisfy.

The goal of Solomon's biographical account is to spare readers from a lifetime of running after hollow dreams and climbing ladders of success that lead away from God. The book of Ecclesiastes serves as a powerful reminder of what's truly important.

1 These are the words of the Teacher, a son of David, king in Jerusalem. ²The Teacher says,
"Useless! Useless!
Completely useless!
Everything is useless."

³What do people really gain
from all the hard work they do
here on earth?

Things Never Change

⁴People live, and people die,
but the earth continues forever.
⁵The sun rises, the sun sets,
and then it hurries back to
where it rises again.
⁶The wind blows to the south;
it blows to the north.
It blows from one direction and
then another.
Then it turns around and
repeats the same pattern,
going nowhere.
⁷All the rivers flow to the sea,
but the sea never becomes full.
⁸Everything is boring,
so boring that you don't even
want to talk about it.
Words come again and again to our
ears,
but we never hear enough,
nor can we ever really see all we
want to see.
⁹All things continue the way they
have been since the
beginning.
What has happened will happen
again;

"Now, everything has been heard, so I give my final advice: Honor God and obey all his commands, because this is all people must do."

BECOMING RECOMMENDS

BOOKS & MUSIC

BOOKS

BLUE LIKE JAZZ

by Donald Miller

Have you ever wondered if the Christian faith is still relevant in our post-modern culture? Are you thirsty for a genuine encounter with God? Do you resent being lumped in with flashy televangelists and harshly judgmental people just because you call yourself a Christian? If so, *Blue Like Jazz* will help you deconstruct the familiar stereotypes and give you a fresh perspective on life and faith. This candid, heartfelt book details Miller's struggle to develop a faith that goes beyond traditional religion and invites readers to pursue a God who is an approachable friend, not a distant spectator.

HINDS' FEET ON HIGH PLACES

by Hannah Hurnard

When life seems challenging, this allegory by Hannah Hurnard is a comforting reassurance that you can persevere. The story follows Much Afraid, along with her companions Sorrow and Suffering, on a journey to the High Places. A loving Shepherd guides them with a gentle voice as they travel, encountering enemies and gathering memorial stones as they mark their progress. Along the way, these travelers overcome their weaknesses and find their faith strengthened. This book is encouraging and a great reminder to keep putting one foot in front of the other when life seems hard.

MUSIC

AWAKEN

by Natalie Grant

Awaken captures Grant's desire for women to discover their life's purpose, make a difference for Christ, and exercise the freedom to follow their dreams. The inspiration behind *Awaken* comes from Grant's exposure to the issue of human trafficking, both international and domestic. While only one song, "Home," was obviously inspired by this tragedy, Grant's newfound passion is evident from the first note to the last. In addition to "Home," don't miss "Live for Today"; "Bring It All Together," Grant's duet with Wynonna Judd; or the poignant song "Held," which builds a case for faith even when God seems silent.

"This book is a reminder to keep putting one foot in front of the other when life seems hard."

WHAT'S IN A word?

Ecclesiastes 1:14 "Chasing the wind" is a phrase used to describe the fleeting nature of life. Life passes by quickly, and any attempt to grab hold of it is as difficult as grasping for the wind.

there is nothing new here on earth.
[10]Someone might say,
"Look, this is new,"
but really it has always been here.
It was here before we were.
[11]People don't remember what happened long ago,
and in the future people will not remember what happens now.
Even later, other people will not remember what was done before them.

Does Wisdom Bring Happiness?

[12]I, the Teacher, was king over Israel in Jerusalem. [13]I decided to use my wisdom to learn about everything that happens on earth. I learned that God has given us terrible things to face. [14]I looked at everything done on earth and saw that it is all useless, like chasing the wind.
[15]If something is crooked,
you can't make it straight.
If something is missing,
you can't say it is there.
[16]I said to myself, "I have become very wise and am now wiser than anyone who ruled Jerusalem before me. I know what wisdom and knowledge really are." [17]So I decided to find out about wisdom and knowledge and also about foolish thinking, but this turned out to be like chasing the wind.

[18]With much wisdom comes much disappointment;
the person who gains more knowledge also gains more sorrow.

Does "Having Fun" Bring Happiness?

2 I said to myself, "I will try having fun. I will enjoy myself." But I found that this is also useless. [2]It is foolish to laugh all the time, and having fun doesn't accomplish anything. [3]I decided to cheer myself up with wine while my mind was still thinking wisely. I wanted to find a way to enjoy myself and see what was good for people to do during their few days of life.

Does Hard Work Bring Happiness?

[4]Then I did great things: I built houses and planted vineyards for myself. [5]I made gardens and parks, and I planted all kinds of fruit trees in them. [6]I made pools of water for myself and used them to water my growing trees. [7]I bought male and female slaves, and slaves were also born in my house. I had large herds and flocks, more than anyone in Jerusalem had ever had before. [8]I also gathered silver and gold for myself, treasures from kings and other areas. I had male and female singers and all the women a man could ever want. [9]I became very famous, even greater than anyone who had lived in Jerusalem before me. My wisdom helped me in all this.

[10]Anything I saw and wanted, I got for myself;
I did not miss any pleasure I desired.
I was pleased with everything I did,
and this pleasure was the reward for all my hard work.
[11]But then I looked at what I had done,
and I thought about all the hard work.
Suddenly I realized it was useless, like chasing the wind.
There is nothing to gain from anything we do here on earth.

Maybe Wisdom Is the Answer

[12]Then I began to think again about being wise,
and also about being foolish and doing crazy things.
But after all, what more can anyone do?
He can't do more than what the other king has already done.
[13]I saw that being wise is certainly better than being foolish,
just as light is better than darkness.
[14]Wise people see where they are going,
but fools walk around in the dark.
Yet I saw that
both wise and foolish people end the same way.

fun FACTS

Eating disorders are among the key health issues facing young women today.

(www.4women.gov)

¹⁵I thought to myself,
"What happens to a fool will
happen to me, too,
so what is the reward for being
wise?"
I said to myself,
"Being wise is also useless."
¹⁶The wise person and the fool
will both die,
and no one will remember either
one for long.
In the future, both will be
forgotten.

HEALTH

The Problem of Pain

When you're injured, you experience acute pain—an uncomfortable sign that something has gone wrong in your body. The pain usually subsides after a few moments or gradually over time. But sometimes the pain doesn't go away. Chronic pain continues long after the injury heals and can sometimes exist even without a specific injury or illness, resulting in discomfort, irritability, fatigue, stress, and depression. This kind of suffering has a way of affecting a person's disposition, so it's important to be sensitive and gracious to everyone because you never know what hidden pain a person is dealing with. The next time you're around a difficult person, consider the possibility of pain in her life—physical or emotional. And remember that compassion and love can help heal any wound.

Is There Real Happiness in Life?

¹⁷So I hated life. It made me sad to think that everything here on earth is useless, like chasing the wind. ¹⁸I hated all the things I had worked for here on earth, because I must leave them to someone who will live after me. ¹⁹Someone else will control everything for which I worked so hard here on earth, and I don't know if he will be wise or foolish. This is also useless. ²⁰So I became sad about all the hard work I had done here on earth. ²¹People can work hard using all their wisdom, knowledge, and skill, but they will die, and other people will get the things for which they worked. They did not do the work, but they will get everything. This is also unfair and useless. ²²What do people get for all their work and struggling here on earth? ²³All of their lives their work is full of pain and sorrow, and even at night their minds don't rest. This is also useless.

²⁴The best that people can do is eat, drink, and enjoy their work. I saw that even this comes from God, ²⁵because no one can eat or enjoy life without him. ²⁶If people please God, God will give them wisdom, knowledge, and joy. But sinners will get only the work of gathering and storing wealth that they will have to give to the ones who please God. So all their work is useless, like chasing the wind.

There Is a Time for Everything

3 There is a time for everything,
and everything on earth has
its special season.
²There is a time to be born
and a time to die.
There is a time to plant
and a time to pull up plants.

3There is a time to kill
  and a time to heal.
There is a time to destroy
  and a time to build.
4There is a time to cry
  and a time to laugh.
There is a time to be sad
  and a time to dance.
5There is a time to throw away stones
  and a time to gather them.
There is a time to hug
  and a time not to hug.
6There is a time to look for
  something
  and a time to stop looking for it.
There is a time to keep things
  and a time to throw things away.
7There is a time to tear apart
  and a time to sew together.
There is a time to be silent
  and a time to speak.
8There is a time to love
  and a time to hate.
There is a time for war
  and a time for peace.

God Controls His World

9Do people really gain anything from their work? 10I saw the hard work God has given people to do. 11God has given them a desire to know the future. He does everything just right and on time, but people can never completely understand what he is doing. 12So I realize that the best thing for them is to be happy and enjoy themselves as long as they live. 13God wants all people to eat and drink and be happy in their work, which are gifts from God. 14I know that everything God does will continue forever. People cannot add anything to what God has done, and they cannot take anything away from it. God does it this way to make people respect him. 15What happens now has happened in the past,
  and what will happen in the future has happened before.
  God makes the same things happen again and again.

Beauty Becomes Her

Your New Style

Have you ever noticed that your hair never looks better than when you walk out of a salon? It can be difficult to recreate the look the stylist gives you, but it's not impossible! Find out what types of products were used to give your hair its great look. Knowing the right tools to use will help improve your hair's appearance. In the same way, it's important to know and use the spiritual tools that will strengthen your relationship with God. Prayer, praise, worship, fasting, silence, journaling, and studying God's Word can all help to build and change your faith.

Unfairness on Earth

16I also saw this here on earth:
Where there should have been
  justice, there was evil;
  where there should have been
  right, there was wrong.
17I said to myself,
God has planned a time for every
  thing and every action,
  so he will judge both good
  people and bad.
18I decided that God leaves it the way it is to test people and to show them they are just like animals. 19The same thing happens to animals and to people; they both have the same breath, so they both die. People are no better off than the animals, because everything is useless. 20Both end up the same way; both came from dust and both will go back to dust. 21Who can be sure that the human spirit goes up to God and that the spirit of an animal goes down into the ground? 22So I saw that the best thing people can do is to enjoy their work, because that is all they have. No

one can help another person see what will happen in the future.

Is It Better to Be Dead?

4 Again I saw all the people who were mistreated here on earth.
I saw their tears
   and that they had no one to
      comfort them.
Cruel people had all the power,
   and there was no one to comfort
      those they hurt.
²I decided that the dead
   are better off than the
      living.
³But those who have never been
      born
   are better off still;
they have not seen the evil
   that is done here on earth.

Why Work So Hard?

⁴I realized the reason people work hard and try to succeed: They are jealous of each other. This, too, is useless, like chasing the wind.
⁵Some say it is foolish to fold your
      hands and do nothing,
   because you will starve to death.
⁶Maybe so, but I say it is better to be
      content
   with what little you have.
Otherwise, you will always be
      struggling for more,
   and that is like chasing the
      wind.

⁷Again I saw something here on
      earth that was useless:
⁸I saw a man who had no family,
no son or brother.
He always worked hard
   but was never satisfied with
      what he had.
He never asked himself, "For whom
   am I working so hard?
   Why don't I let myself enjoy
      life?"
This also is very sad and useless.

Friends and Family Give Strength

⁹Two people are better than one,
   because they get more done by
      working together.
¹⁰If one falls down,
   the other can help him up.
But it is bad for the person who is
      alone and falls,
   because no one is there to help.

¹¹If two lie down together, they will
      be warm,
   but a person alone will not be
      warm.
¹²An enemy might defeat one person,
   but two people together can
      defend themselves;
a rope that is woven of three
      strings is hard to break.

Fame and Power Are Useless

¹³A poor but wise boy is better than a foolish but old king who doesn't listen to advice. ¹⁴A boy became king. He had been born poor in the kingdom and had even gone to prison before becoming king. ¹⁵I watched all the people who live on earth follow him and make him their king. ¹⁶Many followed him at first,

but later, they did not like him, either. So fame and power are useless, like chasing the wind.

Be Careful About Making Promises

5 Be careful when you go to worship at the Temple. It is better to listen than to offer foolish sacrifices without even knowing you are doing wrong.
²Think before you speak,
   and be careful about what you
      say to God.
God is in heaven,
   and you are on the earth,
   so say only a few words to God.
³The saying is true: Bad dreams
   come from too much
      worrying,
   and too many words come from
      foolish people.

⁴If you make a promise to God, don't be slow to keep it. God is not happy with fools, so give God what you promised. ⁵It is better not to promise anything than to promise something and not do it. ⁶Don't let your words cause you to sin, and don't say to the priest at the Temple, "I didn't mean what I promised." If you do, God will become angry with your words and will destroy everything you have worked for. ⁷Many useless promises are like so many dreams; they mean nothing. You should respect God.

Officers Cheat Each Other

⁸In some places you will see poor people mistreated. Don't be surprised when they are not treated fairly or given their rights. One officer is cheated by a higher officer who in turn is cheated by even higher officers. ⁹The wealth of the country is divided up among them all. Even the king makes sure he gets his share of the profits.

Wealth Cannot Buy Happiness

¹⁰Whoever loves money
   will never have enough money;

fun FACTS

Back in 1975, the average Pell Grant picked up 47% of a student's tuition. Today's grant averages only 25%.

(Reader's Digest)

Whoever loves wealth
will not be satisfied with it.
This is also useless.
[11]The more wealth people have,
the more friends they have to
help spend it.
So what do people really gain?
They gain nothing except to
look at their riches.
[12]Those who work hard sleep in
peace;
it is not important if they eat
little or much.
But rich people worry about their
wealth
and cannot sleep.

[13]I have seen real misery here on
earth:
Money saved is a curse to its owners.
[14]   They lose it all in a bad deal
and have nothing to give to their
children.
[15]People come into this world with
nothing,

WHAT'S IN A word?

Ecclesiastes 5:1 "Be careful" is a reminder to be respectful and behave righteously when you worship God (and always!). This verse says it's better to listen than to offer "foolish sacrifices," so pay close attention to what you do and say.

and when they die they leave
with nothing.
In spite of all their hard work,
they leave just as they came.
[16]This, too, is real misery:
They leave just as they came.
So what do they gain from
chasing the wind?
[17]All they get are days full of sadness
and sorrow,
and they end up sick, defeated,
and angry.

Enjoy Your Life's Work

[18]I have seen what is best for people
here on earth. They should eat and

drink and enjoy their work, because the life God has given them on earth is short. [19]God gives some people the ability to enjoy the wealth and property he gives them, as well as the ability to accept their state in life and enjoy their work. [20]They do not worry about how short life is, because God keeps them busy with what they love to do.

6 I have seen something else wrong here on earth that causes serious problems for people. [2]God gives great wealth, riches, and honor to some people; they have everything they want. But God does not let them enjoy such things; a stranger enjoys them instead. This is useless and very wrong. [3]A man might have a hundred children and live a long time, but what good is it if he can't enjoy the good God gives him or have a proper burial? I say a baby born dead is better off than he is. [4]A baby born dead is useless. It returns to darkness without even a name. [5]That baby never saw the sun and never knew anything, but it finds more rest than that man. [6]Even if he lives two thousand years, he doesn't enjoy the good God gives him. Everyone is going to the same place.

[7]People work just to feed
themselves,
but they never seem to get
enough to eat.
[8]In this way a wise person
is no better off than a fool.
Then, too, it does a poor person
little good
to know how to get along in life.
[9]It is better to see what you have
than to want more.
Wanting more is useless—
like chasing the wind.

ETIQUETTE 101

MANNERS AT THE GYM

You've joined a fitness center—that's great! But before you step on the treadmill, mind your manners. First and foremost, wipe up your sweat. There's nothing worse than your moist mark left behind, so carry a towel at all times. Limit your time on equipment to thirty minutes if others are waiting. Reset weight machines after use to the lowest setting to prevent injury to others. Clean up after yourself, keeping personal items in a locker and putting towels in available receptacles. Be on time for scheduled classes, and definitely obey all posted rules of the health club.

Who Can Understand God's Plan?

¹⁰Whatever happens was planned
long ago.
Everyone knows what people are
like.
No one can argue with God,
who is stronger than anyone.
¹¹The more you say,
the more useless it is.
What good does it do?
¹²People have only a few useless days
of life on the earth; their short life
passes like a shadow. Who knows what
is best for them while they live? Who
can tell them what the future will
bring?

Some Benefits of Serious Thinking

7 It is better to have respect
than good perfume.
The day of death is better than the
day of birth.
²It is better to go to a funeral
than to a party.
We all must die,
and everyone living should think
about this.
³Sorrow is better than laughter,
and sadness has a good
influence on you.
⁴A wise person thinks about death,
but a fool thinks only about
having a good time.
⁵It is better to be criticized by a wise
person
than to be praised by a fool.
⁶The laughter of fools
is like the crackling of thorns in
a cooking fire.
Both are useless.

⁷Even wise people are fools
if they let money change their
thinking.

⁸It is better to finish something
than to start it.
It is better to be patient
than to be proud.
⁹Don't become angry quickly,
because getting angry is foolish.

¹⁰Don't ask, "Why was life better in
the 'good old days'?"
It is not wise to ask such
questions.

¹¹Wisdom is better when it comes
with money.
They both help those who are
alive.
¹²Wisdom is like money:
they both help.
But wisdom is better,
because it can save whoever has
it.

¹³Look at what God has done:
No one can straighten what he
has bent.
¹⁴When life is good, enjoy it.
But when life is hard,
remember:
God gives good times and hard
times,
and no one knows what
tomorrow will bring.

Become INVOLVED

PregnancyCenters.org

PregnancyCenters.org offers a place where visitors can locate a network of crisis pregnancy centers around the United States and Canada. These centers help women make decisions for life when they are faced with an unwanted pregnancy. This site also operates a free hotline that is available 24/7 to answer women's questions on abortion, pregnancy tests, STD's, adoption, parenting, medical referrals, housing, and many other issues.

If you want to get involved protecting the lives of the unborn, you can train to be a phone consultant or a counselor at a pregnancy center. You can also volunteer to greet women as they come in, talk with them after they receive a free pregnancy test, and encourage them to consider carrying their babies to term. Consider joining with your local center to spread the message of abstinence to local teens by collaborating on community campaigns and speaking opportunities.

At the Web site, you can enter your zip code to find the location and phone number of a crisis pregnancy center near you. The center may need office help, fundraisers, community liaisons, or donations of baby items, especially diapers and formula.

To get involved in the fight for little lives, stop by www.pregnancycenters.org.

It Is Impossible to Be Truly Good

¹⁵In my useless life I have seen both of these:
I have seen good people die in spite
   of their goodness
and evil people live a long time
   in spite of their evil.
¹⁶Don't be too right,
   and don't be too wise.
   Why destroy yourself?
¹⁷Don't be too wicked,
   and don't be foolish.
   Why die before your time?
¹⁸It is good to grab the one and not
      let go of the other;
   those who honor God will hold
      them both.

¹⁹Wisdom makes a person stronger
   than ten leaders in a city.

²⁰Surely there is not a good person
      on earth
   who always does good and never
      sins.

²¹Don't listen to everything people
      say,
   or you might hear your servant
      insulting you.
²²You know that many times
   you have insulted others.

²³I used wisdom to test all these
      things.
   I wanted to be wise,
      but it was too hard for me.
²⁴I cannot understand why things are
      as they are.
   It is too hard for anyone to
      understand.
²⁵I studied and tried very hard to
      find wisdom,
   to find some meaning for
      everything.
   I learned that it is foolish to be evil,
      and it is crazy to act like a
         fool.
²⁶I found that some women are worse
      than death
   and are as dangerous as traps.
   Their love is like a net,

and their arms hold men like
   chains.
A man who pleases God will be
   saved from them,
   but a sinner will be caught by
      them.
²⁷The Teacher says, "This is what I learned:
   I added all these things together
      to find some meaning for
         everything.
²⁸While I was searching,
   I did not find one man among
      the thousands I found.
   Nor did I find a woman among all
      these.
²⁹One thing I have learned:
God made people good,
   but they have found all kinds of
      ways to be bad."

Obey the King

8 No one is like the wise person
   who can understand what
      things mean.
Wisdom brings happiness;
   it makes sad faces happy.
²Obey the king's command, because you made a promise to God. ³Don't be too quick to leave the king. Don't support something that is wrong, because the king does whatever he pleases. ⁴What the king says is law; no one tells him what to do.
⁵Whoever obeys the king's command
   will be safe.
   A wise person does the right
      thing at the right time.
⁶There is a right time and a right
      way for everything,
   yet people often have many
      troubles.
⁷They do not know what the future
      holds,
   and no one can tell them what
      will happen.
⁸No one can control the wind
   or stop his own death.
No soldier is released in times of
   war,
   and evil does not set free those
      who do evil.

Balancing Act

Fear Factor

Is there a change you've wanted to make, but you're afraid to actually make it? Maybe you've thought about moving or switching jobs, but you're apprehensive about what might happen. Your life is too precious to be controlled by any "fear factor." Being afraid of new people and experiences robs you of new opportunities. Psalm 27:1 says the Lord protects and saves you, so you never need to be afraid. If you move and don't like your new surroundings, look forward to your next move while making the best of this one—you may end up loving it! If you accept a new job and it isn't all you hoped it would be, take advantage of the opportunity to bring a fresh and creative approach to that job. You have one life to live. God wants you to go for it!

Seven ways to...

Put Others First

1. Be quick to listen and slow to speak.

2. Hold doors open for other people.

3. Let someone go in front of you in line.

4. Give more than you keep.

5. Yield to other drivers, even the pushy ones.

6. Respond kindly to someone who is rude.

7. Look for little ways to respond to the needs of others.

Justice, Rewards, and Punishment

⁹I saw all of this as I considered all that is done here on earth. Sometimes people harm those they control. ¹⁰I saw the funerals of evil people who used to go in and out of the holy place. They were honored in the same towns where they had done evil. This is useless, too.

¹¹When evil people are not punished right away, it makes others want to do evil, too. ¹²Though a sinner might do a hundred evil things and might live a long time, I know it will be better for those who honor God. ¹³I also know it will not go well for evil people, because they do not honor God. Like a shadow, they will not last. ¹⁴Sometimes something useless happens on earth. Bad things happen to good people, and good things happen to bad people. I say that this is also useless. ¹⁵So I decided it was more important to enjoy life. The best that people can do here on earth is to eat, drink, and enjoy life, because these joys will help them do the hard work God gives them here on earth.

We Cannot Understand All God Does

¹⁶I tried to understand all that happens on earth. I saw how busy people are, working day and night and hardly ever sleeping. ¹⁷I also saw all that God has done. Nobody can understand what God does here on earth. No matter how hard people try to understand it, they cannot. Even if wise people say they understand, they cannot; no one can really understand it.

Is Death Fair?

9 I thought about all this and tried to understand it. I saw that God controls good people and wise people and what they do, but no one knows if they will experience love or hate.

²Good and bad people end up the same—
those who are right and those who are wrong,
those who are good and those who are evil,
those who are clean and those who are unclean,
those who sacrifice and those who do not.

The same things happen to a good person
as happen to a sinner,
to a person who makes promises to God
and to one who does not.

³This is something wrong that happens here on earth: What happens to one happens to all. So people's minds are full of evil and foolish thoughts while they live. After that, they join the dead. ⁴But anyone still alive has hope; even a live dog is better off than a dead lion!

⁵The living know they will die,
but the dead know nothing.
Dead people have no more reward,
and people forget them.
⁶After people are dead,
they can no longer love or hate
or envy.
They will never again share
in what happens here on earth.

Enjoy Life While You Can

⁷So go eat your food and enjoy it;
drink your wine and be happy,
because that is what God wants you to do.
⁸Put on nice clothes
and make yourself look good.
⁹Enjoy life with the wife you love. Enjoy all the useless days of this useless life God has given you here on earth, because it is all you have. So enjoy the work you do here on earth. ¹⁰Whatever work you do, do your best, because you are going to the grave, where there is no working, no planning, no knowledge, and no wisdom.

Time and Chance

¹¹I also saw something else here on earth:
The fastest runner does not always win the race,
the strongest soldier does not always win the battle,
the wisest does not always have food,
the smartest does not always become wealthy,

what do you value?

Put a star next to anything you handle well or is a quality you already have.

Put a circle next to anything you don't handle well or is an attribute that seems out of reach for you.

___ Confidence	___ Beauty
___ Humility	___ Responsibility
___ Flexibility	___ Boldness
___ Physical fitness	___ Cool-headed logic
___ Passion	___ Enthusiasm
___ Compromise	___ Bravery
___ Smarts	___ Fashion sense
___ Faithfulness	___ Cooperation
___ Wealth	___ Adaptability
___ Honesty	___ Consistency

MORE STARS: YOU'RE A GLASS-HALF-FULL KIND OF WOMAN. You recognize your strengths, and you're willing to name them. You value looking for the good in things and try to see the best in yourself and others. You know you can't be good at everything and are willing to work on your weaknesses.

MORE CIRCLES: YOU TEND TO SEE THE GLASS AS HALF-EMPTY. You focus more on things you can't do than on those you can. Sometimes you are too hard on yourself. You value being realistic and thinking things through before jumping in, both of which are positive qualities.

Three or more stars next to words like CONFIDENCE, LOGIC, RESPONSIBILITY, OR SMARTS means you're a left-brain thinker. You analyze each situation, think before you act, and plan carefully so everything goes smoothly.

Three or more stars next to words like PASSION, BOLDNESS, BRAVERY, OR ENTHUSIASM means you're a right-brain thinker. You enjoy spontaneous activities, think outside the box, and appreciate creativity.

Three or more stars next to words like BEAUTY, PHYSICAL FITNESS, WEALTH, OR FASHION means you place value on appearances. For good or bad, you assess others and yourself by what's on the outside. You need to be careful not to let the love of superficial things dominate your value system.

Three or more stars next to words like HUMILITY, CONSISTENCY, HONESTY, OR FAITHFULNESS means you place value on your relationships with God and others. You always try to be yourself and work hard to make sure your actions reflect your beliefs.

Three or more stars next to words like COMPROMISE, COOPERATION, ADAPTABILITY, OR FLEXI-BILITY means you value being a team player. You're able to make situations work because you can find the middle ground that benefits everyone. You are able to figure out what's truly important to you and are willing to compromise on the non-essentials.

and the talented one does not
always receive praise.
Time and chance happen to
everyone.
[12]No one knows what will happen
next.
Like a fish caught in a net,
or a bird caught in a trap,
people are trapped by evil
when it suddenly falls on them.

Wisdom Does Not Always Win

[13]I also saw something wise here on earth that impressed me. [14]There was a small town with only a few people in it. A great king fought against it and put his armies all around it. [15]Now there was a poor but wise man in the town who used his wisdom to save his town. But later on, everyone forgot about him. [16]I still think wisdom is better than strength. But those people forgot about the poor man's wisdom and stopped listening to what he said.

[17]The quiet words of a wise person
are better
than the shouts of a foolish
ruler.
[18]Wisdom is better than weapons of
war,
but one sinner can destroy much
good.

10 Dead flies can make even
perfume stink.
In the same way, a little foolishness
can spoil wisdom.
[2]The heart of the wise leads to right,
but the heart of a fool leads to
wrong.
[3]Even in the way fools walk along
the road,
they show they are not wise;
they show everyone how stupid
they are.
[4]Don't leave your job
just because your boss is angry
with you.
Remaining calm solves great
problems.

[5]There is something else wrong that
happens here on earth.
It is the kind of mistake rulers
make:
[6]Fools are given important positions
while gifted people are given
lower ones;
[7]I have seen servants ride horses
while princes walk like servants
on foot.
[8]Anyone who digs a pit might fall
into it;
anyone who knocks down a wall
might be bitten by a snake;
[9]anyone who moves boulders might
be hurt by them;
and anyone who cuts logs might
be harmed by them.
[10]A dull ax means
harder work.
Being wise will make it easier.
[11]If a snake bites the tamer before it
is tamed,
what good is the tamer?

[12]The words of the wise bring them
praise,
but the words of a fool will
destroy them.

Q: I HAVE A CHRISTIAN FRIEND WHO IS HAVING AN AFFAIR. SHOULD I TALK TO HER ABOUT IT?

A: You do not have to condone sin by keeping it a secret, but there is a fine line between bringing it up in love and being critical or judgmental. The saying, "Hate the sin, but love the sinner" may seem trite, but it's true. Confront the person lovingly and directly (do not gossip about her!) and be prepared for her to react angrily out of guilt. Offer to stand with her if she chooses to repent and make amends, and be strong enough to remain a friend—possibly at a distance—if she decides not to change.

What's the POINT?

¹³A fool begins by saying foolish
things
and ends by saying crazy and
wicked things.
¹⁴A fool talks too much.
No one knows the future,
and no one can tell what will
happen after death.
¹⁵Work wears fools out;
they don't even know how to get
home.

The Value of Work

¹⁶How terrible it is for a country
whose king is a child
and whose leaders eat all
morning.
¹⁷How lucky a country is whose king
comes from a good family,
whose leaders eat only at
mealtime
and for strength, not to get
drunk.

¹⁸If someone is lazy, the roof will
begin to fall.
If he doesn't fix it, the house
will leak.

¹⁹A party makes you feel good,
wine makes you feel happy,
and money buys anything.

²⁰Don't make fun of the king,
and don't make fun of rich
people, even in your
bedroom.
A little bird might carry your
words;
a bird might fly and tell what
you said.

Boldly Face the Future

11 Invest what you have,
because after a while you
will get a return.
²Invest what you have in several
different businesses,
because you don't know what
disasters might happen.

³If clouds are full of rain,
they will shower on the earth.

Ecclesiastes 11:9

Do you always feel like you are waiting for the next thing to come along before you can be truly happy? Do you feel as if life is on hold until you achieve that next goal, land the perfect job, find a great guy, or discover your hidden talents? God wants you to experience the abundant life right now, no matter what your circumstances. In this exact moment, you have already been equipped by God to do great things. You don't have to wait until you are older! You don't have to focus your time and energy on what you don't have yet; you can enjoy what you do have today. So many people look back on their younger days and long for them again, saying they never realized how good they had it until after the time was gone. Live for today! Be happy while you are young. Examine your life and enjoy the blessings in it. Rejoice in the beautiful creation around you, in the relationships God has given you, and in the talents he has blessed you with. Revel in the fact that you are alive, that God loves you, and that you can do great things through him.

What's the POINT?

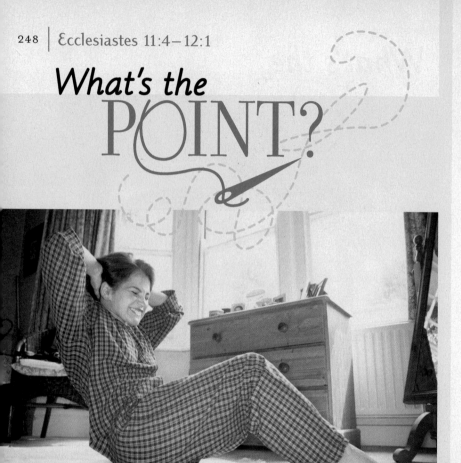

Ecclesiastes 12:14

Want to know a great way to lose weight? Confess to God all the wrong things you've done. Really! After you do, you'll feel so much lighter that you'll practically float! Gone is the weight of the world from your shoulders. You can move on to bigger and better things—guilt-free! You know that old cliché, "You can run, but you cannot hide"? Well, it really is true. At least when it comes to God. He knows everything about you—the very, very good and the really, really bad. Nothing is a secret from him, and the day will come when he will hold everyone accountable for their words and actions. Since God knows it all anyway, wouldn't it be a good idea to go ahead and 'fess up now? God will forgive your sins if you ask him to, and you can trust him to never bring them up again. He will cleanse you from all the wrongs you have done, every single one (1 John 1:9). And if you admit what you have done wrong sooner rather than later, you get to live with a whole lot more freedom and a whole lot less guilt. The next time you make a mistake that disappoints God, don't carry it around with you; confess it right away and live in the freedom God has for you!

A tree can fall to the north or south,
but it will stay where it falls.
[4]Those who wait for perfect weather
will never plant seeds;
those who look at every cloud
will never harvest crops.

[5]You don't know where the wind will blow,
and you don't know how a baby grows inside the mother.
In the same way, you don't know what God is doing,
or how he created everything.
[6]Plant early in the morning,
and work until evening,
because you don't know if this or that will succeed.
They might both do well.

Serve God While You Are Young

[7]Sunshine is sweet;
it is good to see the light of day.
[8]People ought to enjoy every day of their lives,
no matter how long they live.
But they should also remember this:
You will be dead a long time.
Everything that happens then is useless.
[9]Young people, enjoy yourselves while you are young;
be happy while you are young.
Do whatever your heart desires,
whatever you want to do.
But remember that God will judge you
for everything you do.
[10]Don't worry,
and forget the troubles of your body,
because youth and childhood are useless.

The Problems of Old Age

12 Remember your Creator while you are young,
before the days of trouble come
and the years when you say,

"I find no pleasure in them."
2When you get old,
    the light from the sun, moon,
        and stars will grow dark;
    the rain clouds will never seem
        to go away.
3At that time your arms will shake
    and your legs will become
        weak.
Your teeth will fall out so you
        cannot chew,
    and your eyes will not see
        clearly.
4Your ears will be deaf to the noise
        in the streets,
    and you will barely hear the
        millstone grinding grain.
You'll wake up when a bird starts
        singing,
    but you will barely hear singing.
5You will fear high places
    and will be afraid to go for a
        walk.
Your hair will become white like
        the flowers on an almond
        tree.
    You will limp along like a
        grasshopper when you walk.

Your appetite will be gone.
Then you will go to your everlasting
        home,
    and people will go to your
        funeral.
6Soon your life will snap like a silver
        chain
    or break like a golden bowl.
You will be like a broken pitcher at
        a spring,
    or a broken wheel at a well.
7You will turn back into the dust of
        the earth again,
    but your spirit will return to
        God who gave it.

8Everything is useless!
    The Teacher says that
        everything is useless.

Conclusion: Honor God

9The Teacher was very wise and taught the people what he knew. He very carefully thought about, studied, and set in order many wise teachings. 10The Teacher looked for just the right words to write what is dependable and true.

11Words from wise people are like sharp sticks used to guide animals. They are like nails that have been driven in firmly. Altogether they are wise teachings that come from one Shepherd. 12So be careful, my son, about other teachings. People are always writing books, and too much study will make you tired.

13Now, everything has been heard,
    so I give my final advice:
Honor God and obey his commands,
    because this is all people must
        do.
14God will judge everything,
    even what is done in secret,
    the good and the evil.

WHAT'S IN A word?

Ecclesiastes 12:11 "Nails" refers to the hooks used in tents for hanging clothes, pots, and other everyday household items. The mental "nails" or "pegs" of wisdom are intended to provide stability and a sound perspective on life.

WISE WORDS

Don't Judge by Outward Appearances

Have you ever sat in a busy airport or mall and watched people pass by? Just by looking at people, you can guess all kinds of things about their professions and lifestyles. But they are just guesses. To really know someone, you have to go much deeper. Proverbs 31:30 says, "Charm can fool you, and beauty can trick you, but a woman who respects the LORD should be praised." God knows that it's easy for us to get caught up in superficial impressions and outer beauty, but it's important to remember that appearances can be deceptive. That's why the Bible challenges us to look at the inner person of the heart, the place where true beauty resides.

Song of Songs

Love. True love. Song of Songs is a love story between a young girl and her lover that explores their intense passion and longing. The language is vibrant and robust, and the passionate exchange of descriptive words between the bride and groom has been known to make more than a few people blush. In fact, because of its explicit language, some ancient and modern sages prohibited men from reading the book before they turned thirty!

While Song of Songs is a love story between a man and a woman, it can actually be read on several levels. Reflected in this tale of love, courtship, and marriage is a picture of the relationship between Jesus Christ and his bride, the church. Another interpretation views the book as a description of God's love for Israel.

Fortunately, you don't have to examine all the meanings in order to understand and appreciate the Song of Songs. Whether or not its characters are allegorical, this song narrates the splendor of marriage and celebrates the love and sexual intimacy between married couples. While Song of Songs is rich with romantic and sexual imagery, the book in no way encourages extramarital activity. Rather, it embraces and affirms sexual pleasure within the confines of marriage.

Enjoy reading this love song as both a beautiful story honoring human love and as a reminder of God's overwhelming love for you.

1

Solomon's Song of Songs.

The Woman Speaks to the Man She Loves

²Kiss me with the kisses of your
mouth,
because your love is better than
wine.
³The smell of your perfume is
pleasant,
and your name is pleasant like
expensive perfume.
That's why the young women
love you.
⁴Take me with you; let's run
together.
The king takes me into his
rooms.

Friends Speak to the Man

We will rejoice and be happy with
you;
we praise your love more than
wine.
With good reason, the young
women love you.

The Woman Speaks

⁵I'm dark but lovely,
women of Jerusalem,
dark like the tents of Kedar,
like the curtains of Solomon.
⁶Don't look at how dark I am,
at how dark the sun has made
me.
My brothers were angry with me
and made me tend the
vineyards,

"I found the one I love."

BOOKS

WHEN WALLFLOWERS DANCE

by Angela Thomas

Angela Thomas's books are a lot like rich, hot cocoa on a cold, drizzly day. They make you feel warm inside and out, and they reach directly for the heart of every reader. A self-proclaimed former wallflower, Thomas encourages women to see themselves as beautiful in God's eyes. In When Wallflowers Dance, the follow-up to the best-seller Do You Think I'm Beautiful?, this mother of four challenges women to step out of the corners and dance, to celebrate the life God has designed for them, and to appreciate the truly beautiful people they are becoming.

CAPTIVATING: UNVEILING THE MYSTERY OF A WOMAN'S SOUL

by John and Stasi Eldredge

In the heart of every woman is the deep desire to be treated like a princess. That's the premise of John and Stasi Eldredge's Captivating, a companion volume to John's book about masculinity, Wild at Heart. This time, it's the woman's turn. The Eldredges contrast your desire for adventure and romance with the reality that life is often more about duties and demands. Captivating looks at Eve's role before Adam and Eve sinned and encourages you to restore your feminine heart in order to have more freedom, strength, peace, and beauty in your life.

MUSIC

ALL ABOUT LOVE

by Steven Curtis Chapman

In a romantic mood? Pop All About Love into the CD player and give it a spin. After sixteen years of marriage, Steven Curtis Chapman decided to write an album of love songs to his wife Mary Beth—and let her be the executive producer of the project. From his heartfelt plea to God in "How Do I Love Her?" to the song about the day his wife was born, "11-6-64," this album will melt your heart. Chapman also does a fun cover of The Proclaimers' pop hit "I'm Gonna Be (500 Miles)" and includes his classic "I Will Be Here."

Thomas challenges women to celebrate the life God has designed for them and to appreciate the truly beautiful people they are becoming.

so I haven't tended my own
    vineyard!
[7]Tell me, you whom I love,
    where do you feed your sheep?
    Where do you let them rest at
      noon?
    Why should I look for you near your
      friend's sheep,
    like a woman who wears a veil?[n]

The Man Speaks to the Woman

[8]You are the most beautiful of
    women.
    Surely you know to follow the
      sheep
    and feed your young goats
      near the shepherds' tents.
[9]My darling, you are like a mare
    among the king's stallions.
[10]Your cheeks are beautiful with
    ornaments,
    and your neck with jewels.
[11]We will make for you gold
    earrings
    with silver hooks.

The Woman Speaks

[12]The smell of my perfume spreads
    out
    to the king on his couch.
[13]My lover is like a bag of myrrh
    that lies all night between my
      breasts.
[14]My lover is like a bunch of flowers
    from the vineyards at
      En Gedi.

WHAT'S IN A word?

Song of Songs 2:1 The "Plain of Sharon" was an area known for its flowers and rich, life-giving land. The woman is saying that she is only one among a field of other beautiful women.

The Man Speaks

[15]My darling, you are beautiful!
    Oh, you are beautiful,
    and your eyes are like doves.

The Woman Answers the Man

[16]You are so handsome, my lover,
    and so pleasant!
    Our bed is the grass.
[17]Cedar trees form our roof;
    our ceiling is made of juniper
      wood.

The Woman Speaks Again

2   I am a rose in the Plain of
      Sharon,
    a lily in the valleys.

The Man Speaks Again

[2]Among the young women, my darling
    is like a lily among thorns!

The Woman Answers

[3]Among the young men, my lover
    is like an apple tree in the
      woods!
  I enjoy sitting in his shadow;
    his fruit is sweet to my taste.
[4]He brought me to the banquet room,
    and his banner over me is love.
[5]Strengthen me with raisins,
    and refresh me with apples,
    because I am weak with love.
[6]My lover's left hand is under my
    head,
    and his right arm holds me
      tight.

The Woman Speaks to the Friends

[7]Women of Jerusalem, promise me
    by the gazelles and the deer
  not to awaken
    or excite my feelings of love
    until it is ready.

The Woman Speaks Again

[8]I hear my lover's voice.
    Here he comes jumping across
      the mountains,
    skipping over the hills.

What's the POINT?

Song of Songs 2:16

Have you heard people say that to make a marriage successful, the partners have to work out a 50-50 arrangement? Well, those numbers tell only half the story. A marriage that honors God and both spouses is one that requires 100 percent from the husband and 100 percent from the wife. Everything. All of you. The whole package. Your body, your heart, your mind, your dreams, your desires. Nothing held back. In order for two people to be truly united, they both have to give up their own agendas, their own priorities, and their own desires to have their needs met first. Real love in marriage must be self-sacrificing. Husbands and wives need to be willing to lay down their own lives for each other. It's not always easy to put someone else first, but it is so rewarding in the end! Are you ready to give up what you want? Can you abandon the desire for your needs to take priority over your partner's needs? That degree of self-lessness requires a heart, mind, and soul commitment, but your sacrifice will be richly rewarded. When you reach the point of laying down your desires for someone else, you'll experience the depth of love that is found in Song of Songs.

1:7 veil This was the way a prostitute usually dressed.

Living with Long-Term Illness

KAYLA'S STORY

After returning from a trip, I noticed that I could not feel the left side of my head, face, and arm. I thought it was because of all the traveling and stress, but then I began to have a sharp, piercing pain in my head.

I decided to visit a neurologist, and the tests showed that I had multiple sclerosis (MS). I had just turned thirty, and I didn't have time to think about a long-term illness. The reality of MS didn't really sink in until my mother did some research and recommended some herbal and vitamin supplements. I immediately felt better, and I was able to control my symptoms without special medication.

I lived with MS for more than five years before it began taking a heavy toll on my body. Then, within a few months, I found myself losing my train of thought and struggling with my speech. Medical tests showed the MS was in my spine and brain. I was immediately put on steroids, taught to self-administer shots, and began taking anti-anxiety medication to help control my fear of shots. God constantly poured out his grace on me as he walked me through painful situations that I could have never endured in my own strength.

In dealing with tremendous fatigue and the flu-like side effects of the medication, I have continually had to rely on God's Word; it's the only way I can survive. It gives me hope and strength to face each day. I hold on to Psalm 139:5 as a promise of God's nearness: "You are all around me—in front and in back—and have put your hand on me." Whenever I experience shooting pains in my head and legs, I remember 2 Chronicles 20:15: "The battle is not your battle, it is God's." His power is alive and working in me, and I know he is stronger than my disease.

I'm feeling the best I've felt in years, and my last checkup showed evidence of physical improvement. In the midst of this disease, the Lord continues to show himself true and faithful.

> I FOUND MYSELF LOSING MY TRAIN OF THOUGHT AND STRUGGLING WITH MY SPEECH.

What's the POINT?

9My lover is like a gazelle or a young deer.
  Look, he stands behind our wall
peeking through the windows,
  looking through the blinds.
10My lover spoke and said to me,
  "Get up, my darling;
  let's go away, my beautiful one.
11Look, the winter is past;
  the rains are over and gone.
12Blossoms appear through all the land.
  The time has come to sing;
  the cooing of doves is heard in our land.
13There are young figs on the fig trees,
  and the blossoms on the vines smell sweet.
Get up, my darling;
  let's go away, my beautiful one."

The Man Speaks

14My beloved is like a dove hiding in the cracks of the rock,
  in the secret places of the cliff.
Show me your face,
  and let me hear your voice.
Your voice is sweet,
  and your face is lovely.
15Catch the foxes for us—
  the little foxes that ruin the vineyards
  while they are in blossom.

The Woman Speaks

16My lover is mine, and I am his.
  He feeds among the lilies
17until the day dawns
  and the shadows disappear.
Turn, my lover.
  Be like a gazelle or a young deer
  on the mountain valleys.

The Woman Dreams

3 At night on my bed,
  I looked for the one I love;
I looked for him, but I could not find him.
2I got up and went around the city,
  in the streets and squares,

Song of Songs 3:5

If you are deathly allergic to chocolate but you absolutely love it, would it be a good idea to keep a stock of candy bars in your nightstand? Of course not! So if you are single and want to remain pure, why would you torment and tempt yourself by hanging out at nightclubs, reading novels with explicit sex scenes, or watching tons and tons of romantic movies? Although this biblical warning to not awaken romantic urges too soon is most often applied to teenagers, it is for anyone who is a God-seeking single, no matter how old you are. Stay the course! Guard your heart! Don't torture yourself by overindulging in romantic media and tempting situations that make you constantly long for a mate and stir you up physically and emotionally when there's not a husband-to-be in sight. You may have spent so many years being single and celibate that you are about to give up and give in, but keep in mind that remaining sexually pure until marriage has great payoffs that make it well worth the wait. Remember—purity is not about seeing how close you can get to the edge; it's about seeing how far away from it you can stay.

looking for the one I love.
I looked for him, but I could not
find him.
³The watchmen found me as they
patrolled the city,
so I asked, "Have you seen the
one I love?"
⁴As soon as I had left them,
I found the one I love.
I held him and would not let him go
until I brought him to my
mother's house,
to the room where I was born.

The Woman Speaks to the Friends

⁵Women of Jerusalem, promise me
by the gazelles and the deer
not to awaken
or excite my feelings of love
until it is ready.
⁶Who is this coming out of the
desert
like a cloud of smoke?

Who is this that smells like myrrh,
incense,
and other spices?
⁷Look, it's Solomon's couch"
with sixty soldiers around it,
the finest soldiers of Israel.
⁸These soldiers all carry swords
and have been trained in war.
Every man wears a sword at his side
and is ready for the dangers of
the night.
⁹King Solomon had a couch made for
himself
of wood from Lebanon.
¹⁰He made its posts of silver
and its braces of gold.
The seat was covered with purple
cloth
that the women of Jerusalem
wove with love.
¹¹Women of Jerusalem, go out and see
King Solomon.
He is wearing the crown his
mother put on his head

on his wedding day,
when his heart was happy!

The Man Speaks to the Woman

4 How beautiful you are, my
darling!
Oh, you are beautiful!
Your eyes behind your veil are like
doves.
Your hair is like a flock of goats
streaming down Mount
Gilead.
²Your teeth are white like newly
sheared sheep
just coming from their bath.
Each one has a twin,
and none of them is missing.
³Your lips are like red silk thread,
and your mouth is lovely.
Your cheeks behind your veil
are like slices of a pomegranate.
⁴Your neck is like David's tower,
built with rows of stones.
A thousand shields hang on its walls;
each shield belongs to a strong
soldier.
⁵Your breasts are like two fawns,
like twins of a gazelle,
feeding among the lilies.
⁶Until the day dawns
and the shadows disappear,
I will go to that mountain of myrrh
and to that hill of incense.
⁷My darling, everything about you is
beautiful,
and there is nothing at all
wrong with you.
⁸Come with me from Lebanon, my
bride.
Come with me from Lebanon,
from the top of Mount Amana,
from the tops of Mount Senir
and Mount Hermon.
Come from the lions' dens
and from the leopards' hills.
⁹My sister, my bride,
you have thrilled my heart;
you have thrilled my heart
with a glance of your eyes,
with one sparkle from your
necklace.

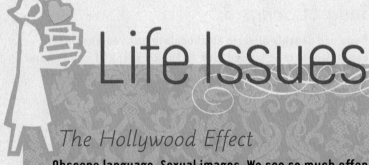

Life Issues

The Hollywood Effect

**Obscene language. Sexual images. We see so much offensive
material on TV and in films that we don't even feel shocked
anymore. If the screenplay is funny or stirs our emotions, we
tend to overlook all the garbage. It's the "Hollywood effect,"
and it can numb our sensitivity to unhealthy words and
images. We need to be wise media consumers, able to look
beyond the surface. What do the movies you watch advocate?
What worldview do the characters have? Are they people
whose lives you emulate? Are the relationships the kind that
can last a lifetime, or are they based on nothing more than a
chemical reaction? Philippians 4:8 says to think about the
things that are "good and worthy of praise" and "true and
honorable and right and pure and beautiful and respected."
Think about that the next time you reach for the remote.**

▶▶ **3:7 couch** Something like a bed carried by slaves on which the king lay or sat while traveling.

RELATIONSHIPS

Expand Your Family

When tragedy strikes, disappointment comes, or you find yourself in a jam, whom do you call first? For many of us, it would be family: a parent, a sibling, or even a cousin. But in our ever-expanding twenty-first century world, "family" has been redefined to include others with whom you share close relationships. Roommates, co-workers, and even church family can fill in the gaps in your support system if your parents live too far away or are no longer alive. You may think this is a modern concept, but see Proverbs 27:10 for advice on this very topic. Expanding your family circle can be an amazing way to deepen relationships. The best way to start? Be "family" to someone else in need.

10Your love is so sweet, my sister, my bride.
   Your love is better than wine,
   and your perfume smells better than any spice.
11My bride, your lips drip honey;
   honey and milk are under your tongue.
   Your clothes smell like the cedars of Lebanon.
12My sister, my bride, you are like a garden locked up,
   like a walled-in spring, a closed-up fountain.

WHAT'S IN A word?

Song of Songs 4:1 "Doves"
When Solomon tells his beloved that her eyes are like doves, he is saying that her eyes are not only beautiful but also pure and innocent.

13Your limbs are like an orchard of pomegranates with all the best fruit,
   filled with flowers and nard,
14nard and saffron, calamus, and cinnamon,
   with trees of incense, myrrh, and aloes—
   all the best spices.
15You are like a garden fountain—
   a well of fresh water
   flowing down from the mountains of Lebanon.

The Woman Speaks

16Awake, north wind.
   Come, south wind.
Blow on my garden,
   and let its sweet smells flow out.
Let my lover enter the garden
   and eat its best fruits.

The Man Speaks

5 I have entered my garden, my sister, my bride.
I have gathered my myrrh with my spice.

I have eaten my honeycomb and my honey.
   I have drunk my wine and my milk.

The Friends Speak

Eat, friends, and drink;
   yes, drink deeply, lovers.

The Woman Dreams

2I sleep, but my heart is awake.
   I hear my lover knocking.
"Open to me, my sister, my darling,
   my dove, my perfect one.
My head is wet with dew,
   and my hair with the dampness of the night."
3I have taken off my garment
   and don't want to put it on again.
I have washed my feet
   and don't want to get them dirty again.
4My lover put his hand through the opening,
   and I felt excited inside.
5I got up to open the door for my lover.

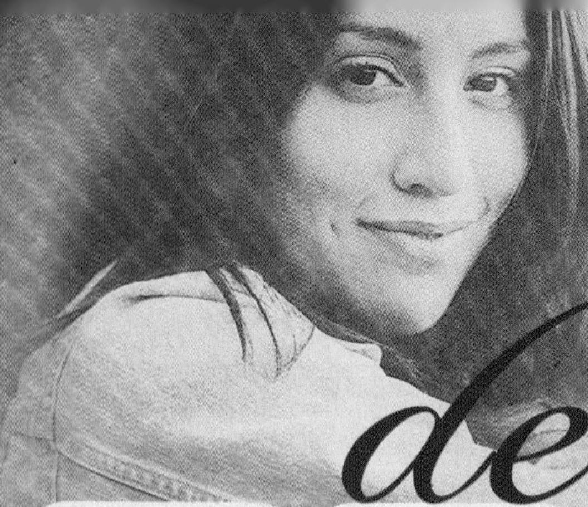

"The reason angels can fly
is that they take themselves so lightly."
–*G.K. Chesterton*

december

It's *World AIDS Day.* Learn more about what you can do at www.data.org. 1	2	3	Don't forget to set up a Christmas gift budget before you begin shopping. 4	5
6	*Invite a friend to attend a Christmas Eve service with you.* 7	8	Get involved with www.angeltree.com. 9	10
11	Do something extra special for people who have a birthday in December. 12	Learn more about *Hanukkah* by researching it on-line. 13	*Make time to bake Christmas cookies.* 14	Mail your Christmas cards and gifts by today so they arrive in time! 15
Read Psalm 100. Share your joy with a friend. 16	17	Pray for a person of influence: It's Steven Spielberg's birthday. 18	Go with your friends to look at outdoor Christmas displays in your area. 19	20
21	It's the first day of winter. Enjoy the coolest season of the year. 22	Finish up that last minute Christmas shopping! 23	*Christmas Eve.* Celebrate this time with your family, if possible. 24	*Christmas Day.* Reflect on how God has made himself real to you this year. 25
Take advantage of all those after-Christmas sales. 26	What New Year's resolutions do you want to make for the upcoming year? 27	Pray for a person of influence: It's Denzel Washington's birthday. 28	Invite some friends to go skating—on ice, if possible. 29	30
New Year's Eve. Enjoy the friends God has blessed you with! 31				

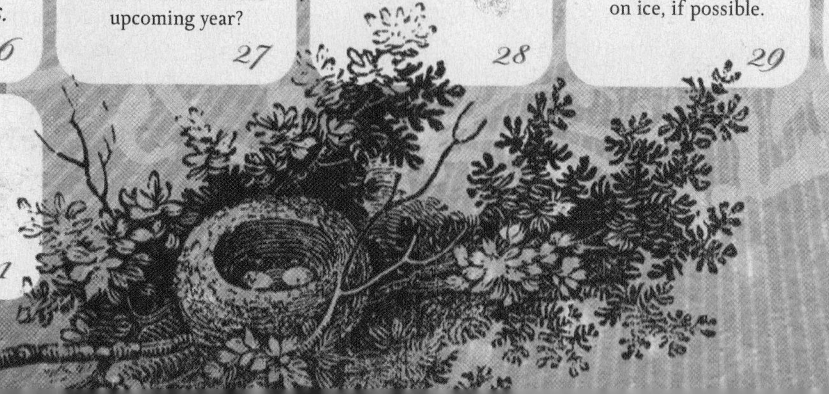

Myrrh was dripping from my
hands
and flowing from my fingers,
onto the handles of the lock.
[6] I opened the door for my lover,
but my lover had left and was
gone.
When he spoke, he took my
breath away.
I looked for him, but I could not
find him;
I called for him, but he did not
answer.
[7] The watchmen found me
as they patrolled the city.
They hit me and hurt me;
the guards on the wall took
away my veil.
[8] Promise me, women of Jerusalem,
if you find my lover,
tell him I am weak with love.

The Friends Answer the Woman

[9] How is your lover better than other
lovers,
most beautiful of women?
How is your lover better than other
lovers?
Why do you want us to promise
this?

The Woman Answers the Friends

[10] My lover is healthy and tan,
the best of ten thousand
men.
[11] His head is like the finest gold;
his hair is wavy and black like a
raven.
[12] His eyes are like doves
by springs of water.
They seem to be bathed in cream
and are set like jewels.
[13] His cheeks are like beds of spices;
they smell like mounds of
perfume.
His lips are like lilies
flowing with myrrh.
[14] His hands are like gold hinges,
filled with jewels.

His body is like shiny ivory
covered with sapphires.
[15] His legs are like large marble posts,
standing on bases of fine gold.
He is like a cedar of Lebanon,
like the finest of the trees.
[16] His mouth is sweet to kiss,
and I desire him very much.
Yes, daughters of Jerusalem,
this is my lover
and my friend.

The Friends Speak to the Woman

6 Where has your lover gone,
most beautiful of women?
Which way did your lover turn?
We will look for him with you.

The Woman Answers the Friends

[2] My lover has gone down to his
garden,
to the beds of spices,
to feed in the gardens
and to gather lilies.
[3] I belong to my lover,
and my lover belongs to me.
He feeds among the lilies.

The Man Speaks to the Woman

[4] My darling, you are as beautiful as
the city of Tirzah,
as lovely as the city of Jerusalem,
like an army flying flags.
[5] Turn your eyes from me,
because they excite me too
much.
Your hair is like a flock of goats
streaming down Mount Gilead.
[6] Your teeth are white like sheep
just coming from their bath;
each one has a twin,
and none of them is missing.
[7] Your cheeks behind your veil
are like slices of a pomegranate.
[8] There may be sixty queens and
eighty slave women
and so many girls you cannot
count them,

Worship the Creator

Sitting quietly under a tree, on a mountaintop, or at the beach can be a breathtaking experience. Being surrounded by God's creation can make you feel closer to the creator. Psalm 8 describes the intricacies of God's handiwork, including his most significant creation: human life. We are his masterpiece! When we see God's creativity reflected in the variety of the human race and see his power in the miraculous ways our bodies work, we have yet another reason to worship the Lord. "I praise you because you made me in an amazing and wonderful way" (Psalm 139:14).

9but there is only one like my dove,
  my perfect one.
She is her mother's only
  daughter,
the brightest of the one who
  gave her birth.
The young women saw her and
  called her happy;
the queens and the slave women
  also praised her.

HEALTH
Sizing Up Self-Image

Eating disorders—including anorexia, bulimia, and binge eating—affect millions of women. One of the key causes is a poor self-image. According to *Health* magazine, women tend to overestimate the size of their bodies. When fifty average-sized women were asked to estimate the width of a box during a study at St. George's Hospital Medical School in London, they had no problem sizing things up. But when the same fifty women were asked to estimate the width of their bodies, they guessed that their waists were twenty-five percent larger and their hips were sixteen percent larger than they actually were. Obviously, our perception can be quite skewed when it comes to self-image. That's why it's important to know what God says and thinks about you. Not only is God's assessment of your value and worth steady and accurate, it's also eternal. He loves you just as you are.

The Young Women Praise the Woman

10Who is that young woman
  that shines out like the dawn?
She is as pretty as the moon,
  as bright as the sun,
  as wonderful as an army flying
    flags.

The Man Speaks

11I went down into the orchard of nut
    trees
  to see the blossoms of the
    valley,
to look for buds on the vines,
  to see if the pomegranate trees
    had bloomed.
12Before I realized it, my desire for
    you made me feel
  like a prince in a chariot.

The Friends Call to the Woman

13Come back, come back, woman of
    Shulam.
  Come back, come back,
  so we may look at you!

The Woman Answers the Friends

Why do you want to look at the
    woman of Shulam
  as you would at the dance of two
    armies?

The Man Speaks to the Woman

7 Your feet are beautiful in sandals,
    you daughter of a prince.
  Your round thighs are like jewels
    shaped by an artist.
2Your navel is like a round drinking
    cup
  always filled with wine.
  Your stomach is like a pile of
    wheat
  surrounded with lilies.
3Your breasts are like two fawns,
  like twins of a gazelle.
4Your neck is like an ivory tower.

Your eyes are like the pools in
Heshbon
near the gate of Bath Rabbim.
Your nose is like the mountain of
Lebanon
that looks down on Damascus.
⁵Your head is like Mount Carmel,
and your hair is like purple
cloth;
the king is captured in its folds.
⁶You are beautiful and pleasant;
my love, you are full of delights.
⁷You are tall like a palm tree,
and your breasts are like its
bunches of fruit.
⁸I said, "I will climb up the palm tree
and take hold of its fruit."
Let your breasts be like bunches of
grapes,
the smell of your breath like
apples,
⁹ and your mouth like the best
wine.

The Woman Speaks to the Man

Let this wine go down sweetly for
my lover;
may it flow gently past the lips
and teeth.
¹⁰I belong to my lover,
and he desires only me.
¹¹Come, my lover,
let's go out into the country
and spend the night in the
fields.
¹²Let's go early to the vineyards
and see if the buds are on the
vines.
Let's see if the blossoms have
already opened
and if the pomegranates have
bloomed.
There I will give you my love.
¹³The mandrake flowers give their
sweet smell,
and all the best fruits are at our
gates.
I have saved them for you, my lover,
the old delights and the new.

What's the POINT?

Song of Songs 8:14

In the last verse of this book, the woman urges her lover to hurry up. She is eager to meet with him, spend time with him, and pour out her love on him. You may be eager for your love to hurry up, too. If you are married or in a relationship, there are probably issues you wish your partner would hurry up and resolve. If you are single, you may be waiting for your love to hurry up and get here! Regardless of your situation, it is important to take note of the heightened sense of anticipation this woman has for the one she loves. She is not sitting back quietly waiting. No, she is calling to him with a sense of eagerness. If you are in a relationship, that may mean deciding to put aside your tendency to criticize. Instead, encourage your husband or boyfriend to be the man God wants him to be! You can be excited about the changes you can already foresee. For those who are waiting for a man of God to love and marry, you can eagerly anticipate what the Lord has in store. Whether you find true love or not, you can decide to maintain that sense of excitement about what God has for you next.

MONEY

Save Without Thinking

If you think you need to have hundreds or even thousands of dollars to make a savings account worthwhile, you need to think again. Small amounts of money add up over time. For example, did you know that if you save twenty dollars a week for thirty years and earn just five percent interest, you will end up with almost seventy-three thousand dollars? Now that's a lot of dough in return for saving less than three dollars a day! There are many ways to save that much and more. One of the best things you can do is to take advantage of an employer-sponsored 401(k) or savings plan that allows you to automatically put money away. If you don't see the money in your paycheck, you're a lot less likely to spend it. Look around for simple things you can do to cut out excess spending: Brew your coffee at home. Brown-bag it at work. Call during off-peak hours. Use only ATMs that don't charge a fee. Pay bills on time, or even a little early, to avoid late charges. Swap services with a friend; exchange a night of baby-sitting for having your oil changed. A few dollars here and there really add up, especially with consistent effort!

8 I wish you were like my brother
who fed at my mother's
breasts.
If I found you outside,
I would kiss you,
and no one would look down on
me.
²I would lead you and bring you
to my mother's house;
she is the one who taught me.
I would give you a drink of spiced
wine
from my pomegranates.

The Woman Speaks to the Friends

³My lover's left hand is under my
head,
and his right arm holds me
tight.
⁴Women of Jerusalem,
promise not to awaken
or excite my feelings of love
until it is ready.

The Friends Speak

⁵Who is this coming out of the
desert,
leaning on her lover?

The Man Speaks to the Woman

I woke you under the apple
tree
where you were born;
there your mother gave birth to
you.
⁶Put me like a seal on your heart,
like a seal on your arm.
Love is as strong as death;
jealousy is as strong as the
grave.
Love bursts into flames
and burns like a hot fire.
⁷Even much water cannot put out
the flame of love;
floods cannot drown love.
If a man offered everything in his
house for love,
people would totally reject it.

The Woman's Brothers Speak

[8]We have a little sister,
and her breasts are not yet grown.
What should we do for our sister
on the day she becomes engaged?
[9]If she is a wall,
we will put silver towers on her.
If she is a door,
we will protect her with cedar boards.

The Woman Speaks

[10]I am a wall,
and my breasts are like towers.
So I was to him,
as one who brings happiness.
[11]Solomon had a vineyard at Baal Hamon.

Most women average just 600 mg of calcium each day, far less than the recommended amount.

(The Well Street Journal)

He rented the vineyards for others to tend,
and everyone who rented had to pay
twenty-five pounds of silver for the fruit.
[12]But my own vineyard is mine to give.
Solomon, the twenty-five pounds of silver are for you,
and five pounds are for those who tend the fruit.

The Man Speaks to the Woman

[13]You who live in the gardens,
my friends are listening for your voice;
let me hear it.

The Woman Speaks to the Man

[14]Hurry, my lover,
be like a gazelle
or a young deer
on the mountains where spices grow.

Beauty: A SHORT STUDY JOURNAL

Have you ever thought about true beauty? More than a great haircut, radiant skin, or the latest fashion, what qualities make a woman truly beautiful? Here are some questions to help you look at important truths about yourself and life-changing truths about God. Take a minute to think through these questions, reflect on your life, and meditate on Scripture. You may want to devote an entire afternoon to this study. We're hoping you'll revisit it from time to time to celebrate your growth and shed light on the journey ahead.

List three things you like about your face, your body, or your overall appearance. What is it about each feature that you appreciate?

If you could change one thing about your physical appearance, what would you change? Why?

When you think about your appearance each day, do you tend to give more attention to the features you like or those you don't like? Why? Which would be healthier for you to focus on?

If you rated the importance of all the characteristics you look for in friends, how would you rate physical appearance?

1 2 3 4 5 6 7 8 9 10

What qualities are more important in a friend than attractiveness?

It's easy to think that because a woman is attractive or well groomed, she probably has it all together. It may seem that she is somehow more important, valuable, or likable because of her physical appearance. The truth is that a person may look great on the outside but struggle with many issues—including appearance—on the inside.

The Bible makes it clear that you can't judge people by appearances. Proverbs 31:30 says, "Charm can fool you, and beauty can trick you, but a woman who respects the LORD should be praised."

Have you ever been tricked by charm or beauty? Have you ever met women who are physically attractive, but their unattractive behavior and attitudes taint their beauty? Explain.

Why do you think Proverbs 31:30 says that "a woman who respects the LORD should be praised"?

When God looks at you, do think he is more concerned with your outer physical appearance or your inner spiritual appearance? Why?

Where do you think true beauty comes from?

Pop culture sends many false messages about beauty. These messages tell us that our beauty is measured by the size we wear, the brand we buy, or the way we look.

What are some of the unhealthy and false beliefs about beauty that are prevalent in films, advertisements, magazines, and on television? Which of these beliefs have you bought into?

God longs to adorn you with true beauty—the kind that isn't based on time or trends or the world's opinion of what is beautiful. First Peter 3:3-4 says, "It is not fancy hair, gold jewelry, or fine clothes that should make you beautiful. No, your beauty should come from within you—the beauty of a gentle and quiet spirit that will never be destroyed and is very precious to God."

What have you done in the last few weeks to cultivate your true, inner beauty?

In what ways are you allowing God to work in your life to cultivate your true beauty?

God already sees you as beautiful! He thinks you are fantastic—a magnificent work of art and a masterpiece of his creation. Did you know that God delights in you just the way you are? In fact, Zephaniah 3:17 says that God rejoices over you! He sings and feels joyful about you!

In what ways has God made you even more beautiful through your relationship with him?

What steps can you take to see yourself as beautiful, the way God sees you?

Purpose: A SHORT STUDY JOURNAL

Have you ever taken time to think about your purpose? Have you ever considered why you're *really* here? The questions in this study journal will help you look at important truths about yourself and life-changing truths about God. Take a minute to think through these questions, reflect on your life, and meditate on Scripture. You may want to devote an entire afternoon to this study. We're hoping you'll revisit it from time to time to celebrate your growth and shed light on the journey ahead.

Make a list of five things you love most about your life. Why do those things bring you joy?

_____
_____
_____
_____
_____
_____
_____

List the names of five people you love. What makes those relationships so important to you?

_____
_____
_____
_____
_____
_____
_____
_____

What do you love most about your job? Your hobbies? Your friends?

_____
_____
_____
_____
_____
_____
_____

When you look to the future, what do you aspire to be or do?

_____
_____
_____
_____
_____
_____

Do you have a five- or ten-year plan for your life? If so, what does it look like?

_____
_____
_____
_____
_____
_____

When people truly encounter God, their lives are often marked by significant changes. Some people alter their behavior, activities, or habits. Other people change their relationships or priorities. If you've known God since childhood, the changes you've experienced may have come about more gradually. Reflecting on your life, how has knowing God changed you?

_____
_____
_____
_____
_____
_____

Knowing God also has a way of changing what drives you. Instead of being driven by things like money or your reputation, you are likely to discover that you are motivated by pleasing God and spreading his fame. He wants you to live your life with eternity in mind, knowing that the things of this world will pass away.

Do you think God has a plan for your life? If so, what does that plan look like?

How does God's plan for your life compare with the five- or ten-year plan you outlined? In what ways are they the same? In what ways are they different?

The Bible makes it clear that God has a plan and a purpose for your life! In fact, Ephesians 1:10–12 says:

> His goal was to carry out his plan, when the right time came, that all things in heaven and on earth would be joined together in Christ as the head. In Christ we were chosen to be God's people, because from the very beginning God had decided this in keeping with his plan. And he is the One who makes everything agree with what he decides and wants. We are the first people who hoped in Christ, and we were chosen so that we would bring praise to God's glory.

Circle every mention of Christ in this passage. According to this scripture, what is your real purpose?

Clearly, you were designed to glorify God! He created you to praise him not just on Sunday mornings, but also throughout the week's activities and relationships. A life that glorifies God is a life that displays his characteristics. People will see God in your attitude and actions as you demonstrate love, joy, peace, patience, kindness, goodness, faithfulness, gentleness, and self-control (see Galatians 5:22–23).

Scripture makes it clear that your purpose isn't just to know Jesus on your own, but also as part of a family of believers. In 1 Timothy 3:14–15, Paul writes, "Although I hope I can come to you soon, I am writing these things to you now. Then, even if I am delayed, you will know how to live in the family of God. That family is the church of the living God, the support and foundation of the truth."

Why do you think God prioritizes community with other believers? How does being part of the family of God help and strengthen you? List specific lessons you've learned because of someone else's influence or record a time you were able to help another Christian grow.

God often works in your life through your relationships with others. In fact, it's often through those relationships that your faith is put on display. Loving God is directly linked with loving other people. In Matthew 22:37–40, Jesus gave two rules to live by: "'Love the Lord your God with all your heart, all your soul, and all your mind.' This is the first and most important command. And the second command is like the first: 'Love your neighbor as you love yourself.' All the law and the writings of the prophets depend on these two commands."

In what ways do these two commandments go together? Is it possible to truly love your neighbor without loving God? Is it possible to truly love God without loving your neighbor? Why or why not?

How does building healthy relationships with others allow you to fulfill your God-given purpose?

In the space provided, draw a picture of what a healthy relationship between you, God, and others looks like:

When you reflect on the picture above, can you think of any situations where you've allowed your relationships to suffer for one reason or another? Why is it important to God that these relationships be restored?

Proverbs 17:9 says, "Whoever forgives someone's sin makes a friend, but gossiping about the sin breaks up friendships."

Is there anyone you need to forgive? Do you need to reconcile or make peace with anyone? If so, make a note about the person or situation below. Take some time to pray, and ask God what you need to do to improve the relationship.

Your purpose is to know God and grow in your relationship with him and other believers. God also wants you to make him known to other people! In fact, Matthew 28:18–20 records some of Jesus' final words: "Then Jesus came to them and said, 'All power in heaven and on earth is given to me. So go and make followers of all people in the world. Baptize them in the name of the Father and the Son and the Holy Spirit. Teach them to obey everything that I have taught you, and I will be with you always, even until the end of this age.'"

What does it mean to "go and make followers of all people"? According to this passage, how does telling others about Jesus fit into God's purpose for your life?

Is there anyone in your life that God has been nudging you to share your faith with? If so, who? What's stopping you?

In the following space, write a short purpose statement for your life. Look back over the Bible verses from this study, and then craft a statement that captures your life's mission.